European Corporate Law

European Company Law Series

VOLUME 5

Editor

Steef M. Bartman, Attorney-at-Law, Emeritus Professor of Company Law at Leiden Law School and Professor of Corporate Group Liability at Maastricht University, the Netherlands.

Introduction

The European Company Law Series is closely linked to the bimonthly journal European Company Law, also published by Kluwer Law International.

Contents/Subjects

The series covers subjects of company law in a broad sense, including insolvency, co-determination and securities law. Topical issues such as merger control, corporate governance, and piercing the corporate veil have been covered.

Objective of Series

Analysis of topical or complex subjects in European company law.

Readership

Academics; regulators; practitioners.

The titles published in this series are listed at the end of this volume.

European Corporate Law

Fourth Edition

Adriaan Dorresteijn
Mieke Olaerts

Bastiaan Kemp
Thomas Biermeyer
Marcus Meyer-Erdmann
Tomas Arons

Wolters Kluwer

Published by:
Kluwer Law International B.V.
PO Box 316
2400 AH Alphen aan den Rijn
The Netherlands
E-mail: lrs-sales@wolterskluwer.com
Website: www.wolterskluwer.com/en/solutions/kluwerlawinternational

Sold and distributed by:
Wolters Kluwer Legal & Regulatory U.S.
7201 McKinney Circle
Frederick, MD 21704
United States of America
E-mail: customer.service@wolterskluwer.com

ISBN 978-94-035-3223-3

e-Book: ISBN 978-94-035-3224-0
web-PDF: ISBN 978-94-035-3225-7

Table of Contents

List of Abbreviations

AG	Aktiengesellschaft
AktG	Aktiengesetz
All E.R.	All England Law Reports
APA	Asset Purchase Agreement
ASB	British Accounting Standards Board
BetrVG	Betriebsverfassungsgesetz
BGB	Bürgerliches Gesetzbuch
BGBL	Bundesgesetzblatt
BGHZ	Entscheidungen des Bundesgerichtshofes in Zivilsachen
BIICL	British Institute of International Comparative Law
BRIS	The Business Registers Interconnection System
BRRD	Bank Recovery and Resolution Directive
BTA	Business Transfer Agreement
BV	Besloten vennootschap met beperkte aansprakelijkheid
BW	Dutch Civil Code
CA 2006	Companies Act 2006
CBC	Cross-Border conversion
CBD	Cross-Border division
CBM	Cross-Border merger
CIC	Community Interest Company
CJEU	Court of Justice of the European Union
COMI	Centre of Main Interests
Commission	European Commission
CRD IV	Capital Requirements Directive

CSE	Comité Social et Économique
CSR	Corporate Social Responsibility
CV	Commanditaire vennootschap
DCC	Dutch Civil Code
DTI	Department of Trade and Industry
EBA	European Banking Authority
EBOR	European Business Organization Law Review
EC	European Community
ECB	European Central Bank
ECFR	European Company and Financial Law Review
ECGI	European Corporate Governance Institute
ECJ	European Court of Justice (abbreviation previously used for the CJEU)
ECL	European Company Law
ECR	Official Reports of Cases Before the Court of Justice in English
EEA	European Economic Area
EEC	European Economic Community
EEIG	European Economic Interest Grouping
EIRO	European Industrial Relations Observatory
EIOPA	European Insurance and Occupational Pensions Authority
EMCA	European Model Company Act
EP	European Parliament
ESAP	European Single Access Point
ESMA	European Securities and Markets Authority
ESOS	Employee Share Ownership Schemes
EU	European Union
EUR	Euro
EWC	European Works Council
GAAP	Generally Accepted Accounting Principles (US)
GIE	groupement d' intérêt économique
GmbH	Gesellschaft mit beschränkter Haftung
GmbHG	Gesetz betreffend die Gesellschaften mit beschränkter Haftung
HGB	Handelsgesetzbuch
IAS	International Accounting Standards
IASB	International Accounting Standards Board
IASC	International Accounting Standards Committee
IFRS	International Financial Reporting Standards

IR	Integrated Reporting
KG	Kommanditgesellschaft
KgaA	Kommanditgesellschaft auf Aktien
LMA	Loan Market Association
LLP	Limited Liability Partnership
LP	Limited Partnership
LPA	Limited Partnerships Act
Ltd	Private Limited Company
M&A	Merger & Acquisition
MIFID	Markets in Financial Instruments Directive
MIFIR	Markets in Financial Instruments Regulation
MitbestG	Mitbestimmungsgesetz
MNE	Multinational enterprise
MOMIG	Gesetz zur Modernisierung des GmbH-Rechts und zur Bekämpfung von Missbräuchen
NJ	Nederlandse Jurisprudentie
NJW	Neue Juristische Wochenschrift
NRE	Loi sur les Nouvelles Régulations Économiques
NV	Naamloze vennootschap
OECD	Organisation for Economic Co-operation and Development
OHG	Offene Handelsgesellschaft
OJ	Official Journal of the European Union
PA	Partnership Act
PartG	Partnerschaftsgesellschaft
Plc	Public Limited Company
S. Com. por A.	Sociedad comanditaria por acciones
SA	Société anonyme, sociedad anónima, spólka akcyjna
SAPA	Società in accomandita per azioni
SARL	Société a responsabilité limitée
SAS	Société par actions simplifiée
SC	Sociedad regular colective
SCA	Société en commandité par actions
SCE	Societas Cooperativa Europaea (European Cooperative Society)
SCIC	Société coopérative d'intérêt collectif
SCS	Société en commandite simple
SE	Societas Europaea (European Company)
SEAG	SE Ausführungsgesetz

SEC	Sociedad en comandita
SEC	U.S. Securities and Exchange Commission
SKA	Spólka komandytowo-akcynja
SL (or SRL)	Sociedad de responsabilidad limitada
SLNE	Sociedad Limitada Nueva Empresa
SMEs	Small- and Medium-Sized Enterprises
SNC	Société en nom collectif
SPA	Società per azioni, Share purchase agreement
sp. z o.o.	Spólka z ograniczoną odpowiedzialnocią
sp.j.	Spólka jawna
sp.k	Spólka komandytowa
sp.p.	Spólka partnerska
SPV	Special purpose vehicle
SRL	Società a responsabilità limitata, Société à responsabilité limitée, Società a responsabilità limitata
TEU	Treaty on European Union
TFEU	Treaty on the Functioning of the European Union
UK	United Kingdom
US	United States
VAT	Value-Added Tax
VOF	Vennootschap onder firma
WOR	Wet op de ondernemingsraden
XBRL	eXtensible Business Reporting Language
ZGR	Zeitschrift für Unternehmens- und Gesellschaftsrecht
ZIP	Zeitschrift für Wirtschaftsrecht

Preface

Since the publication of the first edition of this book, almost thirty years ago, many changes have taken place in the area of European corporate law. In hindsight, one can say that the first edition was dealing with a somewhat rudimentary version of European corporate law. Since then, we have seen major developments, such as the introduction of the European Company, rules on cross-border mergers, divisions, and conversions as well as rules regarding employee involvement. The financial crisis of 2008 and its aftermath gave rise to extensive European Union (EU) regulation of banks and other financial institutions. The EU rules on accounting, strongly influenced by international accounting standards as they are, have been modernized in order to contain non-financial reporting obligations with a view to sustainability and other social responsibility concerns of undertakings.

Notwithstanding the impact of harmonization by EU legislation, many subjects are still left to the regulatory competence of the Member States. Hence, national corporate laws within the EU (and the EEA)[1] differ from one another, partly with regard to rather practical matters such as the authorization of documents, time limits for decision making, and board structures. But they are also different with regard to key issues such as the duties and liabilities of directors and the interest of company groups against the interest of the individual companies within the group. Accordingly, the book contains sections on some key elements of the corporate laws of a few Member States: Germany, France, and the Netherlands.

As at the completion of the previous edition, a few words must be spent on the position of the United Kingdom in this book. On the day the UK left the EU, 'all EU laws which are directly applicable in the UK and all laws which have been made in the UK in order to implement our obligations as a member of the EU are converted into domestic law (...)'.[2] The effects of Brexit, in regard to the topics dealt with by this book, can only be assessed more years from now. Therefore, the UK is still featured in this

1. The European Economic Area (EEA) Agreement provides for the inclusion of EU legislation covering the free movement of goods, services, persons, and capital.
2. *Legislating for the United Kingdom's Withdrawal from the European Union*, Department for Exiting the European Union, March 2017, 31.

book in the same way as in the previous edition but that might change with the next edition of this book.

This book is primarily designed for those at university or others in legal practice who wish to acquire a better understanding of corporate law within the EU and its common characteristics as well as some of the similarities and differences between the various national legal systems. Therefore, we describe some of the main issues of corporate law at the EU level as well as at the national level. The latter, of course, cannot be done in a comprehensive way because it would not only represent a task far greater than we could have coped with but it would also be disproportionate to the aims of the book. Even the laws of the restricted number of Member States we have included will be, out of necessity, dealt with in a rather eclectic way and the same applies to the UK.

The revision of the third edition of this book has been taken on by a new team of authors. Their professional expertise has enabled us to elaborate on subjects of which the importance is growing, notably corporate governance, cross-border business combinations and group law in Chapters 6, 8 and 10 respectively.

Most of the updating and revision for the fourth edition was done by Adriaan and Mieke. Tomas contributed to Chapter 3 (the sections on capital markets), Bastiaan was co-author of the revised Chapter 6, Marcus updated Chapter 7 and Thomas, Marcus and Bastiaan updated and expanded Chapter 8.

We thank the co-authors of the previous editions for their excellent contributions we were able to build on for this edition of the book.

Dr Adriaan Dorresteijn, Emeritus Professor Utrecht University
Dr Mieke Olaerts, Professor Maastricht University; Of Counsel DVDW
Dr Bastiaan Kemp, Professor Maastricht University;
Attorney-at-law at Loyens & Loeff
Dr Thomas Biermeyer, Partner at AKD Benelux;
Assistant Professor Maastricht University
Dr Marcus Meyer-Erdmann, Senior Researcher at European Trade Union Institute
Tomas Arons, Professor Utrecht University; Of Counsel to Vereniging
van Effectenbezitters
April 2022[3]

3. The book is updated during 2021 and the first three months of 2022.

CHAPTER 1

Introduction

I SCOPE AND FOCUS OF THE BOOK *EUROPEAN CORPORATE LAW*

1.01 European corporate law, like any corporate law, consists of legal norms relating to certain types of business organizations. In other words, corporate law provides the legal structure of a business enterprise. In general, corporate law includes all incorporated forms of business organizations and thus encompasses more than just company law. For the purposes of this book, corporate law is used in this broad sense. It includes, for example, the law on partnerships, merger regulation and the role of employees in corporate decision-making. The focus of this book is, as the title suggests, on 'European' corporate law. However, we have added some sections on the United Kingdom (UK) to our analysis even though, due to Brexit, the UK is no longer a Member State of the European Union (EU). UK company law, however, is influenced by the European harmonization programme and in its turn has had an influence on that programme which is reflected, for example, by the Takeover Directive. For these reasons, we felt that UK law could not be completely left out.

1.02 European corporate law as defined above is in fact for a great deal national law. Although many business activities are carried out across borders, most business organizations are subject to national laws of the Member States.

As the Court of Justice of the European Union (CJEU) stated in the *Daily Mail* case:

> [It] should be borne in mind that, unlike natural persons, companies are creatures of the law and, in the present state of Community law, creatures of national law. They exist only by virtue of the varying national legislation which determines their incorporation and functioning.[1]

1. Case C-81/87 (*K. v. The Treasury and Commissioners of Inland Revenue, ex parte Daily Mail and General Trust plc)* (1989) I All E.R. 328.

There are, however, exceptions to this principle. The EU[2] introduced business organizations that are primarily governed by European law as to their formation and functioning. The most important one is the European Company (Societas Europaea (SE)). Its Statute (2001) prevails over national law, although several issues are still referred to national law, that is, the law of the Member State in which the SE has its registered office.[3] Other business organizations under European law are the European Cooperative Society (Societas Cooperativa Europaea (SCE)), which was introduced in 2003, and the European Economic Interest Grouping (EEIG), which dates back to 1985.[4]

1.03 Much older exceptions to the rule that national law governs companies are the 'inter-state enterprises', which are partly disentangled from domestic law. The *'Société européenne pour le financement du materiel ferroviaire'* (Eurofima) was founded in 1956 by a convention among several European countries. According to the convention, this company is subject to the law of the country in which it is seated (Switzerland), but only insofar as this law does not contravene the convention. The shares of Eurofima are held by the national railways of the contracting states.[5] A similar regime applies to the *Société Internationale de la Moselle.* Subsequent to the 1956 convention between France, Germany and Luxembourg, it is incorporated under German law, albeit the German government is obliged to safeguard the rights of the shareholders in the event that German company law is changed.[6]

1.04 Notwithstanding these exceptions, the observation made by the CJEU in *Daily Mail* is correct for the majority of companies. Furthermore, even European and international companies, although not primarily based on national law, must be registered in one of the Member States, which adds a national element to them. European corporate law thus encompasses both EU law and all national corporate laws. Nevertheless, for a basic understanding of this area of law, it is not required to study all national corporate laws in detail because business organizations tend to show a fundamentally similar set of legal characteristics.[7] Within the EU, the harmonization programme has contributed significantly to this phenomenon.

2. The abbreviation EU (European Union) will be used even where EC (European Community) would be more appropriate as being one of the communities the EU is built upon. The consolidated version of the Treaty on European Union is published in the OJ 2016 C202, http://eur-lex.europa.eu/collection/eu-law/treaties.html.
3. Regulation (EC) No. 2157/2001 on the Statute for a European Company (SE).
4. Regulation (EEC) No. 2137/85 and Regulation (EC) No. 1435/2003.
5. Eurofima (European Company for the Financing of Railroad Rolling Stock) was originally founded for a period of fifty years, but in 1984 the members of the Convention approved to extend this period for an additional fifty years, www.eurofima.org (16 Mar. 2021).
6. Moselle Convention of 27 Oct. 1956, *Bundesgesetzblatt* 1956 II, 1838. Georges Ripert, *Droit Commercial,* Tome 1 par Rene Roblot, No. 1724. Ignaz Seidl-Hohenveldern, *Corporations in and under International Law,* Cambridge: Grotius Publications, 1987, 112–114; Christoph Engel, 'Internationale öffentliche Unternehmen', *RabelsZeitschrift* 80 (1995): 495–544, mentions several other examples of international companies based on a treaty between states.
7. J. Armour et al., 'What Is Corporate Law', in R. Kraakman et al., *The Anatomy of Corporate Law: A Comparative and Functional Approach,* Third Edition (Oxford: Oxford University Press, 2017), chapter 1.

1.05 Corporate law, approached comparatively, cannot be understood properly without reference to the entrepreneur *pur sang*, the sole trader, or the sole proprietor. Similarly, attention has to be given to the non-corporate forms of business organizations, partnerships or firms. These subjects are dealt with very briefly in this chapter and more in depth both within the EU and the UK in Chapter 2. In the section on partnerships, some introductory remarks are made on companies and other incorporated forms of business organizations, which are the main subject of this book. The relevant harmonization programme within the EU is discussed in Chapter 3. As illustrated, corresponding directives and regulations are not confined to company law but can also be found in related areas such as taxation and financial services. Business organizations under Community law are highlighted in Chapter 4. The focus is on the EEIG, the SE and the SCE. Chapters 5 and 6 deal with selected topics regarding companies under national laws: namely, the formation and financing of companies and their management structures, including the issue of corporate governance. In Chapter 7, the involvement of employees, being one of the most controversial issues, is discussed. Employee involvement in some of the Member States represents an element of corporate law with a bearing on the decision-making structure. Other Member States traditionally had little experience with employee involvement, but a 2002 directive established a general framework for informing and consulting employees.[8] The dynamics of the business enterprise are highlighted in Chapter 8 on cross-border business combinations, takeovers and restructuring tools. The annual accounts, also in their consolidated form, are the subject of Chapter 9. Lastly, Chapter 10 provides a review of the law of groups. With the acknowledgement of groups of companies and other legal entities, the law has certainly been challenged to its limits in dealing with economic reality caused by the fact that a company within the group is both legally independent and simultaneously functions as part of a larger economic entity.

As mentioned above, for a basic understanding of European corporate law, it is not necessary to study all national laws in detail. However, in some areas, especially those where there is less or no harmonization, references to national law are needed to explain the issues at stake. The purpose of this book does not require including references to the national laws of all or most of the EU Members States, therefore the focus is on the laws of selected jurisdictions: France, Germany and The Netherlands. References to UK law are also included as is explained in the Preface to this book and in paragraph 1.01. Other jurisdictions are mentioned occasionally.

II TYPES OF BUSINESS ORGANIZATIONS AND TERMINOLOGY

1.06 After this brief overview of the subsequent chapters, it is necessary to return to the principal idea. In general, a business enterprise may be carried on either by a natural person, the sole trader or the sole proprietor, or by a business organization – the latter being any legal entity involving two or more persons, such as a partnership or a

8. Directive 2002/14/EC.

private or public limited liability company. In the case of the sole trader, the entrepreneur is the owner of the assets belonging to the business, and he or she personally bears all the risks. There is no legal distinction between a sole trader's private and business capital. The sole trader sometimes is subject to special rules, depending on the nature of the business. For taxation purposes, a sole trader may be obliged to keep books, for instance, in connection with value added tax (VAT). If a sole trader is rendering professional services as a lawyer, a physician or an accountant, rules applicable to these professions may have an impact on the way the business is organized. Those who are engaged in commercial activities may have an obligation to register with a commercial register, keep books and draw up a balance sheet once a year. Nevertheless, the sole trader is the simplest way to carry on a business, and its use is widespread. It does not require incorporating a company or involving a notary. In 2018, there were slightly more than 25 million small- and medium-sized enterprises (SMEs) in the EU (SMEs are enterprises having fewer than 250 employees). Of these, 93% were micro SMEs (fewer than 10 employees). In the non-financial business sector, SMEs accounted for 99.8% of all enterprises in the EU in 2018 and employed more than 97 million people in the EU.[9] It is likely that sole traders run most of the micro-class enterprises.

1.07 An entrepreneur may seek to cooperate and share the risks of a business enterprise with others for several reasons. Such cooperation is generally considered to be a partnership. The UK Partnership Act (PA) 1890, for example, defines a partnership as the relation that subsists between persons carrying on a business in common with a view of profit.[10] In most Member States, a partnership is a non-incorporated form of a business organization. As outlined in Chapter 2, several continental jurisdictions distinguish between commercial and other partnerships. The former refers to partnerships included in the Commercial Codes, while the latter concerns those partnerships that are ruled by the Civil Codes. Partnerships generally can sue or be sued under their firm's name, even where they do not have a legal personality. Chapter 2 contains further details about commercial partnerships.

1.08 The particular branch of a business organization that is set up under foreign law can be regarded, for pragmatic reasons, as another non-incorporated business organization. For example, the English branch of a French company or the Dutch branch of a Belgian partnership is not incorporated under the law of the UK or the Netherlands. In the first example of the English branch of a French company, the company remains incorporated in France, it merely registers a branch of that French company in the UK as it wants to do business there through a branch office. Contracts, proprietary rights, other rights and also debts will then be regarded as rights and debts of the French company. The European Commission has taken harmonizing measures regarding disclosure requirements for branch offices. They are discussed in Chapter 3. Branch

9. European Commission, Annual Report on European SMEs 2018/2019, 15–17. The figures mentioned relate to the EU-28, meaning that the UK was included in the report.
10. Section 1 *Partnership Act* 1890, accessible at http://www.legislation.gov.uk.

offices should, however, be distinguished from subsidiaries. If a company is incorporated in France, it may form a new company under UK law in order to do business in the UK. In such case, the second company is not a branch but a subsidiary of the French company. A subsidiary is a separate legal person, being a company of which the first company (the parent company) holds a majority of the shares. Consequently, business conducted by the UK company results in rights and debts for the account of that subsidiary.

1.09 Incorporation, in general, means the creation of a corporation; that is, a legal person separate and distinct from its members. The requirements for incorporation may vary depending on the type of legal person to be incorporated. As to companies, they are incorporated either by registration or by notarial deed. Generally, registration is a prerequisite for acquiring legal personality, such as for the SE and companies under the national law of several Member States. In other countries, incorporation takes place by a notarial deed, although in most countries registration in addition to a notarial deed is also required before the company actually comes into existence.[11] Similar to the SE, the EEIG is incorporated by registration (*see* paragraphs 4.04 and 4.17). The issue of formalities and requirements for the incorporation of companies and EEIGs is dealt with in Chapter 4.

1.10 Companies can be classified in several ways: for instance, limited companies, as opposed to unlimited companies, a distinction made in the UK. If a company is registered as an unlimited company, then there is no limit on the liability of its members.[12] In other Member States, members of some types of companies are not liable for the obligations of the company, but they may be obliged to contribute to the assets.[13] Managing partners of a German limited partnership with shares (*Kommanditgesellschaft auf Aktien* (KGaA)), as well as its equivalents in other continental Member States, are liable for the obligations of the partnership, which, in many other respects, resembles a company (*see* paragraphs 2.47 and 2.48). Another division is between public companies and private limited liability companies. Public companies are companies incorporated as such, and they are generally subject to stricter requirements than private companies, particularly with regard to capital and company structure. Traditionally, in most countries, only public companies were therefore allowed to be listed on a stock exchange. This picture is slowly changing since private companies in some countries can also be listed on the stock exchange.[14] Private

11. Examples are United Kingdom: CA 2006, sections 7–9 and 16; *Polish Commercial Companies Code (Kodeks spólek handlowych)*, Third bilingual edition (Warszawa: Wydawnictwo C.H. Beck, 2004), Articles 163 and 306; *Belgian Companies Code* (*Wetboek van Vennootschappen en Verenigingen*), Article 2:5; Articles 2328, 2331 and 2462 *Italian Civil Code (Codice Civile)*. According to the *Dutch Civil Code* (*Burgerlijk Wetboek*) Articles 6:64 and 6:175, a company comes into existence by force of the notarial deed only. Registration is obligatory but not a prerequisite.
12. Section 3 UK Companies Act 2006.
13. For example, Articles 6:55 and 6:56 Dutch Civil Code.
14. A prerequisite will be that the shares of the private company are freely transferable which depends on the relevant legislation. For example, the Dutch BV is allowed to state in the articles that its shares are freely transferable, Dutch Civil Code, Article 2:195(1).

companies are generally better suited for SMEs that do not have to call for funding on the capital market. The rules for private limited liability companies are generally more flexible allowing the incorporators to set up a company with internal rules that are tailored to their needs, for example regarding calling a general meeting and distributing profits.

1.11 The original idea behind the private company is that formation takes place by *intuitu personae* and that a rather concise and flexible statute reflects its personal character, enabling its members to regulate the company's internal affairs. For instance, the first statute in Europe concerning the private company - the 1892 German *GmbHGesetz*, creating the *Gesellschaft mit beschränkter Haftung* (GmbH) - is still valid and consists of less than ninety sections.[15] In comparison, the 1965 German *Aktiengesetz* (AktG) concerning the public company - the *Aktiengesellschaft* (AG) - has more than 400 sections.[16] In French company law, one can find similar differences between the private company - *société à responsabilité limitée* (SARL) - and the public company - *société anonyme* (SA).[17] By way of contrast, in the UK, both types are governed by the same statute, now the Companies Act 2006. Under this Act, a public company is one whose certificate of incorporation states that it is a public company and has been duly registered as such. Requirements for registration include the authorized minimum capital. All other registered companies are private companies to which many provisions of the Companies Act do not apply.[18] Italy and the Netherlands initially regulated the private company by copying most of the rules for the pre-existing public company. Later on, they allowed for a more flexible regime for private companies, albeit maintaining a rather voluminous set of rules for this form of company.[19] The Polish Commercial Companies Code also shows a tendency to regulate the private company extensively, although it retains certain personal elements such as the right of an individual shareholder to inspect the books and documents of the company.[20]

1.12 In several jurisdictions, the idea to return to the original concept of a restricted and flexible statute for the private company has been put forward, owing to the

15. *Gesetz betreffend die Gesellschaften mit beschränkter Haftung* (GmbHG), from 20 Apr. 1892, accessible at http://www.gesetze-im-internet.de.
16. *Aktiengesetz* (AktG) from 6 Sep. 1965. The second Book, i.e., thirteen sections, concerns the KGaA, which possesses some of the characteristics of both a public company and a limited partnership (*see* paragraph 2.47).
17. French Commercial Code, Articles L223-1–L223-43 (SARL) and L225-1–L225-270 (SA), accessible at http://www.legifrance.gouv.fr.
18. CA 2006, s. 4.
19. Italy: Legislative Decree No. 6 of 17 Jan. 2003 'Riforma organica della disciplina delle società di capitali e società cooperative, in attuazione della legge delega 3 ottobre 2001, n. 366', published in the Official Journal No. 17 on 22 Jan. 2003 (Supplement No. 8). The Netherlands: Wet vereenvoudiging en flexibilisering van 18 juni 2012, Stbl. 2012, 299. The introduction of the private company in the Netherlands in 1971 served to evade disclosure requirements, which were at the time expected to pertain exclusively to public companies, P. van Schilfgaarde, J. Winter, J.B. Wezeman & J. Schoonbrood, *Van de BV en de NV*, no. 9 (Deventer: Seventeenth edition, 2017). For Belgium: L. Dabin & A. Benoit-Moury, *Jura Europae: Company Law Volume II* (loose leaf) (München: Beck, 1964-Belgium), no. 20.
20. *Polish Commercial Companies Code*, Article 212(1) Third bilingual edition (Warszawa: Wydawnictwo C.H. Beck, 2004).

enhanced freedom of establishment for companies within the EU and the needs of the business community. In some countries, company statutes have been adapted in order to introduce new types of private companies.[21] The freedom of establishment and various types of public and private companies are further discussed in Chapter 2 and throughout this book, where applicable.

1.13 Lastly, companies may also fall into different categories based on factual criteria, such as their size or the type of industry they belong to, but this discussion is beyond the scope of this book. Such facts cannot remain completely overlooked, as they may intertwine with company law. Therefore, the classification of companies is expanded in three directions. First, companies may be closed or open companies. Closed companies, also called closely held companies, feature a limited number of shareholders, and the transfer of shares to outsiders is barred, unless all shareholders agree. This, of course, requires contractual arrangements or specific provisions in the articles of the company.[22] Private companies are not, by their very nature, closed companies, but they are better suited to be shaped into closed companies than public companies. Closed companies may be created for several reasons, for example, in order to gain tax benefits or where the partners in a joint venture aim to keep their cooperation exclusive. Second, companies with only one shareholder (member) can be seen as a separate category. A company, by its origin, is a vehicle for cooperation, as is shown by its etymology. However, the concept of a general meeting of shareholders has little meaning when all shares are held by one individual or by another company. Separate EU legislation has been enacted to enable such single member (private) companies in all Member States and to subject these companies to specific rules, as seen in Chapter 3. Third, companies may belong to a group. Groups are mostly built on share ownership, that is, one company - the parent company - holding the shares in other companies, which are commonly called subsidiaries. Based on shareholdership and other legal and factual bonds, such a group may act as an economic entity (*see* Chapter 10).

21. T. van Duren, 'The Light Vehicle Competition', *European Company Law* 1, no. 4 (December 2004): 153-161.
22. Y. Guyon, 'Données juridiques: Essai d'une problématique de la société fermée', in *Propositions pour une société fermée européenne*, sous la direction de Jeanne Boucourechliev (Luxembourg: Office des publications officielles des Communautés européennes, 1997), 37 *et seq.*

CHAPTER 2

Business Organizations Within the EU and the UK

I INTRODUCTION

2.01 The word 'company' means an association of persons who engage in a joint activity, commercial or otherwise. In essence, the term 'company law' may be used to cover the legal regulation of all such activities. This is the case in continental legal systems, apart from legal forms like associations. Each country, however, does allow certain specific forms under which joint economic activities may be carried out, and these are generally divided into partnerships and companies. The essential, but not universal, distinction between these two generic forms is that partnerships are based on individual agreements among the partners, whereas companies are organizations that exist independently of their members and depend on capital resources. In other words, the distinction is between partnerships, personal companies, and capital companies, but all are regarded as companies. In various continental languages, the generic term 'company' covers both partnerships and capital companies, such as the French *société,* the Italian *società*, the German *Gesellschaft* and the Polish *spółka.*

2.02 The United Kingdom (UK), however, deriving its commercial law from a different heritage, treats partnerships and companies as entirely different entities for the purpose of legal regulation. Company law is regarded as applicable only to two specific types of organizations: public and private limited companies, whereas partnerships are basically regarded as contractual activities. The importance of this different approach is that in most continental legal systems there is some overlap in the regulation of partnerships and companies, whereas there is a complete dichotomy in the UK. Although it is perfectly permissible in the UK for a partnership to use the words '& Co' in its name, it still does not constitute a company within the UK's narrow definition of the word for legal purposes.

A Civil and Commercial Law

2.03 Another difference is that continental legal systems draw, or used to draw, a distinction between civil and commercial law whereas such a distinction is not made in the UK. In France, for example, Article L210-1 of the Commercial Code states: 'The commercial nature of a company shall be determined by its form or by its objects.' The second sentence adds: 'General partnerships, limited partnerships, limited liability companies and joint-stock companies are commercial by virtue of their form, irrespective of their objects.' Any such organization that does not comply is therefore of a civil nature, such as the French silent partnership (*see* paragraph 2.18). There are differences between commercial and civil organizations, so this distinction is more than just one of form. For example, in France, commercial organizations must submit themselves to the scrutiny of a special branch of the judiciary (*tribuneaux de commerce*), and, in Germany, the courts have no discretion to waive penalties originating from a contractual agreement if the debtor is a merchant (*Kaufmann*), although they have this option in other cases.[1]

2.04 The methods used by Member States to demarcate between civil and commercial law regarding business organizations differ slightly. An example of how France makes this distinction is mentioned in the previous paragraph. Another example is Germany, where every person carrying on a commercial business is deemed a merchant (*Kaufmann*). In addition, a business is, in any event, a commercial business if its name is registered with the commercial registry.[2] The rules applicable to merchants do apply to general and limited partnerships (LPs) and capital companies alike.[3] The Spanish Civil Code allows partnerships with civil objects to have the same form as commercial partnerships, in which case the provisions of the Commercial Code apply insofar as they do not contravene those of the Civil Code. By contrast, public and private companies are simply declared commercial by Spanish law.[4] Similar to other continental countries, Italy used to have a civil code and a commercial code that applied specifically to the merchant (*commerciante*). By the 1942 law reform, the concept of merchant was replaced by the concept of a commercial entrepreneur *(imprenditore commerciale)* and a separate commercial code no longer existed. Entrepreneurs *(imprenditori)* are defined as persons who are professionally engaged in an organized economic activity in order to produce or exchange goods or services.[5] According to Italian law, commercial entrepreneurs are subject to a special legal framework

1. Articles L721-1 *et seq.* French Commercial Code; German Commercial Code (*Handelsgesetzbuch*) Section 348 and Section 343 of the German Civil Code (*Bürgerliches Gesetzbuch,* BGB). The Belgian Companies Code (*Wetboek van Vennootschappen en Verenigingen*) of 2019 does no longer differentiate between civil and commercial law.
2. Sections 1 and 2 German Commercial Code (*Handelsgesetzbuch,* or HGB).
3. Section 6 German Commercial Code, section 3 German Stock Corporations Act (*AktG*), section 13(3) German Limited Liability Companies Act (*GmbHG*).
4. Article 1670 of the Spanish Civil Códe (*Codigo Civil*). Article 2 Capital Companies Act *(Ley de Sociedades de Capital* as amended by *Ley 5/2021)*, accessible at https://www.boe.es.
5. Article 2082 Italian Civil Code *(Codice civile)*.

regarding, *inter alia*, registration, accounting, commercial agency and bankruptcy. Small and agricultural entrepreneurs are exempted from part of these rules, and the legal framework does not, as a matter of principle, apply to intellectual professionals.[6]

2.05 The common law system in operation in the UK does not make a distinction similar to those distinctions discussed in the previous paragraph. Instead, there is a practical distinction between profit-making and non-profit-making organizations. Both are enacted in the Companies Act 2006 (non-profit companies limited by guarantee, section 5 UK Companies Act 2006). In fact, a partnership can only be formed 'with a view of profit',[7] and only one form of a private company, the company limited by guarantee, is designed for non-profit-making organizations. Thus, whereas an association of lawyers would be regarded as a civil partnership in Belgium or France, it would be a partnership in England in exactly the same way as an association of market traders.

B Legal Personality and Limited Liability

2.06 A substantive distinction in the various forms of business organizations available in Europe is between those forms that are given legal personality and those that are not. In all countries, the capital companies have this type of personality conferred by law, whereas partnership forms have either no such personality or a modified form of it. Legal personality in its fullest sense means that the company is a separate and wholly distinct legal person from that of its members. It alone makes contracts, owns property and employs people. What follows is an even more important concept of limited liability of those members. Members (shareholders) whose liability is limited by shares are only liable to contribute to the assets up to the amount, if any, unpaid on their shares. Consequently, the company's creditors have recourse to the assets of the company, but not to assets owned by its shareholders or directors. The corollary is that creditors of the shareholders (and the directors), in principle, have no recourse to the assets of the company.[8]

2.07 As stated in the previous paragraph, some forms of partnerships may have legal personality but in a modified form. Such partnerships may make contracts, own property and employ people like any other legal person, but they differ in an important aspect: their members are liable for the debts incurred by the partnership. The same applies to the European Economic Interest Grouping (EEIG), which resembles the partnership form in several aspects (*see* paragraph 4.02 *et seq.*). Modified legal personality thus enables a partnership to operate in the same way as other legal

6. Articles 2195, 2083, 2135 Italian Civil Code. G.F. Campobasso, *Diritto Commerciale. 1. Diritto dell'Impresa.* Settima Edizione, UTET Giuridica, Wolters Kluwer Italia S.r.l. 2015, 41–45.
7. Section 1 of the PA 1890, accessible at http://www.legislation.gov.uk.
8. *See* for the general aspects regarding this asset partitioning, J. Armour et al., 'What Is Corporate Law?', in R. Kraakman et al., *The Anatomy of Corporate Law: A Comparative and Functional Approach,* Third Edition (Oxford: Oxford University Press, 2017), sections 1.2.1–1.2.2.

persons while the liability of its members is a guarantee for its creditors. Therefore such partnerships do not have to raise capital in order to be creditworthy.

C Principal Forms of Business Organization

2.08 It is possible to characterize the principal forms of business enterprise available in the various countries, bearing in mind the above factors. There are four principal types: general partnerships, limited partnerships, private companies and public or stock companies. Each form is discussed in turn. There are divisions within some of these and not all national forms fit exactly into one mould, particularly some hybrid forms, which are dealt with separately. There has also been a trend to introduce new and modified forms of business organizations into existing legal systems.

2.09 Four factors account for the tendency to introduce new and modified forms. First, countries were urged to limit the joint and several liability of the partners of large firms in professional services who were faced with substantial damages awards. Germany and Poland, for instance, introduced the *Partnerschaftsgesellschaft* (PartG) and the *spółka partnerska* (sp. p.), respectively.[9] These are very similar to general partnerships but exclude joint and several liability of a partner for negligence concerning professional performance of one of the other partners. In the UK, the *Limited Liability Partnership* (LLP) has been designed for the same purpose, but its use is not limited to certain regulated groups of professionals such as auditors, lawyers and medical doctors. Notwithstanding its name, the LLP is a legal person that has much less in common with the UK partnership than it has with the private company.[10]

2.09a Second, several Member States have undertaken to develop forms of business organizations that suit small- and medium-sized enterprises (SMEs) more than the traditional forms. Even the private company is often thought to share too many features with the public company, such as capital requirements and board structure, to effectively function for the benefit of SMEs. Thus, simplified and new types of companies have been introduced which are subject to less formal requirements and enjoy more freedom to insert tailor-made provisions into the companies' articles. The enhanced flexibility is offset by the imposition of limitations, such as the prohibition of using the capital market for funding and issuing shares in bearer form.[11] Examples are

9. Germany: Gesetz vom 25 July 1994 (BGBl. I S. 1744) as amended; many references are made to the regulation of the *Offene Handelsgesellschaft* (*OHG*). Polish Commercial Companies Code, Articles 86–101.
10. Limited Liability Partnerships Act 2000. J. Freeman, 'Limited Liability Partnerships in the United Kingdom: Do They Have a Role for Small Firms?', in J.A. McCahery, Th. Raaijmakers & E.P.M. Vermeulen (eds), *The Governance of Close Corporations and Partnerships* (Oxford: Oxford University Press, 2004), 293 *et seq.* and G. Morse, 'Limited Liability Partnerships and Partnership Law Reform in the United Kingdom', in J.A. McCahery, Th. Raaijmakers, & E. P.M. Vermeulen (eds), *The Governance of Close Corporations and Partnerships* (Oxford: Oxford University Press, 2004), 317 *et seq.*
11. F. Wooldridge, 'Some New Types of Company and Partnership in France and Germany', *International and Comparative Corporate Law Journal* 3, no. 2 (2001): 211 *et seq.*

the *société par actions simplifiée* (SAS), introduced by the French legislature, and the German public company (AG), which has been made accessible for SMEs by abolishing the requirement that at least five persons need to take part in its formation.[12] Similarly, subcategories of the private company have been created, such as the Spanish new enterprise limited liability company (*Sociedad Limitada Nueva Empresa* (SLNE)). The SLNE is a simplified version of the private company with respect to, *inter alia*, its formation procedure and decision-making features.[13] A similar approach has been taken by the German legislature by allowing a *Gesellschaft mit beschränkter Haftung* (GmbH) to be founded without initial capital. Several restrictions apply until the company has built up reserves equal to the level of the statutory minimum capital (*haftungsbeschränkte Unternehmergesellschaft*).[14] Another example of a simplified private company is the Italian *società a responsabilità limitata semplificata* introduced in 2012.[15] It is formed by a notarial deed according to a standard template *(Tabella A)* provided by ministerial decree.[16] The capital must be a minimum of EUR 1, but less than EUR 10,000.[17]

2.09b Third, what are known as social enterprises have gained momentum in several Member States. These enterprises can be distinguished from mainstream enterprises in that they have a primary and explicit social purpose. Accordingly, the aim of their economic activities is to benefit society. Social enterprises have limits on distribution of profits and/or assets in order to prioritize the social aim over profit-making. In its 2011 Communication Social Business Initiative, the European Commission calls the social economy and social innovation one of its main concerns and signals 'the growing desire of Europeans for their work, consumption, savings and investments to be more closely attuned to and aligned with "ethical" and "social" principles'.[18]

For policy objectives, the Commission coined the term 'social enterprise' to cover the following types of businesses:

- those for which the social or societal objective of the common good is the reason for commercial activity, often in the form of a high level of social innovation;
- those where profits are mainly reinvested with the view to achieving a social objective; and

12. Articles L227-1 *et seq.* French Commercial Code and Gesetz für kleine Aktiengesellschaften und zur Deregulierung des Aktienrechts, 2 Aug. 1994.
13. Ley 7/2003, de 1 de abril, de la sociedad limitada Nueva Empresa por la que se modifica la Ley 2/1995, de 23 de marzo, de Sociedades de Responsabilidad Limitada.
14. Section 5a GmbhG, inserted in 2008 by the act to modernize private company law and to curb abuse (*Gesetz zur Modernisierung des GmbH-Rechts und zur Bekämpfung von Missbräuchen (MoMiG)*. 'Renovating the German Private Limited Company', *German Law Journal* 9, no. 9 (2008): Special Edition.
15. Article 2463*bis* Italian Civil Code, introduced by Law Decree 1/2012.
16. Decreto Ministero della Giustizia 23/06/2012 n° 138, G.U. 14/08/2012.
17. Article 2463*bis*(3) Italian Civil Code. Serra, L. *Società a responsabilità limitata semplificata*, AltalexPedia, 2013.
18. Brussels, 25.10.2011 COM(2011) 682 final.

- where the method of organization or ownership system reflects their mission, using democratic or participatory principles, or focusing on social justice.[19]

Several Member States have developed specific legal forms or 'legal statutes' that can be adopted by different types of organizations such as the French *Société coopérative d'intérêt collectif* (SCIC). The UK has adapted the company form to facilitate the *Community Interest Company* (CIC).[20]

2.09c Fourth, the Court of Justice of the European Union (CJEU) has enhanced the freedom of establishment for companies by several landmark rulings to the effect that no Member State can withhold its citizens from using company forms of other Member States (*see* paragraphs 2.54 *et seq.*). This certainly is another stimulus for legislators to make their business organizations more attractive and flexible.[21] It enforces the trend to deregulate private companies, for instance, by abandoning the mandatory minimum capital for this type of company thereby copying the traditional position of the UK Private limited company (Ltd). France has not included this requirement for the *société a responsabilité limitée* (SARL).[22] Similarly, the Dutch legislature has modified the provisions for the *besloten vennootschap met beperkte aansprakelijkheid* (BV) by eliminating most of the capital requirements and by simplifying decision-making rules.[23] Even the UK has taken steps to further enhance the attractiveness of its Ltd. The Companies Act 2006 has simplified decision making for private companies and abolished the requirement to have a company secretary.[24]

2.10 As already mentioned in paragraph 2.08, this chapter is structured around the principal forms of a business organization. The starting point is partnerships, followed by companies and hybrid forms. Important aspects of the company forms are addressed again in Chapters 5 *et seq.* Following this classification of national business organizations, business organizations under European Union (EU) law are also described, although they are presented in more detail in Chapter 4. The EU has had a long-standing effect on national company law because of its harmonization programme. The effects of the harmonization programme are briefly outlined in this chapter but are discussed in greater depth in Chapter 3. The final part of this chapter examines the extent to which the freedom of establishment, as guaranteed by the Treaty on the Functioning of the European Union (TFEU), has been accomplished.

---

19. *Ibid.*, 2–3.
20. European Commission, *A Map of Social Enterprises and Their Eco-Systems in Europe* (Luxembourg: Publications Office of the European Union, 2015), 51 *et seq.* France: Titre II ter, Loi n° 47-1775; UK: introduced by the Companies Act 2004. Section 6 UK Companies Act 2006. Further: A. Argyrou, *Social enterprises in the EU. Law promoting stakeholder participation in social enterprises* (Instituut voor Ondernemingsrecht nr. 111) (dissertation, Utrecht), Deventer: Wolters Kluwer 2018.
21. J.A. McCahery & E.P.M. Vermeulen, 'The Evolution of Closely Held Business Forms in Europe', in J.A. McCahery, Th. Raaijmakers & E.P.M. Vermeulen (eds), *supra* n. 10, at 191 *et seq.* Also, T. van Duren, 'The Light Vehicle Competition', *European Company Law* 1, no. 4 (2004): 153–161.
22. Article L223-2 French Commercial Code. T. van Duren, *supra* n. 21.
23. The new legislation for the BV came into force on 1 Oct. 2012.
24. Explanatory Notes to the Companies Act 2006, 9 and 79.

II PARTNERSHIPS

2.11 Partnerships are those organizations that, whether or not they have legal personality, do not confer the privilege of limited liability upon their members. For that reason alone, they are generally not a popular medium for ordinary commercial transactions such as a distribution agreements. Nor are they suitable for very large organizations, despite very few practical restrictions on size. However, fiscal transparency may motivate enterprises to use general partnerships, especially for joint ventures, because, in such cases, the partners are granted tax deductions for losses suffered by the joint venture enterprise. The use of partnerships to avoid mandatory disclosure of annual accounts is not possible because the scope of the harmonized rules for financial reporting extends to partnerships where all members who have unlimited liability are public or private companies (*see* paragraph 9.28).[25] As a rule, partnerships have not been subject to any EU harmonization programme.

2.12 A common feature of all partnerships is that they are, in essence, personal relationships and, as a result, the assignment of a partner's share is usually restricted without agreement from the other partners. This follows from the partnership's contractual basis. Once agreed, as a rule, a contract can only be modified with the consent of each party to the contract and this, of course, also applies to the partnership contract. Partnerships are sometimes characterized as 'the most dangerous' (because of the partners' liability) and the 'most closed' (because it is not possible to transfer a partner's share unless all the other partners agree) of the 'company' forms.[26]

2.13 Partnership law offers the essential attributes for coordinating the economic activity of two or more persons.[27] It provides for a decision-making mechanism comprising both the internal management structure and the authority of partners to represent the firm. Moreover, partnership law creates a pool of assets for the benefit of the firm's creditors. For classification purposes, it is important to note that these attributes may vary from those that are rather rudimental and weak to more solid and sophisticated features. The law concerning simple partnership forms, such as the silent commercial partnership, confers such 'rudimental' mechanism to the partnership by granting each partner the power to manage the partnership's business, but not the authority to bind other partners by contracting with third parties. More developed types, such as the general partnership, have both elements and, therefore, each of the partners can bind the other partners or the partnership unless a clause in the partnership contract states otherwise. It must be noted, however, that partnership law, by using default terms, generally leaves substantial freedom for the partners to agree on the internal constitution of the firm. This flexibility enables partnerships to function for

25. Directive 2013/34/EU, Preamble recital 5.
26. M. Cozian, A. Viandier & F. Deboissy, *Droit des sociétés*, 27e édition (Paris: LexisNexis, 2012), no. 1204, regarding the société en nom collectif. The term 'companies' is used here in the generic sense, as previously mentioned in paragraph 2.01.
27. H. Hansmann & R. Kraakman, 'The Essential Role of Organizational Law', in J.A. McCahery, Th. Raaijmakers & E.P.M. Vermeulen (eds), *supra* n. 10, at 24 *et seq.*

a wide spectrum of business enterprises, ranging from family businesses and professional firms to joint ventures created by transnational enterprises.

2.14 As for the pool of assets, creditors of simple partnership forms are very unlikely to gain access to a great deal of the assets, as the partners may remain the owners of the assets, notwithstanding the fact that the assets are placed at the disposal of the partnership. The pool is then restricted to assets acquired during the term of the partnership's activities, and these assets are co-owned only as long as they are not divided. Creditors of the firm can lay claim to these assets. If they are not fully paid, then they may also lay claim to a partner's assets, but these must be shared with that partner's creditors. The creditors of a partner may also lay claim to that partner's share of the co-owned assets. In other words, the separation between the simple partnership's assets and the assets of its partners is easily permeable. By contrast, partnership forms enjoying legal personality own the property that is brought into the partnership and only the firm's creditors may lay claim to this property.[28]

2.15 The simple forms of partnership: civil partnership and silent commercial partnership are dealt with briefly in the following paragraph. Partnerships in the UK are described in paragraphs 2.19–2.23. The continental general partnership and the limited partnership are discussed in paragraphs 2.24–2.34 and 2.35–2.39, respectively.

A Civil Partnerships and 'Silent' Commercial Partnerships

2.16 In continental jurisdictions where a distinction is made between civil and commercial law (*see* paragraph 2.03), civil partnerships, that is, those that do not have commercial objects as defined by each country, are regarded essentially as a matter of agreement between the partners.[29] They are governed by civil rather than commercial codes. For instance, the Italian civil partnership, the *società semplice,* is the basic form of cooperation where the object is not commercial. Registration is mandatory, but it is not a prerequisite for the existence of the partnership.[30] In Spain, the civil partnership has no legal personality as long as it remains silent, but it is regarded as having legal personality if it operates in the name of the partnership.[31]

2.17 More importantly for our purposes, several countries have one or more forms of 'silent' commercial partnerships which are regarded as a matter of agreement rather than status because these partnerships can exist without being registered and without using the firm's name. It should be said, however, that these are not the mainstream forms of a general partnership in those countries.

28. H. Hansmann & R. Kraakman, 'Organizational Law as Asset Partitioning', *European Economic Review* 44 (2000): 807 *et seq.*
29. Note that 'civil partnership' has a different and specific meaning in the UK: The Civil Partnership Act 2004 defines this as a relationship between two people of the same sex ('civil partners'), which is formed when they register as civil partners.
30. Articles 2251–2290 Italian Civil Code. G.F. Campobasso, *Diritto Commerciale. 2. Diritto delle Società*, Nona Edizione, UTET Giuridica, Wolters Kluwer Italia, 56.
31. Article 1669 Spanish Civil Code.

2.18 A few examples may illustrate what silent commercial partnerships entail. In France, the *société en participation,* or silent partnership, is a purely private arrangement that does not need to be disclosed to anyone. It has no assets distinct from those of its partners, who retain title to their contributions so that each partner merely makes his or her assets available to the partnership. There may be undivided assets held in co-ownership by the partners. This occurs if assets are initially acquired by one or more partners acting in their own name because they cannot act in the name of the partnership without losing its silent status, followed by a transfer of ownership to all partners. The French silent partnership is effectively an agreement between the partners, subject to general rules of contract and a few mandatory provisions for partnerships in general. However, if the silent partnership has a commercial character (*see* paragraphs 2.03–2.05), default rules of a general partnership apply, unless otherwise agreed upon.[32] The silent partnership is used for business affairs such as joint marketing agreements. As already mentioned, partners must contract with third parties in their own name. In addition, third parties cannot sue a partner whom they have not dealt with personally unless that partner either led them to believe that he or she was involved in or made a profit from the transaction, or that the existence of the partnership had been voluntarily disclosed to the general public. This is known as a *société en participation ostensible.*[33] The Spanish silent partnership, or *sociedad civil interna,* is similar to the French silent partnership because it is an agreement subject to the general rules of contract. It has no assets and the patrimonial rules of the Civil Code apply.[34] Germany has a slightly different form of silent partnership, the *stille Gesellschaft.*[35] It is designed for an association between an active businessperson (the general partner) and a financial backer. In many respects, this type of partnership resembles a limited partnership in that the undisclosed partner is liable only to the other partner for the amount agreed in their contract, but not to third parties.

B General Partnerships in the UK

2.19 Civil partnerships are unknown in England, and no partnership is capable of having even a modified legal personality. A partnership is defined simply as 'the relation which subsists between persons carrying on a business in common with a view of profit'.[36] Companies, in the English law sense of the word, are excluded from this definition. There are no formal requirements for the formation of an English partnership. As stated earlier, an English partnership arises from an agreement between two or more persons, legal or natural, that they will carry on a business in common with the purpose of creating profit. The agreement may be expressed by way of a formal deed, or it may simply be inferred from the course of dealings, in which those involved act as

32. Articles 1871 and 1871-1 French Civil Code.
33. Article 1872-1 French Civil Code.
34. Articles 1669 and 392 Spanish Civil Code.
35. *See* sections 230–237 German Commercial Code.
36. Section 1 PA 1890.

partners, even if they themselves are not aware of the fact that this makes them partners. In general, questions as to whether or not a partnership exists will usually arise where either a creditor wishes to sue the other 'partners' on a contract made by one of them, or there is an internal dispute that requires a partnership obligation to be imposed in order to achieve its accomplishment. In such cases, it should be noted that simply sharing the profits of a business is neither a conclusive proof of a partnership nor the co-ownership of land.[37]

2.20 The essential characteristics that apply to an English partnership are twofold. First, every partner is an agent of his or her fellow partners in respect of any transaction carried out in the ordinary course of the partnership business.[38] Thus, any act within the ordinary authority of a partner will bind all the other partners. In addition, anyone who is not actually a partner, but who is represented as such to third parties, for example, a salaried partner, will also have that binding authority.[39] This concept also applies to a partner who acts outside a partner's ordinary authority, but who has been presented as having additional authority by the other partners.

The second concept is that partners among themselves are regarded as being in a fiduciary position. This means that they owe each other absolute duties of honesty and disclosure over and above the standard duties of care. Any partner who makes any unauthorized profit from a partnership transaction must account for that amount to the other partners, who do not need to prove either fault or loss. These two concepts are the reason for most disputes concerning the existence or liability of a partnership.

2.21 An English partnership is, as the partnerships mentioned in paragraphs 2.16–2.18, largely a matter of agreement between the partners. The Partnership Act (PA) of 1890 not only provides a few compulsory provisions but also includes several implied terms as to management and finance in default. All partners have equal management rights unless there is an agreement to the contrary. If a partnership agreement makes no provision for its duration, it is known as a partnership at will and can be dissolved at any time by a notice issued by one of the partners.[40] If the partnership is deemed not to be at will, then mutual consent is required for dissolution, except where the causes mentioned in the PA are involved.[41]

2.22 Although an English partnership is simply a relationship, it does have a name, known as the firm's name, under which it can sue and be sued. Although it is subject to the general regime for business names, there are no special requirements for the choice of the firm's name. The partners are fully liable for all the debts of the firm. Property that is brought into the partnership by the partners or acquired on account of the firm is known as partnership property. The partners hold it as co-owners, and every partner has the right to have that property applied in payment of partnership debts.[42]

37. Section 2 PA 1890.
38. Section 5 PA 1890.
39. Section 14 PA 1890.
40. Section 26 PA 1890.
41. Section 32 PA 1890.
42. Section 20 and 39 PA 1890.

In cases of insolvency, where the partners cannot pay the firm's debts or their own, there are two sets of creditors: the personal creditors of each partner and the partnership's creditors. There are also two estates: the partnership's assets and each individual partner's assets.

All the partners are entitled to share equally in the capital and profits of the business and must contribute equally towards the losses unless otherwise agreed.[43] A partnership is dissolved by termination of the venture, passing of an agreed time period and upon the death or bankruptcy of a partner, unless otherwise agreed. Furthermore, as already mentioned, a partnership for an indefinite period will be dissolved upon notice given by a partner. Lastly, the court may order a dissolution. Dissolution is followed by liquidation of the partnership, resulting in settling the partnership's accounts among the partners.[44]

2.23 In 2003, it was proposed that the PA 1890 be replaced. According to the Law Commission (actually, the Law Commission and the Scottish Law Commission), the act was not devised for larger partnerships, and the lack of entity status for partnerships under the law of England and Wales was criticized as being an anomaly. Although a draft bill was attached to the Law Commission's report, no such bill has been introduced to the Parliament. The Law Commission issued a further Joint Consultation Paper on proposals to reform the Limited Partnerships Act (LPA) of 1907. Although the government in 2006 announced its decision to implement the limited partnership law reforms recommended by the Law Commission, the recommendations with respect to the general partnership law reform have not been taken forward.[45] Since then, only two of the Law Commission's recommendations were implemented. The Legislative Reform Order 2009 made a certificate of registration as conclusive evidence that a limited partnership had been formed as of the date shown on the certificate and requires all new limited partnerships to include 'Limited Partnership', 'LP' or equivalent at the end of their names.[46]

C Continental General Partnerships

2.24 The standard form of general partnerships in continental legal systems is different from the English form. The reason for this is that they require some form of registration, and some countries confer legal personality upon the partnership. The French and Belgian *société en nom collectif* (SNC)[47] and the Spanish *sociedad regular colectiva*

43. Section 24 PA 1890.
44. Sections 33 *et seq.* and 44 PA 1890.
45. *Partnership Law: A Joint Report*, 2003 Law Com No. 283 and Scot Law Com No. 192. The report on limited partnerships included a draft bill. The consultation papers and the report are available from the Law Commission's website, https://www.lawcom.gov.uk/project/partnership-law (accessed 29 March 2021).
46. https://www.lawcom.gov.uk/project/partnership-law (accessed 29 March 2021).
47. Articles L210-1 and L210-6 French Commercial Code, Articles 2:5 and 2:6 *Belgian Companies Code*.

(SC)[48] have legal personality, as opposed to the German *Offene Handelsgesellschaft* (OHG), the Dutch *vennootschap onder firma* (VOF), the Italian *società in nome collettivo* (SNC) and the Polish *spółka jawna* (sp.j.).[49] None of these legal systems, however, confers limited liability upon the partners, and so general partnerships are economically transparent in the same manner as a partnership under English law. Legal personality, which goes hand in hand with unlimited liability, is called modified or reduced legal personality. The main difference is restricted to the ownership of partnership property. If the partnership is a legal person, the partnership is the owner of property brought into the partnership, as opposed to co-ownership by partners of a partnership without legal personality. It should be noted that UK partnerships, which are subject to Scottish law rather than English law, although identical in every other way to English firms, do have legal personality reflecting the continental influence in that legal system.[50]

2.25 Notwithstanding the differences regarding registration requirements and legal personality, the continental forms of partnerships are similar in many ways to those in the UK. The partnership must operate under a firm name, but, in some countries, an extension to the name, such as *en compagnie,* is mandatory in order to indicate the character of the business organization.[51] In conformity with the basic pattern, the partners of a general partnership have *unlimited liability* and each has a *right of management* unless there is an agreement to the contrary.[52] As with the execution of any contract, the partners have obligations towards each other to act in accordance with standards of good faith. Obligations towards the partnership include the obligation to contribute to the partnership and to refrain from competing with the partnership unless agreed otherwise.[53]

2.25a The right of management of the partners will in many cases be limited by the partnership contract. For example, the French SNC has a presumption of equal management,[54] and each partner has wide powers to bind the partnership. In practice, however, the agreement will contain provisions appointing one or more partners, or even third parties, as managers *(gérants)* of the business. In such case, the management rights of the other partners are excluded. However, they retain the possibility to remove a non-partner manager by a simple majority decision.[55]

---

48. Articles 116 and 122 Spanish Commercial Code. The Commercial Code frequently uses *compañia,* but its synonym *sociedad* is also used. In the Civil Code, *sociedad* is used.
49. Section 19 German Commercial Code; Articles 15 *et seq.* Dutch Commercial Code; Articles 2291 *et seq.* Italian Civil Code; Articles 22 *et seq.* Polish Commercial Companies Code.
50. Section 4(2) PA 1890.
51. For example, Article L221-2 French Commercial Code; Article 126 Spanish Commercial Code; Section 19 German Commercial Code; Article 24 Polish Commercial Companies Code.
52. For example, Articles L221-1 and 3 French Commercial Code; Articles 127 and 129 Spanish Commercial Code; Section 114 and 128 German Commercial Code; Article 7A:1676 Dutch Civil Code; Article 4:10 Belgian Companies Code.
53. For example, section 112 German Commercial Code; Dutch Supreme Court 19 Oct. 1990, NJ 1990, 21 *Koghee v. Akkoca;* Articles 136 and 137 Spanish Commercial Code; Article 56 Polish Commercial Companies Code; Article 2301 Italian Civil Code.
54. Articles L221-3 *et seq.* French Commercial Code.
55. Article L-221-12 French Commercial Code.

2.26 The partners may bind the partnership when *dealing with third parties* within the objects of the partnership unless the power to do so is limited by the partnership contract. In some jurisdictions, such limitations generally have no effect on third parties (e.g., Germany, Poland, France), whereas elsewhere limitations may be invoked if duly disclosed (e.g., the Netherlands).[56]

2.27 Limitations of a partner's right of representation may stem not only from the original partnership contract but also from an additional agreement. Such limitations are, for instance, a maximum amount to which a single partner can bind the partnership or the exclusion of real estate transactions by a single partner. The partnership contract may even bar a partner from the right to represent the partnership or determine that a partner is authorized to represent the partnership only in cooperation with another partner. As already mentioned, countries differ in the effect such limitations have on the position of third parties.

2.28 The *patrimonial regime* of a general partnership depends on it having a legal personality in the first place. If so, the partnership owns all assets contributed by the partners or otherwise acquired by the partnership. There are, however, no capital requirements, except for those that may originate from the regulation of specific professions or industries, such as insurance. Even without legal personality, the patrimonial regime of a general partnership may resemble that of a legal person because it can have legal capacity, which may come close to legal personality. For example, the OHG has no legal personality, but it is treated as having legal personality in many respects, especially in relation to third parties, such as its ability to incur obligations, take legal action or be sued. Partnership assets are held in the firm's name and all the partners form a community of joint co-owners *(Gesamthandsgemeinschaft)*.[57] Co-owned assets are no longer at the disposal of a single partner, and creditors of the firm may lay claim on this 'pool of assets'.[58] A similar regime applies to the Dutch general partnership *(vennootschap onder firma)*.[59]

2.29 Partnership law generally provides for default rules on the *distribution of profits and losses*. Traditionally, partnership law presumes that the distribution of both profits and losses is made according to the proportion of the capital contributions of the partners. A partner who provides only services, rather than capital, is treated like the capital partner with the lowest capital contribution unless there is an express agreement to the contrary. This is still the basic rule in France, Belgium, the Netherlands, Italy and Spain. In Spain, however, a partner providing only services is not liable for

56. Articles L221-4 and L221-5 French Commercial Code; Section 125 and 126 German Commercial Code; Article 17 Dutch Commercial Code and Article 25 Trade Register Act *(Handelsregisterwet)*; Article 29 Polish Commercial Companies Code.
57. Section 124 German Commercial Code. The same applies to the Polish general partnership *(sp.j.)*, Article 8 Polish Commercial Companies Code.
58. Section 719 German Civil Code.
59. Article 7A:1655 Dutch Civil Code and Dutch Supreme Court 17 Dec. 1993, NJ 1994, 301. Under Italian law, partnerships are also deemed to hold assets in the firm's name, G.F. Campobasso, *Diritto Commerciale. 2. Diritto delle Società*, Nona Edizione, UTET Giuridica, Wolters Kluwer Italia S.r.l. 2015; 44–47.

losses at all, again, unless otherwise agreed.[60] In Italy, the position of a partner providing services has to be determined by the court where the partnership contract does not provide for that partner's share of profits and losses.[61] Modern partnership law, such as that of Poland, provides for a different rule: all partners have an equal share of profits and losses unless the partnership agreement stipulates another distribution arrangement. The German solution has elements of both systems: the capital partners receive a fixed percentage of their contribution before the rest of the profits, if any, are distributed equally. The partners are also equally liable for losses.[62] It is important to note that these are mainly default rules, so the partners are free to choose a distribution that fits the objects of their partnership. However, in several jurisdictions, it is explicitly prohibited to agree in such a way to exclude a partner from profit distribution or to let only one partner receive all the profits ('societas leonina').[63]

2.30 The provisions on the *dissolution of general partnerships* mirror the contractual character, even where a partnership enjoys legal personality. For example, the French SNC is dissolved by causes such as the end of the period for which the partnership has been formed or by other causes envisaged by the drafters of the contract – such causes may equally lead to the dissolution of a company. However, a partnership may also be dissolved upon the dismissal of a manager who is a partner, or upon the bankruptcy or death of a partner. If the participation of one of the partners has become impossible, the personal relationship is supposed to end. If the relationship seriously deteriorates because of a disagreement between the partners which paralyses the firm, then the court may decide to dissolve the partnership.[64]

2.31 In many cases, the remaining partners may wish to continue the partnership without the participation of the bankrupt or deceased partner. In such cases, the partnership will continue to exist if the partnership contract provides for it or if the remaining partners unanimously decide to carry on its existence.[65]

2.32 In the event that a managing partner is dismissed from the SNC, the dismissed manager may decide to withdraw from the partnership and demand the repayment of his or her participation, the value of which will be determined in accordance with the rules set out in the Civil Code.[66]

---

60. Article 1844-1 French Civil Code; Article 4:4 Belgian Companies Code; Article 7A:1670 Dutch Civil Code; Articles 140 and 141 Spanish Commercial Code.
61. Article 2263(2) Italian Civil Code.
62. Article 51 Polish Commercial Companies Code; Section 120–122 German Commercial Code.
63. For example, Article 1844-1 French Civil Code; Article 4:2 Belgian Companies Code; Article 2265 Italian Civil Code; and, implicitly, Article 51 Polish Commercial Companies Code. Exemption from losses may also be prohibited, e.g., by Article 1844-1 French Civil Code. The term 'societas leonina' refers to one of Fontaine's tales, M. Cozian, A. Viandier & F. Deboissy, *supra* n. 26, at no. 141.
64. Article 1844-7 French Civil Code; Articles L221-12, L221-15 and L221-16 French Commercial Code.
65. Articles L221-12, L221-15 and L221-16 French Commercial Code.
66. Article L221-12 French Commercial Code and Article 1843-4 French Civil Code.

Other countries have similar provisions concerning the dissolution of general partnerships.[67] In addition, each partner has the right to withdraw from the partnership; that is, to terminate the contract, albeit within certain constraints, such as a term that must be taken into account. The constraints are generally more restrictive if the partnership is formed for a limited period. A partner's withdrawal has, in principle, an effect on that partner's participation, but the partnership continues to exist if more than one partner remains and if the partnership contract provides for continuation.[68]

2.33 Upon the death of a partner, his or her heirs may acquire the rights and obligations of the deceased partner in relation to the partnership. The partnership contract may provide for this situation, for instance, by continuation of the partnership with one of the heirs. Alternatively, where continuation of the partnership is agreed upon excluding the heirs, the latter may be entitled to reimbursement of the share of the deceased partner.[69] Such provisions, however, may conflict with the terms of the will of the deceased partner or with family law provisions. For that reason, the Commission has recommended that Member States ensure the continuity of the partnership as a going concern in the event of the death of a partner.[70]

2.34 The dissolution must be published in order to inform the creditors of the partnership and is followed by *liquidation of the partnership's assets*. One or more liquidators must be appointed. As a rule, all partners become liquidators, unless the partnership agreement provides otherwise. Liquidation generally deprives the partnership of its legal capacity in order to take part in any activities other than selling its assets and paying its debts. By its nature, the partnership includes the liability of the partners in the event that the partnership's assets do not bring in sufficient financial means to satisfy the creditors. A surplus will be distributed among the partners. If the partnership is a legal person, it continues to exist until liquidation is completed. Even where the partnership has no legal personality, it must function as an entity until the liquidation procedure is completed.[71]

67. Sections 131–133 German Commercial Code; Article 1700 Spanish Civil Code and Article 221–224 Spanish Commercial Code; Articles 7A:1683–1686 Dutch Civil Code; Articles 58–61 Polish Commercial Companies Code; Articles 4:16-4:19 Belgian Companies Code.
68. Sections 131 and 132 German Commercial Code; Article 225 Spanish Commercial Code; Articles 7A:1683 and 1686 Dutch Civil Code; Articles 58 and 59 Polish Commercial Companies Code; Articles 4:18 *et seq.* Belgian Companies Code; Articles 2272, 2273 and 2284–2290 Italian Civil Code.
69. An example is Article 4:18(2) Belgian Companies Code.
70. Recommendation 94/1069/EC. *See also* the *Better Environment for Enterprises* communication by the European Commission to the European Parliament, Brussels 7 Nov. 2002 COM(2002) 610 final.
71. Articles 1844-8 and 1844-9 French Civil Code; Section 733–735 German Civil Code; Articles 227 *et seq.* Spanish Commercial Code; Articles 3:166 *et seq.* Dutch Civil Code; Articles 82–83 Polish Commercial Companies Code; Articles 2275–2280 Italian Civil Code.

D Limited Partnerships (LPs)

2.35 It has been illustrated that the major disadvantage of the general partnership form is that the partners have unlimited liability for the debts of the firm. It is not, therefore, possible to invest in such a firm without assuming such liability. Consequently, countries have an alternative form of partnership: the LP, which allows some partners to enjoy limited liability for the partnership's debts in the same way as a shareholder of a capital company. The common theme in such partnerships is that there are two types of partners: general partners and limited partners, the latter enjoying limited liability, but restricted management rights. The general partners have management rights and are called managing partners. Among the general partners, the general partnership rules apply.[72]

2.36 LPs of the countries that are used as examples are named and abbreviated as follows:

- Belgium: *commanditaire vennootschap* (CommV) or SComm.
- France: *société en commandite simple* (SCS).
- Germany: *Kommanditgesellschaft* (KG).
- Italy: *società in accomandita semplice* (SAS).
- The Netherlands: *commanditaire vennootschap* (CV).
- Poland: *spółka komandytowa* (sp.k.).
- Spain: *sociedad en comandita* (SEC).
- UK: *limited partnership* (LP).

In all countries, except for the UK, these forms contain the Latin word *commenda*, reflecting the medieval origins of the LP.[73]

2.37 All these forms are modifications of the relevant general partnership form. LPs are rarely used in some countries, for example, France and the UK, but are more popular in others, such as Germany.[74] The LP may, for instance, be indicated when a partner of a general partnership wishes to retire but the remaining partners cannot reimburse the retiring partner's share. To keep this share at the disposal of the partnership, the retiring partner's status can be changed into that of a limited partner.

---

72. Articles L222-1 *et seq.* French Commercial Code; ss 161 *et seq.* German Commercial Code; s 4 Limited Partnerships Act 1907; Articles 145–150 Spanish Commercial Code; Article 19 Dutch Commercial Code; Articles 102 *et seq.* Polish Commercial Companies Code; Articles 4:22-4:24 Belgian Companies Code; Articles 2313 and 2318 Italian Civil Code.
73. *See* on the medieval commenda and its even older origins J.H. Pryor, 'The Origins of the Commenda Contract', *Speculum* 52, no. 1 (January 1977): 5–37 (accessible at http://www.jstor.org/stable/2856894).
74. The limited partnership form in the UK was introduced much later than in other countries by the Limited Partnerships Act of 1907 (limited partnership). Limited partnerships are rare in the UK, principally because by the time they were introduced their role had been superseded by the private limited company. For France, M. Cozian, A. Viandier & F. Deboissy, *supra* n. 26, at no. 1250. The popularity of the German *Kommanditgesellschaft* is partly due to the combination with a private company as a general partner. *See infra*, paragraph 2.46.

This way, limited liability can be created without having to adopt the often less flexible structure of a capital company. A capital company could also have unwanted tax consequences because partnerships are generally regarded as transparent for taxation purposes – that is, the partners and not the partnership are liable for tax – whereas companies themselves are subject to taxation.[75]

2.38 The limited partner is principally liable only up to the amount of his or her contributions, which must be in cash or in kind. The agreed contribution of the limited partner cannot be delivered by way of performing services, as this would involve management participation, which is generally prohibited and conflicts with the idea of a determinable amount of the contribution. In order to avoid misleading third parties, it is not permitted to use the name of the limited partner in the name of the partnership. Aside from a few exceptions, violation of this provision may lead to the loss of the limited liability status.[76] However, to properly inform third parties, some details about the limited partner(s) and their contribution must be mentioned in the documents, which the partnership has to file with the commercial registry. National provisions range from requiring publication of the name and the contribution of each of the limited partners,[77] to more extensive information, such as the total amount of the limited partners' contributions.[78]

2.39 Limited partners may lose their status not only by lending their name to the firm but also by representing the partnership in dealings with third parties. Strict rules may apply, such as in Belgium, France, the Netherlands and the UK, where limited partners are not permitted to represent the partnership when dealing with third parties, not even when limited partners are granted a power of attorney by the general partners, without risking their limited liability status.[79] However, Germany, Poland and Italy permit limited partners to represent the firm if they have a power of attorney. If a limited partner deals with third parties without such power, he or she will be personally liable for the transaction, but this will not, as in other jurisdictions, lead to a loss of limited liability for the debts of the partnership.[80]

---

75. On problems of taxation of partnerships in cross-border situations, *see* P. Essers & G.T. Meussen, 'Taxation of Partnerships/Hybrid Entities', in J.A. McCahery, Th. Raaijmakers & E.P.M. Vermeulen (eds), *supra* n. 10, at 415 *et seq.*
76. For example, Article L222-6 French Commercial Code.
77. Article 1835 French Civil Code and L222-4 French Commercial Code; Section 162 German Commercial Code; s. 8 and 9 Limited Partnerships Act.
78. Article 10 Dutch Trade Register Act (*Handelsregisterwet*).
79. Article L 222-6 French Commercial Code; Article 148IV Spanish Commercial Code; Article 4:25 Belgian Companies Code; s. 6(1) Limited Partnerships Act.
80. Section 170 German Commercial Code and BGHZ 17, 392 *et seq.*; Article 118 Polish Commercial Companies Code; Article 2320 Italian Civil Code.

III COMPANIES

A Private Companies

2.40 Private companies are those forms of business organizations designed for small or medium concerns which require limited liability and legal personality but do not require access to public funding through the general capital markets. Financing comes from contributions by the members themselves or, alternatively, through bank finance. Each country has this type of company, but some, for example, Belgium and France, have severe restrictions on the transferability of the members' interests.[81] They can, therefore, be regarded as closed companies or as capital companies, which retain many of the features of a personal company or partnership. Other countries, such as the UK, Germany and Italy, have no such mandatory restrictions, although many companies adopt some form of restriction on transfers in their charters. The capital requirements in some countries are less rigid in comparison with public companies, and the UK, France and the Netherlands, in fact, do not prescribe a minimum capital at all. In general, the private company forms are very popular and are used by the vast majority of companies, although the limited liability advantages are often negated by the requirement of banks for personal guarantees by the members.

2.41 The various national forms of private companies that are used by way of example in this book are:

- Belgium: *besloten vennootschap or société à responsabilité limitée* (BV/SRL).
- France: *société a responsabilité limitée* (SARL).
- Germany: *Gesellschaft mit beschränkter Haftung* (GmbH).
- Italy: *società a responsabilità limitata* (SRL).
- The Netherlands: *besloten vennootschap met beperkte aansprakelijkheid* (BV).
- Poland: *Spółka z ograniczoną odpowiedzialnocią* (spółka z o.o./sp. z o.o.).
- Spain: *sociedad de responsabilidad limitada* (S.R.L. or S.L.).
- UK: *private limited company* (Ltd).

B Public or Stock Companies

2.42 Public or stock companies are available in each Member State and the UK. Although there are far fewer of these than private companies, in economic terms they are very significant. These companies are designed for larger enterprises which have access to all the capital markets for raising finance in terms of both equity capital from shareholders and loan capital from bondholders. They are genuine capital companies in that there usually are a large and diverse number of shareholders who, although they, economically speaking, 'own' the company, cannot, in reality, manage or control

81. Article 5:63 Belgian Companies Code; Article L223-14 French Commercial Code.

it. This separation of ownership and control requires complex structures for the governance of such companies.[82] The debate on corporate governance finds its origins here, and corporate scandals, such as the Enron, Ahold and Parmalat scandals, demonstrated the need for appropriate control mechanisms.[83] Because of their economic importance, public companies are also subject to far greater controls in such areas as mergers and creditor protection. In general, they also have a large number of employees and the question of the role of employees in the company has to be addressed. However, this, of course, is not limited to the public company form.

2.43 In legal terms, the common characteristics of public companies include the free transferability of shares and securities (access to public investment requires it), an elaborate system of control and minority shareholder protection, controls on raising and maintaining equity capital, the need to compel disclosure of information to members and to the public, and detailed rules as to the presentation and auditing of accounts.[84] In certain areas, the various national forms of public companies are very similar because national laws have been harmonized, or, perhaps more accurately, approximated, as the result of the implementation of EU directives and EU case law. These areas include questions of corporate capacity, share capital, the preparation and auditing of accounts, mergers, conversions and divisions, and the admission of public companies' securities to the appropriate stock exchanges.

2.44 In other areas, however, they remain disparate where either no such harmonization has been attempted (e.g., loan capital) or on issues where there has been a failure by various governments to reach an agreement (e.g., the management structure). With the exception of the UK, each of the national public company forms is regulated by codes or chapters of codes separate from those of the national private companies.

2.45 The various national forms of public or stock companies that are used by way of example in this book include:

- Belgium: *naamloze vennootschap/société anonyme* (NV/SA).
- France: *société anonyme* (SA).
- Germany: *Aktiengesellschaft* (AG).
- Italy: *società per azioni* (SPA).
- The Netherlands: *naamloze vennootschap* (NV).
- Poland: *spółka akcyjna* (SA).
- Spain: *sociedad anónima* (SA).
- UK: *public limited company* (Plc).

---

82. The consequences of the separation of ownership and control were researched for the first time by A. Berle & G.C. Means, *The Modern Corporation and Private Property*, with a new introduction by M.L. Weidenbaum & M. Jensen (New Brunswick/London: Transaction Publishers, 1991). The original publication is from Harcourt, Brace & World, 1932.
83. *The Economist*, 15 July 2002, 'A Guide to Corporate Scandals'; *Washington Post*, 14 Oct. 2004, 'Ahold Settles SEC Fraud Charges. Dutch Grocer Is Not Fined Because of Its Cooperation'. *See also* the European Corporate Governance Institute (ECGI) at www.ecgi.org/.
84. The common structure of company law among many jurisdictions is set out in J. Armour et al., 'What Is Corporate Law', in R. Kraakman et al., *supra* n. 8, chapter 1.

IV HYBRID FORMS

A Companies Acting as General Partner

2.46 Companies having legal personality may be partners in one of the forms of partnership set out previously. Thus in the UK, for example, the general partner in a limited partnership might itself be a limited company – thus, in effect, having complete limited liability. In Germany, for instance, this combination of a company and a limited partnership, known as the GmbH & Co. KG, has become popular. This form has a GmbH as the general partner and individuals as limited partners, who are usually also members of the GmbH. This form is widespread because it combines the advantages of a partnership (such as a simple capital structure) with the limited liability provided by the GmbH. Indeed, a natural person as a general partner would be fully liable for the acts of the partnership. Furthermore, the limited partners of the KG are allowed to act as directors of the general partner, that is, the GmbH. They thus exercise control over the general partner. Any problems caused by the fact that the management board of the GmbH is not accountable to the limited partners of the KG are usually overcome because they are often also members of the GmbH. Apart from combinations, such as the GmbH & Co. KG, there are some other specific forms available for a business enterprise, which combine elements of companies and partnerships. The main form is a type of LP with shares.

B LPs with Shares

2.47 LPs with shares are, in effect, combinations of partnerships and public companies. They are unknown in the UK, which, as mentioned above, treats the two forms as entirely separate. The continental approach of treating all these forms as types of a company allows for greater flexibility. The French *société en commandité par actions* (SCA) is a good illustration of this and is briefly discussed here.[85] The Commercial Code constitutes the hybrid character of the SCA, where the first provision on the SCA declares that where it is compatible with the special provisions, both the rules on LPs and public limited companies apply to it. Because of its mixed nature, the managing partners cannot assign their shares, except with the consent of all other members, whereas the limited partners (shareholders) have freely transferable shares in the same way as those in an SA. The special provisions, however, render the SCA very flexible compared to the SA. The managing partner(s) can be a legal person, for instance, a SARL, and the articles of the SCA may confer extensive powers to such partner(s), including the exclusive right to appoint and dismiss managers. This, of course,

85. Articles L226-1 *et seq.* French Commercial Code.

guarantees the general partner(s) a very strong position vis-à-vis the shareholders, who are only partly compensated by the obligation to establish a supervisory board composed of at least three shareholders.[86] The SCA is sometimes used as a listed company and is considered to offer generally temporary protection against a takeover, due to the weak position of its shareholders. In the event that an SA is transformed into an SCA, the shareholders have the right to opt out.[87]

2.48 In Germany, the LP with shares is known as the KGaA,[88] in Spain as the *sociedad comanditaria por acciones* (S. Com. por A.), in Poland as the *Spółka komandytowo-akcyjna* (SKA) and in Italy as the *società in accomandita per azioni* (SAPA).[89] The Spanish version was modernized in 1989 and is primarily a modification of the public company, the *sociedad anónima*, because they are both categorized as *sociedades de capital* and regulated by the same act.[90] The powers of the managing partners are the same as those of the directors of a public company.[91] In Poland, the position of the general or managing partner(s) is regulated by the provisions on the general partnership, as opposed to other matters, such as the share capital, the supervisory board and the general assembly, which are covered by the provisions for the public or joint-stock company.[92] Similar to the general partners of the Spanish form, the general partners of an Italian SAPA have the same rights and obligations as directors of the public company.[93] In the Netherlands, the LP with shares was abolished in 1971 to prevent the use of this partnership form as an alternative to companies in order to evade harmonized company law. Belgium abolished this partnership form in 2019 when the new Companies Code was enacted.[94]

V BUSINESS ORGANIZATIONS UNDER EU LAW

2.49 The EU legislature has enacted several regulations in order to create legal forms for business organizations under EU law. Primarily, EU law governs such business organizations, which may transfer their registered seat from one Member State to another. By 1985, the first of these business organizations, the EEIG, was introduced. The EEIG aims to enable cooperation between entrepreneurs and/or enterprises from

86. Articles L226-2 and L226-4 French Commercial Code.
87. M. Cozian, A. Viandier & F. Deboissy, *Droit des sociétés*, 33e édition (Paris: LexisNexis, 2020), no. 955.
88. Sections 278 *et seq.* AktG.
89. Article 1 Capital Companies Act *(Ley de Sociedades de Capital* as amended by *Ley 5/2021);* Articles 169 *et seq.* Spanish Commercial Code; Articles 125 *et seq.* Polish Commercial Companies Code; Articles 2452 *et seq.* Italian Civil Code.
90. The Capital Companies Act *(Ley de Sociedades de Capital).*
91. Article 252 *Ley de Sociedades de Capital.*
92. Article 126 Polish Commercial Companies Code.
93. Article 2455 Italian Civil Code. The SAPA is not frequently used: G.F. Campobasso, *Diritto Commerciale. 2. Diritto delle Società.* Nona Edizione, UTET Giuridica, Wolters Kluwer Italia S.r.l. 2015, 548–549.
94. *Wetboek van vennootschappen en verenigingen*, Belgisch Staatsblad/Moniteur Belge 04.04.2019, no. 33239.

different Member States. Almost twenty years later, in 2001, the Regulation on the Statute of the European Company, the *Societas Europaea* (SE), was adopted. It took the European institutions almost three decades of debate and negotiations to reach this milestone. The SE is a capital company and is meant to facilitate the restructuring of enterprises at a European level. The third business organization under EU law is the European Cooperative Society, the *Societas Cooperativa Europaea* (SCE), a vehicle for cooperation of natural persons or national cooperative organizations. The SCE regulation, adopted in 2003, applies as of 18 August 2006.[95] The EEIG, the SE and the SCE are dealt with further in Chapter 4.

VI IMPACT OF THE EU

2.50 Whereas developments at the EU level seemed to have come to a halt during most of the 1990s, considerable progress has been made since then.[96] In hindsight, it can be said that the adoption of the Directive on the European Works Council (1994) paved the way for the SE because it took away the 'employee participation bug' which has infected many proposals in the field of company law to halt their progress.[97] The birth of the SE also brought life to long-pending proposals, such as the Tenth Directive on cross-border mergers. By 2008, it was concluded that the EU harmonization programme yielded a considerable number of directives, ranging from disclosure requirements and annual financial statements to mergers and divisions and takeover bids. The impact of this EU legislation on national company laws is evident and, since then, several directives have been amended and/or simplified.[98] Most recently, enabling the use of digital tools and processes in companies has led to Directive (EU) 2019/1151 and Directive (EU) 2019/2121 governing matters such as online formation and registration and the online completion of certain steps in the process of mergers, divisions and conversions.[99] Harmonization has certainly led to modernization of national laws, for instance, in relation to accounting and financial reporting, takeover bids and capital markets. In some cases, it has had a spill-over effect, where countries extended implementation of EU legislation beyond the prescribed areas; notably, by further applying provisions of the directive aimed at public companies to private companies.

95. The European Commission has also launched proposals for a *European Association* (EA) and a *European Mutual Society*, OJ 1992, C 223/52 and OJ 1992, C 99/40.
96. J. Wouters, 'European Company Law: Quo Vadis?', *Common Market Law Review* 37 (2000): 257–307. For the ups and downs of the harmonization programme, *see also* C. Timmermans, 'First Water van Gerven Lecture', *Company Law as Ius Commune?*, Leuven Centre for a Common Law of Europe, accessible on the website of the Ius Commune Research School, www.iuscommune.eu. A thorough analysis of the state of harmonization in the 1990s is offered by R.M. Buxbaum et al. (eds), *European Economic and Business Law, Legal and Economic Analyses on Integration and Harmonization* (Berlin/New York: Walter de Gruyter, 1996).
97. The metaphor is from J. Wouters, *supra* n. 96, at 263.
98. *See* the 2012 Action Plan for an overview, European Commission, Action Plan: European company law and corporate governance – a modern legal framework for more engaged shareholders and sustainable companies, COM(2012) 740 final, 2–3.
99. Member States need to transpose the 2019 directives in their national laws by August 2021 and January 2023 respectively.

Nevertheless, harmonization has its drawbacks, the most obvious being the risk of 'petrification' of harmonized national law. Drafting and adopting a revised version of a directive may be as burdensome and time-consuming as drafting a new one. This is particularly true when directives or amendments are very detailed. Therefore, the Commission, in its 1985 White Paper on Completing the Internal Market, already featured another approach to law-making in order to minimize harmonization efforts by limiting it to the essentials and relying more on the mutual recognition of national regulations and standards.[100]

2.51 The actual effect of the harmonization programme on the development of corporate law within the EU is difficult to assess. Critics mention the lack of harmonization in core topics, such as directors' duties and shareholder remedies.[101] Others point out peculiarities of national law that may last even where they should have been overruled by harmonization. For instance, the contractual origin of companies, which is still clearly visible in the legal system of countries such as France, may be hard to reconcile with the strict limitation of annulment of companies imposed by the First Directive, and it may take a long time before legal practice conforms to such harmonization.[102]

2.52 Although the various forms of partnerships and companies under national laws of the Member States and the UK have many features in common, a number of differences also mark them and each is a purely national form of organization. These two factors have created basic problems that have been brought into focus by the existence and ideals of the EU, in particular the freedom of establishment. The first problem stems from the differences in national laws and relates to the creation of the single market itself - ideally, in light of the single market, all companies and partnerships operating under various national laws of the Member States should be operating under the same rules. This is expressed by the concept of a level playing field so that, for example, a German AG and a French SA should be subject to the same controls and restrictions. The second problem arises from the fact that purely national forms require registration in, and governance by, a particular Member State. Thus, for a company that wishes to operate in several Member States, the problem has been, in principle, that it could not move from one Member State to another without being wound up entirely and then set up again in the appropriate form in another Member State.

2.53 The answers to these problems are in different stages of development. To solve the level playing field issue, the EU adopted the previously mentioned harmonization

100. This approach was announced in relation to the free movement of goods, COM(85) 310 final, 14 June 1985 White Paper from the Commission to the European Council, *Completing the Internal Market*, 19 *et seq.*
101. L. Enriques, 'EC Company Law Directives and Regulations: How Trivial Are They?' (May 2005). *ECGI – Law Working Paper* No. 39/2005, http://ssrn.com/abstract = 730388.
102. M. Bolzard, 'Incidence des normes européennes sur la liberé de constitution des sociétés en droit francais', *Revue des Sociétés* no. 1 (January/February 2005), 1 *et seq.*; J.V. Louis, 'Ensuring Compliance and Implementation by Member States', in R.M. Buxbaum et al., *supra* n. 96, at 1 *et seq.*

programme, which has been successful to a certain point. To compensate, as it were, for the fact that companies are purely national forms, the SE and other business organizations under EU law were introduced in order to facilitate cross-border cooperation and restructuring. Nevertheless, the problem remained partly unresolved for the national entities, except in terms of setting up a branch in another Member State or merging cross-border. The Commission, in 2004, launched a public consultation on a draft (Fourteenth) Directive on the cross-border transfers of seats but the outcome led the responsible commissioner to the conclusion that there was no need for action at the EU level on this issue, *inter alia,* due to the effects of the CJEU judgment in *Sevic [2003]*, enabling cross-border mergers (*see* paragraph 8.60).[103] Since then, case law clarified that the right of establishment entails, to a certain extent, the cross-border conversion of companies (*see* paragraph 2.68). This formed the stimulus for the codification of this instrument by the Codification Directive (EU) 2017/1132 (*see* paragraph 3.19a). The effects of a cross-border conversion of a company are similar to a transfer of the seat from one state to another. A conversion indeed requires a company governed by the law of country A, having its seat in country A, to meet the criteria as set by country B in order to be subject to the law of country B, resulting in having its seat in that country (*see* paragraphs 8.84 *et seq.*).

VII THE RIGHT OF ESTABLISHMENT WITHIN THE EU

2.54 Regarding the mobility of national companies within the EU, Articles 49 and 54 of the TFEU are relevant. They expressly grant companies the right of secondary establishment in another Member State, for example, through a branch, agency or subsidiary. The CJEU, in *Commission v. France* (1986), regarded this right as being paramount over national tax considerations.[104] However, the right to primary establishment of companies, as afforded to individuals by Article 49, is not acknowledged fully.

2.55 The right to freedom of establishment within the EU is contained in Article 49 of the TFEU itself.[105] This gives self-employed individuals the right to set up a business in any Member State, including the right to set up a company or partnership. This right of primary establishment for individuals has been confirmed by the CJEU in the *Reyners* case (1974).[106] Article 49 provides as follows:

---

103. European Commission, Public consultation on the transparency and level of fees in cross-border transactions in the EU. Feedback Statement, Brussels, 16 February 2018 (accessible at: https://ec.europa.eu/info/sites/default/files/2017-cross-border-transactions-fees-summary-of-responses_en.pdf).
104. Case C-270/83 (*Commission v. France*) (1986).
105. The freedom of establishment is dealt with in the Trade and Cooperation Agreement (TCA) between the EU and the UK. What this agreement might imply for companies is sketched by K. Engsis Sørensen, 'Free Movement of Companies Under the New Trade and Cooperation Agreement Between the EU and the UK', *European Company Law Journal* 18, no. 4 (2021): 117–124.
106. Case C-2/74 (*Reyners v. Belgian State*) (1974).

> Within the framework of the provisions set out below, restrictions on the freedom of establishment of nationals of a Member State in the territory of another Member State shall be prohibited. Such prohibition shall also apply to restrictions on the setting-up of agencies, branches or subsidiaries by nationals of any Member State established in the territory of any Member State.
>
> Freedom of establishment includes the right to take up and pursue activities as self-employed persons and to set up and manage undertakings, in particular companies or firms within the meaning of the second paragraph of Article 54, under the conditions laid down for its own nationals by the law of the country where such establishment is effected, subject to the provisions of the chapter relating to capital.

Article 54 then provides as follows:

> Companies or firms formed in accordance with the law of a Member State and having their registered office, central administration or principal place of business within the Union shall, for the purposes of this Chapter, be treated in the same way as natural persons who are nationals of Member States.
>
> 'Companies or firms' means companies or firms constituted under civil or commercial law, including cooperative societies, and other legal persons governed by public or private law, save for those which are non-profit-making.

The question as to whether this provision allows for the primary establishment (i.e., full mobility) of 'companies or firms' is addressed in the following paragraphs.

2.56 The right of primary establishment would allow a company to be able to move from one Member State to another without having to alter its charter or, at least, its legal personality. Given that a single harmonized system of company law does not yet exist throughout the EU, the solution would require, for example, Belgium to recognize a French incorporated company that chose to move all its offices, management and operations to Belgium as if it were a Belgian company, but without requiring it to actually become a Belgian company.

2.57 Traditionally, two conflicting doctrines of private international law operate within the EU regarding the recognition of companies. The first, known as the doctrine of incorporation, provides that a foreign company, created in accordance with a foreign legal system and having its registered office in that foreign state, is recognized as such by the host country. Under this principle, a company incorporated and registered, for example, in Spain is regarded as a Spanish company by the Netherlands, even if it is operating, in all senses of the word, only within the Netherlands.[107]

107. According to the *Impact Assessment on the Directive on the Cross-border Transfer of Registered Office*, Commission Staff Working Document, Brussels 12 Dec. 2007 SEC(2007) 1707, 9, the incorporation doctrine is followed by other Member States, including Denmark, Finland and the Czech Republic. German courts apply the incorporation doctrine where companies from other Member States are concerned, C. Teichmann, 'Report from Germany', *European Company Law (ECL)* 5, no. 4 (2008): 189. Furthermore: L.A. Martinez Giner, 'Spanish Companies and Private International Law', in G. Maisto (ed.), *Residence of Companies Under Tax Treaties and EC Law*, EC and International Tax Law Series, IBFD 2009, 753 *et seq.*

2.58 The second doctrine, which operates in various forms in other Member States, is that of the *'siege réel'* or real seat. Under this doctrine, the recognition of a company depends on it conforming to the requirements of the country in which it has chosen to locate its real centre of activities or management decision-making. Thus, if the Spanish incorporated and registered company from the previous example moved its real seat of operations to France, it would only be recognized as a corporation there if it complied with French law. Traditionally, Belgium, France, Germany, Poland and Spain used to adhere to the real seat approach. It generally implies that the cross-border transfer of the registered office is not allowed, unless the real seat is simultaneously transferred, but this would result in the winding-up of the company. It must be mentioned, however, that the real seat doctrine is on the retreat, and Member States adhering to it differ in how they apply the doctrine. Germany abandoned the real seat requirement for companies in 2008.[108] In Spanish legal doctrine, it is argued that the incorporation doctrine actually prevails, and the same applies in Poland.[109] In France, an important committee has proposed to abandon the real seat requirement in favour of the incorporation doctrine.[110] Belgium already deleted the real seat requirement in 2019.[111] In Italy, a mixed approach is implemented by the 2003 law reform, requiring that interpretation and application of the provisions regarding foreign companies are to be made in accordance with the principles of the EU legal system. Consequently, the real seat approach for foreign companies having their head office and/or principal operations in Italy is derogated for companies under the law of an EU Member State.[112]

2.59 If all Member States adopted the incorporation theory, then movement of companies from one country to another without losing their corporate status in the process would be much easier. The *'siége réel'* system, in effect, requires dissolution and re-formation in the host state. In practice, other differences between the Member States, for example, regarding the role of employees in the management of companies, make primary establishment difficult to achieve, despite the wording of Article 54 of the TFEU. Against this background, the CJEU refrained from taking up the question as to which system should prevail in the case of *R v. The Treasury, ex parte the Daily Mail* (1988).[113]

---

108. E. Wymeersch, 'The Transfer of the Company's Seat in European Company Law', *ECGI – Law Working Paper* No. 08/2003, March 2003 (www.ssrn.com). *The Impact Assessment on the Directive on the Cross-border Transfer of Registered Office,* 9. Gesetz zur Modernisierung des GmbH-Rechts und zur Bekämpfung von Missbräuchen (MoMiG) which amended s. 4a GmbHG and s. 5 AktG accordingly.
109. Article 17(1) of the Polish International Private Law of 2011 states that a legal person is subject to the law of the state where it has its seat. In Polish legal doctrine, it is assumed that 'seat' means the seat as stated in the articles.
110. Haut Comité Juridique de la Place Financière de Paris, https://www.hcjp.fr/en/home (accessed August 2021).
111. Article 110 Belgian International Private Law Code.
112. The real seat approach derives from the second part of the first paragraph of Article 25 Law No. 218 of 31 May 1995 on the Reform of the Italian System of Private International Law but is now superseded by principles of EU law, according to Article 2507 Italian Civil Code.
113. *R v. The Treasury, ex parte the Daily Mail* (1989) 1 All E.R. 328.

2.60 In the *Daily Mail* case, a UK company wished to transfer all its central management to the Netherlands without losing its status as a UK incorporated company. The practical reason for this was the desire to switch its residence for tax purposes. Under UK law, no company could move its residence for tax purposes without the Treasury's consent, which was refused. The company argued that this consent requirement was contrary to Articles 52 and 58 (now 49 and 54) of the Treaty. In its judgment, the CJEU agreed on the narrow point that the Treaty did preclude a Member State from hindering the movement of one of its companies to another Member State, but it took the view that, because the two countries concerned have the incorporation theory of recognition, there were no problems in recognition. On the broader issue of the general right of establishment, the court was more cautious and was of the opinion that, until the incorporation versus *siège réel* issue was resolved by a future convention or legislation, full primary establishment could not be achieved. Such a convention, proposed in 1968 under the old Article 220 (now repealed) of the Treaty, has never been pursued.

2.61 More recent case law, however, shows a fundamental switch in policy. Starting with the 1999 *Centros* case, the CJEU removed some of the obstacles to mobility.[114] A 2018 study confirms that the real seat doctrine is losing ground. It is established in virtually all Member States that the real seat theory can no longer be applied to companies incorporated in another Member State.[115] A host Member State adhering to a real seat doctrine may not prevent or unduly hinder an inbound movement of a company incorporated under the legislation of the company's home Member State. However, home Member States may, for tax reasons, in particular, prevent the outbound movement of the real seat of companies incorporated under its own legislation. According to the CJEU, exit taxation may represent, if certain conditions are met, a justified restriction to the freedom of establishment, grounded on the balanced allocation of taxing rights according to territoriality.[116]

2.62 The interpretation given by the judgments of the CJEU concerning Articles 49 and 54 TFEU (then Articles 43 and 48 of the EC Treaty) can be summarized as follows.

If a company has its registered office in Member State *A* and is formed in accordance with the law of Member State *A*, then Member State *B*:

114. Case C-212/97 (*Centros Ltd v. Erhvervs- og Selskabsstyrelsen*) (1999), Case C-208/00 (*Überseering BV v. Nordic Construction Company Baumanagement GmbH* (NCC)) (2002), Case C-167/01 (*Kamer van Koophandel en Fabrieken voor Amsterdam v. Inspire Art Ltd*) (2003). K. Baelz & T. Baldwin, 'The End of the Real Seat Theory (Sitztheorie): The European Court of Justice Decision in Ueberseering of 5 Nov. 2002 and Its Impact on German and European Company Law', *German Law Journal* 12 (1 Dec. 2002): Private Law (www.germanlawjournal.com).

115. Study on the cross-border transfers of registered offices and cross-border divisions of companies – Final Report, 5 Feb. 2018, JUST/2015/PR/01/0003, 40.

116. The Polbud judgment and the freedom of establishment for companies in the European Union: problems and perspectives, Study for the JURI committee of EP by Policy Department for Citizens' Rights and Constitutional Affairs Directorate-General for Internal Policies of the Union PE 608.833 – 22 Oct. 2018.

- *cannot refuse to recognize* that company, even when its entire business is carried on by a branch in Member State *B*, thus evading the (more restrictive) rules for incorporation in Member State *B* (*Centros*);
- *cannot deny legal capacity* to that company, even when it is deemed, according to the law of Member State *B*, to have moved its actual centre of administration (its real seat) to that Member State *B;* Member State *B* must *recognize the legal capacity of the company* to be the same as it enjoys under the law of Member State *A* (*Überseering*);
- *cannot impose disclosure requirements* on the branch of that company which go beyond the disclosure obligations provided for by the Eleventh Directive (on branches);
- *cannot impose conditions* on that company provided for in domestic company law relating to minimum capital and directors' liability, irrespective of the reasons for which that company was formed in Member State *A* and the fact that it carries on its activities almost exclusively in Member State *B* (*Inspire Art*);
- *cannot deny the right to convert* a company formed in Member State A to a company under the law of Member State *B* if Member State *B* allows 'internal' conversions of companies (*Cartesio* case). In turn, Member State *A* may not require the winding-up or liquidation of a company incorporated in that state with the aim or effect of preventing it from converting into a company under the law of Member State *B* (*Vale* and *Polbud*).

To explain the summary above, the cases mentioned are briefly discussed in the paragraphs that follow.

2.63 In the *Centros* case, Mr and Mrs Bryde, a Danish couple residing in Denmark, registered a private company named Centros Ltd in England and Wales. The company's registered office was situated in the UK at the home of a friend of Mr Bryde. Centros's capital was divided into two shares, held by Mr and Mrs Bryde. Mrs Bryde was the director of Centros. During the summer of 1992, Mrs Bryde requested the *Erhvervs- og Selskabsstyrelsen* (the Trade and Companies Board), falling under the Danish Department of Trade, to register a branch of Centros in Denmark. The board refused that registration on the grounds, *inter alia*, that Centros, which does not trade in the UK, was in fact seeking to establish not a branch but a principal establishment in Denmark, by circumventing the national rules concerning, in particular, the payment of the minimum capital required for Danish private companies. Centros brought an action before the court (*Østre Landsret*) against the refusal of the board to give effect to that registration. Because the court upheld the arguments of the board, Centros appealed to the Danish Supreme Court (*Højesteret*). The Supreme Court referred questions about the interpretation of the relevant articles of the EC Treaty to the CJEU for a preliminary ruling. This ruling, paraphrased in the previous paragraph, is as follows:

> It is contrary to Articles 52 and 58 of the EC Treaty for a Member State to refuse to register a branch of a company formed in accordance with the law of another

Member State in which it has its registered office but in which it conducts no business where the branch is intended to enable the company in question to carry on its entire business in the State in which that branch is to be created, while avoiding the need to form a company there, thus evading application of the rules governing the formation of companies which, in that State, are more restrictive as regards the paying up of a minimum share capital. That interpretation does not, however, prevent the authorities of the Member State concerned from adopting any appropriate measure for preventing or penalising fraud, either in relation to the company itself, if need be in cooperation with the Member State in which it was formed, or in relation to its members, where it has been established that they are in fact attempting, by means of the formation of a company, to evade their obligations towards private or public creditors established in the territory of the Member State concerned.

2.64 The *Überseering* case[117] originated from a conflict between Überseering BV and Nordic Construction Company Baumanagement GmbH (NCC). Überseering, a Dutch private company, acquired a piece of land in Düsseldorf (Germany), which it used for business purposes. By way of a project management contract, Überseering engaged NCC to refurbish a garage and a motel on the site. The contractual obligations were performed, but Überseering claimed that the paintwork was defective. Überseering unsuccessfully sought compensation from NCC for the defective work, and it brought an action before the Regional Court *(Landgericht Düsseldorf)*. However, prior to this, two German nationals residing in Düsseldorf had acquired all the shares in Überseering. The *Landgericht* dismissed the action, as did the *Oberlandesgericht* (Higher Regional Court). It found that Überseering had transferred its actual centre of administration to Düsseldorf once two German nationals acquired its shares. The *Oberlandesgericht* found that, as a company incorporated under Dutch law, Überseering did not have legal capacity in Germany and, consequently, could not bring legal proceedings there. Überseering appealed to the German Supreme Court *(Bundesgerichtshof)*, which referred the case to the CJEU for a preliminary ruling. The ruling, which has been paraphrased in paragraph 2.61, is as follows:

1. Where a company formed in accordance with the law of a Member State ('A') in which it has its registered office is deemed, under the law of another Member State ('B'), to have moved its actual centre of administration to Member State B, Articles 43 EC and 48 EC preclude Member State B from denying the company legal capacity and, consequently, the capacity to bring legal proceedings before its national courts for the purpose of enforcing rights under a contract with a company established in Member State B.
2. Where a company formed in accordance with the law of a Member State ('A') in which it has its registered office exercises its freedom of establishment in another Member State ('B'), Articles 43 EC and 48 EC require Member State B to recognise the legal capacity and, consequently, the capacity to be a party to legal proceedings which the company enjoys under the law of its State of incorporation ('A').

117. Case C-208/00 (*Überseering BV v. Nordic Construction Company Baumanagement GmbH* (NCC)) (2002).

2.65 In the *Inspire Art* case,[118] Inspire Art Ltd, a company governed by the law of England and Wales, requested registration of its branch in the Netherlands. The *Kamer van Koophandel en Fabrieken voor Amsterdam* (Amsterdam Chamber of Commerce and Industry) concluded that Inspire Art was subject to the obligation to record its description as a *formeel buitenlandse vennootschap* (formally foreign company) and to use that description in its business dealings, as provided by the *Wet op de Formeel Buitenlandse Vennootschappen* (Formally Foreign Companies Act). This Act defined a formally foreign company as a capital company formed under laws other than those of the Netherlands, which carries on its activities entirely, or almost entirely, in the Netherlands and does not have any real connection with the state in which it is registered. Various obligations are imposed on a formally foreign company, concerning, *inter alia*, the company's registration in the commercial register, the minimum share capital and the drawing up and publication of the annual documents. Inspire Art refused to fulfil the registration requirements as a formally foreign company because such requirements conflict with the freedom of establishment. The case was brought before the Subdistrict Court *(Kantongerecht)*, which referred to questions about the applicability of Articles 43 and 48 EC Treaty to the CJEU. It was also questioned whether the requirements imposed by Dutch law could be justified under Article 46 of the Treaty due to the alleged involvement of public policy. The ruling by the CJEU, already paraphrased in paragraph 2.61, is as follows:

1. It is contrary to Article 2 of the Eleventh Council Directive 89/666/EEC of 21 December 1989 concerning disclosure requirements in respect of branches opened in a Member State by certain types of company governed by the law of another State for national legislation such as the Wet op de Formeel Buitenlandse Vennootschappen (Law on Formally Foreign Companies) of 17 December 1997 to impose on the branch of a company formed in accordance with the laws of another Member State disclosure obligations not provided for by that directive.
2. It is contrary to Articles 43 EC and 48 EC for national legislation such as the Wet op de Formeel Buitenlandse Vennootschappen to impose on the exercise of freedom of secondary establishment in that State by a company formed in accordance with the law of another Member State certain conditions provided for in domestic company law in respect of company formation relating to minimum capital and directors' liability. The reasons for which the company was formed in that other State, and the fact that it carries on its activities exclusively or almost exclusively in the Member State of establishment, do not deprive it of the right to invoke the freedom of establishment guaranteed by the Treaty, save where the existence of an abuse is established on a case-by-case basis.

2.66 The cases described in the previous paragraphs all concern the same type of situation: a company is formed and registered in accordance with the law of one Member State, while it carries on all or almost all of its activities (its real seat) in another Member State. This situation can only exist where Member States allow

118. Case C-167/01 (*Kamer van Koophandel en Fabrieken voor Amsterdam v. Inspire Art Ltd*) (2003).

domestic companies to migrate their real seat to another country. For obvious reasons, only Member States adhering to the incorporation doctrine will do so. If the host Member State also favours this doctrine, no problem will arise provided the company complies with the law of its country of origin. However, even the incorporation doctrine does not always guarantee unprejudiced hospitality. Some host Member States tried to restrict avoidance of their national requirements for private companies, such as a minimum capital, by refusing to register the branch of such a company (*Centros*) or imposing certain requirements of national law upon registration of such a branch (*Inspire Art*). The CJEU deems these actions to be in conflict with the freedom of secondary establishment, as guaranteed by the TFEU. If the host country adheres to the real seat doctrine, then the problem becomes more fundamental because, when strictly applied, it prohibits the recognition of a company that does not have its real seat in the country in which it is registered. The host country may then deny, for instance, the company's capacity to start legal proceedings, as in the *Überseering* case. According to CJEU, the TFEU also precludes this. The judgments of the CJEU may have relaxed the (secondary) right of establishment, but still have not eradicated all restrictive policies of the Member States. Member States may continue to prevent their domestic companies from migrating their real seat to another Member State while retaining their original domestic status *(Cartesio, see* paragraph 2.65) and as discussed later in Chapter 4, even the SE is required to have its real seat in the Member State in which it has its registered office. Nevertheless, the CJEU certainly stimulated competition for incorporations within the EU, which may be illustrated by the 2008 amendment to the German GmbHG (Limited Liability Companies Act), allowing the GmbH and the AG to have their real seat outside Germany.[119]

2.67 In 2006, the *Cartesio* case was lodged with the CJEU concerning an LP, which sought to transfer its central administration (real seat) from Hungary to Italy, while remaining registered in Hungary. The Hungarian authorities refused to register the new address of Cartesio on the ground that such a transfer is not possible under Hungarian law. Under Hungarian law, the seat of companies or other legal entities of a commercial nature, such as LPs, is the place where the central administration of that entity is situated.[120] The question referred to the CJEU is whether Articles 43 and 48 of the EC Treaty (now 49 and 54 TFEU) preclude national rules that make it impossible for a company constituted under national law to transfer its real seat to another Member State while retaining its status as a company governed by the law of the state of incorporation.[121] The CJEU repeated elements of the *Daily Mail*, thereby acknowledging the power of a Member State to define the connecting factor required of a company, if it is to be regarded as incorporated under the law of that Member State, and also the connecting factor required if the company is to be subsequently able to maintain that status. Consequently, a Member State has the power of not permitting a company

119. Gesetz zur Modernisierung des GmbH-Rechts und zur Bekämpfung von Missbräuchen (MoMiG) which amended § 4a GmbHG accordingly. *See also* C. Teichmann, *supra* n. 107, at 189.
120. As set out in the *Cartesio* judgment, CJEU 16 Dec. 2008, C-210/06, paragraphs 11–19.
121. Case C-210/06 (*Cartesio*), paragraph 99.

governed by its law to retain that status if the company moves its seat to the territory of another Member State. Nevertheless, where such a company aims to convert into a form of company that is governed by the law of the host Member State, the law of the Member State of incorporation may not require the winding-up or liquidation of that company in preventing it from converting.[122] The CJEU, therefore, classifies this form of relocation to be covered by the right of establishment. As a matter of course, it depends on the law of the host Member State whether such conversion can be effected. It must be noted, however, that the relocation of a company can always be realized indirectly, i.e., through the founding of a subsidiary in the host Member State, thereafter merging the parent company into the subsidiary.[123]

2.68 The CJEU in Case C-378/10 (*Vale*) had to answer questions relating to facts that are the opposite of *Cartesio*. Vale Costruzioni S.r.l. was incorporated and registered in Rome. Some years later, in 2006, the company discontinued business in Italy and applied to be removed from the Italian register. The company was removed from the register in which it was noted that 'the company had moved to Hungary'. After removal, the director and another person incorporated Vale Építési Kft. and asked the Hungarian commercial court to register this company, together with a statement that Vale Costruzioni S.r.l. was the predecessor in law of Vale Építési Kft. The commercial court refused to register the company on the grounds that a company incorporated and registered in Italy could not transfer its seat to Hungary and could not be registered as the predecessor in law of the Hungarian company. Upon appeal by Vale Építési Kft., the Hungarian Supreme Court referred preliminary questions to the CJEU as to whether Articles 49 and 54 TFEU preclude legislation or practices of the host Member State that prohibit a company incorporated in another Member State from transferring its seat to the host Member State and continuing to operate under the laws of that Member State.[124] As in previous judgments, the CJEU repeated that companies are creatures of national law and, consequently, a Member State has the power to define the connecting factors required of a company to be regarded as incorporated under its national law and to maintain that status.[125] The CJEU concluded that national legislation enabling companies to convert their legal form, but does not allow companies governed by the law of another Member State to do so, falls within the scope of Articles 49 and 54 of the TFEU. In such case, companies are treated differently according to whether the conversion is of a domestic or cross-border nature. Its likely effect is to deter companies having their seat in another Member State from exercising freedom of establishment.[126] Since Hungarian law provides for domestic conversions only, it amounts to an unjustified restriction on the exercise of that freedom, and the refusal to register Vale Costruzioni S.r.l. as the predecessor in law of Vale Építési Kft. is incompatible with the

122. *Ibid.*, paragraphs 112 and 113.
123. E. Werlauff, 'Relocating a Company Within the EU', *European Company Law* 5, no. 3 (2008): 136–139.
124. Case C/378-10 (*Vale*) (2012), paragraph 16.
125. Case C/378-10 (*Vale*) (2012), paragraphs 27–29. This is again confirmed in Case C-371/10 (*National Grid Indus*) (2011).
126. Case C/378-10 (*Vale*) (2012), paragraphs 33 and 36.

said articles of the TFEU.[127] The CJEU acknowledged that cross-border conversions pose specific problems because such conversions presuppose the consecutive application of two national laws.[128]

2.69 In case C-106/16 *(Polbud)*, the CJEU confirmed that the right of establishment allows for cross-border conversion of companies. The general meeting of Polbud, a Polish company, decided to transfer the seat of the company to Luxembourg. The envisaged transfer was to re-register the company in Luxembourg. Polbud's request to be removed from the Polish commercial registry was rejected because the transfer did not include its real seat (head office), which would remain in Poland. According to the CJEU, the right of establishment is applicable if the host state (Luxembourg) accepts the registration of a company formed in accordance with the law of another Member State while the location of the real head office of that company remains unchanged. In such case, Poland may only refuse to remove the registration from the commercial registry if it is justified by overriding reasons in the public interest, if it is appropriate for ensuring the protection of the interests of creditors, minority shareholders and employees of the company, and if it does not go beyond what is necessary to attain that objective.[129] According to the CJEU, the Polish refusal did not meet these criteria. The CJEU further held that, according to the Polish Companies Code, a resolution of the shareholders to transfer the registered office to another Member State entails the winding-up of the company at the conclusion of a liquidation procedure. This implies that a company, if it is not liquidated, wishing to transfer its registered office to another Member State cannot be removed from the commercial register. Such a rule is in conflict with the right of establishment as already held by the CJEU in *Cartesio* (*see* paragraph 2.67).[130]

127. *Ibid.*, paragraphs 52–57.
128. *Ibid.*, paragraph 37. Here the CJEU avoided the issue whether, according to Italian law, Vale Costruzioni S.r.l. actually ceased to exist following its removal from the Italian register and, consequently, before the Hungarian company was incorporated (paragraphs 19–20).
129. Case C-371/10 (*National Grid Indus*) (2011).
130. Case C-106/16 (*Polbud*) (2017). Luxembourg at the time was adhering to the real seat doctrine, which means that the envisaged transfer could not be realized anyway.

CHAPTER 3

The Harmonization Programme Within the EU

I INTRODUCTION[1]

3.01 The idea that one could speak of European corporate law would have remained mainly hypothetical if not for the harmonization programme carried out by the European Union (EU).[2] To grasp the significance of the developments in EU legal instruments, one should observe not only the harmonization of company law of the Member States but also European legislation with respect to securities regulation, financial services, taxation, social policy, insolvency and competition, as it often pertains to corporate law or its context. Moreover, an EU institutional supervisory framework for the functioning of banks, the European Banking Union (EBU), was established after the 2008 financial crisis. At its core is the European Central Bank (ECB)[3] as the direct supervisor of EU banks.[4]

Nonetheless, one should be cautious so as not to overestimate what has been achieved. The harmonization programme does not cover all important issues of corporate law. Moreover, its actual significance depends on how EU legislative measures are implemented into national law and how their observance is dealt with.[5] Harmonization is not an end in itself and the same goes for the creation of European

1. More detailed books on the issues dealt with in this chapter are: N. Luca, *European Company Law*, Second edition (Cambridge University Press, 2021) and S. Grundmann, *European Company Law: Organization, Finance and Capital Markets*, Ius Communitatis Series, Second edition (Antwerpen/Oxford: Intersentia, 2012).
2. It is explained in Chapter 1, footnote 2, that 'EU' is used even where 'EC' might be appropriate.
3. Article 127(6) TFEU.
4. *See* European Council conclusions on completing EMU Adopted on 18 Oct. 2012, EUCO 156/12.
5. E. Werlauff, *EU Company Law: Common Business Law of 28 states*, Second edition (Copenhagen: Djøf Publishing, 2003), *Introduction*; L. Enriques, 'EC Company Law Directives and Regulations: How Trivial Are They?', *University of Pennsylvania Journal of International Law* 27, no. 1 (2006).

business organizations, notably the European Company (Societas Europaea (SE)). They serve towards the creation of an internal market - with free movement of goods, persons, services and capital - as a necessary, but an intermediary step in light of the task of the EU to promote, *inter alia,* sustainable development based on balanced economic growth and to aim at full employment.[6]

A The Legal Basis of European Legislation

3.02 European legislation must have a legal basis in the Treaty on European Union (TEU) and the Treaty on the Functioning of the European Union (TFEU), the primary legal sources of the EU. Directives and regulations are therefore regarded as secondary legislation. For directives and regulations in the area of company law, the legal basis is often found in Article 50 of the TFEU. However, the legal basis may be found in other provisions of the TFEU if the subject at hand so requires. The preamble of secondary legislation always clarifies which legal basis is used and for what reason. In the following paragraphs, Article 50 and other articles of the TFEU that have served as a legal basis for company law harmonization in the EU are briefly discussed.

3.03 The legal basis for the EU's activities concerning company law is primarily Article 50(2)(g) of the TFEU. This provision requires the European institutions to reduce the restrictions on the freedom of establishment and to issue directives requiring Member States to amend their laws, in order to comply with the terms of the directive to this effect. According to paragraph (g), the European Parliament (EP) and the Council, by means of directives, have 'to coordinate to the necessary extent the safeguards which, for the protection of the interests of members and others, are required by Member States of companies or firms with a view to making such safeguards equivalent throughout the Community'. The European institutions have always fostered an extensive interpretation as to the scope of this provision, and the European Commission regards the rights of employees as included among the interests referred to in this article.[7] The tasks set out in Article 50 TFEU function 'to attain freedom of establishment'. That might entail more than equivalence of safeguards for the protection of members, shareholders, employees and creditors throughout the EU. As stated in a 1992 publication by the Commission:

> Gradually, (...) the Community's sights have been set higher, going beyond mobility. The object is to find the legal formulas which permit restructurings between groups from different Member States. The creation of a Community legislative framework for cross-border activities by enterprises and for cooperation between enterprises from different Member States, will make it easier for European enterprises to pool the resources that are available in several Member States and hence be competitive not only in Europe, but also then in the world at large.

6. Article 3(3) TEU.
7. K. Gleichmann, *Perspectives on European Company Law,* Forum Internationale (Deventer/Boston: Kluwer Law and Taxation Publishers, 1990), 4, 5 and 7.

> It is no longer the mere alignment of domestic laws that is being sought, but the creation of a truly European company law.[8]

3.04 Directives based on Article 50 TFEU can be adopted by the European Council, according to the ordinary legislative procedure laid down in Article 294 TFEU. As a rule, this procedure allows the Council to act by a qualified majority.[9] Article 50 TFEU also provides the legal basis for legislation with respect to financial services. However, in this area, Article 53 TFEU also plays a role, which calls, *inter alia*, for the mutual recognition of formal qualifications to pursue activities as self-employed persons. In order to broaden the legal base and accelerate the establishment of the internal market, the Single European Act of 1986 added a provision, now Article 114 TFEU, allowing the adoption of measures (directives and/or other instruments) for the approximation of provisions in Member States 'which have as their object the establishment and functioning of the internal market'. Fiscal provisions, provisions relating to the free movement of persons or the rights and interests of employed persons fall outside the scope of this article. The directive on shareholder rights in listed companies was enacted on the basis of this article and Article 50 TFEU.[10]

3.05 Furthermore, Article 115 TFEU allows for a wide area of discretion for European legislation that may even cover the areas exempted from the competence provided by Article 114 TFEU. It can justify the adoption of any directive 'for the approximation of such laws, regulations or administrative provisions of the Member States as directly affect the establishment or functioning of the internal market'. The restriction put forward by the 'directly affect' stipulation is mainly symbolic because the EU institutions avail themselves of the extensive interpretation, which merely requires that measures have to be useful for European integration.[11] Article 115 TFEU, however, deviates from the ordinary legislative procedure and stipulates that the Council act unanimously, thus granting a veto to every Member State.[12] Furthermore, the additional competence granted by Article 153 TFEU should be mentioned. In order to achieve the objectives of the social policy of the EU, as laid down in Article 151 TFEU, the EP and the Council may adopt, *inter alia*, directives containing minimum requirements. An example is the directive regarding information and consultation of employees, which is discussed in Chapter 7.

---

8. Commission of the European Communities, *Conditions for Business Cooperation: Public Procurement* (Brussels, 1992) (CO-62-91-003-EN-C), 4.
9. Unanimity may be required if the Commission advises negatively on amendments to the proposed directive, Article 294(9) TFEU. *See* the website of the European Parliament on the legislative procedures, http://www.europarl.europa.eu/aboutparliament/en.
10. Directive 2007/36/EC, at the time the legal basis was Articles 44 and 95 TEU (now Articles 50 and 114 TFEU).
11. K.J. Hopt, 'European Community Legal Harmonisation and the Business Enterprise', in K.J. Hopt & E. Wymeersch (eds), *European Company and Financial Law* (Berlin/New York: Walter de Gruyter, 1991), 12.
12. Unless otherwise determined by the TEU, the Council shall act by a qualified majority, Article 16(3) TEU.

3.06 Lastly, attention should be drawn to Article 352 TFEU. This provision grants complementary powers for action to be taken where the Treaties (TEU and TFEU) have not provided the necessary powers to attain an objective set out in the Treaties. Similar to Article 115 TFEU, it requires unanimous action by the Council but, unlike Article 115, prior consent of the EP. There are certain limitations, however, for the European institutions to fall back on this 'flexibility clause'.[13] The provision of what is now Article 352 TFEU has been resorted to, among other things, for the adoption of the regulations constituting the European Economic Interest Grouping (EEIG) and the SE because there was no other legal basis for these regulations.[14]

B European Legal Instruments

3.07 The TFEU contains provisions that are directly applicable to the Member States (and individuals), such as the prohibition on distorting competition within the common market because such behaviour would restrict the freedom of establishment.[15] Further, the TFEU empowers its institutions to enact general measures of legislation (secondary legislation), especially directives and regulations. The basic rule articulated in Article 288 states:

> To exercise the Union's competences, the institutions shall adopt regulations, directives, decisions, recommendations and opinions.

Regulations, as a rule, are directly applicable, unlike directives, which must be transposed by the Member States before they can have effect. However, upon a Member State's failure to take the appropriate steps, not only the Commission but also an individual may invoke the directive against the State, though only if it contains clear and unconditional obligations. Thus, in such case, a directive may have direct effect, creating individual rights that are protected by the national courts against Member States, as was decided in *Van Gend & Loos v. The Netherlands* (1963).[16] An individual cannot invoke direct effect against other individuals or companies.[17]

13. Opinion 2/94 [1996] ECR I-1795 of the CJEU on the accession of the EU to the ECHR. *See also*, A. Dashwood et al., *Wyatt & Dashwood's European Union Law* (Hart Publishing: Oxford and Portland Oregon, 2011), Ch. 5 C.
14. Regulation (EEC) 2137/85 and Regulation (EC) 2157/2001, at the time, the legal basis was Article 308 TEC.
15. Articles 101 and 49 TFEU respectively.
16. Case C-26/62 (*Van Gend & Loos v. The Netherlands)* (1963); according to A. Dashwood et al., *supra* n. 13, Ch. 8 I, 'It is difficult to overstate the importance of *van Gend en Loos*'.
17. Case C-152/84 (*Marshall v. Southampton and South-West Hampshire Area Health Authority)* (1986). *See* on the binding force of directives: S. Prechal, *Directives in European Community Law. A Study of Directives and Their Enforcement in National Courts* (Oxford: Clarendon Press, 1995), 19 *et seq.*

1 Directives

3.08 For the harmonization of company law and its related areas mentioned in paragraph 3.01, with the exception of policy on competition, directives are the main legal instruments used. According to Article 288 TFEU, a directive is binding as to the result to be achieved upon each Member State, to which it is addressed, leaving the choice of form and methods to the national authorities. According to the Court of Justice of the European Union (CJEU) in *Francovich* (1991), Member States can be held liable for non-compliance with implementing such obligations.[18] Due to the supremacy of EU law, directives have what is known as a blocking effect because Member States do not have an option of enacting national legal provisions that are not in accordance with the directives.[19]

3.09 Company law directives originally contained detailed provisions focusing on specific safeguards, such as capital requirements. Gradually, however, directives showed a more flexible approach because the gap between diverging national company laws could not always be bridged by providing uniform solutions. Hence, sometimes alternative provisions were included which enable the Member States, or even companies, to choose between several options provided for in a directive.[20] Another way to reach a compromise is to set minimum standards, leaving it to the Member States whether or not they want to impose more stringent rules ('gold plating'). More recently, directives concentrate not so much on reaching a harmonized set of national rules but on removing obstacles to cross-border transactions. They tend to be more principle-based, as opposed to rule-based, as is illustrated by the 2004 Thirteenth Directive on takeovers.[21] Article 3 of this directive covers a set of principles Member States have to comply with, for example, equal treatment of all shareholders of the offeree company in the case of a takeover bid. How to achieve this is in principle left to the Member States.[22] To further the aims of these principle-based directives, the Commission may be empowered to adopt implementing measures.[23] An example of such a multilevel approach is the regulation of the financial services sector, including, *inter alia,* the market for securities. Consequently, the directives providing the framework principles are followed by directives or regulations containing implementing measures (*see* paragraphs 3.50 *et seq.*).

18. Joint Cases C-6/90 and C-9/90 *(Francovich)* (1991). *See* for subsequent case law on the conditions for establishing liability for non-compliance: A. Dashwood et al., *supra* n. 13, Ch. 9 V C.
19. Case C-6/64 *(Costa/Enel)* (1964). R.M. Buxbaum & K.J. Hopt, *Legal Harmonisation and the Business Enterprise* (Berlin and New York: Walther De Gruyter, 1988), 242.
20. Directive (EEC) 78/660. On the effect of options, *see* Steef M. Bartman, 'The Impact of Optional EU Law Making on National Company Law', *European Corporate Law* 5, no. 6 (December 2008): 271–276.
21. Already in this sense: V. Edwards, *EC Company Law*, Oxford EC Law Library, edited by F.G. Jacobs (Oxford: Clarendon Press, 1999), 8 *et seq.*
22. Directive 2004/25/EC (as amended), Preamble (26).
23. Directive 2004/25/EC (as amended), Preamble (28).

3.10 In addition, two concepts related to EU law-making should be briefly mentioned here: codification and recasts. *Codification* in EU law is understood as bringing a directive or another legislative act and all its amendments together in a single new act. This is called vertical codification. Horizontal codification occurs when two or more acts covering related subjects are incorporated into a single new act. In both cases, the codification process starts with a consolidated text, a non-official document produced by the Publications Office. The consolidated text includes all amendments for the convenience of the reader. On the basis of that text, a new act might be prepared and then it must pass through the stages of an accelerated legislative process.[24] Such a fast-track adoption of codification instruments is allowed because no changes of substance may be made to the instruments affected by codification.[25] *Recasting* also brings an act with its amendments (vertical) or two or more related acts (horizontal) together in a single new act. However, unlike codification, it involves new substantive changes, as amendments are made to the original act or acts during the preparation of the recast text. The subsequent legislative procedure enables the legislative authority to concentrate its attention on the new parts of the legislative proposal.[26]

3.11 Regulators often tend to overregulate and EU legislation is certainly affected by that phenomenon. In its 2016 Communication on better regulation, the Commission states: 'The European Union has frequently been criticised - often rightly - for producing excessive and badly written regulation (...). Concentrating on measures that are really necessary and not doing things that have only marginal benefits or can be better done at the national, regional or local level in Member States, also frees up space and means that collectively the institutions can mobilise more quickly to address new circumstances (...).' The Commission also mentions that reducing the adoption of new rules is necessary: '(...) the number of proposals for regulations and directives made by the Commission for adoption by the European Parliament and the Council (...) has declined from 159 in 2011 to 48 in 2015.'[27] According to the 2021 Work Programme of the Commission, better regulation remains on the agenda of the EU.[28]

2 Regulations

3.12 A regulation is a powerful legal instrument. According to Article 288 TFEU, regulations have general application, because they are binding and directly applicable in all Member States. In principle, they have direct effect and are deemed to be

24. Interinstitutional Agreement of 20 Dec. 1994, Accelerated working method for official codification of legislative texts OJ 1996, C 102/2.
25. Brussels, 3.12.2015, COM(2015) 616 final.
26. Interinstitutional Agreement of 28 Nov. 2001 on a more structured recasting technique for legal acts, OJ 2002 C 77/1. An example is Directive 2012/30/EU on the maintenance and alteration of the capital of public companies, which is the recast of the original Second Council Directive of 1976 and several amendments.
27. Better Regulation: Delivering better results for a stronger Union, Brussels 14.9.2016 COM(2016) 615 final, quotes from 2 and 3.
28. Brussels, 19.10.2020 COM(2020) 690 final.

incorporated into the national legal order. Their validity does not depend on national procedures, and the courts must safeguard the rights of individuals created by regulations. It must be admitted, however, that some or parts of regulations need implementing rules to be adopted by the Member States in order to ensure effective application. For example, Member States must designate the competent authority to issue the certificate that is required in the event that the SE transfers its registered office to another Member State.[29] In general, regulations serve for the enactment of legal norms that supersede national law and are pre-emptive to national legislation in the area concerned. In the field of corporate law, regulations have been used for several purposes. In the first place, for the creation of business organizations under Community law, notably the EEIG and the SE. These are discussed in Chapter 4. Furthermore, Regulation EC 1606/2002 enables the Commission to decide on the applicability of international accounting and reporting standards within the EU, as seen in Chapter 9. Regulations are also used in the area of capital markets (*see* paragraphs 3.44 *et seq.*). Lastly, regulations play a dominant role in the implementation of the treaty provisions regarding competition. The regulation most relevant here is the Merger Regulation, which is discussed in Chapter 8.

3 *Recommendations and Opinions*

3.13 Besides directives and regulations, two other legal instruments have been resorted to in the field of corporate law, as provided by the TFEU: recommendations and opinions. Article 288 TFEU provides for recommendations and opinions to be delivered by the European institutions. These instruments have no binding force, but they may serve as guidance for the interpretation of national law or EU law. Moreover, they may anticipate EU legislation. Among the early examples is the 1977 recommendation by the Commission, containing a European Code of Conduct relating to transactions in transferable securities which was followed by European legislation on insider dealing in 1989.[30] Noteworthy is the Commission's recommendation on the role of non-executive or supervisory directors of listed companies and on the committees of the (supervisory) board.[31] The same applies to the recommendation concerning remuneration of directors of listed companies.[32] The last example to be mentioned here is the 2014 Recommendation on a new approach to business failure and insolvency.[33] The Recommendation invited Member States to put effective pre-insolvency procedures in place to help viable debtors to restructure in order to avoid insolvency and to allow a second chance for entrepreneurs in no more than three years after insolvency. After an evaluation of the effects of the recommendation, a Directive on restructuring and insolvency was adopted in 2019.[34] In addition to recommendations, opinions can

29. Articles 69 and 8(8) SE Regulation.
30. Recommendation 77/534/EEC and (EEC) 89/592.
31. Recommendation 2005/162/EC.
32. Recommendation 2009/385/EC.
33. Recommendation C(2014) 1500 final, 12.3.2014.
34. Directive (EU) 2019/1023 amending Directive (EU) 2017/1132.

be issued by several European institutions. For instance, the Commission may issue opinions to Member States regarding social policy, and the ECB may submit opinions to other EU institutions and to national authorities.[35]

4 Judicial Decisions

3.14 Important factors to also consider when discussing the EU regulatory landscape are decisions of the CJEU. The CJEU is among the institutions that carry out the tasks entrusted to the Community.[36] Article 19 of the TEU reads that the court 'shall ensure that in the interpretation and application of the Treaties the law is observed'.[37] The CJEU has jurisdiction to give preliminary rulings, at the request of courts or tribunals from Member States, on the interpretation of EU law. Similarly, it rules on actions brought by a Member State, an institution, or a natural or legal person (Article 19(3)TEU). The system of preliminary rulings is detailed in Article 267 TFEU. These preliminary rulings deal with questions concerning the interpretation of the Treaties and the validity and interpretation of acts of the institutions, bodies, offices or agencies of the EU. Where such a question is raised before a court or tribunal of a Member State, that court or tribunal may request the CJEU to give a ruling. Such court or tribunal is obliged to bring the matter before the CJEU when there is no judicial remedy under national law.

3.15 The CJEU has decided on several cases involving company law. Member States have been criticized for failing to implement company law directives. Several preliminary rulings on the interpretation of company law directives have been issued, notably, in regard to the First, the Second, and the Fourth Directive. Furthermore, some cases pertain to the interpretation of the treaty provisions concerning the right of establishment. Among these are the landmark judgements (*Centros, Überseering, Inspire Art, Cartesio* and *Vale*) dealt with in Chapter 2.[38] Lastly, a case of significant importance is *Marleasing* (1990).[39] The court held that in interpreting the provisions of national law, which implement company law directives, national courts are bound to interpret their law in the light of the text and purpose of the underlying directive. This judgment

35. Articles 159 and 132(1) TFEU.
36. Article 13 TEU.
37. According to Article 19 TEU, the CJEU includes the Court of Justice (known as European Court of Justice, abbreviated ECJ), the General Court (previously named Court of First Instance) and specialized courts. The General Court has limited jurisdiction in comparison to the ECJ and its decisions can be appealed to the ECJ (Article 256 TFEU). A specialized court is the Civil Service Tribunal, having jurisdiction over employment disputes between the EU and its civil servants (Council Decision 2004/752/EC, OJ 2004, L 333/7).
38. An overview of CJEU cases involving corporate law issues is attached to L. Enriques, 'EC Company Law Directives and Regulations: How Trivial Are They?' (May 2005). *ECGI – Law Working Paper* No. 39/2005, http://ssrn.com/abstract=730388.
39. Case C-106/89 (*Marleasing S.A. v. La Comercial International Alimentation S.A.*) (1989).

challenges the tendency of courts and lawyers not to invoke the procedure for preliminary rulings if they are unaware that national provisions refer to EU law.[40]

3.16 The court's jurisdiction also pertains to conventions between Member States, if such conventions provide for it. This is the case with the 1968 Brussels Convention on jurisdiction and the enforcement of judgments in civil and commercial matters.[41] In *Powell Duffryn plc v. Wolfgang Petereit* (1992), the court decided that Article 17 of the Brussels Convention covers a choice of forum clause in a company's articles in relation to disputes between the company and its shareholders.[42] The court held that the relationship between a company and its shareholders, as embodied in the articles, is contractual, qualifying the jurisdiction clause as an agreement under the Brussels Convention. This even applies to shareholders who voted against the adoption of the clause or who acquired their shares afterwards. By becoming and remaining a shareholder, a person consents to adhere to the provisions of the company's articles and the decisions taken by its organs, regardless of his or her objections to a certain clause or decision. The ruling of the court enables companies to use the choice of forum clause in order to enhance legal predictability and to stimulate concentration of litigation in disputes with its shareholders. Most of the Convention's original field of application is now covered by the Brussels I Regulation (EC) No 44/2001 on jurisdiction and the recognition and enforcement of judgements in civil and commercial matters.[43]

3.17 As is clear from *Marleasing*, decisions of national courts also have to be taken into account for a thorough assessment of the development of European corporate law. The conduct of the national courts is the decisive factor in the role played by the CJEU because the national courts can bring a case before the European court based on the preliminary procedure of Article 267 TFEU. In theory, national courts could play an important role in the process of 'integration from below', meaning that case law concerning the interpretation of national corporate law gradually follows a uniform pattern, more or less, within the Community. In reality, hardly any such patterns can be observed and even where company law is harmonized, national courts may be responsible for diverging developments.[44] The EU has taken initiatives to promote that courts of the various Member States discuss their experiences and has established a European Judicial Network in civil and commercial matters.[45]

40. Further: A. Dashwood et al., *supra* n. 13, Ch. 8 II on the duty of consistent interpretation. *See also* Buxbaum & Hopt, *supra* n. 19, at 269.
41. Most of the Convention's original field of application is now covered by Council Regulation (EC) 44/2001.
42. Case C- 214/89 (*Powell Duffryn plc v. Wolfgang Petereit*) (1992).
43. OJ 2001, L 012.
44. K.J. Hopt, 'European Community Legal Harmonisation and the Business Enterprise', in K.J. Hopt & E. Wymeersch (eds), *European Company and Financial Law* (Berlin/New York: Walter de Gruyter, 1991), 22.
45. 2001/470/EC: Council Decision of 28 May 2001 establishing a European Judicial Network in civil and commercial matters, OJ 2001, L 174. For more information: https://e-justice.europa.eu/ejncivil (accessed 23 April 2021).

5 *European Model Company Act*

3.18 Some countries make use of model acts in order to enhance harmonization of substantive company law rules. A model act is generally a company law act which regulates all issues of company law and can be used by states to shape their national laws. This system is successfully used in the United States where the Model Business Corporation Act (MBCA) was set up by the section on Business Law of the American Bar Association. The MBCA forms the basis for business corporation statutes in thirty-two states.[46] Inspired by this example, scholars from twenty-two EU Member States, acting as the European Model Companies Act (EMCA) Group, published a model act in 2017. The act is according to its introduction:

> ...designed as a free-standing general company statute that can be enacted by Member States, either substantially in its entirety or by adoption of selected provisions.[47]

The EMCA is an academic endeavour and not endorsed by the European legislator, and the group of scholars are independent. It is therefore not a 'mandatory harmonisation instrument'[48] but rather a top-down voluntary harmonization attempt. So far it is not clear to what extent the model act is used by national legislators or corporate practice. It offers interesting insights, however, into the different types of company law regulation available in the EU Member States, and it also provides for common denominators. Its provisions touch upon all areas of company law: from incorporation to dissolution of the company and many issues in between such as provisions on directors' liability, financing and company groups.

II HARMONIZED COMPANY LAW

3.19 Having discussed the potential EU level legislative instruments that can be used to achieve harmonization, we look closer into the actual harmonization in the area of European company law and the instruments used to achieve this. The harmonization of the company laws of the Member States started in the 1960s. At the time, the Commission envisaged a program of harmonizing directives affecting various aspects of company law. The directives were numbered. Therefore, older literature often refers to the first, second, third (and so on) company law directives. However, although the First Directive was the first to be adopted in 1968,[49] the numerical order of the planned directives was not strictly followed. Not all of the proposed directives survived the political debate and some were therefore withdrawn by the Commission. Furthermore,

46. *See* Model Business Corporation Act (2016 Revision): Official Text with Official Comment & Statutory Cross-References (americanbar.org).
47. The European Model Company Act (EMCA)—a tool for European integration, introduction, 1. | https://link.springer.com/article/10.1007/s12027-018-0521-8#Sec2
48. The European Model Company Act (EMCA)—a tool for European integration https://link.springer.com/article/10.1007/s12027-018-0521-8#Sec2
49. Directive (EEC) 68/151.

modernization of company law requires legislation not thought of at the outset of the programme and as a consequence, several later directives, such as the Shareholders Rights Directive, were adopted without being numbered under the original programme.

3.19a The results of the original harmonization programme are as follows:

First Directive (disclosure of certain documents, the validity of obligations entered into by a company and the nullity of the company) 1968/151/EEC
Second Directive (maintenance and alteration of public companies' capital) 1977/91(EEC)
Third Directive (domestic mergers of public companies) 1978/855(EEC)
Fourth Directive (annual accounts of companies) 1978/660/EEC
(Fifth Directive (structure of public companies) withdrawn)
Sixth Directive (divisions of public companies) 1982/891/EEC
Seventh Directive (consolidated annual accounts of companies) 83/349/EEC
Eighth Directive (approval of persons responsible for carrying out statutory audits of accounting documents) 1984/253/EEC
(Ninth Directive (links between undertakings and in particular to groups) withdrawn)
Tenth Directive (cross-border mergers) 2005/56/EC
Twelfth Directive (single-member companies) 1989/667 EEC
Thirteenth Directive (takeover bids) 2004/109/EC.

A caveat is needed here. First, the directives listed have for a great deal been amended and/or codified by newer legislation. An important example is the Codification Directive (EU) 2017/1132 containing the (often amended) provisions originally to be found in the First, Second, Third, Sixth and Tenth Directives. As a matter of course, we refer in this book to legislation currently (2022) in force.[50] Second, the harmonization programme does not cover company law as a whole because certain aspects are left to national law, for instance, the liability of company directors. Third, it is good to keep in mind that corporate law, being the subject of this book, encompasses more than just company law. Therefore, also directives, regulations and case law regarding areas such as capital markets (*see* Part III of this chapter) and the role of employees (*see* Chapter 7) are relevant for understanding how and to what extent business organizations are regulated by EU law. Turning back to actual company law: the main themes of current EU harmonizing legislation are briefly set out in sections A–F which follow. The main issues that have been harmonized and discussed below are related to: the formation of companies and their capital, disclosure requirements and financial statements, issues of corporate governance and shareholders, mergers and divisions, conversions and seat transfers, insolvency and restructuring.

50. In the previous edition of this book, the legislation history was set out in more detail. An up-to-date overview is offered by https://ec.europa.eu/info/business-economy-euro/doing-business-eu/company-law-and-corporate-governance_en.

A Formation and Capital

3.20 Traditionally, national laws have regarded companies as a form of cooperation between two or more persons in line with the literal definition of 'company'. As a consequence, the formation of a company in several Member States required a minimum of two persons or, in the case of a public company, sometimes even more.[51] However, if only one person is economically involved, the requirement of multiple shareholderships upon formation or later on does not reflect reality. Therefore, Directive 2009/102/EC (as amended) requires Member States to allow for the single-member private company in order to enable the individual entrepreneur to enjoy limited liability by incorporating his or her business (Article 2 of Directive 2009/102/EC). Accordingly, its application is confined to private companies, but it also applies to public limited companies if a Member State allows such company to have a sole member (Article 6). If a company has become a single-member company after incorporation, this fact and the identity of the sole member must be filed or registered and publicized (Article 3). Contracts between the sole member and the company as represented by that sole member must be recorded in minutes or drawn up in writing. Member States need not apply this to current operations concluded under normal conditions (Article 5). Member States may maintain special provisions or sanctions for cases where a natural person is the single member of several companies ('one person group') or where a single-member company is the sole member of a company (Article 2). Some Member States offer an alternative for the formation of a single-member company by providing that an entrepreneur may set up an undertaking the liability of which is limited to a sum dedicated to a stated activity. The safeguards laid down for such undertakings must be equivalent to those imposed by the Directive in regard to companies (Article 7). Accordingly, if a Member State allows for this alternative, the sole entrepreneur can separate his or her personal liability from that of the business. An example is the French regime laid down in the Commercial Code, Articles L526-6 *et seq.* *(l'entrepreneur individuel à responsabilité limitée)*.

3.21 Rules regarding the formation of companies were originally harmonized in the first company law directive and are now taken up in the Codification Directive 2017/1132. In order to modernize the formation procedure, Article 13g of Directive (EU) 2017/1132 requires Member States to ensure that formation of companies may also be carried out fully online although this facility may be limited to the type of companies mentioned in Annex IIA of the directive. As a matter of course, several ancillary measures are necessary for online formation. For instance, the identity of the persons applying for the formation has to be validated and the appointment of directors has to be verified. These measures are set out in Article 13g. Furthermore, Member States must make templates available for the online formation of companies. For the sake of clarity, it is determined that these templates are subject to national law (Article

51. S. Grundmann, *supra* n. 1, at 324.

13h). The harmonization of the formation procedure is further discussed in Chapter 5 of this book.

3.22 Since the liability of shareholders in a public or private company is limited, it is not surprising that national legislators have tried to redress abuses for a long time. Because the measures taken showed considerable disparities, the EU, starting with the Second Directive as mentioned in paragraph 3.19a, has enacted legislation in order to ensure protection for both shareholders and creditors of those companies. In fact, the Codification Directive (EU) 2017/1132[52] contains four categories of detailed provisions. First, information must be available to enable any interested person to be informed about the composition of the capital of the company. Second, a minimum capital must be subscribed. Third, the Codification Directive aims to maintain the capital by prohibiting any reduction by distribution to the shareholders, where the latter are not entitled to it, and by imposing limits on the company's rights to acquire its own shares. Fourth, the Codification Directive ensures the equal treatment of shareholders in the same position and the protection of creditors in case of alteration of the capital. The result is a harmonized level of capital requirements for the public company, yet it does not apply to private companies, as they fall outside its scope. The provisions mentioned above can be found in Title I, Chapter IV of the Codification Directive (EU) 2017/1132.

B Disclosure and Financial Statements

3.23 As mentioned in paragraph 3.19, companies must disclose certain documents and particulars upon formation, but this applies equally to changes in these data and to several other events during a company's existence. Disclosure occurs by submitting data (documents and information) to the central register which has to be installed by each Member State. In such commercial or companies (or business) register, files are opened for each company recorded in that register. Directive (EU) 2017/1132 contains provisions on how disclosure should take place and how access to data can be obtained. To start with, all registered companies must be identifiable by a European unique identifier (Article 16(1)), and all registers are interconnected by an EU-wide infrastructure as prescribed by Article 22–24 of the Codification Directive (EU) 2017/1132.[53] The data submitted by a company is to be kept by the register in the file in electronic form, irrespective of the form in which it is submitted, and all data is to be publicly available (Article 16(2)(3)). Copies of the data may be obtained from the register on application. The price of copies of the basic data mentioned in Article 14 may not exceed the administrative costs of the copies (Article 16a and 19). Member States must ensure that the filing of the basic data mentioned in Article 14 can be

52. Directive (EU) 2017/1132 as amended and corrected by Directives (EU) 2019/1023, (EU) 2019/1151, (EU) 2019/2121 and Corrigendum OJ L 20, 24.1.2020. Directive (EU) 2019/2121 must be transposed by the Member States by January 2023.
53. The infrastructure is The Business Registers Interconnection System (BRIS), https://ec.europa.eu/cefdigital/wiki/display/CEFDIGITAL/Business+Registers+Interconnection+System (accessed 20 May 2021).

completed online, without the necessity for an applicant to appear in person for any authority or body (Article 13j). Member States may maintain other forms of filing for data not mentioned in Article 14 (Article 13j(5)).

3.24 Directive (EU) 2017/1132 further determines that a company may only rely on the data against third parties when disclosure is completed. On the one hand, protection is therefore offered to a company if it fulfils its disclosure obligations. On the other hand, third parties may rely on data of which the disclosure formalities have not yet been completed. For instance, a board member may be authorized to represent the company in dealings with third parties but only jointly with another person. As long as this restriction is not duly disclosed, a third party may rely on the representation by a single board member unless the company proves that the third party had knowledge of the restriction (Article 16(5)).

3.25 Directive (EU) 2017/1132 contains several provisions about what companies have to disclose, as is already shown briefly in paragraph 3.19. Apart from the formation of a company, many other events, changes and developments during a company's lifespan trigger disclosure requirements that are also harmonized by provisions of the Codification Directive. To name a few, the opening of a branch in another Member State triggers disclosure requirements in both the home state of the company and the state where the branch is registered. Companies must provide information on mergers, divisions and conversions whether they happen on a domestic level or cross-border. Furthermore, information with regard to winding-up or insolvency proceedings and the striking-off of a company from the register must be disclosed. In the following paragraphs 3.26–3.29, several disclosure requirements are discussed in more detail. The articles mentioned are all from Directive (EU) 2017/1132.

3.26 Upon *formation*, the statutes (articles) or the instrument of incorporation of a public limited company must contain information on, *inter alia*, the objects of the company, the company's capital and the rules governing the appointment of directors or others who are responsible for representing the company towards third parties (Article 3). Also, information about the registered office and several details about the shares of the company, such as limitations on the transfer of shares, has to be provided in the statutes (articles) or the incorporation document. It is allowed, however, to include these data in a separate document (Article 4). The documents mentioned here have to be disclosed by the company together with various other data such as any amendments to these documents, the appointment, termination of office and particulars of board members, the accounting documents for each financial year and the winding-up of the company (Articles 14 and 15). In principle, Article 14 applies only to public companies, but Member States may extend the application to private companies.[54] Formation and related disclosure requirements are further discussed in Chapter 5.

54. Article 18(1) refers to Annex II where, besides public and private companies, some limited partnerships with shares are mentioned.

3.27 Opening of a *branch*, such as the creation of a subsidiary, is one of the possibilities in which companies may exercise the right of establishment in another Member State. Among the data to be disclosed in the Member State where the branch is opened are the address and the activities of the branch, the name and the legal form of the company and the register in which the company file is kept. Furthermore, the appointment and termination of office of the persons who are authorized to represent the company and the accounting documents of the company as drawn up, audited and disclosed pursuant to the law of the Member State by which the company is governed (Articles 30 and 31). Member States must ensure that the registration of a branch of a company governed by the law of another Member State can be fully carried out online (Article 28a(1)). The rules for disclosure of data concerning branches apply to both public and private companies.[55]

3.28 Opening and termination of *winding-up or insolvency proceedings* of a company must be made available by the register. The same applies in principle to the striking-off of the company from the register. Such information must be made available EU-wide through the system of interconnection of the registers (Article 20). National law determines the consequences for branches established in another Member State than the state where the company is registered. However, if a company is struck off the register, its branches must similarly be deleted from the register except if the striking-off happens due to the conversion of the company, a merger or division or a cross-border transfer of its registered office (Article 34). As a matter of course, branches can also be opened by companies governed by the law of non-EU states. If such company is comparable to the types of companies listed in Annex II of the directive, then the disclosure requirements are comparable to what should be disclosed if a branch is opened by a company from a Member State (Article 36).

3.29 If a company participates in a *conversion, merger or division*, various documents are to be drawn up and part of these must be disclosed and made publicly available in the register together with other data, such as the envisaged legal form resulting from the operation. Here again, Member States must ensure that these requirements can be fulfilled fully online (Articles 86g, 123, 160g). After the operation is completed, information regarding the results must be entered into the registers. For example, in the case of a cross-border conversion, this entails the registration of the converted company in the register of the destination Member State whereas, in the register of the departure Member State, the date of striking-off or removal of the company from the register must be entered (Article 86p).[56] It must be noted that the rules for cross-border conversions apply to both public and private companies whereas the rules for mergers and divisions, irrespective of whether they are domestic or cross-border, apply to public limited companies only.[57] Conversions, mergers and divisions of companies are further dealt with in Chapter 8 of this book.

55. Article 29 refers to the companies listed in Annex II of the Directive.
56. Similar provisions apply to the cross-border merger, Article 130 and the cross-border division, Article 160p.
57. These companies are listed in Annex I of Directive (EU) 2017/1132.

3.30 Lastly, the harmonization of disclosure requirements also encompasses the financial statements which companies have to prepare and publish regularly. The rules regarding financial statements are laid down in a separate Directive 2013/34/EU, which is known as the Accounting Directive. Directive 2013/34/EU prescribes what is required from companies and groups of companies regarding their financial statements, consolidated financial statements and related reports. Financial statements and how they are to be published are described in Chapter 9 of this book.

C Corporate Governance, Including Shareholders

3.31 Corporate governance is generally understood as the way companies are managed and controlled. There is not one uniform corporate governance system at the EU level. The division of powers, as discussed further in Chapter 6, is largely left to the law of the Member States. Member States have drawn up codes dealing with corporate governance and stewardship that fit into their national mould.[58] Consequently, the EU has not taken action to further an EU-wide corporate governance code. Nevertheless, several aspects related to corporate governance issues have been harmonized. Issues that have been addressed at the EU level are: the rights of shareholders of listed companies, minimum standards for takeover bids, and specific rules on corporate governance and remuneration for banks and investment firms. In addition, the Commission has installed an expert group on technical aspects of corporate governance and has launched an online platform for information sharing.[59] As already mentioned in paragraph 3.13, there are also several recommendations by the Commission related to corporate governance issues, such as the recommendation on the role of non-executive or supervisory directors of listed companies and on the committees of the (supervisory) board,[60] and the recommendation concerning remuneration of directors of listed companies.[61]

3.32 In order to strengthen shareholder rights, there is an EU directive that contains provisions regarding transparency, proxy voting rights, participation in general meetings via electronic means and the exercise of cross-border voting rights.[62] This directive is generally referred to as the Shareholder Rights Directive. The original directive was revised in 2017 in order to encourage long-term shareholder engagement and to regulate identification of shareholders by the company, a process which is often burdensome because shares can be held by numerous intermediaries. Moreover, the directive addresses institutional investors and asset managers in order to further disclosure of their policy on shareholder engagement and how they exercise their

58. All codes can be accessed via the website of the ECGI - European Corporate Governance Institute, https://ecgi.global/content/codes (accessed 25 May 2021).
59. https://ec.europa.eu/info/business-economy-euro/doing-business-eu/company-law-and-corporate-governance_en (accessed 25 May 2021).
60. Recommendation 2005/162/EC.
61. Recommendation 2009/385/EC.
62. Directive 2007/36 EC.

voting rights. Lastly, the directive provides for the obligation of Member States to ensure that shareholders have an effective say on remuneration policy.[63]

3.33 An important development in the area of corporate governance is that the subject matter is no longer restricted to the division of powers within the company and to the way in which companies are managed and controlled. Gradually, the corporate governance debate is taking on a broader dimension, not only just examining the internal function of the company but also becoming outward-looking by formulating principles on how companies should act in view of societal interests. This can be illustrated by the way the Shareholders Rights Directive deals with the topic of remuneration. In paragraph 29 of the preamble, it is explained what is at stake with remuneration (of directors) apart from technical aspects like who has to decide on it:

> The remuneration policy should contribute to the business strategy, long-term interests and sustainability of the company and should not be linked entirely or mainly to short-term objectives. Directors' performance should be assessed using both financial and non-financial performance criteria, including, where appropriate, environmental, social and governance factors.[64]

Another example of this is what is known as the 'sustainable corporate governance initiative'. In 2020, a study on directors' duties and sustainable corporate governance was published. This study was commissioned by the European Commission. It led to the sustainable corporate governance initiative of the Commission to improve the existing company law and corporate governance framework in the EU. The goal of this initiative is to come up with proposals to enable companies to focus on long-term sustainable value creation rather than short-term benefits.[65] The initiative started with a public consultation in early 2021. So far it has led to a proposal for a directive on Corporate Sustainability Due Diligence[66] (*see* further paragraph 10.27). Corporate governance and the position of shareholders are further detailed in Chapter 6 of this book.

D Mergers and Divisions of Limited Liability Companies

3.34 The EU harmonization covers mergers of public companies, whether they are domestic or cross-border. The merger type regulated at the EU level is a legal procedure by which two or more companies are merged into one company. The latter may be one of the merging companies (merger by acquisition) or a newly formed company (merger by formation of a new company). In both cases, the consequences are the same. The merging companies are wound up without going into liquidation, and all their assets

63. Directive (EU) 2017/828 amending Directive 2007/36/EC.
64. Directive (EU) 2017/828. *See also* https://ec.europa.eu/growth/industry/sustainability_en (accessed May 2021).
65. *See* https://ec.europa.eu/info/law/better-regulation/have-your-say/initiatives/12548-Sustainable-corporate-governance_en.
66. Proposal for a Directive on Corporate Sustainability Due Diligence and amending Directive (EU) 2019/1937COM (2022) 71 final.

and liabilities are transferred to the acquiring company or the newly incorporated (or formed) company. We note that in the case of a merger by formation, the newly incorporated company therefore also functions as an acquiring company. When the merger procedure is completed, the shareholders of the merging companies are automatically issued shares in the acquiring company or the new company, and they might be paid in cash if certain conditions are met. If the acquiring company already holds 90% or more of the shares of the merging companies, however, the procedure and the consequences of the merger may, in principle, be simplified. The same applies where all shares of the merging companies are held by one person or the shareholders of the merging companies hold their shares in the same proportion in all merging companies. The merger methods are further discussed in paragraphs 8.46 *et seq.*

3.35 The opposite of the merger is the division, although the legal procedure effectuating a division is almost identical to the merger procedure. A division entails that the company being divided sees all or part of its assets and liabilities transferred to more than one company. A specific form is the division by separation. This happens if the company being divided transfers part of its assets and liabilities to one or more acquiring companies in exchange for the issue of shares in the acquiring company or companies. As is the case with mergers, an acquiring company can be existing or newly formed. *See* paragraphs 8.55 *et seq.* for a more detailed explanation of division methods.

3.36 Mergers and divisions are governed by the Codification Directive 2017/1132, and the relevant provisions are rather detailed. The harmonization is aimed at strengthening legal certainty of the merger and division procedures and at the protection of the stakeholders of the companies participating in these operations.[67] The interests of stakeholders and third parties require that several documents and particulars are published and provisions relating those to documents and particulars are included in the directive.[68] To enable cross-border mergers and divisions, the directive provides additional rules for issues such as the applicable law and the authorities responsible for supervising and control of the operation.[69] In the Codification Directive (EU) 2017/1132, Chapters I and II of Title II are dedicated to domestic mergers and cross-border mergers respectively. Chapters III and IV in the same title deal with domestic and cross-border divisions respectively.[70]

3.37 Mergers and divisions as discussed here should be distinguished from other operations such as share transactions which may result in a takeover or asset deals that may lead to the transfer of assets and even liabilities to another company. Such business transactions are, in principle, governed by national law, rules for trading at

67. Directive (EU) 2017/1132, Preamble paragraphs 61 and 73.
68. For example, Article 92 prescribing the publication of the draft terms of a merger. When in the case of a merger the acquiring company already holds 90% or more of the outstanding shares of the merging companies the procedure can be simplified, Articles 113 and 115.
69. For example, Articles 127 and 128, dealing with the scrutiny of the legality of the merger and the designation of the authorities that may issue the pre-merger certificate.
70. Directive (EU) 2017/1132 as amended by Directive (EU) 2019/2121.

stock exchanges, and international private law. They do not encompass a legal procedure comparable to harmonized mergers and divisions. Yet, the term merger is often used in a generic way, meaning a number of transactions whereby control of one or more companies or their business enterprise is transferred to another company. The financial press often uses the term 'merger' in this sense, but the wider meaning of 'merger' can also be found in EU policy documents or in legislation for other areas such as competition law.[71]

3.38 Mergers and divisions are further discussed in Chapter 8 of this book, which deals with the wider subject of cross-border cooperation and acquisitions. A few remarks remain to be made here. First, although the harmonized rules for domestic mergers and divisions apply to public limited companies only (Article 87 and 135), the provisions covering cross-border mergers and divisions apply to both public and private companies (Article 119 and 160b). [72] Second, the merger provisions of Directive (EU) 2017/1132 oblige Member States to regulate mergers whereas the directive does not require Member States to introduce the division procedure into their legislation. But if they do, they must comply with the directive for the operations to which the directive applies. [73]

E Conversions and Transfer of Seat

3.39 As explained in Chapter II, paragraphs 2.54 *et seq.*, the right of establishment as granted by the TFEU to companies and firms is put to a test several times in cases judged by the CJEU. These cases were primarily oriented to issues connected with the seat of a company, mostly related to the question of whether the right of establishment means that the seat of a company can be transferred across borders. In *Cartesio*, the CJEU held that a Member State has the power to determine that a company governed by its law will lose that status if it moves its seat to the territory of another Member State. However, a Member State may not require the winding-up or liquidation of a company if that company aims to convert into a form of company governed by the law of the host Member State. In fact, the CJEU paved the way to greater cross-border mobility of companies by *Cartesio* and the cases that followed, *Vale* and *Polbud* (*see* paragraphs 2.67–2.69), by changing the perspective from transfer of seat to conversion.[74] The result of a cross-border conversion actually is the transfer of the seat of a company.

The CJEU held that conversion of a company governed by the law of a Member State into a company governed by the law of another Member State is, in principle,

71. Most notably in competition law: Regulation (EC) 139/2004 is called the Merger Regulation, but it also covers other operations than mergers, as discussed in this chapter.
72. The Third Directive and the Sixth Directive were applicable to public companies only. During the codification leading up to Directive 2017/1132 apparently no attention was paid to the limited scope of the Third and Sixth Directives and no changes were made in that respect.
73. The division has always been optional for Member States, Sixth Directive, 82/891/EEC.
74. J.L. Hansen, 'The Vale Decision and the Court's Case Law on the Nationality of Companies', *European Company and Financial Law Review* 1 (2013): 1–17.

covered by the right of establishment (Articles 49 and 54 TFEU) because, in principle, certain conditions apply. Most notably, the host Member State has to have a provision for the internal conversion of companies, for instance, to convert a private company into a public company. If this is the case, the host Member State may not refuse the conversion if the converted company meets the same requirements as the host Member State imposes on domestic companies. This was established by the CJEU in *Vale* and *Polbud* (*see* paragraphs 2.68 and 2.69). This case law made a cross-border transfer of seat in fact possible in those Member States that had rules on conversion in place. It also paved the way for European harmonization of conversions.

3.40 To enable cross-border conversions, Directive 2019/2121 amended the Codification Directive (EU) 2017/1132 by inserting provisions on this matter. They are placed in Title II, Chapter I, Articles 86a *et seq.* of the Codification Directive. Like the provisions for cross-border mergers and divisions, the provisions apply to both public and private companies (Article 86b).

3.41 The procedure to be followed to realise a cross-border conversion is similar to the procedure for a cross-border merger or division. Nevertheless, the consequences of a conversion differ from the effects of the other operations. The merger or division procedure leads to one or more companies winding up or being formed whereas the conversion implies that the existence of a single company as a legal person is continued. Therefore all assets and liabilities of that company will be those of the converted company, the members (shareholders) will, in principle, continue to be members of the converted company, and the rights and obligations arising from employment contracts or employment relationships will be those of the converted company (Article 86r). The (cross-border) conversion is further discussed in Chapter 8 of this book.

F Insolvency and Restructuring

3.42 Directly applicable EU legislation is enacted in the area of insolvency and restructuring to secure that cross-border insolvency proceedings operate efficiently and effectively. The Insolvency Regulation (Recast) prevents forum shopping by taking away incentives for parties involved in an insolvency case to transfer assets or judicial proceedings from one Member State to another to obtain a more favourable position. In addition, the international jurisdiction of a court in a Member State to open insolvency proceedings and the recognition of those proceedings in other Member States is established. Furthermore, the powers of 'insolvency practitioners' are dealt with as well as the law which is applicable in certain situations. [75]

3.43 On top of the procedural rules for insolvency and restructuring, Directive 2019/1023 aims to harmonize material rules for insolvency and restructuring of

75. Regulation (EC) No 1346/2000 recast as Regulation (EU) 2015/848.

business enterprises.[76] Member States are required to install early warning tools in order to signal to debtors and entrepreneurs that urgent action is needed (Article 3). Where there is a likelihood of insolvency, debtors must have access to a preventive restructuring framework. This should enable them to restructure their debts or business and restore their viability, without prejudice to other solutions for avoiding insolvency, thereby protecting jobs and maintaining business activity (Article 4). During restructuring, debtors should remain in control of their assets and day-to-day operations of their business (Article 5). Member States have to ensure that debtors may benefit from a stay of individual enforcement actions (Article 6). Furthermore, they have to designate a national judicial or administrative authority that is competent to confirm negotiated restructuring plans. Creditors whose rights are affected can vote on the adoption of such a plan (Articles 8–15). Article 11 is among the directive's most important provisions. It regulates what is known as a cross-class cram-down. If a restructuring plan is not approved by the affected parties in every voting class, then it may nevertheless be confirmed by a judicial or administrative authority upon the proposal of the debtor or with the debtor's agreement. Confirmation makes the plan binding upon dissenting voting classes but only if the restructuring plan fulfils the conditions laid down in Article 11 of Directive 2019/1023. Among these are that dissenting voting classes of affected creditors are treated at least as favourably as any other class of the same rank and more favourably than any junior class.

III CAPITAL MARKETS

3.44 For companies and businesses in general, the functioning of capital markets is essential. Companies may need to attract loans and other debt financing as well as equity. Capital markets are supposed to provide these financial means. Notwithstanding their importance to the economy, capital markets in the EU are for the greater part organized along national lines. This contrasts with the free movement of capital as being one of the fundamental freedoms of the EU.[77] With a view to removing these obstacles, the Commission according to its 2020 Action Plan aims to complete the Capital Markets Union (CMU) in order to get money (investments and savings) flowing across the EU for the benefit of consumers, investors and companies, regardless of where they are located. Market-based financing is essential to sustain the recovery of businesses and the return to long-term growth and to finance the green and digital transitions of the economy. In addition, the CMU can contribute to a more inclusive and resilient society, notably by helping to meet the challenges posed by an ageing population. Lastly, integrated capital markets are crucial for the EU's global competitiveness and its autonomy.[78]

76. Directive (EU) 2019/1023.
77. Green Paper *Building a Capital Markets Union*, Brussels, 18.2.2015, COM(2015) 63 final, 4.
78. *A Capital Markets Union for people and businesses-new action plan*, Brussels, 24.9.2020 COM(2015) 590 final.

3.45 The measures proposed in the Action Plan should lead to an integrated CMU by the end of 2022.[79] Among the steps to be taken are the following:

- making companies more visible to cross-border investors by setting up a European single access point (ESAP). This platform is to provide seamless, EU-wide access to all relevant information, including financial and sustainability-related information, disclosed to the public by companies, including financial companies;
- simplifying listing rules for small and innovative companies on SME growth and regulated markets;
- encouraging more long-term and equity financing from institutional investors;
- directing SMEs to alternative providers of funding (e.g., via crowdfunding platforms);[80]
- integrating national capital markets into a genuine single market by making the outcome of cross-border investment more predictable as regards insolvency proceedings;
- facilitating shareholder engagement by introducing a harmonized definition of 'shareholder', and clarifying and harmonizing the rules governing the interaction between investors, intermediaries and issuers as regards the exercise of voting rights and corporate action processing;
- improving cross-border settlement services by reviewing the Central Securities Depositories Regulation;[81]
- enhancing the single rulebook for capital markets and stronger supervisory coordination or direct supervision by the European Supervisory Authorities (ESAs).[82] [83]

3.46 Another important factor for the functioning of capital markets is the availability of usable and reliable information for market participants. The importance of financial reporting need not be explained here but dealt with in Chapter 9. A rather new phenomenon which affects capital markets is corporate sustainability reporting. Regulation (EU) 2020/852 establishes criteria for determining whether an economic activity qualifies as environmentally sustainable. This way it is possible to establish the

79. Annex to *A Capital Markets Union for people and businesses-new action plan*, Brussels, 24.9.2020 COM(2015) 590 final.
80. Cf. Regulation (EU) 2020/1503 amending Regulation (EU) 2017/1129 and Directive (EU) 2019/1937 [2020].
81. Regulation (EU) No 909/2014 amending Directives 98/26/EC and 2014/65/EU and Regulation (EU) No 236/2012 [2014].
82. These are: the European Securities and Markets Authority (ESMA), the European Banking Authority (EBA), and the European Insurance and Occupational Pensions Authority (EIOPA).
83. Annex to *A Capital Markets Union for people and businesses – new action plan*, Brussels, 24.9.2020 COM(2015) 590 final; *Green Paper Building a Capital Markets Union*, Brussels, 18.2.2015, COM(2015) 63 final; Communication *Unleashing the potential of Crowdfunding in the European Union*, COM (2014) 172. A critical analysis is presented by D. Ramos Muñoz, Shadow Banking: The Blind Spot in Banking and Capital Markets Reform, *ECFR* 13, no. 1 (2016): 157–196.

degree to which investing in a company is environmentally sustainable. This regulation is important for financial market participants such as insurance companies, investment firms or credit institutions, to name a few. [84] These financial market participants and financial advisers have to be transparent with regard to the integration of sustainability risks and the consideration of adverse sustainability impacts in their processes. They have to provide sustainabilityrelated information regarding financial products to their clients under the sustainabilityrelated disclosures in the financial services sector regulation.[85]

3.47 As part of the European Green Deal[86] aiming to get Europe climate-neutral by 2050, the Commission submitted a proposal for a Corporate Sustainability Reporting Directive (CSRD) in 2021. If the directive is adopted, then it will make sustainability reporting by companies more consistent.[87]

3.48 After the 2008 financial crisis and its aftermath, the difficulties of EU-wide cooperation and coordination of supervisors became apparent. This led to the creation of three European Supervisory Authorities: the European Banking Authority (EBA), the European Securities and Markets Authority (ESMA), and the European Insurance and Occupational Pensions Authority (EIOPA).[88] In addition, the Single Supervisory Mechanism was created, which transfers supervisory tasks for 'significant' banks in the euro area and other participating Member States to the ECB.[89] This competence of the ECB is an important pillar of the 'Banking Union'. Another feature of the Banking Union is a mechanism for an integrated and effective decision-making process in case systemically important credit institutions fail.[90]

3.49 Investor protection and regulation of the financial services market are also important for the functioning of the capital markets. The EU set out its policy with regard to these issues in its 1999 Action Plan.[91] The plan was aimed at creating a common legal framework for integrated securities and derivatives markets and a single set of financial statements for listed companies. Consequently, listed companies are obliged to prepare their financial statements in accordance with International Accounting Standards (IAS) in order to allow 'fair value accounting' (*see* paragraph 9.17).

3.50 The following EU legislation contains requirements regarding information and transparency as well as rules aimed at protecting investors against abusive behaviour by other financial market participants:

---

84. Regulation (EU) 2020/852 amending Regulation (EU) 2019/2088 [2020]. The relevant market participants are summarized in Article 2 of Regulation (EU) 2019/2088.
85. Regulation (EU) 2019/2088.
86. COM/2019/640 final.
87. The proposal is part of the 2018 Action Plan: Financing Sustainable Growth, COM(2021) 189 final.
88. Regulations (EU) 1092/2010, 1093/2010, 1094/2010 and 1095/2010.
89. Credit institutions are deemed significant if, *inter alia*, the total value of their assets exceeds EUR 30 billion, Article 6(4), Regulation (EU) 1024/2013.
90. The Single Resolution Mechanism (SRM), Directive 2014/59/EU and Regulation (EU) 806/2014.
91. *Financial Services: Implementing the Framework for Financial Markets: Action Plan*, COM(1999)232, 11 May 1999.

the 2014 Market Abuse Regulation;[92]
the 2017 Prospectus Regulation;[93]
the 2014 Markets in Financial Instruments Directive II (MiFID II);[94]
the 2013 revised Transparency Directive.[95]

The Market Abuse Regulation covers financial instruments admitted to trading on regulated markets (stock exchanges) or on other trading facilities. This regulation is aimed at preserving market integrity and curbing market abuse. Therefore, it contains rules on insider dealing, unlawful disclosure of inside information and market manipulation. The Prospectus Regulation relates, *inter alia*, to the admission of securities to listing, which requires prior publication of a prospectus. The Markets in Financial Instruments Directive II ensures protection for investors by establishing conduct of business obligations and creates a single passport for investment firms, enabling them to operate across the EU. The Revised Transparency Directive sets out uniform rules for the disclosure of information, in particular yearly and half-yearly company financial reporting, by issuers of securities throughout the EU. More details on the four pieces of legislation are provided in the paragraphs that follow.

3.51 First, the Market Abuse Regulation in Article 7(1)(a) defines insider information regarding financial instruments or issuers of financial instruments as:

> information of a precise nature, which has not been made public, relating, directly or indirectly, to one or more issuers or to one or more financial instruments, and which, if it were made public, would be likely to have a significant effect on the prices of those financial instruments or on the price of related derivative financial instruments.

Such definitions also apply to information regarding commodity derivatives and emission allowances.

Issuers of financial instruments must draw up an insider list, consisting of employees who have access to inside information and others who have such access by performing tasks as advisors, accountants or credit rating agencies (Article 18). Member States must prohibit any person who possesses inside information from using it either by transactions for their own account or for the account of a third party or by disclosing that information or using it for 'tipping' (Articles 8 and 14). In addition, the issuers of financial instruments must inform the public as soon as possible of inside information that directly concerns the issuer (Article 17).

Market manipulation, as defined in Article 12, is, *inter alia*, entering into a transaction, placing an order or any other behaviour:

- gives, or is likely to give, false or misleading signals as to the supply of, demand for, or price of, a financial instrument; or

92. Regulation (EU) No 596/2014.
93. Regulation (EU) 2017/1129 repealing Directive 2003/71.
94. Directive 2014/65/EU amending Directive 2002/92/EC; Directive 2011/61/EU.
95. Directive 2004/109/EC amending Directive 2001/34/EC; Directive 2013/50/EU.

- secures, or is likely to secure, the price of one or several financial instruments at an abnormal or artificial level.

Member States must prohibit any person from engaging in market manipulation (Article 15).

Each Member State must designate a single administrative competent authority for the purpose of the Market Abuse Regulation (Article 22). The competent authorities of the Member States must cooperate with each other and with ESMA (Article 25).

3.52 Second, the Prospectus Regulation concerns rules on the drafting, approval and distribution of the prospectus. Issuers can obtain a 'single passport'. The regulation covers a wide range of securities of both an equity and non-equity nature (Article 1). Member States may not allow any offer of securities to be made to the public within their territory without prior publication of a prospectus, although some small offers are exempted (Article 3). The information that the prospectus must contain is set out in the regulation and its delegated acts (Articles 6, 13 and 16). No prospectus may be made public before the competent authority of the home state of the issuer has approved it (Article 20). The home Member State's approval serves as a 'single passport' because it is valid for a public offer or an admission to trading in other Member States (Article 20).[96]

3.53 Third, the Markets in Financial Instruments Directive (MiFID II) covers undertakings providing investment services to third parties or performing investment activities through the establishment of a branch in the EU (Article 1). For providing these services or performing these activities on a professional basis, prior authorization in the home Member State is required. Authorized firms must be registered in the Member States and every authorization must be notified to ESMA. Investment firms having legal personality must have their head office in the same Member State as their registered office. A firm without legal personality must have its head office in the Member State where it actually carries out its business (Articles 5(4)). The authorization represents a single passport because it is valid for the entire EU (Article 6). In order to become authorized, capital and organizational requirements must be met, and rules and procedures for fair and orderly trading must be established (Articles 14–16). Member States must ensure that authorized firms comply with the provisions ensuring investor protection.[97] Furthermore, the directive provides for the authorization by Member States of certain systems as a regulated market and for the admission of financial instruments to trading (Articles 44 and 51). Detailed matters, such as the reporting of transactions to the competent authorities, are governed by the Markets in Financial Instruments Regulation (MiFIR).[98]

---

96. *See* for the results: *Consultation on the Review of the Prospectus Directive*, 18/02/2015–13/05/2015, – Feedback statement on the public online consultation, at http://ec.europa.eu/finance/consultations/2015/prospectus-directive/index_en.htm (accessed May 2016).
97. Articles 24–30 Regulation (EU) 600/2014.
98. Regulation (EU) 600/2014.

3.54 Fourth and last, the Transparency Directive (as amended) harmonizes transparency requirements related to information about issuers of listed securities. These issuers should provide for a regular flow of information. The annual financial report must be made public four months after the end of a financial year at the latest and must remain publicly available for at least ten years (Article 4). In addition, a half-year report must cover the first six months and must be published three months after that period at the latest (Article 5). Issuers active in the extractive or logging of primary forest industries have to report yearly on payments made to governments (Article 6). Member States must ensure that the issuer is notified about 'major holdings', being shareholders acquiring or disposing of shares thereby passing certain thresholds (Article 9). The information contained in the notification must be made public by the issuer (Article 12).

CHAPTER 4

Business Organizations under EU Law

I INTRODUCTION

4.01 There are several types of business organizations governed by European law which were briefly introduced in paragraph 2.49. In this chapter, several of these European business organizations, namely the European Economic Interest Grouping (EEIG), the *Societas Europaea* (SE) and the *Societas Cooperativa Europaea* (SCE) are discussed (*see* paragraphs 4.02, 4.13 and 4.44, respectively). These business organizations have several features in common: first, they are primarily governed by European Union (EU) law, they can transfer their registered seat from one Member State to another, and their formation requires a cross-border element. Their European character, however, is weakened by the fact that not all aspects of these business types are covered by European law. Consequently, the respective regulations often refer to rules provided for under national law.

II EUROPEAN ECONOMIC INTEREST GROUPING

4.02 The idea of a supranational business organization was realized for the first time by the introduction of the EEIG. The EEIG is a 'modest' legal form, offering a flexible and light structure for cross-border cooperation. The EEIG is governed by Regulation (EEC) 2137/85, which required the Member States at the time to take appropriate measures to enable the formation of an EEIG by mid-1989.[1] By its nature, the EEIG is a vehicle for cooperation among enterprises in different Member States. Formation of an EEIG entails few formalities and no initial capital to be contributed. Subsequently, the members have unlimited joint and several liability. A grouping, like a general partnership, has capacities, distinct from its members, to have rights and obligations of

1. OJ 1985, L 199.

all kinds, to make contracts or accomplish other legal acts, and to sue and be sued. It is left to the national law of the Member States to determine whether the EEIG has legal personality.[2] Article 40 of the Regulation secures fiscal transparency, meaning that the profits and losses of a grouping are taxable only in the hands of its members. The purpose of the EEIG must be limited to facilitating or developing the economic activities of its members. Its purpose is not to make profits for itself, and its activities must not be more than ancillary to the economic activities of its members. The structure of the grouping is simple, and there are only two mandatory bodies: the members and the manager(s).

4.02a Credit is given to the French for the invention of such an easy-to-operate legal form for cooperation as its introduction was inspired by the French *groupement d'intérêt économique* (GIE). The GIE was introduced in France in 1967 and has been successful,[3] even in the field of international cooperation. A well-known example of the latter is *Airbus,* which was originally formed in 1970 as a GIE by several European aircraft builders. The enterprise developed into what is now Airbus Group SE, registered in the Netherlands and listed on stock exchanges in France, Germany and Spain.[4]

4.03 The European character of the EEIG is secured by the provision that the grouping 'shall be formed upon the terms, in the manner and with the effects laid down in this Regulation', as stated in Article 1 of Regulation (EEC) 2137/85. The regulation has precedence over national law and is directly applicable in all Member States. For this reason, the EEIG is supposed to offer 'legal neutrality', placing its members on an equal footing insofar as no one is operating in a more familiar legal environment.[5] However, this is only partially true because the binding provisions of the regulation do not cover all aspects of the EEIG. The issues that are dealt with in the regulation are:

- the conditions governing the constitution of a grouping;
- certain aspects of its internal operation;
- the protection of third parties and members.

Even for these aspects, provisions of national law may complete the regulation. In addition, many important matters, such as the consequences of liability and insolvency, are referred completely to national law.

2. Article 1. For example, under German law the EEIG is not a legal person. *See* C. Müller-Gugenberger & P. Schotthöfer, *Die EWIV in Europa. Texte und Erläuterungen aus rechtsvergleichender Sicht,* 1 Auflage (München: Verlagsgruppe Jehle-Rehm, 1995) (*Die EWIV in Europa*), 661 and 686; Commission of the European Communities, EEIG. *The Emergence of a New Form of European Cooperation* (Brussels/Luxembourg: 1993), 16.
3. G. Ripert & R. Roblot, *Traité de Droit Commercial,* par Michel Germain, Tome 1, Volume 2, 18e édition, 2002, no. 2054.
4. On 27 May 2015 at the Annual General Meeting of Shareholders of Airbus Group N.V., the conversion into a European Company was approved with a majority of 99.99%, Annual Report 2015 and Registration Document 2015 of Airbus Group.
5. Communication from the Commission, 97/C 285/10, OJ 1997, C 285, Ch. II.

A Formation and Publication

4.04 Parties intending to form a grouping must conclude a contract and register it in the Member State in which the official address of the EEIG is established.[6] The contract for the formation of the grouping and its internal organization is governed by the national law of the Member State in which its official address is situated.[7] The contract must include the name of the grouping, preceded or followed by the words 'European Economic Interest Grouping' or by the initials 'EEIG'[8] and the official address. In addition, the contract must include the objects for which the grouping is formed, the name of each member of the grouping, as well as other information relating to the members and the duration of the grouping. If the last provision is absent, it is assumed that the duration is indefinite.[9] If national law provides for the nullity of the grouping, its nullity must be established or declared by judicial decision. However, the court must, where it is possible for the affairs of the grouping to be put in order, allow time to permit that to be done.[10]

4.05 A contract for the formation of a grouping must be filed at the commercial registry, together with several other documents and particulars, notably: notice of the appointment of the manager or managers, their names and other identification particulars required by the law of the Member State in which the register is kept. In addition, notifications that managers may act alone or that they must act jointly must be filed, as well as any information concerning the termination of any manager's appointment.[11] Any grouping establishment carrying on business activities in a Member State other than that in which its official address is situated must be registered in that other Member State. This 'secondary' registration is carried out simply by submitting copies of the documents that must be filed for its 'primary' registration, together with, if necessary, a translation conforming with the practice of the registry where the establishment is registered.[12] Upon its primary registration, the EEIG is formed and possesses the legal capacities described previously.[13] Thus, from that

6. Articles 1 and 6.
7. Article 2(1). This provision does not bar the members from agreeing that certain legal relationships underlying the contract such as regarding distribution of costs and insurance will be governed by the law of another state. *See* on this E. Werlauff, *EU Company Law: Common Business Law of 28 states*, Second edition (Copenhagen: Djøf Publishing, 2003), 121.
8. The mandatory words or acronym should be in the national language. In Danish: *Europæisk økonomisk firmagruppe* (EØFG), Dutch: *Europees Economisch Samenwerkingsverband* (EESV), French: *groupement européen d'intérêt économique* (GEIE), in German: *Europäische wirtschaftliche Interessenvereinigung* (EWIV), in Polish: *Europejskie Zgrupowanie Interesów Gospodarczych*; in Spanish: *agrupación europea de interés económico* (AEIE), in Italian: *Gruppo Europeo di Interesse Economico* (GEIE). The CJEU ruled that inclusion of additional elements in the name may be required by national law, Case C-402/96 *(EITO)* (1997).
9. Article 5.
10. Article 15.
11. Articles 6, 7, 9 and 39, Communication from the Commission, 97/C 285/10, OJ 1997, C 285 (further: Commission, *EEIG*), 73 and 74.
12. Article 10.
13. Article 1.

moment on, it may also assume obligations that have arisen out of activities carried out on behalf of the grouping before its registration. If the grouping does not assume these obligations, the persons who carried out those activities will bear unlimited joint and several liability for them.[14]

4.06 After registration, several particulars must be published in the national gazette, such as the mandatory minimum content of the contract, the number, date and place of registration, and almost all of the documents and particulars that have to be filed at the registry.[15] Although publication is not a prerequisite for its existence, it is essential for the functioning of the EEIG in relation to third parties. Pursuant to the First Directive, the documents and particulars that must be published may be relied on by a grouping against third parties under the conditions laid down by the applicable national law.[16] Following the publication in the national gazette, notice that a grouping has been formed must be given to the *Official Journal of the EU.*[17]

4.07 The contract must designate the official address of the EEIG. It must be situated in the EU, either where the grouping has its central administration or where one of the members has its central administration or, in the case of a natural person, the place of that person's principal activities, provided that the grouping carries on activities there.[18] The second option, thus, makes it legal for an EEIG to conduct its activities by using the infrastructure of one of its members. The official address may be transferred within the EU as long as the new address fulfils the conditions mentioned above. Such transfer will result in a change of applicable law if the address is moved from one Member State to another. In that case, a transfer proposal must be drawn up and filed, and the proposed address must be published. The decision to transfer may only be taken two months after publication, and the members must decide on it unanimously. During the two-month period, a competent authority of the Member State in which the EEIG is registered may oppose its transfer, but only on grounds of public interest and if the law of the Member State so provides.[19] If no objection is raised, the transfer may be carried out by registering the EEIG in the transferee Member State. Until the cancellation of the old address is published, third parties may continue to rely on that address, unless they have actual knowledge of the transfer.[20]

14. Article 9(2).
15. Article 8.
16. Article 25.
17. Articles 8 and 11, The Official Journal of the EU, previously the Official Journal of the EC.
18. Article 12. Note that the EEIG Regulation uses 'Community' where now European Union should be read.
19. Articles 13 and 14. Spain, the UK, and Ireland have exercised this option, *Die EWIV in Europa, supra* n. 2, at 595, 631, 740. However, it is argued that in other Member States authorities may intervene as well, e.g., to take legal steps to ensure that the grouping complies with tax obligations, *see* D. van Gerven, 'The European Economic Interest Grouping (EEIG): The First European Legal Vehicle for Cooperation Between Enterprises', in D. van Gerven & C.A.V. Aalders (eds), *European Economic Interest Grouping* (Deventer/Boston: Kluwer Law and Taxation Publishers, 1990), 73. *See further* 120, 138, 204, 236, 259.
20. Article 14.

4.08 As already mentioned, the regulation requires the activity of the grouping to be ancillary to the economic activities of its members, and its purpose may not be to make profits for itself. Therefore, partners wanting to start a new economic activity that is not connected with their own activities would have to set up another type of business organization, such as a company. The ancillary role must not be interpreted too narrowly, that is, in the sense of 'accessory' or of 'less importance'.[21] The regulation does not prohibit the EEIG from completely, though temporarily, taking over some of its members' activities. This can be the case for the purposes of performing work on site in the construction industry, for example.[22] In accordance with this ancillary character, a grouping may not direct a group, that is, exercise the power of management or supervision over the activities of the members or the activities of another undertaking. Shareholding in another undertaking is allowed only insofar as it is necessary for the achievement of the grouping's objective and if it is done on its members' behalf. The grouping is also prohibited from being a member of another grouping, in order to avoid a complicated chain of liabilities in an international context.[23]

4.08a In addition, two specific prohibitions apply. The grouping may not employ more than 500 people, a limitation that stems from German law concerning employee representation on the supervisory board. Without this limitation, employee representation would be obligatory for a grouping employing more than 500 people and having its official address in Germany, as opposed to non-German groupings employing more than 500 people.[24] Second, a grouping may not be used by a company for granting loans to the director of that company or for the transfer of property between the company and a director, when those transactions are restricted or controlled under the Member State's laws governing companies.[25] This clause was inserted at the request of the UK and reflects certain sections of the Companies Act. In general, a Member State may impose appropriate sanctions in order to prevent abuse or circumvention of its national laws by a grouping.[26]

4.09 The membership of a grouping may consist of only three categories:

- companies or firms within the meaning of the second paragraph of Article 54 TFEU (ex Article 48 TEC);
- other legal bodies that have been formed in accordance with the law of a Member State and that have their registered or statutory office and central administration in the EU;
- natural persons who carry on a business activity or who provide services in the EU.[27]

21. Commission, *EEIG, supra* n. 11, at 47.
22. Communication from the Commission, 97/C 285/10, OJ 1997, C 285, Ch. II(3).
23. Commission, *EEIG, supra* n. 11, at 59.
24. D. van Gerven, *supra* n. 19, at 13.
25. Article 3.
26. Preamble of the regulation.
27. Article 4(1).

In practice, these are not serious limitations because a wide range of legal entities is included, that is, not only business organizations but also non-profit-making organizations and legal bodies governed by public law to the extent that they pursue an economic activity.[28] However, entities formed in accordance with the law of a 'third country', such as a Delaware incorporated company, cannot be members of an EEIG.[29] To participate, they would first have to constitute one of the entities mentioned above in accordance with the law of a Member State.

The cross-border dimension of the grouping is secured by the requirement that the enterprises concerned are situated in at least two different Member States.[30]

4.09a The members of a grouping have unlimited joint and several liability for its debts and other liabilities. New members incur all existing liabilities unless a clause is added in the formation contract exempting a new member from liabilities that originated prior to that new member's admission.[31] Former members of an EEIG remain liable for five years following their withdrawal for liabilities arising out of the grouping's activities during the period of their membership.[32] Creditors may not proceed against a current or former member for payment before the liquidation of a grouping is concluded, unless they have first requested payment from the grouping and payment has not been made within an appropriate period.[33]

As already mentioned, national law determines the consequences of the liability of members and former members, such as the recourse a member may take against co-members if that member has paid more than his or her share.

B Structure

4.10 The mandatory bodies of a grouping are the members acting collectively in a general meeting and the manager(s), but the contract for the formation may provide for other bodies as well. The members, acting as a body, may make any decision for achieving the objects of the grouping.[34] Each member has one vote. The contract for the formation, however, may give more than one vote to certain members, provided that one single member does not hold the majority of the votes.[35] For several decisions, unanimity is always required. For example, to amend the objects of the grouping, transfer its official address to another Member State, change the number of votes allotted to each member, or decide on the admission of new members. For other decisions, the contract may set forth different rules but, where it fails to do so,

28. D. van Gerven, *supra* n. 19, at 15.
29. But an 'associate membership' can be created via underlying agreements, E. Werlauff, *EU Company Law*, *supra* n. 7, at 122.
30. Article 4(2).
31. Article 26(2) and 7 sub j.
32. Article 34.
33. Article 24.
34. Article 16.
35. Article 17(1).

unanimity may also be required.[36] The members have full freedom to organize their meetings, and they can regulate their own methods of decision making, which may take place, apart from at meetings, by other means, such as voting by post or teleconference.[37]

4.10a The grouping is managed by one or more natural persons, appointed by a contract or by the decision of its members. Member States may allow legal persons to be managers on the condition that such legal persons designate one or more natural persons to represent them. Those persons are liable as if they were the managers of the grouping concerned. The appointment and removal of the managers are determined by the contract for its formation or, failing that, by the unanimous decision of the members.[38] Each of the managers may represent the grouping in dealings with third parties and bind the grouping acting on behalf of it. The rules concerning acts not falling within the objects of the grouping or the limitations that can be relied on as against third parties reflect the provisions of the First Directive.[39] The law of the Member State in which the EEIG has its official address governs the liability of the managers towards its members.[40] For this purpose, the general provisions for the duties of managers of legal persons may apply to the managers of an EEIG. As an alternative, Member States may also rely on the provisions pertaining to the partners of a partnership.[41] In addition, special provisions may apply, for instance, in the case of bankruptcy.[42] Towards third parties, the liability of the grouping and/or its managers is, of course, subject to the law applicable according to private international law.[43]

C Involvement of Employees

4.11 In contrast to the SE and the SCE, the EEIG is not subject to special European legislation concerning the involvement of employees. Consequently, national law governs this matter. It must be noted, however, that Community law certainly has a

36. Articles 17(2) and (3) and Article 26(1).
37. Commission, *EEIG, supra* n. 11, at 12.
38. Article 19.
39. Article 20, *see* paragraph 3.23 of this book.
40. Article 2(1).
41. An example of the first is Article 9 Book 2 of the Dutch Civil Code: 'Each officer or managing director shall be responsible to the legal person for the proper performance of the duties assigned to him (...).' An example of the second is Article 144 of the Spanish Commercial Code which states that 'damage to the Company's interests caused by malice, abuse of power or gross negligence on the part of one of the partners shall result in that partner being liable (...)'.
42. For example, Article 2:138 of the Dutch Civil Code, which applies to the EEIG and states that each managing director is liable if the management has 'manifestly performed its duties improperly'.
43. In the case of non-contractual liability, this will normally be the *lex loci delicti, see* E. Werlauff, *EU Company Law, supra* n. 7, at 428; D. van Gerven, *supra* n. 19, at 45. For jurisdictional matters, *see* Regulation (EU) No. 1215/2012 (Brussels I Regulation). Further: on the law applicable on contractual obligations: Regulation (EC) No. 593/2008 (Rome I) and Regulation (EC) No. 864/2007 (Rome II) dealing with the law applicable to non-contractual obligations.

bearing on the role of employees. Due to a 1994 directive, Community-scale undertakings may have an obligation to establish a European works council (EWC) or an alternative procedure for information and consultation of employees. Dependent on specific circumstances, employees of an EEIG or of its members may take part in such councils or procedures. On the national scale, another directive requires Member States to meet minimum requirements for employees' right to information and consultation.

The involvement of employees is further discussed in Chapter 7.

D Perspectives of the EEIG

4.12 The introduction of the EEIG at Community level aims to facilitate cross-border cooperation, especially for small- and medium-sized enterprises (SMEs).[44] This intention is perfectly justified by the global trend to increase intercompany cooperation.[45] The flexibility regarding formation, operation and financing of an EEIG should make this legal form particularly accessible to SMEs.[46] Through cooperation, they are able to match the advantages of large enterprises without any loss of independence. However, international cooperation among SMEs is not as universal as might be expected. Lack of communication between businesspeople operating small enterprises and differences in conditions for doing business from one country to another present obstacles. Legal barriers do not seem to play much of a role here.[47]

By 1997, the European Commission reported that with more than 800 EEIGs being set up, this legal form was still not being optimally used. The Commission advised the EEIG for firms wishing to cooperate as a 'consortium' in order to participate in public contracts and programmes financed by public funds.[48] Regarding the sectors of activity in which the members of groupings operate, an earlier survey indicates a predominance in the service sector. There are various types of activities that may be assigned to a grouping. However, it is most frequently used as a means of providing services for its members or third parties, but also for distribution, research and production.[49] The number of EEIGs is constantly growing. By July 2017, more than

44. Commission, *EEIG, supra* n. 11. Positive on the perspectives for the EEIG in practice are Gugenberger & Schotthöfer, *Die EWIV in Europa. Texte und Erläuterungen aus rechtsvergleichender Sicht,* no. 21–25. Note that because of the introduction of the EEIG, EU policy has shifted from SMEs to entrepreneurs. *See also* R. Aernoudt, *European Enterprise Policy: From SME Policy to Entrepreneurship Policy* (Antwerp/Oxford/New York: Intersentia, 2003).
45. S.E. Huyzer et al., supra n. 1, at 11.
46. Commission, *EEIG, supra* n. 11, at 8.
47. Commission DG III – Industry, Eurostat, Panorama of EC industry 1993: an extensive review of the situation and outlook of the manufacturing and service industries in the European Community, Publications Office, 1993, 99–106.
48. Participation of European Economic Interest Groupings (EEIGs) in public contracts and programmes financed by public funds, COM(97) 434 final, OJ 1997, C 285.
49. Commission, *EEIG, supra* n. 11, at 23 and 35. According to H. Zahorka, a few 'megatrends' are, *inter alia,* the use of the EEIG for IT-based virtual firms and for cooperation between self-employed professionals, EWIV-Konferenz, Frankfurt, 5 Nov. 2004, http://www.libertas-institut.com/de/Praesentationen/HJ_Zahorka.pdf (accessed May 2016).

2,500 EEIGs were founded. A few Member States counted for most of these, notably Belgium (507), Germany (450) and France (319).[50]

III EUROPEAN COMPANY

4.13 In the context of an integrated market, the Commission proposed, in 1970, the Statute for the European Company, officially named the *Societas Europaea* (SE).[51] The idea was to create a supranational business organization to enable enterprises to restructure their businesses at the European level. The original proposal was very ambitious. The Commission suggested that the statute should cover all aspects of modern company law to avoid the application of divergent national laws, but the proposal was substantially amended and weakened in that respect before it was eventually adopted in 2001. As a result, the SE Regulation on the Statute for the SE and the SE Directive supplementing the statute with regard to the involvement of employees entered into force on 8 October 2004.[52] Both the regulation and the directive are based on Article 308 of the EC Treaty (now Article 352 TFEU). Under this provision, the Council may take appropriate measures by a unanimous decision, in order to achieve EU objectives where the treaties do not provide the necessary powers to do so.[53]

4.14 The original proposal raised much debate on employee involvement and other issues, such as the law of groups, which were part of the first draft. Therefore, the proposal proved to be 'non-negotiable', and it was substantially amended over the years in order to improve its political credibility.[54] Compared to the original proposal, later proposals were far less comprehensive and referred to national law more often.[55] Eventually, about thirty options were worked in, where Member States may follow patterns of domestic company law. The provisions concerning employee involvement were removed altogether from the regulation on the SE Statute in order to form the substance of a separate directive: the SE Directive. Although the SE is not the first type

50. Furthermore in 2017 the following number of EEIGs were present in: Spain (231), Italy (231), the Netherlands (201) and the UK (267). EEIG Statistics from the European EEIG Information Centre (at LIBERTAS – European Institute GmbH), www.ewiv.eu – www.libertas-institut.com (accessed August 2021).
51. OJ 1970, C 12411; Supplement to the Bulletin 8-1970 of the European Communities. A preliminary draft was delivered by P. Sanders, 'From Conception to Reality', in J. Rickford (ed.), *The European Company: Developing a Community Law of Corporations: Collected Papers from the Leiden University Unilever Programme 2002* (Antwerp/ Oxford/New York: Intersentia, 2003), 37–39.
52. Council Regulation (EC) No. 2157/2001 *(SE Regulation);* Council Directive 2001/86/ EC (involvement of employees). For the introduction in the Member States *see*: K. Oplustil & C. Teichmann, *The European Company – All over Europe: A State-by-State Account of the Introduction of the European Company* (Berlin: De Gruyter, 2004).
53. The Commission initially proposed to ground the SE Statute on the 'traditional' legal basis of Article 44 (ex Article 54). *See* on the legal basis: A. Wehlau, 'The Societas Europaea: A Critique of the Commission's 1991 Amended Proposal', *Common Market Law Review* 29, no. 3 (1992): 473.
54. J. Rickford (ed.), *supra* n. 51, at 18.
55. Supplement to Bulletin EEC *4175*; OJ 1989, 263/07 and 263/08; OJ 1991, C 176/01, and C 138/08.

of company of a non-national nature, as can be seen from paragraph 1.02 in this book, where reference is made to 'international companies', its introduction is hailed as 'a unique and historic step (...) in European company law'.[56] The introduction of the SE has helped to make the Tenth Directive on cross-border mergers (now incorporated in Directive (EU) 2017/1132) acceptable to the Member States. Even as a draft, the SE also provided a model for another European business organization, the SCE.[57]

4.15 An SE is a public limited liability company with capital divided into shares. Upon registration, it obtains legal personality.[58] Access to the SE is primarily reserved for national public limited companies, which, under certain conditions, are even allowed to transform directly into an SE. Private limited companies and other legal bodies are only allowed to participate in the formation of an SE by forming a holding company or a joint subsidiary, respectively.[59] As already mentioned, an important characteristic of the SE is that it may transfer its registered office within the EU without being wound up.[60] Another hallmark is that the SE offers its founders the option to choose between a one-tier and a two-tier board structure.[61] In addition, the SE features cross-border employee involvement, for which rules are laid down in the accompanying Directive 2001/86/EC.[62]

A Applicable Law

4.16 As with the EEIG, the European character of the SE is secured by the rules determining the applicable law. For the SE, Article 9(1) of the SE Regulation ranks the sources of law. Thus, the SE is primarily governed by the regulation itself and, where the regulation expressly authorizes it, its articles of association.[63] Where matters are not, or not completely, regulated by the SE Regulation, an SE is governed by provisions of the law of the Member State in which the SE has its registered office. In such case, the national provisions adopted specifically to implement EU measures prevail over other national provisions.[64] Second, national company law may apply, insofar as it relates to public companies. Third, the articles of association of the SE may contain additional provisions in the same way as allowed for a domestic public limited

56. E. Werlauff, *SE – The Law of the European Company* (Copenhagen: DJØF Publishing, 2003), 1.
57. Regulation (EC) No. 1435/2003 on the Statute for a European Cooperative Society (SCE) and Council Directive 2003/72/EC (involvement of employees).
58. Articles 1 and 16 of Regulation (EC) No. 2157/2001.
59. Article 2.
60. Article 8, *see* paragraph 2.53 and Chapter 8. Cross-border transfer of the seat is, generally speaking, not an option for companies under national law. They may, however, instead use a cross-border conversion which is allowed under EU law (*see* paragraph 2.66 *et seq.*) and further regulated by Directive (EU) 2019/2021.
61. Chapter 6 of this book deals with board structures in general.
62. Directive 2001/86/ (involvement of employees).
63. W.J.M. van Veen, 'The Law Governing SEs: An Interpretation Based on a Textual Analysis and the Referencing Methodology in the Regulation', *European Company Law* 1, no. 3 (October 2004): 111–116.
64. These implementation measures must be in accordance with the directives applicable to public companies, Article 9(2). *See* further: E. Werlauff, *supra* n. 56, at 23.

company.[65] It is important to note that, for taxation purposes, the SE will be subject to the legislation of the Member State in which it has its registered office. and it will enjoy no more facilities for deduction of losses incurred by establishments abroad than other business organizations.[66]

4.16a As seen next, the most important matters covered by the SE Regulation itself are the formation of the SE, the transfer of the registered office, the board structure and the general meeting. The reader who is familiar with the company law directives, as set out in Chapter 3, will feel at home with many details of the SE Regulation because it contains the essence of the harmonization of company law.[67] According to the SE Regulation, the articles of association of an SE may provide for a number of matters pertaining to the SE's internal organization. Examples include the determination of the board as either one-tier or two-tier (Article 38), the determination of the number of board members (*inter alia,* Article 43(2)) and the determination of the majority required for a decision by the general meeting to amend the articles of association (Article 59(1)).

4.16b The SE Directive must, like any directive, be implemented through appropriate measures by the Member States.[68] The directive ensures that negotiations take place between employee representatives and management on the involvement of employees in the SE. Whenever the negotiations lead to an arrangement that conflicts with the articles of association of the SE, the arrangement prevails and the articles of association must consequently be amended. The high ranking of this agreement is laid down in Article 12(4) of the SE Regulation. An example of such a conflict would be an arrangement leading to more seats on the supervisory body than allowed for by the articles of association (Article 39(4)).

4.16c The highest-ranking provisions of national law are those specifically adopted to implement the SE Regulation and SE Directive. The former attribute the regulation of several matters to the Member States, partly as an option, and partly on a mandatory basis. Examples are the obligation to designate the competent authority to affirm the completion of the formalities for the SE to transfer its registered office (Article 8(8)), the option to require additional publication of the proposal to transfer the registered office (Article 8(2)) and the option to require less than 10% of the subscribed capital for shareholders, in order to demand a general meeting (Article 55(1)).[69] Second in the hierarchy of national law are provisions of company law that are relevant for public

65. Article 9(1c, iii). Where the SE Regulation refers to harmonized law, competition between the law systems of the Member States can hardly occur. *See* C. Tavares da Costa & A. de Meester Bilreiro, *The European Company Statute* (The Hague/London/New York: Kluwer Law International, 2003), 14.
66. Preamble, Recital 20. Directive 90/434/EEC on the common system of taxation applicable to mergers, divisions, and transfers of assets and exchanges of shares concerning companies of different Member States must be amended as to include the SE.
67. Werlauff, *EU Company Law, supra* n. 7, at 75.
68. Article 288 TFEU.
69. According to W. van Veen, more than forty provisions of the SE Regulation refer to the Member States in this way: *supra* n. 63, at 113.

limited liability companies, as specified in Annex I of the SE Regulation. Again, the SE Regulation itself makes several references to the rules of the law of the Member States that are applicable to public limited companies. This way, the SE Regulation invokes harmonized national legislation for issues such as the capital of the SE (Article 5) and the preparation of the annual financial statements (Article 61). However, references are also made to non-harmonized provisions of national law, such as for winding up, liquidation, insolvency, cessation of payments and similar procedures (Article 62).[70] By introducing national provisions that go beyond what is strictly necessary for the SE Regulation's implementation, Member States may try to make the SE an attractive legal form in order to compete with other Member States for SE incorporations.[71]

4.16d It follows from the ranking as laid down in Article 9 of the SE Regulation that the articles of association of the SE might only contain additional provisions regarding matters not covered by the SE Regulation. The same goes for national law, which is applicable pursuant to the SE Regulation. Therefore, it depends a great deal on the Member State in which the SE has its registered office what additional provisions may be allowed in the articles of association (statutes) of the SE.

B Formation and Publication

4.17 Formation of an SE may be undertaken according to several methods. The first four of these are 'primary' formation methods, in the sense that no pre-existing SE is involved, whereas this would be the case if 'secondary' formation applies. Each of these methods is mentioned here, and the relevant provisions of the SE Regulation are highlighted in the following paragraph. An SE can be formed according to the following methods:

(1) *Formation of an SE by merger* between public limited companies. Those companies have to be formed under the law of a Member State and have their registered offices and head offices within the EU. To secure the cross-border dimension, at least two of them must be governed by the law of different Member States (Article 2(1)). The merger may be carried out as an acquisition by one of the merging companies (the acquiring company), which will take the form of an SE upon the completion of the merger, or by formation of a new company, which will have the form of an SE (Article 17).
(2) *Formation of a holding SE* by public and/or private limited companies. As under (1), the companies involved must have been formed under the law of a Member State and have their registered offices and head offices within the EU. At least two of them must be governed by the law of different Member States or have, for at least two years, a subsidiary company governed by the

70. Referral to the national law for public limited companies is to be found in thirty-three provisions of the SE Regulation, W. van Veen, *supra* n. 63, at 114.
71. M. Menjucq, 'Implementation in France of the Regulation on the European Company: A Strategic Interpretation', *European Company Law* 1, no. 3 (October 2004): 117 *et seq.*

law of another Member State or a branch situated in another Member State (Article 2(2)).

(3) *Formation of a subsidiary SE* by companies and firms within the meaning of Article 54 TFEU, including other legal bodies governed by public or private law, safe for those that are not profit-making. The same conditions apply as mentioned under (2): the participating companies, firms and other legal bodies must have their registered offices and head offices within the EU. At least two of them must be governed by the laws of different Member States or have, for at least two years, a subsidiary company governed by the law of another Member State or a branch situated in another Member State (Article 2(3)).

(4) *Conversion into an SE* by a public limited company, if that company has a subsidiary company governed by the law of another Member State for at least two years (Article 2(4)).

(5) *Setting up an SE subsidiary* by an SE (Article 3(2)). As this fifth mode implies the pre-existence of an SE, its formation is sometimes referred to as 'secondary' formation.[72] The same applies when an SE participates in the formation of another SE by way of a merger or by creating a holding SE or a subsidiary SE. The regulation facilitates this by stating that an SE, in this respect, is to be regarded as a public limited company governed by the law of the Member State in which it has its registered office. Therefore, apart from the setting up of a subsidiary SE already mentioned here, the following 'secondary' methods can also be exploited.

(6) *Formation of an SE by merger* between an SE and one or more other SEs, or one or more public limited companies. The requirements are the same as mentioned under (1), so the participating companies must be formed under the laws of a Member State and have their registered offices and head offices in different Member States within the EU.

(7) *Formation of a holding SE* by an SE with one or more other SEs, or together with one or more public or private companies as mentioned under (2).

(8) *Formation of* a *subsidiary SE* by an SE with one or more other SEs, or with one or more companies or legal bodies as mentioned under (3).

It must be noted here that the formation of an SE cannot be completed by registration before the involvement of employees is settled in accordance with the rules set out in the SE Directive.[73] The involvement of employees is explained in paragraphs 4.35 *et seq.*

4.17a To summarize, the SE is not available to natural persons or companies, firms and other legal bodies without 'cross-frontier credentials'.[74] The restriction is understandable in the light of the introduction of the SE as being 'necessary to attain, in the

72. Article 3(2) guarantees that the SE subsidiary can be wholly owned.
73. Article 12(2).
74. J. Rickford, *supra* n. 51, at 22.

course of the operation of the common market, one of the objectives of the Community', according to the previous wording of what is now Article 352 TFEU (ex Article 308 TEC). Moreover, the restriction may help curb the circumvention of national law by using the new form where a company under national law is indicated. However, the cross-border dimension seems to be easy to create because there is no requirement that companies participating in the formation of an SE be independent. The SE Regulation even grants facilities to holding companies merging with wholly owned subsidiaries, as well as with subsidiaries owned for 90% or more.[75] For example, Company A in one Member State may form a subsidiary B in another Member State and after that, both companies may merge into an SE or form an SE by way of a holding company.[76]

4.18 The SE Regulation contains several provisions on the procedure for formation, notably formation by merger and by way of forming a holding company. These provisions are as follows:

- Articles 17–31 on the formation by *merger* are largely similar to the merger provisions in Directive (EU) 2017/1132 (originating from the Third Directive and the Tenth Directive), which are set out in Chapters 3 and 8 of this book. Because of the cross-border dimensions of the merger, Member States may provide for its competent authorities to oppose the merger on grounds of public interest.[77] Member States may also adopt provisions to ensure protection for minority shareholders who have opposed the merger.[78]
- Articles 32–34 govern the formation of an SE as a *holding company*. This is a very different operation, because no company ceases to exist, as is the case with a merger, and the actual decision lies with the shareholders because they must decide whether they intend to contribute their shares in exchange for shares in the SE to be formed.[79] Nevertheless, the procedure shows strong similarities with the merger procedure. The draft terms for the formation of the holding company must contain the same particulars and must be approved by the general meeting of each of the companies involved.[80]
- Articles 35 and 36 governing the formation of a *subsidiary SE* do little more than refer to provisions of national law for the formation of a subsidiary of a public limited liability company.
- Article 37 deals with the *conversion* (transformation) of a public limited company into an SE. The operation does not result in the winding-up of the company or in the creation of a new legal person. The conversion must be

75. Article 31. Note that this article refers to the Third Directive which is absorbed by the codification Directive (EU) 2017/1132.
76. J. Rickford, *supra* n. 51, at 22.
77. Article 19. The grounds mentioned can be, e.g., tax claims, which may be put at risk by the merger.
78. Article 24(2).
79. Article 33(1) and (4).
80. Article 32(2) and (6). The question whether or not a qualified majority is required is discussed by C. Teichmann, 'Minderheitenschutz bei Gründung und Sitzverlegung der SE', *ZGR* 3 (2003): 367 *et seq.*

approved by the general meeting of the company after, *inter alia,* draft terms of conversion and a report on the implications for both shareholders and employees have been drawn up.

4.18a Essential elements of the merging procedure are:

- approval of the draft terms of the merger by the general meeting of each of the merging companies (Articles 20 and 23);
- publication (Article 21);
- examination of the draft terms of merger by independent experts (Article 22);
- protection of creditors and holders of bonds and securities other than shares (Article 24);
- scrutiny of the legality of pre-merger acts and formalities by the national authorities of the participating companies and by the authority of the Member State in which the SE is to be registered after the completion of the merger and the SE is formed (Articles 25 and 26).

Some Member States provide for a special procedure to scrutinize and amend the share exchange ratio or a procedure to compensate minority shareholders but without preventing the completion of the merger. Such procedure could favour shareholders of a merging company to the detriment of shareholders of other participating companies, which may not have access to such procedures under their national law. To reach 'equality of arms', Article 25(3) states that such provisions only apply when accepted by the general meeting of those other companies. If accepted, the decision in the procedure becomes binding on the SE and all of its shareholders.[81] The merger takes effect on the date on which the SE is registered (Article 27) and may not be declared null and void thereafter (Article 30). The issue of employee involvement must be dealt with before registration of an SE (*see* paragraphs 4.35 *et seq.* below).

4.18b The formation of a holding SE differs from the merger procedure, *inter alia,* in relation to the following issues:

- there is no right for the authorities to oppose it on grounds of public interest;
- there is no scrutiny of the legality of the pre-formation formalities (as this is governed by national law);
- the formation depends on decisions taken by individual shareholders, during a period of three months, to contribute their shares and only if more than 50% of the shares of each participating company are contributed (Articles 32 and 33).[82]

81. A special procedure as mentioned by Article 25(3) is the German Spruchverfahren (paragraphs 5–8 and 9–11 SE-AG, modelled after paragraph 15 Umwandlungsgesetz), C. Teichmann, *supra* n. 80.; C.H. Seibt, 'Report from Germany', *European Company Law* 1, no. 3 (2004): 131–134.
82. C. Teichmann, *supra* n. 80, at 388 *et seq.*

4.19 Irrespective of the method of formation, the SE acquires legal personality on the date on which it is registered in the Member State where it has its registered office.[83] For the purpose of its registration, the name of the SE must be preceded or followed by the abbreviation 'SE'.[84] An SE may not be registered until an arrangement for employee involvement has been concluded or when no arrangement could be reached until the applicable rules for employee involvement have been otherwise determined in accordance with the SE Directive.[85] The SE's formation and registration are then published in the manner laid down by the laws of each of the Member States concerned, in accordance with the First Directive (now Directive (EU 2017/1132). In addition, notice of an SE's registration also is published in the *Official Journal of the European Union.*[86]

C The Law Applicable to Formation

4.20 Because companies from different Member States may participate in the formation of an SE, a question may arise as to which law should be applied to the formation. As pointed out before, Article 9 of the SE Regulation gives precedence to the regulation itself, but it does not cover all aspects of the formation procedure. In relation to formation by merger, Article 18 of the SE Regulation states that, for matters not covered, each company involved in the formation is to be governed by the provisions of its domestic law concerning the merger of public companies, as harmonized by the Third Directive (now Directive (EU) 2017/1132). The completion of the merger, however, is subject to the law of the Member State of the proposed registered office of the SE.[87]

4.20a If, for example, a Spanish company merges with a French company into a newly formed SE, matters such as decision making, publication, protection of creditors, scrutiny of the pre-merger acts and formalities, and the striking-off from the register are governed by Spanish and by French law, respectively. However, this will not lead to the completion of the merger, because the SE has to be registered and the *ipso iure* consequences have to be determined. Therefore, Article 26, together with Article 15, provides for additional scrutiny of the legality of the merger by the competent authority of the Member State of the proposed registered office of the SE. If the SE formed by the Spanish and French companies is to be registered in Belgium, then the completion of the merger will be subject to Belgian law.

4.21 One would expect the same approach for the formation of a holding SE, but a provision equivalent to Article 18 is missing in this respect. In any event, however, the procedure preceding the formation of the holding may only be followed according to the rules of the national law of the companies involved. For example, when the general

83. Article 16.
84. Article 11.
85. Article 12(2), Directive 2001/86/EC. *See* paragraph 4.35 below.
86. Articles 13 and 14.
87. Articles 26 and 15.

meeting of a Polish public company approves the draft terms of formation of a holding SE to be registered in Germany, Polish law will govern the decision making on the Polish side, as it would in the case of a merger.[88] Therefore, Article 18 must be read analogously with respect to the formation of a holding SE.

The formation of a subsidiary SE will be governed, like the formation of any subsidiary, by the law of the Member State in which the subsidiary SE will have its registered office.[89] For the participating companies, national provisions apply to the decision making on the formation of a subsidiary as it would with regard to the formation of any subsidiary.

D Widening the Range of Participating Companies

4.22 Article 2(5) offers the option for Member States to provide that a company whose head office is not within the EU may, nevertheless, participate in the formation of an SE. Such company must be formed under the law of a Member State, have its registered office in that Member State, and have a 'real and continuous link with a Member State's economy'. Such company can only be formed and continue its existence under the law of a Member State adhering to the incorporation doctrine.[90] Member States relying on the real seat doctrine will not allow a company registered in that state to have its head office elsewhere. Therefore, those Member States will probably not use this option, as opposed to countries with the incorporation doctrine, such as the Netherlands.[91] Companies having their registered office outside the EU - irrespective of the place of their head office - may not participate in the formation of an SE. As a matter of course, they may become a shareholder of an SE after its formation.

4.22a As a result, a Danish registered public limited company having an establishment in Denmark but its head office in the United States may, according to Danish law, participate in the formation of an SE.[92] The same company may also participate in such formation according to Dutch law. This means, for example, that a Danish *aktieselskab* may merge with a Dutch company in order to form an SE registered in Denmark or the Netherlands for that matter.[93]

88. C. Teichmann, *supra* n. 80, at 388.
89. Article 3.
90. Paragraphs 2.57 *et seq.* Note that such company very likely will have its head office in a country that equally applies the incorporation doctrine because only then will its legal status there be secured.
91. The option is used by Article 2, Uitvoeringswet verordening Europese vennootschap (the Netherlands).
92. Preamble, Recital 23, specifies what is meant by 'a real and continuous link with a Member State's economy'.
93. On the effects of the real seat doctrine in this respect, *see* H.W. Neye & C. Teichmann, 'Der Entwurf für das Ausführungsgesetz zur Europäischen Aktiengesellschaft', *Die Aktiengesellschaft*, Heft 4 (2003): 171.

E Registered Office and Head Office

4.23 The registered office of an SE must be situated at the place specified in its articles of association. It must be located within the Community in the same Member State as its head office. A Member State may impose on SEs registered in its territory the additional obligation of locating the head office and the registered office in the same place.[94]

4.23a To be acceptable for all Member States, the SE Regulation contained the real seat arrangement of Article 7, but, in the preamble, one reads that such is without prejudice to Member States' laws and does not pre-empt any choices to be made for other Community texts on company law. The real seat requirement prevents the SE from moving its head office to another Member State and leaving the registered office where it is in order to avoid a change of applicable law.[95] It also limits the converse movement of 'jurisdiction shopping' by the founders of an SE or by way of transfer of the registered seat only. Therefore, the Delaware effect, which is to be expected where the registered office can be chosen regardless of the actual head office, will not have much impact here.[96]

4.24 In the event that the registered office and the head office of an SE do not coincide, the Member State in which the registered office is located should take appropriate measures to oblige the SE to conform to the prescriptions of the SE Regulation within a specified period. This can be done either by re-establishing its head office in the same Member State as its registered office or by transferring its registered office to the Member State in which the head office is situated.[97] For the latter option, the procedure of Article 8 must be applied. This procedure, resulting in the transfer of the SE, is an important characteristic of the SE. Such transfer does not result in the SE being wound up or in the creation of a new legal person. Crossing the border of a Member State, however, will result in a substantial change in applicable law, because of the regulation's frequent reference to the national law of the registered office.[98] The transfer of an SE is subject to the same rules applicable to the EEIG (*see* paragraph 4.07). The proposal to transfer must be duly published and no decision may be taken

94. Article 7. The stricter requirements – registered office must be the same as the location of the head office – had initially been opted for by e.g., Germany, but have been removed in the course of the company law reform allowing the German GmbH and AG to locate the head office outside Germany.
95. This limitation conflicts with the case law by the European Court of Justice, E. Wymeersch, 'Cross-Border Transfer of the Seat of a Company: Recent EU Case Law and the SE Regulation', in J. Rickford, *supra* n. 51, at 88; E. Werlauff, 'Cross-Border Transfers of SE Companies. Domicile Requirements Contrary to the EC Treaty Right of Establishment', *European Company Law*, no. 3 (October 2004): 121 *et seq.*
96. E. Werlauff, *supra* n. 95, at 109 *et seq.* and, on the definition of head office, 113 *et seq.*
97. Article 64. E. Werlauff, *supra* n. 95, at 115 *et seq.*
98. Article 8.

for two months after publication. Member States have the option to include a provision that its authorities may oppose the transfer on grounds of public interest.[99]

4.24a Article 8 of the SE Regulation, dealing with the transfer of the SE's seat, is far more detailed than its corresponding provisions in the EEIG Regulation. For example, the proposal to transfer an SE must include: (a) the proposed registered office of the SE, (b) the proposed articles of association of the SE, including, where appropriate, its new name, (c) any implication the transfer may have on employee involvement, (d) the proposed transfer timetable, and (e) any rights provided for the protection of shareholders and/or creditors.[100] The transfer to another jurisdiction represents a threat to the creditors of the SE. Although they retain their claims, it may be more difficult to obtain repayment once the SE has crossed borders. Therefore, the SE is to satisfy the interests of creditors and holders of other rights with respect to the SE and ensure that they have been adequately protected, for example, by way of actively informing the creditors in advance or offering them sufficient security upon demand. This protection concerns any liabilities arising prior to the publication of the transfer proposal. A Member State may even extend this protection to liabilities that arise or may arise prior to the transfer.[101]

4.25 The decision on the transfer is taken at the general meeting.[102] The Member States may opt to adopt provisions designed to ensure protection for minority shareholders who oppose a transfer. Once the transfer is decided on, their position vis-à-vis the SE may be rather different because a new set of national rules will be applicable. Of course, opposing shareholders can sell their shares prior to the transfer, but there may not always be a market available. Therefore, protection may be offered over and above the protection that would apply under national company law.[103] Although the Member States tend to rely on existing rules, Germany, for example, has adopted specific provisions in this area.[104]

The transfer procedure has a built-in safety valve because registration in the 'new' Member State can only be effected when a certificate has been submitted by the competent authority of the 'old' Member State, attesting to the completion of the acts and formalities to be accomplished before the transfer.[105] The transfer takes effect from the date of registration of the new office.[106] Upon publication, the new registration may be relied on against third parties. However, they may continue to rely on the old

99. The option will be used by most Member States, e.g., the Netherlands (Article 5 Uitvoeringswet verordening Europese vennootschap).
100. Article 8(2).
101. The Netherlands, Uitvoeringswet, Article 4 offers an instrument of protection which can be used not only up to two months after publication but also for liabilities that may arise until the date of the transfer. Germany extends the protection to fifteen days after the publication of the proposal, SEAG, s. 13(2).
102. Articles 8(6) and 59.
103. Article 8(5); *see also* Werlauff, *supra* n. 95, at 124.
104. The Netherlands has not used this option. Under German law, the SE must offer to repurchase the shares of the opposing shareholders (cash out), SEAG, s. 12(2).
105. Article 8(9).
106. Article 8(10).

registered office as long as the deletion of the SE's registration in the old Member State has not been publicized unless there is proof that they were aware of the new registered office.[107] Between 2000 and 2019, more than 300 cross-border transfers of seat of SEs were counted.[108]

F Capital

4.26 The capital of an SE and its shares are to be denominated in euro and the subscribed minimum may not be less than EUR 120,000. This minimum is meant to secure that the SE has sufficient assets, without making it too difficult for small and medium-sized undertakings to form SEs.[109] If a Member State requires a greater subscribed capital for domestic companies carrying out certain types of activity, such as financial institutions and insurance companies, the higher amount will apply to SEs carrying out such activities and having their registered office in that Member State.[110] The Member States not having the euro as their currency[111] may subject SEs with registered offices within their territory to the same provisions applicable to public limited companies in relation to their capital. In any case, an SE may express its capital in euros as well.[112] The SE Regulation contains no further provisions in relation to capital, and Article 5 refers all other matters to national law.

G Structure: One-Tier or Two-Tier Board

4.27 The structure of the SE consists of the general meeting, combined with either the two-tier system with a management body and a supervisory body or the one-tier system with an administrative body only. The articles of association of the SE determine the choice between these two systems.[113] A Member State without provisions for one of the systems in relation to public companies should adopt appropriate measures for SEs registered within its territory.[114] In other words, Member States are supposed to facilitate both systems for the SE but may apply certain rules of their national system, such as provisions concerning the registration of members of the SE's bodies, their rights and obligations, and conditions for eligibility. Some Member States, such as Germany, having a mandatory two-tier structure for all public companies, have

107. Article 8.
108. T. Biermeyer & M. Meyer, Cross-border Corporate Mobility in the EU: Empirical Findings 2020 (Edition 1) (15 Aug., 2020), 40. Available at SSRN: https://ssrn.com/abstract=3674089 or http://dx.doi.org/10.2139/ssrn.3674089
109. Preamble, Recital 13, Articles 1(2) and 4.
110. Article 4(3).
111. This is because the third phase of the Economic and Monetary Union (EMU) does not apply.
112. Article 67(1). The national currency/euro conversion rate shall be that for the last day of the month preceding the formation of the SE.
113. Preamble, Recital 14 and Article 38.
114. Articles 39(5) and 43(4).

introduced such provisions, thus offering legal certainty and securing for these aspects equal treatment of SEs.[115,116]

4.28 In the two-tier system, the management body (board) is responsible for managing the SE. Member States may adopt rules providing that one or more members from the management body are responsible, as managing directors, for the current (day-to-day) management under the same conditions as the directors of domestic public limited companies. The members of the management body of an SE are appointed and removed by the supervisory body (board), but these powers may lie with the general meeting if a Member State allows the articles of association of the SE to provide for it.[117] The members of the supervisory body are appointed by the general meeting, but this rule does not affect national law permitting minority shareholders or others to appoint some of the members of a company body.[118] Moreover, arrangements for employee participation, having a bearing on the composition of the supervisory board, must be taken into account.[119] The supervisory body oversees the duties performed by the management body, but may not exercise the power to manage the company.[120]

4.29 In the one-tier system, also called a unitary board system, the administrative body (board) has the power to manage the SE. Where the responsibilities of management and those responsible for supervision are automatically separated by the two-tier system, these responsibilities must be clearly defined in the one-tier system.[121] Member States may articulate rules providing that one or more managing directors of the one-tier board are responsible for the day-to-day management under the same conditions as for domestic public limited companies.[122] The general meeting appoints and removes the members of the administrative body unless minority shareholder rights under national law or arrangements for employee participation provide otherwise.[123] Overall, under the one-tier system, the general meeting has direct influence on the election of those persons who are to conduct the company's affairs.

4.30 Several provisions of the regulation are common to the one-tier and two-tier systems (Articles 46–51). Among these are the following:

115. Sections 20 *et seq.* SEAG. S. Maul, 'Konzernrecht der deutschen SE – Ausgewählte Fragen zum Vertragskonzern und den faktischen Unternehmensverbindungen', ZGR 5–6 (2003): 743 *et seq.*
116. DTI, Implementation of the European Company Statute, A Consultative Document, October 2003, 3.40. In the Netherlands, the structure regime, a compulsory governance system for large companies, does not apply to the SE, Memorie van Toelichting, 29,309 no. 3, 3 *et seq.*; *See further*: paragraphs 6.11 *et seq.* According to K. Hopt, in Rickford (ed.), *supra* n. 51, at 52–53, Member States must adopt measures in order to rule out uncertainties.
117. Article 39(2).
118. Articles 40(2) and 47(4).
119. Article 40(2).
120. Article 40(1).
121. Preamble, Recital 14.
122. Article 43(1). For an example of this option, *see* the German implementation Act, s. 40(1) *SE – Ausführungsgesetz*.
123. Article 43(3).

- members of company bodies are not appointed for longer than a six-year period, although reappointment is possible;[124]
- the articles of association (statutes) of the SE may permit a legal person to be a member of one of its bodies, provided that the law of the registered office of the SE does not provide otherwise with respect to public limited companies; the legal person must then designate a natural person to exercise its functions on the board;[125]
- the articles of association must list the transactions that require the authorization of the management body by the supervisory body (two-tier system) or an express decision by the administrative body (one-tier system);
- decision making requires that at least half of the members of a body are present or represented and that decisions are taken by the majority of the members present or represented unless the regulation or the articles provide differently;[126]
- members of the SE's bodies are liable for loss or damage sustained by the SE as a result of breach, on their part, of the obligations attached to their functions; this liability is governed by the provisions applicable to public companies in the Member State in which the SE has its registered office.[127]

4.30a The SE Regulation obliges the SE to draw up a list of transactions which require authorization by the supervisory body or an express decision by the unitary board. Member States may alternatively enact rules providing, though only for the two-tier system, that the supervisory body designates the transactions subject to its authorization.[128] Member States may also determine certain transactions that must be indicated in the articles of association of an SE. Transactions requiring authorization or express decision making, as a rule, generally consist of major business operations, such as large investments, the setting-up, acquisition, disposal or closing down of undertakings, and the raising or granting of loans. Thus, if employee representatives are among the members of the body concerned, the authorization or deliberation requirement can be viewed as a guarantee of their influence.

H Structure: General Meeting

4.31 The general meeting decides on matters for which it has sole responsibility under the SE Regulation or the SE Directive, as implemented.[129] Besides the appointment of members of the SE's management body or bodies, as set out previously, the regulation allocates to the general meeting the decision-making powers concerning the transfer of

124. Article 46.
125. Article 47(1).
126. Article 50(1).
127. Article 51.
128. Germany has used this option, s. 19 SEAG.
129. Article 52.

the SE's registered office, the amendment of its articles of association and the conversion of an SE into a public company under national law.[130] Moreover, where an SE is involved in the formation of another SE by way of a merger or in the formation of a holding SE, it follows from the SE Regulation that the general meeting is the body that decides on this matter.[131] Regarding other matters, the general meeting of the SE has the same powers as the general meeting of a domestic public limited company. This is of special importance for the various matters that are almost completely referred to in national law, most notably the financial statements (annual accounts) and the winding-up of an SE.

4.31a To recapitulate, the following articles of the SE Regulation require a decision of an SE's general meeting:

- Article 8(4): transfer of the SE's registered office.
- Article 23(1): approval of the draft terms of merger, whereby an SE is formed, if an SE is involved in the merger.
- Article 32(6): approval of the draft terms of formation of a holding SE, if an SE is one of the parties involved in such formation.
- Articles 23(2) and 32(6): ratification of the arrangement of employee involvement accompanying the merger or formation of a holding SE, if an SE is involved and its general meeting has reserved the right to ratification.
- Article 40(2), two-tier system: appointment of the members of the supervisory body (of the management body, only if the Member State has opted for it, Article 39(2)).[132]
- Article 43(3), one-tier system: appointment of the members of the administrative body.
- Article 59: amendment of an SE's articles.
- Article 66(6): approval of the draft terms of conversion of an SE into a public limited company and of the articles of that company.

4.32 Decisions of the general meeting are taken by a majority of the votes cast unless the SE Regulation or national law requires otherwise.[133] One of the exceptions concerns the amendment of the articles of association, where a majority of two-thirds of the votes cast is required. However, Member States may require a simple majority, provided that at least half of the subscribed capital is represented.[134] It is important to note that the votes cast do not include votes attached to shares, in respect of which the shareholder has not taken part in the vote, abstained or returned a blank or spoiled

130. Articles 8(4), 59(1), and 66(6).
131. Article 3(1).
132. Note that Article 39(2) deals with both the appointment and removal of members of the administrative body where Articles 40(2) and 43(3) only mention appointment (of members of the supervisory body and the administrative body, respectively).
133. Article 57.
134. Article 59.

ballot.[135] Where an SE has two or more classes of shares, each decision by the general meeting will be subject to a separate vote by each class of shareholders – if the decision of the general meeting affects their class rights.[136] The SE Regulation contains some provisions on convening the general meeting, which normally lies with the bodies of the SE, but can also be initiated by minority shareholders.[137] They may also request that additional items be put on the agenda.[138] Insofar as the organization and conduct of the general meeting, as well as the voting procedures, are not covered by these rules, the law of domestic public limited companies applies.[139]

I Financial Statements, Winding Up and Liquidation

4.33 The preparation of financial statements (accounts) and consolidated financial statements (accounts), including the accompanying management report and the auditing and publication of these documents, is governed by national law, harmonized, as a matter of course, by the directives dealing with these matters (*see* Chapter 9). Listed SEs, just like other listed companies in the EU, will have to comply with International Accounting Standards (IAS/IFRS) (*see* Chapter 9).[140]

4.34 As regards winding up, liquidation, insolvency, cessation of payments and similar procedures, an SE will be governed by the applicable national law, including provisions relating to decision making by the general meeting on those matters.[141] In contrast to the financial statements, here the reference concerns national law that has only been partially harmonized (*see* Chapter 3.42 *et seq.*).

J Involvement of Employees

4.35 As demonstrated in Chapter 7, within the EU, national regimes have always differed considerably within two basic forms of employee involvement.[142] In the first form, there are mechanisms for providing information to and consultation of employees through a representative body, be it a works council or the representatives of trade unions. The second form is called employee participation and encompasses representation of employees at the board level or influencing the selection or appointment of board members. It was feared that the formation of an SE could be used for the evasion of national rules, particularly those of the second form. This could be the case, for example, if a German AG were to merge with a company governed by the law of another Member State that has no equivalent to German employee participation.

135. Article 58.
136. Article 60(1).
137. Articles 54 and 55.
138. Article 56.
139. Article 53.
140. E. Werlauff, *supra* n. 95, at 160.
141. Article 63.
142. SE Directive, Article 1 defines those forms.

Consequently, the German participation system could disappear if no adequate measures are adopted. On the other hand, should EC legislation safeguard all pre-existing rights of employees, the other Member State might fear the export of the German system of employee participation to an SE registered in its territory.

4.36 Therefore, involvement of employees has been a controversial issue for many years. While the debate was still going on, the directive on the EWC was enacted in 1994, and it has certainly helped pave the way for the introduction of the SE.[143] This directive contains a mechanism for the involvement of employees in undertakings with a community dimension. The mechanism is initiated by the formation of a special negotiating body of employee representatives. This body has the task, together with central management, to negotiate on the scope, composition and functions of the EWC, or an equivalent procedure for information and consultation. Should negotiations fail, a list of Subsidiary Requirements (standard rules) which are included in the Annex to the directive, would apply. The EWC is further discussed in Chapter 7, but it is important to note that this system of negotiations, combined with a fallback on standardized rules, is copied in the SE Directive (Directive 2001/86/EC supplementing the SE Regulation).[144]

4.37 The preamble of the SE Directive explains that the creation of an SE simultaneously implies the necessity to introduce information and consultation procedures at a transnational level, as well as the preservation of existing participation rights within the companies establishing the SE. However, in the latter case, the parties may decide otherwise.[145] Employee rights in force before the establishment of an SE should provide the basis for employee rights of involvement in the established SE, according to the 'before-and-after principle'. Consequently, that approach applies not only to the initial formation of an SE but also to structural changes in an existing SE.[146]

4.38 The directive extensively regulates the negotiating procedure. The responsibility to take the necessary steps to start negotiations lies with the organs (corporate bodies) of companies participating in the formation of an SE.[147] As a matter of course, information must be provided. The SE Directive determines that these negotiations must take place as soon as possible after publishing the draft terms of merger or creating a holding company or after agreeing to a plan to form a subsidiary or transform into an SE. Information must be given on the identity of the participating companies, the subsidiaries or establishments concerned and the number of their employees.[148] A special negotiating body must be established in accordance with the provisions of the directive. The members of this body must be in proportion to the number of workers

143. Directive 94/45/EC.
144. P.L. Davies, 'Employee Involvement in the European Company', in J. Rickford (ed.), *supra* n. 51, at 67 *et seq.*; E. Werlauff, *supra* n. 95, at 133 *et seq.*; C. Tavares da Costa & A. de Meester Bilreiro, *supra* n. 65, at 73 *et seq.*
145. Preamble, Recitals 6 and 7.
146. Preamble, Recital 18.
147. Article 3(1).
148. *Ibid.*

employed in each Member State by the participating companies and their relevant subsidiaries or establishments.[149] Once the negotiating body is established, negotiations may commence, and they may continue for six months. The parties may decide, however, to extend this period for up to one year.[150]

4.39 The negotiating body decides on the outcome of the negotiations. Decisions may be taken by an absolute majority, provided that such a majority also represents an absolute majority of employees. Should the results lead to a reduction of participation rights, a qualified majority is required. This varies among the different methods of forming an SE.[151] The negotiating body may also decide not to open negotiations or to terminate negotiations already opened in order to rely on the rules on information and consultation in force in the Member States where the SE has employees. Here again, a qualified majority is required.[152] Should the negotiations fail or if the parties so agree, the Standard Rules, which have to be implemented by each Member State, apply. The Standard Rules are to be found in the Annex to the SE Directive.[153] Included are rules for the composition of the body representing the employees (Part 1 of the Standard Rules), for information and consultation (Part 2), and for participation (Part 3).

4.39a To summarize, the following options have to be taken into account:

(1) the negotiations lead to either (a) an agreement on employee involvement or (b) an agreement that the Standard Rules apply;
(2) if the negotiations produce no result or the (extended) period for negotiations expires, then the Standard Rules apply;
(3) if the negotiating body decides to terminate the negotiations or not to open them at all, then there would be no special employee involvement provisions for the SE, but national legislation will be applicable.[154]

4.40 The Standard Rules limit the competence of the representative body to cross-border issues: 'questions which concern the SE itself and any of its subsidiaries or establishments situated in another Member State or which exceed the powers of the decision-making bodies in a single Member State'.[155] Against this background, it might be expected that comparable formulas will constitute parts of agreements on information and consultation. In general, management will not easily agree on more involvement of employees than prescribed by the Standard Rules, while the negotiating body

149. Article 3(2).
150. Article 5.
151. Article 3(4).
152. Article 3(6).
153. The Standard Rules in the Annex to the SE Directive are almost identical to the Subsidiary Requirements in the Annex to the Directive on the EWC.
154. Several examples are described by L.L. Hansen, 'Employee Involvement and the Formation of a European Company: The Competition Between the Approaches of Different Member States When a European Company Is Formed Through International Merger', *European Company Law*, no. 3 (October 2004): 126 *et seq.*
155. SE Directive, Annex, Part 2(a).

will not be adamant about accepting lower standards. Therefore, the negotiations have been described as 'bargaining in the shadow of the law'.[156]

4.41 The Standard Rules apply, as already mentioned, when the parties so agree, when the negotiation period expires without result, or when negotiations have never begun due to a decision of the negotiating body.[157] The issue of participation is dealt with in Part 3 of the Standard Rules, but these rules will apply only when the following additional criteria are met:

- In the case of a transformation of a public company into an SE, employee participation is relevant where national rules for employee participation apply to the transforming public company.[158] Part 3(a) confirms that all the existing rules 'shall continue to apply to the SE'. There is no option for the negotiating body or management to decide not to have that employee participation in the SE.[159]
- In the case of a merger, if the existing participation rules in one or more participating companies cover at least 25% of all employees involved in the merger unless the negotiating body decides to lower this threshold.[160]
- For the setting up of a holding SE or a subsidiary SE, the threshold is set at 50% coverage, but here, again, the negotiating body may decide to apply Part 3 even when less than 50% of all employees involved are covered by the pre-existing system(s) of participation.[161]

If there was more than one form of participation within the companies involved in the formation of an SE, the special negotiating body would decide which of those forms must be established in the SE.[162]

Member States may opt out of the application of Part 3 of the Standard Rules in the case of a merger, thus preventing the 'import' of the system of employee participation, as determined by the Annex.[163] The option, if used, would prevent registration of an SE in the case of a merger, unless none of the participating companies is governed by participation rules or an agreement on employee involvement has been concluded, including participation rules.[164]

4.42 Lastly, the rules on the involvement of employees in the SE form an 'indissociable complement' to the SE Regulation and must be applied concomitantly.[165] Their application is secured because an SE cannot be registered unless the involvement of

156. *See* Davies, *supra* n. 144, at 77.
157. Article 7(1).
158. Article 7(2)(a).
159. Article 3(6), 4(4), Part 3(a).
160. Article 7(2)(b).
161. Article 7(2).
162. *Ibid.*
163. Article 7(3) and Preamble, Recital 9.
164. SE Regulation, Article 12(3). *See* on this option, J. Rickford (ed.), *supra* n. 51, at 28.
165. SE Regulation, Preamble, Recitals 19 and 22.

employees has been determined. As already pointed out, this requires that an agreement be concluded, that the standard rules apply, or that a valid decision has been taken by the negotiating body to rely on national legislation.[166] Whenever the articles of association of the SE conflict with an arrangement for employee involvement, the latter prevails and the articles must be amended.[167]

4.42a Rules of the SE Directive and of the EWC Directive do not cumulate. Where an SE is an undertaking with a Community dimension and therefore falls within the ambit of the EWC Directive, the rules from this directive give way to an agreement on employee involvement but apply where no agreement is concluded.[168] Provisions of national legislation on the participation of employees, other than those implementing the SE Directive, do not apply to an SE. However, the SE Directive does not prejudice other rights concerning the involvement of employees provided for by national legislation.[169]

K Perspectives of the SE

4.43 The SE is supposed to facilitate the restructuring of business enterprises at a European level and simplify group structures. Therefore, the SE may replace a series of national companies, all working under different rules. In addition, it offers enhanced flexibility because it can move its registered seat to another Member State. Finally, the SE represents a 'European identity' not associated with companies under national law.[170] On the downside, there is the potentially lengthy negotiating procedure on employee involvement,[171] as well as the manifold references to national law, leaving substantial differences between SEs in the various Member States and the lack of a separate tax regime.[172] How these pros and cons will be perceived in practice and to what extent the SE will be used remains to be seen.[173] By October 2021 more than 3,400 SEs had been established, again an increase in comparison to the 2,615 mentioned in

166. SE Regulation, Article 12(2).
167. SE Regulation, Article 12(4).
168. SE Directive, Article 13(1).
169. SE Directive, Articles 13(2) and (3). *See* on national rules Chapter 9 of this book.
170. Most of these pros can be found in the Preamble of the SE Regulation. *See also* Commissioner F. Bolkestein, 'The New European Company: Opportunity in Diversity', in J. Rickford (ed.), *supra* n. 51, at 41-42; C. Tavares da Costa & A. de Meester Bilreiro, *supra* n. 65, at 59.
171. The negotiating procedure has proven not to be an impediment to the formation of sizeable SEs, especially in Germany: J. Reichert, 'Experience with the SE in Germany', *European Company Law* 5, no. 6 (December 2008): 297-304.
172. F. Bolkestein, 'The New European Company', *op. cit.*, 43, mentions initiatives to amend taxation directives as to include the SE and SCE, resulting in Directive 2003/123/EC and a Commission proposal of October 2003 to amend the Merger Directive. *See also* the survey on the taxation of the Societas Europaea, International Bureau of Fiscal Documentation 2003, http://europa.eu.int/comm/taxation_customs/taxation/company_tax/developments.htm.
173. *See* for a rather optimistic perspective *Die Aktiengesellschaft*, Heft 4 (2003): 169 *et seq.* as well as C. Tavares da Costa & A. De Meester Bilreiro, *supra* n. 65, at 175-178. On issues related to the implementation of the SE Directive: *Communication from the Commission on the Review of Council Directive 2001/86/EC of 8 Oct. 2001 Supplementing the Statute for a European Company with Regard to the Involvement of Employees*, Brussels, 30 Sep. 2008, COM(2008) 591(final) and

the 2014 edition of this book (and 284 SEs in the 2009 edition).[174] Several large businesses use the legal form of the SE as the top holding company, such as Airbus Group SE, BASF SE, Schneider Electric SE and Getlink SE (the former Groupe Eurotunnel SE). The majority of SEs, however, had no employees upon registration, which raises concerns that the obligations under the SE Directive will not be complied with, because they apply to the period of formation of the SE.[175]

4.43a In 2010, the Commission forwarded a report to the Council and the European Parliament on the application of the SE Regulation.[176] The report sums up practical problems related to setting up an SE. These are, for instance, the rather high minimum capital requirement, the lack of the option to form an SE by way of cross-border division, and the period of at least two years during which a company must have had a subsidiary or branch in another Member State in order to convert into an SE or to participate in a cross-border merger.[177] Moreover, further problems are caused by the lack of clarity and the complexity of the SE Statute. Article 2 of the Statute refers to a 'subsidiary', but without providing a proper definition of the term. The Commission announced the plan to propose potential amendments to the SE Statute and the SE Directive by 2012. The 2012 Action Plan, however, proposed nothing more than the launch of an information campaign to increase awareness of the SE and the opportunities it offers.[178] In appreciating this campaign, Article 69 of the SE Regulation comes to mind. It requires the Commission, five years after the entry into force of the Regulation at the latest, to analyse in particular the appropriateness of the following:

(a) allowing the location of an SE's head office and registered office in different Member States;
(b) broadening the concept of 'merger' in Article 17(2), in order to also admit other types of merger, such as types of 'merger' – actually divisions – mentioned by the Sixth Directive;
(c) revising the jurisdiction clause in Article 8(16), when necessary, because relevant sources of law have been adapted;

---

the reports and minutes of the Group of Experts 'SE – European Company' on the implementation of the SE Directive, accessible at http://ec.europa.eu/employment_social/labour_law/documentation_en.htm.

174. Database on http://ecdb.worker-participation.eu.
175. COM(2008)591(final), 7 and 8.
176. *Report from the Commission to the European Parliament and the Council on the application of Council Regulation 2157/2001 of 8 October 2001 on the Statute for a European Company (SE)*, COM(2010) 676 and the *Accompanying Commission Staff Working Document*, Brussels, 17 Nov. 2010.
SEC(2010) 1391 final.
177. Report COM(2010) 676, paragraph 3.1.
178. *Action Plan: European company law and corporate governance – a modern legal framework for more engaged shareholders and sustainable companies*, COM(2012) 740 final, paragraph 4.5. *See also* the website of the Commission on setting up a European Company, https://europa.eu/youreurope/business/running-business/developing-business/setting-up-european-company/index_en.htm.

(d) allowing more freedom to the Member States to accept provisions in the articles of an SE, even when such provisions are not permitted for national public companies.

IV EUROPEAN COOPERATIVE SOCIETY

4.44 In the wake of the drafts for the SE Statute, the Commission launched proposals for a European Association (EA), a European Cooperative Society (SCE) and a European Mutual Society (EMS) by 1992, to be followed by a proposal for a European Foundation (FE) in 2012. The 1992 proposals were amended in 1993, following the comments of the Economic and Social Committee.[179] However, after screening the pending legislative proposals, the Commission withdrew the proposals for an EA and EMS by 2005.[180] The 2012 proposal for the FE was also taken off of the legislative agenda by 2014, due to the failure of the Member States to reach a consensus.[181] In 2003, the SCE Regulation and the ECS Directive were adopted.[182]

4.44a The SCE and the withdrawn EMS can be regarded as business organizations for the cooperation of natural persons who act according to principles different from those of other economic subjects. These principles embody the notion of man taking priority over capital by allotting voting rights to persons independent of their share of the capital.[183] Together with foundations and associations, cooperative societies and mutual societies are sometimes referred to as the Social Economy.[184] Unlike capital companies, they do not offer investor-driven structures, but they spring from the economic and social needs of their members and are generally managed in accordance with the principle of 'one member, one vote'.

4.45 The SCE has the status of a legal person, and it is a company with its capital divided into shares. The members are only liable up to the amount of their shares unless the articles of association impose stricter liability. The purpose of the SCE is to fulfil its members' needs and to further their business and/or social activities. Except where the articles of association provide otherwise, the SCE is not allowed to serve non-members.[185] There are no severe restrictions for participating in the formation of an SCE. An SCE may be formed 'from scratch' by five or more natural persons residing

179. OJ 1992, C 99 and 1993, C 236 and OJ 1993, C 236.
180. Communication *Outcome of the screening of legislative proposals pending before the Legislator*, Brussels, 27.9.2005, COM(2005) 462 final.
181. The proposal: Brussels, 8.2.2012 COM(2012) 35 final. Withdrawal: Annex 2 to the Commission Work Programme 2015, Strasbourg, 16.12.2014, COM(2014) 910 final.
182. Regulation (EC) 1435/2003 (Statute for a European Cooperative Society (SCE)) and Directive 2003/72/EC (involvement of employees).
183. Preamble of the regulation concerning the Statute of the European Cooperative Society as amended.
184. Cooperatives are among the legal forms used for social enterprises, *see* https://www.euricse.eu (accessed December 2021).
185. Article 1 ECS Regulation.

in at least two Member States. It may also be formed by one or more natural persons, together with one or more companies, firms and other legal bodies, or by two or more of those companies, firms or legal bodies. The law of at least two different Member States must govern the participating companies, firms and legal bodies. The SCE may also be formed by a merger between cooperatives or by conversion of a cooperative. As with the SE, Member States may provide that a legal body, the head office of which is not in the Community, may participate in the formation of an SCE (*see* paragraph 4.22).[186]

4.46 In many respects, the SCE Regulation is similar to its SE counterpart, for example, regarding the applicable law, the structure of the SCE with the same option between a one-tier and a two-tier system, plus an accompanying directive on the involvement of employees.[187] However, the cooperative nature of the society is reflected in several specific provisions, for example, the acquisition and loss of membership. The articles of association may contain certain conditions for membership, such as subscription of a minimum amount of capital.[188] When a member leaves the SCE, he or she may be entitled to repayment of his or her part of the subscribed capital, reduced in proportion to any losses.[189] Another example of expressing the cooperative nature is seen in the 'one member, one vote rule', which is the principle laid down in Article 59(1). However, if the law of the Member State in which the SCE has its registered office so permits, the articles of association may provide for multiple votes, though within certain limits, for example, no member may exert more than 30% of the voting rights.[190] Because of its decision-making characteristics, it may not be easy for a cooperative to find investors willing to take shares. Therefore, the articles of association may allow for members that do not regularly make use of the services of the SCE (non-user members). However, collectively such members may not have more than 25% of the total voting rights.[191]

186. Article 2.
187. Articles 8 and 36.
188. Article 14(2).
189. Article 16.
190. Article 59(2).
191. Article 59(3).

CHAPTER 5

Formation and Financing of Companies

I INTRODUCTION

5.01 This chapter analyses some features with regard to the formation procedure of private and public limited liability companies as harmonized by the European Union (EU). For this purpose, the relevant provisions of the Consolidation Directive (EU) 2017/1132 ('Directive 2017/1132') are outlined and attention is drawn, by way of illustration, to some of the particularities evident in national laws.[1] The provisions of Directive 2017/1132 related to the formation and financing of companies apply partly to both private and public companies and partly to only public companies.[2] The provisions requiring disclosure of certain documents and particulars upon formation apply to both categories of companies. The same applies to the provisions that restrict the grounds to claim that obligations entered into on the company's behalf are not binding upon it. The directive furthermore restricts those situations in which nullity of the company can be ordered. These rules apply to private and public companies alike. On the other hand, Directive 2017/1132 requires only public companies to provide specific information in the statutes, also known as the articles of association, or in the deed of incorporation or a separate document. Equally, the provisions on the maintenance and alteration of capital apply only to public companies. According to Article 1 of Directive 2017/1132, all these provisions concern the safeguarding of the interests of the company's shareholders and third parties (*see also* paragraphs 3.20–3.22).

1. Although this chapter discusses the formation of public companies and of private companies separately, these two procedures are almost identical for both public and private companies in the UK, and quite similar in the Netherlands and in Belgium.
2. The Consolidation Directive 2017/1132 (as amended) contains the provisions originally enacted by the First Directive and the Second Directive, also known as the Capital Directive; *see* paragraphs 3.20 *et seq.*

II PUBLIC COMPANIES

A Formation

5.02 As a rule, a public company can be set up either through its formation or through the transformation (conversion) of an existing legal entity. In the first case, there are two options: (i) the capital can be subscribed only by the members (shareholders), resulting in a closely held public company; or (ii) the initial capital can also be raised by a public subscription of shares, with a view to incorporate it as an open company or a publicly held company. Due to the complexity of its requirements, the latter procedure has rarely been adopted by those interested in setting up public companies. Companies are therefore generally set up in such a way as to have the initial capital subscribed by the founders and only later, once the business has grown sufficiently and more capital is needed than the initial shareholders can or will supply, the shares are listed on the stock market. Therefore, most shares that can be bought on the stock market are shares in existing companies. Such listing is generally referred to as an initial public offering or IPO.

5.03 Directive 2017/1132 does not specify methods of formation but it does prescribe in Article 14(a) that the Member States must ensure that companies disclose their instrument of constitution (incorporation) and the articles of association[3] where they are contained in a different instrument. Accordingly, Article 3 provides that the instrument of incorporation or the articles must contain, at the very least, information regarding:

- the type and name of the company;
- the objects of the company;
- the amount of the subscribed capital, where the company has no authorized capital;
- the amount of the authorized capital, where the company has such capital, and the amount of the subscribed capital at the time the company is incorporated and at the time of any change in the authorized capital;
- insofar as they are not determined by law, the rules governing the number of, and the procedure for appointing, members of the bodies responsible for representing the company with regard to third parties, administration, management, supervision or control of the company and the allocation of powers among those bodies;
- the duration of the company, unless this duration is indefinite.

3. In Directive 2017/1132 'statutes' is used for articles of association. In this book we prefer to use 'articles of association' or simply 'articles' instead of 'statutes' except where the text of the directive is quoted. Otherwise, confusion may rise because 'statute' also means a piece of legislation.

5.04 In addition, Article 4 of Directive 2017/1132 requires that the instrument of incorporation, the articles of association or a separate document published in conformity with the procedural rules stated in Article 16 of the directive, contain the following minimum content:

- the registered office;
- the nominal value and number of the shares subscribed;
- the number of shares subscribed without stating the nominal value, provided that such shares may be issued under national law;
- any special conditions restricting the transfer of shares;
- if there are different classes of shares, the details required in the three points listed above must be provided with regard to each class, as well as the rights attached to the shares of each class;
- an indication as to the type of shares (registered or bearer shares, where both are allowed according to national law) and any provisions pertaining to the conversion of those shares, unless this procedure is provided by law;
- the amount of the subscribed capital paid up at the time of incorporation;
- the nominal value of the shares or, where there is no nominal value, the number of shares issued for a consideration other than in cash, together with the type of the consideration and the name of the contributor;
- the identity of the natural or legal persons by whom, or in whose name, the statutes or the instrument(s) of incorporation have been signed;
- the total amount, or at least an approximation, of the formation costs payable by, or chargeable to, the company and, where appropriate, also the costs before the company is authorized to start operating;
- any special advantage granted to anyone who has been involved in the formation of the company or, where applicable, in transactions leading to the grant of an authorization to commence business.

5.05 Because Directive 2017/1132 provides for a minimum amount of documentation to be disclosed, Member States may require other elements to be added to the documents to be disclosed. In Germany, for instance, the articles of association of an *Aktiengesellschaft* (AG) must also contain provisions stipulating the form that the company's announcements must assume, and the indication of the enterprise's objects must include details as to the type of goods and products to be traded and manufactured, where industrial and commercial enterprises are concerned.[4] In the United Kingdom (UK), the two principal instruments of incorporation are the memorandum of association and the articles of association. In essence, the memorandum of association serves the purpose of stating the subscribers' intention to establish a company and become members of the company. In the case of a company that is to have a share capital, the memorandum of association also demonstrates the members' agreement to

4. Section 23 German Stock Corporation Act (*Aktiengesetz*).

take at least one share each.[5] The memorandum of association must be delivered to the registrar together with an application for registration of the company and certain documents and a statement of compliance.[6]

5.06 Article 10 of Directive 2017/1132 requires that the instrument of incorporation and the company's articles 'shall be drawn up and certified in due legal form', except in those Member States, whose laws provide for preventive control at the time of formation of a company. The same applies to any amendments made to these documents. The EU Member States often provide for a mandatory requirement to notarize the instrument of incorporation and/or the articles. Unlike continental countries, the UK has no concept of a notarial deed but in addition to the requirements set out in Directive 2017/1132, the English system requires a statement of compliance.[7]

B Registration

5.07 Generally speaking, after obtaining the deed of incorporation, the incorporators must file an extract of the deed and articles within a certain time frame, and where appropriate, also file other documents, with a view to having the company *registered* in the commercial register. The commercial register should then register the company, provided that all the documents are properly submitted, and every legal requirement has been duly complied with. Accordingly, an announcement of the registration must be published in the national gazette, designated for that purpose by the Member State.

5.08 *The* Member States should ensure, according to Article 16 of Directive 2017/1132, that files are opened in a central commercial register or companies register for each of the companies to be registered in the register. Member States are also required to facilitate the filing of, *inter alia*, the instrument of incorporation and the articles of association by electronic means, and they must also ensure that copies are obtainable from the register 'by either paper or electronic means' (Article 16a Directive 2017/1132). The disclosure of the instrument of incorporation and the articles of association must be effected by being published in the national gazette or by equally effective means, including a system whereby the information can be accessed through a central electronic platform (Article 14(3) Directive 2017/1132). For further details on registration and disclosure *see* paragraph 3.23 *et seq.*

5.09 On a national level, various types of institutions keep the commercial register and handle the registrations. It can be the (commercial) court, as is the case in Belgium and France; the Chamber of Commerce, as is the case in the Netherlands; or the Registrar

5. Section 8 UK Companies Act 2006 and UK Companies Act 2006 – Explanatory Notes, 6, accessible via http://www.legislation.gov.uk/ukpga/2006/46/notes/contents.
6. Section 9 UK Companies Act 2006.
7. Section 13 UK Companies Act 2006. This statement can be accepted by the registrar as sufficient evidence of compliance. It is an offence to make a false statement of compliance, section 1112 UK Companies Act 2006.

of Companies, which is the competent authority in the UK.[8] Registration is essential for a company to come into existence (*see* paragraph 1.09). In the event that no notarial deed is required, registration assumes particular importance. Therefore, in the UK, the registrar will issue a certificate of incorporation to the company, which is conclusive evidence that all formalities of incorporation have been complied with and that the public company has been registered.[9]

C Substantive Requirements

5.10 A public company can be formed for any purpose, in accordance with the law by which it is governed, by one or more persons acting as founders/subscribers. In some countries, the participation of more than one person is required for the formation of a public company, as opposed to a private company, which can generally be formed as a single-member company. The requirement that more than one person is involved in the formation of a public company has been abandoned by several Member States. The Netherlands allowed for formation of a single-member public company by adapting its legislation in 1986.[10] Germany dropped the requirement that only five persons can form an AG in 1994, and the UK, in 2006, also allowed for a single person to form a public company (and not just a private company).[11] In France, however, the minimum number of founders and shareholders required to form an SA is two.[12] Where national law requires a company to have more than one member, the fact that all shares are held by one member 'shall not lead to the automatic dissolution of the company', according to Article 6 of Directive 2017/1132. A separate directive applies to single-member companies: Directive 2009/102/EC. It ensures that there is a company form in every Member State that can be established by one founder and after formation that has only one member. The company type it applies to is specified in the annex to the directive. For most Member States, this is a private company.

5.11 The capital requirements pertaining to the formation of public limited liability companies are a subject covered by Directive 2017/1132 in Articles 44–86. There is no consensus as to the need to maintain the legal capital regime as now laid down in Directive 2017/1132. Studies on this subject have led to opposite conclusions. In 2004, a study on the merits of this legal capital regime system was published by an interdisciplinary working group of experts led by Jonathan Rickford and supported by the British Accounting Standards Board (ASB) and the Company Law Centre at the British Institute of International Comparative Law (BIICL). According to this study, a legal capital regime is costly, redundant and defective. In practice, creditors do not widely rely on this regime and, according to the report, it tends to produce 'inconsistent

8. Sections 1060 *et seq.* Companies Act 2006. Further: Articles R210-1 and R741-1 *et seq.* French Commercial Code; Article 3 *Handelsregisterwet* (the Netherlands).
9. Sections 14–16 UK Companies Act 2006.
10. Article 2:64(2) Dutch Civil Code, Act as of 16 May 1986, Stb. 275.
11. Section 2 German Stock Corporation Act and section 7 UK Companies Act 2006.
12. Article L225-1 French Commercial Code.

results as between companies within the Member States and between different Member States within the EU'. According to Rickford, creditors in the UK could 'rely on fiduciary duties and wrongful trading, plus robust liquidation procedures'.[13] The opposite conclusion was drawn by the Working Group 'Kapital in Europa' directed by Marcus Lutter. This group of German and other European company law experts carried out a study on the benefits of fixed legal capital and its related specifics. The conclusions achieved by this study, which was published in 2006, are that the concept of fixed legal capital has a useful function.[14] These differences in opinion also led to different regimes for private companies among the Member States as discussed further on in this chapter. The harmonization of minimum capital requirements incorporated in Directive 2017/1132 is only applicable to public companies. Therefore, Member States are free to establish capital requirements for private companies.

5.12 Article 45 of Directive 2017/1132 provides that the Member States must require a minimum share capital to be subscribed upon incorporation of a public company.[15] This minimum may be not less than EUR 25,000. Member States have implemented differing amounts for this minimum capital requirement. For instance, the minimum share capital that must be subscribed upon the formation of a public company in Germany is EUR 50,000 and in the Netherlands, EUR 45,000.[16] Article 48 of Directive 2017/1132 further states that shares issued for a consideration must be paid up at incorporation to at least 25% of their nominal value. Furthermore, shareholders may not be released from the obligation to pay up their contributions except where it occurs in a reduction of the capital within the parameters of the directive (Article 53). Failure to comply with the national provisions pertaining to the minimum capital to be paid up can trigger the company's nullity by court order (Article 11). It may not always be clear when such failure occurs because the directive does not prescribe a time limit within which the amount of consideration in cash must be fully paid.[17] For consideration other than in cash, the time limit is set to within five years after incorporation (Article 48).

5.13 Directive 2017/1132 requires that the subscribed capital consists of cash or of assets capable of economic assessment. To secure the latter's value, any contribution other than in cash must be subjected to an independent expert's report. According to Article 49, the expert's report should contain at least a description of each of the assets comprising the consideration as well as the methods of valuation used. The report must state whether the values arrived at by the application of these methods correspond at least to the number and nominal value or, where there is no nominal value, to the

13. J. Rickford, 'Legal Approaches to Restricting Distributions to Shareholders: Balance Sheet Tests and Solvency Tests', *European Business Law Review* 7 (2006): 179.
14. *See* M. Lutter (ed.), 'Legal Capital in Europe', *European Company and Financial Law Review*, special volume 1 (2006).
15. Some jurisdictions refer to an 'authorized share capital', i.e., a figure that acts as a ceiling on the amount of capital that may be issued (in any case this limit can be augmented through an ordinary resolution). The Dutch Civil Code, Article 2:67(2), states that the authorized [and issued] share capital must at least amount to the minimum capital.
16. Section 7 German Stock Corporation Act; Article 2:67 Dutch Companies Code.
17. E. Werlauff, *EU Company Law – Common Business Law of 28 States*, Second edition (Copenhagen: DJØF Publishing, 2003), 208.

accountable par value and, where appropriate, to the premium on the shares to be issued for them'. The expert is thus required to state whether the value of the assets equals at least the nominal value (or accountable par value) of the shares issued in exchange for these assets. Where the nominal value is kept low, it will not be problematic for the expert to meet this requirement, because then the shares will be issued at a premium, which the expert does not have to include in his or her statement. Article 49 represents a minimum level of protection and does not pertain to all details of consideration other than in cash upon formation. Where the directive states that any consideration other than in cash must be transferred, in full, to the company within five years as of the date of incorporation or the authorization to commence business, Member States may opt for a shorter period. In the Netherlands, payment must take place 'without delay' after subscription. In Germany, however, the five-year term has been implemented.[18]

D Pre-incorporation Transactions

5.14 When a company acquires legal personality, it is fully capable of acting in its own name and is regarded to be a separate legal person, distinct from its members and, as a result, confers limited liability to them.[19] However, the process of establishing a company is far from instantaneous and, therefore, many questions may arise as to the capacity of the company to acquire certain rights or liabilities before the moment of incorporation. Directive 2017/1132 provides a rule with regard to pre-incorporation contracts. Pursuant to Article 7, if: 'before a company being formed has acquired legal personality, action has been carried out in its name and the company does not assume the obligations arising from such action, the persons who acted shall, without limit, be jointly and severally liable, therefore, unless otherwise agreed.' Accordingly, subsequent to obtaining legal personality, the company may assume liability for pre-incorporation transactions. Article 7 aims to ensure that third parties contracting with the company, even before it has acquired legal personality, always have recourse to a debtor.[20]

5.15 There are diverging opinions concerning the choice of the party on whose behalf an action has to be taken for the Article 7 rule to apply: the company as existing prior to incorporation (which may constitute a partnership under national law), or the future legal person. In any event, as noted by Grundmann, the English-language version of the original First Directive (containing the phrase 'before a company being formed has acquired legal personality, action has been carried out in its name') points to the application of what is now Article 7 at least in those cases where action was taken on

18. Article 2:80b(2) Dutch Civil Code and section 36a(2) German Stock Corporation Act.
19. *See* paragraph 1.09 for the moment at which a company comes into existence.
20. E. Werlauff, *supra* n. 17, at 207.

behalf of the future legal person.[21] Further, the assumption of liability by the company does not necessarily require the company's consent, even though the English-language version of Article 7, as well as the German and the French version, seems to suggest this interpretation.[22] Although the assumption of liability does not require the consent of the third party (creditor), it seems that there is a presumption that the third party knew they were dealing with a company. Otherwise, the third party cannot be obliged to accept that a company assumes the position of its 'presumed contractual partner'.[23]

5.15a Although the founders of a French SA do not necessarily have to sign a notarial deed, the pre-registered company is formed the moment the contract is signed, though the SA only acquires legal personality upon registration.[24] Persons who have acted on behalf of the company in formation (*société en formation*), before it has acquired full legal personality, are held jointly and severally liable for those acts, except if the company, after having been properly formed and registered, assumes its obligations thereby entered into.[25] An action on behalf of the future legal person is void under French law; therefore, only actions on behalf of the company prior to registration are legally accepted.[26]

5.15b German company law, with regard to the formation of a public company, sets out two essential criteria in the process of establishing a company. First, the promoters must subscribe to all shares in return for contributions.[27] This subscription has to be recorded by a notary and included in the formation deed. Once all shares are subscribed, the company is established and a *pre-AG* is considered to be formed. However, the *pre-AG* does not have legal personality until registration and whoever acts in its name as such is personally liable.[28] The second requirement is registration and only then the company is granted legal personality, though it is possible to assume rights and liabilities negotiated for it prior to registration. The creditor's consent is not required for this assumption if it takes place within three months after registration and the assumption is communicated to the creditor.[29]

5.15c A public company in the Netherlands is incorporated upon execution of a notarial deed of incorporation.[30] Prior to its incorporation, legal acts may be performed in the name of the company to be incorporated. Legal acts prior to incorporation are binding on the company only if it, after its incorporation, expressly or implicitly, ratifies those acts. Persons who perform such legal acts are bound jointly and severally until

21. S. Grundmann, *European Company Law*, Second edition (Cambridge-Antwerp-Portland: Intersentia, 2012), 156. In his opinion, the wording of Article 9(2) of the EEIG Regulation supports this view.
22. S. Grundmann, *supra* n. 21, at 140–142.
23. E. Werlauff, *supra* n. 17, at 207.
24. Article L 210-6 French Commercial Code.
25. *Ibid.*
26. S. Grundmann, *supra* n. 21 at 140–142.
27. Section 29 German Stock Corporation Act.
28. Section 41(1) German Stock Corporation Act.
29. Section 41(2) German Stock Corporation Act.
30. Article 2:64(2) Dutch Civil Code.

ratification by the company ('*unless the contrary has been stipulated explicitly in respect of that juridical act*'). Even then these persons are liable for any loss sustained by a third party as a result of non-performance by the company, provided that they knew or could reasonably have known that the company could not perform its obligations.[31] Upon incorporation, registration must follow. If the directors fail to meet the obligation to register, they are jointly and severally liable for legal acts binding on the company.[32]

5.15d In the UK, companies are formed and acquire legal personality upon registration.[33] Prior to registration, the company does not exist. Consequently, if the founders of the company (or others) nevertheless enter into contracts on the company's behalf, the company cannot be bound. Such contract has effect, subject to any agreement to the contrary, as one made with the person purporting to act for the company or as agent for it. Accordingly, such person is personally liable under the contract.[34] This provision provides legal certainty for third parties by avoiding the consequences of the contract with a non-existent company being a nullity.

III PRIVATE COMPANIES

A Formation

5.16 Generally, the formation procedure for private companies does not differ much from the procedure for public companies, even though the scope of the relevant section of Directive 2017/1132 is limited to public companies. The instruments of incorporation and the articles of a private company contain roughly the same elements that are required for public companies, and the formalities regarding the execution of the articles are often the same. Thus, the considerations set out above regarding the documents required for the formation of companies, such as the statement of compliance in the UK, apply equally to private companies. If a German private company is formed with the use of template articles of association, then a simplified formation procedure is allowed.

5.17 Directive 2019/1151 introduced provisions with regard to the online formation of companies. These provisions are inserted in Articles 13–13h of Directive 2017/1132. Member States must ensure that online formation is allowed for at least private companies as referred to in Annex IIA of Directive 2017/1132.[35] Formation means the entire process of establishing a company in accordance with national law, including the drawing up of the company's instrument of constitution and all steps necessary for entering the company in the register. In order to facilitate this method of formation, Member States have to provide an electronic identification scheme and a 'template',

31. Article 2:93 Dutch Civil Code.
32. Article 2:69 Dutch Civil Code.
33. Section 7 UK Companies Act 2006.
34. Section 51 UK Companies Act 2006.
35. Articles 13 and 13g Directive 2017/1132 (as amended).

being a model for the instrument of the constitution of a company.[36] Several Member States, including France and the Netherlands, have opted for an extension period ending in August 2022 for the implementation of the online formation provisions.[37] Germany has already adopted legislation allowing for online formation which will be in force as of 1 August 2022. For the formation, a notarial deed will remain essential but the founder or founders may communicate with the notary by means of videoconferencing.[38]

B Registration

5.18 How private companies are registered is generally similar to the registration of public companies. Nevertheless, a few peculiarities should be mentioned here. All documents required to establish a German private company must be submitted electronically to the court for registration in the commercial register.[39] An application may not take place before a quarter of the nominal value on each of the shares has been paid up, representing at least half of the amount of EUR 25,000 which is the minimum capital requirement. Non-cash contributions must be at the free disposal of the company before application.[40] In the UK, the Companies Act 2006 provides that, among the documents to be provided upon application for registration, there must be a statement of capital and initial shareholdings, regarded as a 'snapshot' of a company's share capital at a specific moment.[41] This requirement is similar to that which Article 3 of Directive 2017/1132 prescribes for public companies.[42] The application must be delivered to the registrar of companies electronically or by post.[43] Upon registration, a certificate of incorporation is provided by the registrar.[44] In France, copies of the articles must be delivered to the registrar of the Commercial Registry (*registre du commerce et des sociétés*), together with the instrument appointing the directors, if not in the articles, and a declaration of compliance with all procedural requirements. The company will then be registered. No capital may be withdrawn from the company's bank account before the registry issues a registration certificate; this is called a *Récépissé K Bis* or *Extrait K Bis*.[45] In the Netherlands, a private company comes into existence upon the execution of the notarial deed which contains the articles and

36. Articles 13a, 13b, and 13h Directive 2017/1132 (as amended).
37. https://ec.europa.eu/info/business-economy-euro/doing-business-eu/company-law-and-corporate-governance_en (accessed January 2022).
38. https://dserver.bundestag.de/btd/19/281/1928177.pdf (accessed January 2022).
39. Sections 8a and 8b Handelsgesetzbuch (German Commercial Code); Section 7 German Limited Liability Company Act (*GmbHG*); and section 6 General Terms of Use for the Company Register (accessible at https://www.unternehmensregister.de/ureg).
40. Sections 5 and 7 German Limited Liability Company Act.
41. Sections 9 and 10 UK Companies Act 2006. UK *Companies Act 2006 – Explanatory Notes, supra* n. 5, at 7–8.
42. UK *Companies Act 2006 – Explanatory Notes, supra* n. 5, at 8, 10.
43. https://www.gov.uk/limited-company-formation/register-your-company.
44. Section 15 UK Companies Act 2006.
45. Article L223-8 French Commercial Code; https://www.service-public.fr/professionnels-entreprises/vosdroits/F32886 (accessed January 2022).

the appointment of the directors.[46] The directors are obliged to register the company with the commercial registry which is kept by the Chamber of Commerce. Because the company exists independently from registration, it has legal capacity and can enter into contracts or other legal acts. To minimize risks for third parties, the directors are personally liable for acts of the company as long as the company is not duly registered.[47]

C Substantive Requirements

5.19 In general, a private company may be formed by one or more persons for any legally permissible purpose. National laws may cap the number of members of a private company. For example, in France, the *société a responsabilité limitée* (SARL) may not have more than 100 members. If the company exceeds this threshold, it will be dissolved within one year, unless the situation is normalized during this period. This can be done either by reducing the number of members or by transforming the company into another form, such as the SA, which allows for an extended number of members.[48] German law limits the number of shareholders to three if a private company is formed by the simplified procedure using template articles of association as already mentioned in paragraph 5.16 above.[49] Member States may also place restrictions on the use of the single-member company to prevent abuse, which is feared, in particular, if setting up a cascade of single-member companies, each being the single member of another company, were to be allowed. Thus, in France, a single-member company is not permitted to form another single-member company.[50] To the same effect, the German private company is not allowed to have a legal person as director.[51] In the UK, every company must have at least one director who is a natural person.[52] Dutch law has chosen a different approach by holding the directors of a legal person which is appointed as a director of another legal person personally, jointly and severally liable for the obligations arising out of the directorship of that other legal person.[53] Other restrictions to the use of private companies may follow from the regulation of certain industries, requiring that certain operations may only be carried out by public limited companies. For example, in France, the SARL cannot be utilized for insurance, investment and savings companies (*'sociétés d'assurance, de capitalisation et d'épargne'*).[54]

5.20 Since the provisions of Directive 2017 /1132 relating to the capital of companies pertain only to public limited liability companies, there are no harmonized European

46. Articles 2:177 and 2:242 Dutch Civil Code.
47. Article 2:180 Dutch Civil Code; Article 18 *Handelsregisterwet*.
48. Article L223-3 French Commercial Code.
49. Section 2(1a) German Limited Liability Company Act.
50. L223-5 French Commercial Code.
51. Section 6 German Limited Liability Company Act.
52. Section 155 UK Companies Act 2006.
53. Article 2:11 Dutch Civil Code.
54. Article L223-1 French Commercial Code.

rules for private limited liability companies with regard to a legally required amount of minimum capital. This leaves considerable room for regulatory competition and, accordingly, jurisdictions with different legal backgrounds provide for varied solutions. Against this background, the UK traditionally follows a liberal approach, according to which no minimum capital is required to incorporate a private company, whereas Germany preserved its fixed legal capital of EUR 25,000 during the 2006 modernization of its *Gesellschaft mit beschränkter Haftung* (GmbH) legislation. The proposal to substantially lower the amount was not approved by the German legislature.[55] It was argued that, even though capital requirements may not play a fundamental role in protecting creditors' interests, they also function as a threshold to assure credibility and seriousness, thereby preventing the creation of too many unserious businesses. However, there is an exception, as laid down in section 5a GmbHG (*Gesetz betreffend die Gesellschaften mit beschränkter Haftung*) to facilitate start-ups. To that end, a private company can be formed without minimum capital but with a distinctive name: *Unternehmergesellschaft (haftungsbeschränkt)* or *UG (haftungsbeschränkt)*. This can be literally translated as 'entrepreneur company (limited liability)'.[56] However, for this form, considerable restrictions are imposed on the distribution of profits in order to enable the company to progressively save up or accumulate the minimum nominal capital required for a normal GmbH.

A minimum capital as a requirement to form a SARL in France was abolished in 2003, and the same applies to the minimum capital requirement to form a BV in the Netherlands, which was abolished in 2012.[57] The abolition of the requirement can be regarded against the background of fear that businesses may prefer incorporating abroad, where they would find lower or less restrictive requirements than those they would have to comply with in their own jurisdictions. Governments have been reconsidering the attractiveness and feasibility of domestic company law since the Court of Justice of the European Union (CJEU) liberalized the market for incorporations to a certain extent (*see* paragraph 2.61 *et seq.*). How such a market may function is illustrated by the 'post Centros' significant increase in incorporations in the UK.[58]

5.21 Generally speaking, since the requirements of Directive 2017/1132 with regard to contributions in kind do not apply to private companies, the rules for these contributions tend to be less stringent in comparison with the requirements for contributions in kind made to public companies. The French Commercial Code requires the memorandum of association and articles of association to include a valuation of the contribution, which must be drawn up by, and under the responsibility of, an auditor of the

55. M. Beurskens & U. Noack, 'The Reform of German Private Limited Company: Is the GmbH Ready for the 21st Century?', *German Law Journal* 9, no. 09 (1 Sep. 2008) – Special Edition (accessible at https://germanlawjournal.com).
56. Section 5a German Limited Liability Company Act. 23 Oct. 2008, Beurskens & Noack, *supra* n. 55, at 1083.
57. Act of 18 June 2012, Stb. 2012/299. *See* H. Boschma, L. Lennarts & H. Schutte-Veenstra, 'The Reform of Dutch Private Company Laws: New Rules for the Protection of Creditors', *European Business Organization Law Review* 8 (2007): 590–598.
58. M. Becht, C. Mayer & H. F. Wagner, Where Do Firms Incorporate? (October 2006), CEPR Discussion Paper No. 5875. Accessible at SSRN: http://ssrn.com/abstract=953820.

formation proceedings, appointed by unanimous decision of the founders, being the future members, or by a court order. However, the founders may decide unanimously to not engage an auditor if no contribution in kind exceeds an amount determined by decree, and if the value of all contributions in kind not evaluated by an auditor does not exceed the amount corresponding to half the capital.[59] Under Dutch law, contributions in kind for private companies must be described and evaluated by the founders. They each have to sign the description and this document must be made available at the company's office for inspection by the shareholders.[60] German law requires that contributions in kind be specified in the articles.[61] In the UK, private companies are not subject to requirements such as the valuer's report concerning the adequacy of the consideration as required for public companies.[62]

D Pre-incorporation Contracts

5.22 Because the provisions of Directive 2017/1132 concerning pre-incorporation contracts are applicable to both public and private companies, this matter is generally regulated for private companies in the same way as described above with regard to public companies. This applies to the moment of acquisition of legal personality, the liabilities for pre-incorporation contracts and other aspects related to the liability of founders of private companies.

5.22a If a company is formed by two or more people, different phases in the formation process can be distinguished. Apart from the harmonized rules on pre-incorporation contracts, other legal consequences may then come into play depending on non-harmonized national law. For instance, German law provides for a distinction between two stages before the registration of a GmbH. The first stage is the period starting from the decision of the founders to establish a GmbH, through a preliminary and binding agreement, until the moment when the articles are notarized – pre-formation company ('*Vorgründungs-gesellschaft*'). During this stage and depending on whether or not the founders act with third parties, the founders' agreement and their acts may cumulatively approximate the legal form of a general partnership or even a limited partnership. Because of this, the founders are treated as partners without limited liability. The second stage starts when the notarial deed is executed which leads to a pre-company *('Vor-gesellschaft)'*. The pre-company resembles the future GmbH, except for the legal capacity, which only arises upon registration in the commercial register. At the time of registration of the German GmbH in the commercial register, the rights and obligations of the pre-registered GmbH[63] are wholly transferred 'to the registered GmbH by

59. Article L223-9 French Commercial Code.
60. Article 2:204a Dutch Civil Code. The description of the non-cash contribution does not have to be attached to the notarial deed, unlike in the case of public companies.
61. Section 5 German Limited Liability Company Act.
62. Sections 593 *et seq.* UK Companies Act 2006.
63. This means that from this moment on relevant parts of the German Limited Liability Company Act apply to the pre-GmbH, provided that they do not presuppose legal capacity.

operation of law' and the personal (joint and several) liability of the shareholders who acted in the name of the company expires.[64]

IV FINANCING OF PUBLIC AND PRIVATE COMPANIES

Companies can be financed in various ways. The most obvious is by means of share capital. Another way of financing business activities is by means of bonds or loans. These forms of financing are applicable to both public and private companies as well as listed and non-listed companies, and for that reason, we make for this subject in principal no distinction between the two types of companies. With that said, however, the rules regarding minimum capital and the maintenance of capital differ between public and private companies as has been pointed out in the previous paragraphs.

A Share Capital of Public and Private Companies

5.23 One of the traditional means utilized to finance companies is share capital (also designated as equity), the other is loan capital. All capital companies, by definition, have a share capital which represents a capital fund, contributed to by the members and available to creditors in fulfilment of the company's liabilities to them. Company law provides companies with the power to ensure that this fund is actually contributed to in the first place, the raising capital provisions. Furthermore, it may ensure the maintenance of that capital, i.e., the fund is retained by the company for the benefit of its creditors and not distributed to the members to the extent that it may prejudice the interests of creditors. Usually, the company's capital is divided into shares,[65] which can differ with regard to its form and transferability. The share capital is deemed to include: (i) the nominal value of allotted shares; (ii) the amount of any premium paid; and (iii) the capital reserves, which companies are required to retain. Directive 2017/1132 requires the Member States to enact rules pertaining to both raising and maintaining share capital of public companies. The directive also addresses for public companies the alteration (increase[66] and reduction) of share capital, including purchase and redemption by a company of its own shares, and the financial assistance provided by a company for the acquisition of its own shares by a third party.[67]

---

64. Section 11 German Limited Liability Company Act. *See* G. Wirth, M. Arnold, R. Morshäuser, M. Greene & S. Carl, *Corporate Law in Germany* 2016, revised Third edition (München:Verlag C.H. Beck, 2016); Wolfgang Schon, The Concept of the Shareholder in European Company Law, *European Business Organization Law Review* 1 no. 1 (2000): 3–39, 3.2.
65. Some countries use a term other than 'share' to designate a part of the capital of private companies. For instance, in France, '*part social*', which correspond to '*parts*' or '*quotas*' and in Germany, '*Geschäftsanteil*'.
66. The increase of capital refers to actual addition to the company's capital, thereby excluding the capitalization of reserves and any premiums, which are considered an accounting exercise.
67. Articles 44–86 Directive 2017/1132 (as amended).

5.23a Companies may issue shares with no-par value, i.e., without nominal value.[68] These shares are issued without the indication of a par value, either in the company's articles of association or on the share certificate itself. Among the reasons why some companies issue this type of share is avoidance of liability that companies would have to assume towards shareholders if the share price were to fall considerably below the par value of the shares. Further, the issuance of no-par value shares provides companies with more flexibility to set higher or lower prices for potential public offerings.

B Loan Capital

5.24 The loan capital of a company may include loans from a specific lender, such as a bank or a finance company, as well as bonds issued by the company, which are debt securities[69] that are supposed to be repaid (normally at a fixed date) and attract interest payments rather than dividends. In this respect, there is no difference between a public and a private company, although listed companies generally make a public appeal to financing by not only listing their shares on the stock exchange but also issuing bonds in capital markets. Therefore, what follows applies both to public and private companies. The company may give security to the providers of loan capital in the form of a charge over part or all of the company's assets. Since there is no harmonization at the European level for this type of funding, national laws assume particular relevance and provide for different solutions, for instance, with regard to the types of bonds that can be issued, or even concerning the procedure that is to be followed by the corporate bodies authorized to decide or approve the issuance of bonds. However, national law quite often does not regulate loan capital specifically for companies.[70]

5.25 The decision of a company's board to attract a loan or to issue debt instruments may be subject to the approval of other corporate bodies. For example, under Dutch law, several resolutions of the board of directors of sizable companies are subject to the approval of the supervisory board, including the issuance of debt instruments.[71] The German Stock Corporation Act states that the articles of association or the supervisory board must stipulate that certain types of transactions may only be entered into after receiving the consent of the supervisory board.[72] Hence, attracting loans or issuing debt instruments by German public companies will often need the consent of the supervisory board.

5.26 The fact that loan capital is not extensively regulated, let alone harmonized, is to a certain extent compensated for by the market. The London-based Loan Market

68. Article 47 Directive 2017/1132 (as amended).
69. Securities are financing instruments which offer evidence of debt or equity and are tradable on the financial markets. For instance: shares, bonds, debentures, notes, options and warrants. These financing instruments can be issued by companies, governments or other organizations.
70. E. Werlauff, *supra* n. 17, at 225.
71. Articles 2:164 and 2:274 Dutch Civil Code.
72. Section 111(4) German Stock Corporation Act.

Association (LMA) provides standard loan documentation for syndicated loans (loans offered by a group of lenders) on the primary and secondary markets. Documents, such as standard term sheets, mandate letters, commitment letters and inter-creditor agreements, can be used by members of the LMA, thus allowing lenders and borrowers to focus on the commercial aspects of individual transactions.[73]

5.27 Generally speaking, loan capital can be divided into various categories, and in the following paragraphs, we briefly discuss bonds, convertibles and mezzanines. Bonds and convertibles are securities, i.e., they are financing instruments, which offer evidence of debt and are tradable on the financial markets. Mezzanine financing may partly or wholly consist of securities, such as convertibles, but may also require other instruments.

5.28 A bond is a written and signed promise to pay a certain sum of money on a certain date, or upon the fulfilment of specified conditions. Normally, a company provides collateral for bonds, and the investment is thus not considered risky from an investor's (or a bondholder's) point of view. Accordingly, the interest rate is relatively low. In the case of liquidation, bondholders are paid off before shareholders, and their interest payments are given priority to be paid before shareholders' dividends. Conversely, bondholders do not normally share in any capital growth of the company or in any surplus profits.

5.29 Convertibles are usually convertible bonds or convertible preferred shares, which include an option to convert the security into another form of security, normally common stock, at a fixed price and time. Convertible bonds tend to offer a lower rate of return – compared to ordinary bonds – in exchange for the value of the option to convert the bonds into another form of security. A conversion could lead to an increase in the share capital and turn the creditor into a co-owner of the company, thereby causing shareholder dilution. The issuance of such securities is therefore governed by the share capital increase rules laid down in Directive 2017/1132.[74]

5.30 Mezzanine finance is a hybrid and flexible manner of financing that is treated as a cross between debt and shareholder's equity on the balance sheet. Mezzanine capital is regarded as a form of debt, typically a subordinated loan, i.e., subordinated to a senior bank loan. This means that mezzanine creditors[75] can only be paid off after all senior creditors have been paid in full, which increases the risk of non-repayment of the mezzanine loan. In general, this financing instrument does not require collateral. However, where collateral is required, it is also subordinated.[76] Therefore, mezzanine

73. http://www.lma.eu.com (accessed January 2022). The LMA covers the 'EMEA' markets: Europe, Middle East and Africa.
74. Article 68(4) Directive 2017/1132 (as amended).
75. For instance, investment banks or private equity firms and hedge funds. E. Wymeersch, 'Shareholders in Action: Towards a New Company Paradigm?', *European Company Law* 4, no. 2 (2007): 50–57.
76. If the collateral cannot be subordinated, the mezzanine loan agreement will state that senior lenders have priority on repayment upon execution of the collateral.

loans are significantly more costly than borrowing from a bank. Usually, the mezzanine creditor requires not only a higher interest rate, but also warrants subscribing for equity, or royalties, in order to partake in the success (or failure) of the borrowing company.[77] The combination of these fixed and variable components allows for flexible pricing. As a result, mezzanine loans can be tailored to meet the specific needs of a borrowing company and be adapted to its expected cash flows. The repayment of the principal is normally due at maturity. Although mezzanine financing is a form of debt, it features on the equity side of the balance sheet, thereby strengthening the company's equity ratio, which may improve its senior lending potential.

5.31 Generally speaking, mezzanine capital is a general term for long-term financing instruments, primarily aimed at supporting growth. Accordingly, it is used, *inter alia,* to finance acquisitions, management buyouts, equipment purchases or business expansion. Due to the additional risks that mezzanine capital involves, it is normally provided only to companies with sound financial records, which generate considerable cash flows and have strong management, all regarded as crucial indicators of the company's potential to be successful. The demand for this financing instrument has increased since the beginning of the twenty-first century, and the European Investment Fund provides a specific Mezzanine Facility for Growth.[78]

C Securitization

5.32 Securitization is considered an advanced type of factoring or discounting of debts.[79] It consists of a transaction where the owner – originator/seller (typically banks or corporations) – of certain receivables (for instance, home mortgage loans or consumer credit receivables) sells them to a third party, which is a special purpose vehicle ('SPV'), in exchange for a purchase price to be paid upon its sale. The SPV finances the purchase price of the receivables, usually by issuing marketable bonds or by a bank loan, and secures the borrowing precisely on those receivables. An SPV is normally formed as a public company and is a thinly capitalized company, whose shares are held by somebody other than the originator, for instance by charitable trustees. Thus, an SPV is a different legal entity and not a subsidiary that would have to be consolidated on the originator's balance sheet. Accordingly, the originator cannot be held liable for the SPV's obligations. Overall, the main effect of securitization is that

77. K. Marks, L. Robbins, G. Fernandez & J. Funkhouser, *The Handbook of Financing Growth: Strategies, Capital Structure and M&A Transactions* (Hoboken: John Wiley & Sons, Inc., 2005).
78. https://www.eif.org/what_we_do/equity/mezzanine/index.htm (accessed January 2022). *Mezzanine Finance, Roundtable between Bankers and SMEs*, Enterprise publications, Ref. Ares(2014)78108 – 15/01/2014 and the Commission Communication, *Financing SME Growth – Adding European Value*, Brussels, 29 June 2006 COM(2006) 349 final.
79. The essential difference between factoring and securitization is that the factoring companies raise their finance mostly from banks, while in securitization the SPVs issue bonds secured on the receivables. Moreover, many of the factoring companies are subsidiaries of banks and not single-purpose companies as in securitization. Philip Wood, *The Law and Practice of International Finance Series,* Project Finance, Securitizations and Subordinated Debt', Vol. 5 (2007): 111–120.

the originator transfers the risk of non-payment of the receivables to the investors and, in addition, removes the assets and the borrowing from its balance sheet. This transaction is designated as securitization precisely because the receivables that were non-marketable assets are converted into marketable assets, symbolized by securities (bonds) that the lenders can sell. By resorting to securitization, originators try to gain access to additional financial resources and improve their financial ratios.[80]

D Covered Bonds

5.33 Other financing structures to be considered are covered bonds – known in Germany as *Pfandbrief*[81] – which are debt securities (issued normally by a bank), to be paid 'out of a pool of eligible mortgages',[82] or cash flows from other debt, such as public sector loans. Covered bondholders are entitled to be paid prior to all other creditors. Although similar to the asset-backed securities originating in securitization, they differ in one essential way, i.e., covered bonds must feature on the issuing bank's consolidated balance sheet. The creation of these structures was aimed at making it easier to finance residential property.[83]

E Off-Balance-Sheet Arrangements

5.34 Securitization carried out by separate companies is considered an example of off-balance-sheet arrangements.[84,85] Normally, these arrangements involve the creation of SPVs (as described above) or, in other situations, involve offshore activities projected with a view to serve, among others, economic, legal, tax or accounting purposes. Off-balance-sheet arrangements tend not only to expose a company to benefits but also may represent risks where the company has accepted to back up the SPV's obligations to investors. Both benefits and risks are relevant for a thorough assessment of the financial position of a company or, where appropriate, for the financial position of a group as a whole. After a series of corporate scandals, such as Enron and Parmalat, regulators in the United States and Europe have reacted in such a way as to make risk management one of the most central concerns of board members.[86]

80. P. Wood, *supra* n. 79, at 111–120.
81. Covered bonds originated in German Law in 1769 under the designation: *Pfandbrief*. Nowadays covered bonds are commonly used throughout Europe.
82. P. Wood, *supra* n. 79, at 130.
83. *Ibid.*
84. Preamble, recitals 8 and 9, Directive 2006/46/EC.
85. Other examples of off-balance-sheet arrangements are: (i) outsourcing; (ii) consignment stock arrangements; (iii) take or pay arrangements; (iv) combined sale and repurchase agreement; (v) operating leasing agreement; (vi) risk and benefit-sharing arrangements; (vii) or obligations arising from a contract like debt factoring; and (viii) pledged assets.
86. G. Ferrarini & P. Giudici, Financial Scandals and the Role of Private Enforcement: The Parmalat Case (May 2005). ECGI – Law Working Paper No. 40/2005, Available at SSRN: https://ssrn.com/abstract=730403 or http://dx.doi.org/10.2139/ssrn.730403; J. Coffee, 'A Theory of Corporate Scandals: Why the US and Europe Differ', in J. Armour & J.A. McCahery (eds), *After*

5.35 The European response, leading to the amendment of the former Fourth and Seventh Directives (annual accounts) and the replacement of the former Eighth Directive (statutory audit), embodies, *inter alia*, securing the independence of statutory auditors and requiring boards to report on the internal controls of the company or the group.[87] These issues are addressed in paragraphs 9.24 *et seq*. and paragraph 10.21 of this book. Corporate scandals have been an additional driving force behind International Financial Reporting Standards (IFRS) being applicable to financial reporting and standards being adopted in EU Commission Regulations (*see* paragraphs 9.09 and 9.10).

Enron: Improving Corporate Law and Modernising Securities Regulation in Europe and the US (Oxford: Hart Publishing, 2006), 216–231.

87. K. Hopt, 'Modern Company and Capital Market Problems: Improving European Corporate Governance After Enron', in J. Armour & J.A. McCahery (eds), *supra* n. 86, at 446. Financial Reporting Council, Guidance on Risk Management, *Internal Control and Related Financial and Business Reporting*, Sept. 2014, Available at https://www.frc.org.uk.

CHAPTER 6

The Management and Control of Companies

I INTRODUCTION

6.01 All public and private companies enjoy legal personality (*see* paragraphs 2.06 and 2.07). This enables them to take part in economic life in a way that is similar to natural persons. Companies can enter into contracts with clients, employees and suppliers, can own property and commit tortious acts. However, as companies are legal constructs and not natural persons, systems of decision making have to be put in place in order to determine the company's will and enable the company to be represented towards third parties. To make these systems function, responsibility needs to be allocated to certain corporate bodies and/or natural persons that actually take the decisions and represent the company. Generally, as is described further in this chapter, this power is allocated to the general meeting of shareholders and board of directors, with the latter having the power to represent the company to third parties. On some occasions, a third corporate body can be added: the supervisory board. Large parts of company law are devoted to providing checks and balances and a division of powers among the various corporate actors. There are many similarities between national company laws with regard to how companies are run. The general division of powers often has the same common denominators, although there are also many variations with regard to the details. For example, even though in most jurisdictions shareholders have the same minimum shareholder rights, certain jurisdictions award shareholders and the general meeting stronger decision-making powers whereas other jurisdictions place the primary power with a board of directors.

6.02 This chapter focuses on the division of powers within a company. After a short introduction to the separation between ownership and control and the division of power in general, we start with discussing the board of directors. We first look into the role of the board in general and the different board structures, and from there we discuss the different types of directors, board composition as well as the power of the board of directors to represent the company. Furthermore, we examine the duties of the board and its risks of liability. In the second half of this chapter, we set out the position of shareholders and the role of the general meeting. We first discuss the reasons why shareholders arguably should have voting rights in the company, focusing mainly on the rights-based theory, contractual theory, economic theory and the shareholder democracy theory. Next, the various (types of) shareholder rights are set out, including appointment and dismissal rights, instruction rights and the approval of important board decisions. After these items, we discuss the functions of the general meeting of shareholders and whether the general meeting actually fulfils these functions. Subsequently, we explain how shareholders can exercise their rights in relation to the general meeting, such as how to convene a general meeting, add items to the agenda and vote during the general meeting. Lastly, we set out certain principles regarding shareholder information rights, derivative suits and shareholders agreements.

II OWNERSHIP AND CONTROL

6.03 One of the core characteristics of the company is the delegation of the responsibility to manage the day-to-day operations of the company to the board of directors.[1] As a result in most companies, except for smaller companies where the shareholders are at the same time director, a separation exists between the 'ownership' of the company and the management or 'control' of the company (*see also* paragraphs 2.42 and 2.43).[2] The underlying economic reason for this separation is that shareholders as 'owners' are not able to manage the company themselves and therefore appoint managers that are better and more efficiently able to do so. In part the reason that shareholders are unable to manage the company is due to the fact that coordination costs for shareholders are generally considered relatively high, making it both impractical and expensive for shareholders to take day-to-day decisions regarding the management of the company.[3] In addition, especially in larger companies with a diverse group of (smaller) shareholders, the expertise of managers who are appointed by the shareholders might be higher than the expertise of the shareholders themselves. As a result, it is better for the company – and the shareholders – to delegate management of the company to

1. P.L. Davies, S. Worthington & C. Hare, *Principles of Modern Company Law* (London: Sweet & Maxwell, 2021), 46; J. Armour et al., 'What Is Corporate Law', in R. Kraakman et al (eds.), *The Anatomy of Corporate Law* (Oxford: Oxford University Press, 2017), 11–12; R.C. Clark, *Corporate Law* (Boston: Little, Brown and Company, 1986) 21 *et seq.*
2. The legal implications of which were already discussed by Berle and Means in their renowned book *The Modern Corporation and Private Property*: A.A. Berle & G.C. Means, *The Modern Corporation and Private Property* (Chicago: Commerce Clearing House, Inc., 1932).
3. S. Cools, 'The Dividing Line between Shareholder Democracy and Board Autonomy: Inherent Conflict of Interest as Normative Criterion', *European Company and Financial Review* 11 (2014): 272.

specialized directors instead of keeping full or most of the control over the company themselves.[4]

6.04 The separation of ownership and control within the company increases – from the aforementioned perspectives – the possibilities to manage the company efficiently, but at the same time it creates new challenges and potential costs. Since the authority to manage the day-to-day operations of the company is delegated to the board of directors, a situation arises in which directors, in the absence of control and monitoring mechanisms, may have an incentive to act opportunistically in their own interest rather than in the interests that they should serve. This has been described as one of the principal–agent relationships within the company, with the directors being the agents.[5] The costs resulting from the separation of ownership and control in this relationship are – in short – twofold, namely (i) the costs related to directors acting in their own interest instead of in the interest of the principal, and (ii) the costs related to the principal trying to lower the costs under (i) by monitoring the directors and – if necessary – intervening. A significant part of company law is concerned with the position of the board of directors and shareholders and how the power between these two corporate bodies is divided.

III REGULATING THE DIVISION OF POWER

6.05 National company law provides rules on the division of powers.[6] These rules can take the form of default rules, from which parties can deviate in the articles of association, and mandatory rules, from which parties may not deviate. Mainly, the rules on the division of power are focused on the relationship between the general meeting and the board of directors (and, if installed, the supervisory board), also introducing a system of checks and balances to ensure that the directors do not abuse their powers to the detriment of the company, shareholders and other stakeholders. This has traditionally been considered the area of corporate control or, in modern terms, corporate governance. The law tries, among other things, to balance the autonomy of the board of directors with the power of the general meeting to monitor the board of directors and intervene where necessary. To achieve this, both corporate bodies are granted specific rights as part of the broader system of checks and balances, including for instance the right of the general meeting to be consulted, or the right of prior approval of certain fundamental board proposals, such as an alteration of the

4. D.J. Smythe, 'Shareholder Democracy and the Economic Purpose of the Corporation', 63 *Wash. & Lee L. Rev.* (2006): 1407, 1409.
5. *See* J. Armour et al., 'What Is Corporate Law', in R. Kraakman et al., *supra* n. 1, at 29–30. The other main two principal–agent relationships are the relationship between the majority shareholder as agent and the minority shareholder as principal and the company as agent and the parties with whom the company contracts, such as creditors, employees and customers as principals.
6. On the separation of ownership and management as well as on the related agency problems *see* J. Armour, H. Hansmann & R. Kraakman, 'Agency Problems and Legal Strategies' in R. Kraakman et al., *supra* n. 1, 29 *et seq.*; dealing with the same issues with a focus on closed corporations, *see* G. Bacmann et al., *Regulating the Closed Corporation* (de Gruyter: Berlin, 2014), 83 *et seq.*

company's constitution or a reduction of capital.[7] As part of this division, shareholders combined in the general meeting retain the more crucial control rights, such as the right to - in principle - appoint and dismiss the directors.

6.06 A typical proponent of countries regulating corporate governance by mandatory statutory rules is Germany. The German Stock Corporation Act (*Aktiengesetz*) consists of numerous rules structuring the management system of a public company, including the strict separation of the board of directors and the supervisory board.[8] UK law is more flexible in the sense that it contains fewer mandatory provisions with regard to the division of powers and is supplemented with model articles which can be used by a company to design its own internal system. The corporate governance of a listed company will also be affected by listing rules and corporate governance codes. The latter are often used in addition to the division of powers as set out in mandatory law. Corporate governance codes often deal with a variety of issues, such as auditor independence, financial reporting and independence of non-executive directors. The provisions of the codes are generally not legally binding in a strict sense, but companies falling within the scope of the corporate governance code are expected to 'comply with the Code's provisions', and to 'give a considered explanation' when they deviate from the provisions.[9] This 'comply or explain approach', which the United Kingdom (UK) Corporate Governance Code pioneered, has subsequently been used by many other national corporate governance codes. In addition, there can also be codes applicable to shareholders of listed companies. The UK Corporate Governance Code has for example been complemented by the UK Stewardship Code, addressing the responsibilities of institutional investors.[10]

6.07 National laws provide different methods of regulating these management and control functions of companies. In part, the method chosen will depend on the size of the company and the number of parties participating in the cooperation. Rules applicable to public limited liability companies for example tend to be more prescriptive as this company type is traditionally meant for larger companies with many shareholders (*see* paragraph 2.42). Rules for private limited liability companies are by contrast often more flexible, allowing for deviations and tailor-made solutions to be adopted in the articles of association. The national rules often also depend on the political and socioeconomic policies of each country. For example, one relevant factor is different national perceptions as to who should be involved in the control process, particularly the question of employee participation in that process (*see* Chapter 7). The latter has made it difficult to harmonize the national rules on the division of powers within the European Union (EU). As already mentioned in earlier chapters, an all-encompassing harmonized system of the division of power at the EU level is not in

7. *See* paragraphs 3.20 *et seq.* and Chapter 5.
8. From a historical perspective, it is worth mentioning that German corporate law in the 19th century evolved from a flexible one-tier system to a mandatory two-tier system. *See* C. Teichmann, *Binnenmarktkonformes Gesellschaftsrecht* (De Gruyter: Berlin, 2006), 545 *et seq.*
9. This is the 'comply or explain' approach. *See* UK Corporate Governance Code, 5.
10. Also accessible at: www.frc.org.uk.

place, but there are several EU directives and regulations in the area of company law that do deal with certain aspects of corporate governance. In Chapter 3, we already referred to the Takeover Directive which for example sets out default rules for the role of the board of directors and the general meeting of listed companies in the case of a takeover (*see* paragraph 3.31 *et seq.*).[11] The Shareholder Rights Directive, as the name suggests, harmonizes to some extent the rights of shareholders and the functioning of the general meeting of listed companies.[12] The regulation on the SE also contains certain provisions concerning, for example, board structures and the role of the general meeting.[13] However, many issues such as rules on directors' liability and the specific decision-making rights of the general meeting are left to be regulated by the national law of the Member State where the SE has its registered office (*see* paragraph 4.13 *et seq.*).

6.08 Another interesting initiative is the European Model Company Act (EMCA).[14] As already mentioned in Chapter 3, the EMCA is an academic initiative, with no political authority, to establish a free-standing general company statute that can be enacted by Member States either in its entirety or by the adoption of selected provisions (*See* paragraph 3.18). It is – in essence and similar to the US Model Business Corporation Act and the United Nations Commission on International Trade Law (UNCITRAL) Model Law on arbitration – a tool for better regulation of company law. The EMCA provides a model for a fully texted company act.

IV THE BOARD OF DIRECTORS

A The Role of the Board

6.09 The most basic governance structure of a company consists of two corporate bodies: the general meeting and the board of directors. The general meeting is awarded certain powers among which is the power to appoint the board of directors. The board of directors is the central body of public and of private limited liability companies and is in charge of the day-to-day management and decision-making. The board of directors is generally responsible for the strategy of the company, the investments that have to be made, etc. The board's task also includes taking everyday business decisions such as investment decisions, decisions with regard to the financing of the company, etc. One important power of the board of directors that is relevant in order to manage the company on a daily basis is the power to represent the company, which is discussed later on in this chapter. Company laws are generally rather brief in describing the general tasks of the board.

11. Directive 2004/25/EC.
12. Directive 2007/36/EC.
13. Regulation 20157/2001.
14. Accessible at https://law.au.dk/en/research/projects/european-model-company-act-emca.

6.10 According to Dutch law, for example, the role of the board is to manage the company.[15] For listed companies, the law makes explicit that this includes setting the strategy and the policy of the company.[16] The UK Companies Act 2006 on the contrary does not set out the general role of the board. It instead leaves these issues to be dealt with in the company's articles of association.[17] The model articles[18] do state that 'the directors are responsible for the management of the company's business', and they may use all the powers of the company for that purpose.[19] The Companies Act does, however, contain several provisions on the duties of directors, which are discussed later on in this chapter (*see* paragraphs 6.32 *et seq*). Comparable to the Dutch approach, the German Stock Corporation Act states that the role of the board of directors is to manage the affairs of the company on its own responsibility.[20] The remainder of the board's powers and tasks depends on the way this is divided in national company law in conjunction with the articles of association of the company. The French Commercial Code stipulates for public companies that the board of directors decides on the company's strategy and monitors its implementation.[21] There are differences between company laws where it concerns the further division of powers between the board of directors and the general meeting. Some company laws are very prescriptive in this respect, whereas others leave it up to the company itself to decide in the articles of association. Some company laws, for example, place the residual power with the general meeting.[22] All powers which have then not specifically been assigned by law or the articles of association to another body belong in that case to the powers of the general meeting. When it comes to the division of powers, the general meeting and the board of directors often function as communicating vessels. In some jurisdictions, certain acts are reserved for the board which in other jurisdictions belong to the powers of the general meeting.

B Board Structures

6.11 As mentioned before, in the simplest corporate governance model, there is a board of directors and a general meeting, and the general meeting appoints and dismisses the board of directors. The board can consist of only executive directors, being those who manage the company on a daily basis. However, some jurisdictions mandate, depending on the size of the company or on whether it meets certain other

15. Article 2:129(1) Dutch Civil Code for public companies and Article 2:239(1) Dutch Civil Code for private companies.
16. Article 2:129(1) Dutch Civil Code.
17. I-M Esser & J. Loughrey, 'United Kingdom', in A. Vicari & A. Schall (eds), *Company Laws of the EU* (Munchen/Oxford/Baden-Baden: C.H. Beck, Hart, Nomos 2020), m. 157, 1504.
18. The UK Companies Act is accompanied by model articles providing for standard default rules that companies can use on which to model their internal structure.
19. Model Articles for Private Companies, section 3.
20. Section 76 German Stock Corporation Act.
21. Article L. 225-35 French Commercial Code.
22. This is for example the case in the Netherlands Articles 2:107 and 2:217 Dutch Civil Code.

requirements, that supervisors or monitoring members are added to the board.[23] This has traditionally led to two types of board structures: the dualistic or two-tier model where besides the board of directors and the general meeting a third body is added: the supervisory board and the one-tier system. In the one-tier system, rather than adding a new body, a division of tasks is made within the board of directors distinguishing two types of directors: executives and non-executives. In a two-tier system, it is generally the general meeting that appoints the supervisory board while the supervisory board in its turn appoints and dismisses the management board.[24] In a two-tier board, there is a more clear separation between the monitoring role and the management since these are placed in two separate bodies: a supervisory board and a board of directors which is generally called the management board (instead of the board of directors which term is generally used when referring to a one-tier system).[25] The management board is in charge of the day-to-day management of the company, while the supervisory board monitors the management board and provides the management board with advice. The supervisory board is also often given the power to approve certain board decisions.[26]

6.12 In essence the one-tier and the two-tier board each have their advantages and disadvantages. In a one-tier board, it is said that it is easier to communicate. All directors attend the same meetings and therefore should have the same information,[27] at least in theory. This is different in a two-tier board, where the supervisors are dependent on the information provided by the board of directors.[28] Another difference between the two types of board structure is said to be the independence of the supervisors. In theory, supervisory board members are perceived to be more independent from the board of directors in a two-tier system due to the fact that they sit on separate boards and therefore can operate more independently than non-executive directors who have their meetings together with the executive directors in a one-tier board.[29] Another potential advantage of the two-tier system is that the management and monitoring function of the two boards and their members are rigidly defined and separated, whereas, in the unitary board system, the distinction can become blurred.[30] The non-executive members of a one-tier board monitor the execution of strategic board decisions, which they themselves also have to account for as members of the

23. A. Vicari, *European Company Law* (Berlin/Boston: De Gruyter) 2021, 76 *et seq.*
24. *Ibid.*, 80 *et seq.*
25. In the remainder of this chapter, we also use the term management board when specifically referring to the board in a two-tier system and board of directors when we mean the board in a one-tier system. Where the distinction between the two structures is not relevant, we use the general term board of directors.
26. This is for example the case in the Netherlands according to Articles 2:164 and 2:274 Dutch Civil Code. *See also* in this respect A. Vicari, *supra* n. 23, at 80–81.
27. K.J. Hopt, 'Comparative Corporate Governance: The State of the Art and International Regulation' in A.M. Fleckner & K.J. Hopt, *Comparative Corporate Governance: A Functional and International Analysis* (Cambridge: Cambridge University Press, 2013), 31.
28. Regarding this problem in the Polish two-tier system *see* K. Samol, 'One- or Two-Tier Board System? A Comparative Analysis of the British and Polish Systems of Corporate Governance', *European Company Law* 13, no. 2 (2016): 67–78.
29. *Ibid.*
30. S.M. Bainbridge, 'The Board of Directors', in J.N. Gordon & W.G. Ringe (eds), *The Oxford Handbook of Corporate Law and Governance* (Oxford: Oxford University Press, 2018), 282 *et seq.*

unitary board. Instead, the supervisory board members in the two-tier system supervise acts and decisions that they themselves do not have to account for, because the management of the company, including the strategic part of it, is not the task of the supervisory body to which they belong.

6.13 Both board types have their own advantages and disadvantages.[31] In the past, there has been a lot of debate in the literature regarding the potential superiority of one of these two board structures. However, research shows that it was often difficult to establish that one structure functions better than the other, and there is no conclusive evidence in this respect.[32] The European Commission has therefore always endorsed freedom for companies to choose between either of the board structures.[33] The Commission already announced in 2012 that it had no intention of harmonizing these models.[34] So far the European harmonization directives do not prescribe a specific board structure. One of the few places where board structures are mentioned is in the *Societas Europaea* (SE) Regulation. The SE Regulation allows SEs to choose between a one-tier or a two-tier board structure.[35] The board structures in the SE are further discussed in section 4.27 *et seq.*

6.14 The one-tier board traditionally comes from the Anglo-American legal systems such as in the US and the UK, whereas the two-tier board structure is a traditional feature of the German legal tradition such as in Germany, Austria and, even though it does not fit in the German tradition, the Netherlands.[36] Whether it is due to the introduction of the SE or other corporate governance developments, several countries have made their national laws more flexible with regard to board structures. Nowadays, several countries which traditionally only had a one-tier or a two-tier board structure, also allow companies incorporated under their national law to choose between either of these board structures. Both France and the Netherlands are examples of this. The prevalent board structure in the EU Member States is the one-tier model, either as mandatory or as an alternative to the two-tier model.[37]

6.15 There are also jurisdictions that allow for a hybrid board structure, which is a board structure that takes a middle path between the one-tier and the two-tier board or that has specific features from either model. The traditional Scandinavian model is an example of this. It has two boards: a board of directors and an executive board which

31. C. Gerner-Beuerle & M. Schillig, *Comparative Company Law* (Oxford: Oxford University Press, 2019), 306.
32. A. Vicari, *supra* n. 23, at 73. *See*, for example, the *Report of the High Level Group of Company Law Experts on a Modern Regulatory Framework for Company Law in Europe*; C. Jungman, 'The Effectiveness of Corporate Governance in One-Tier and Two-Tier Board Systems', *ECFR* 3 (2006): 426–474; K.J. Hopt, *supra* n. 27, at 31; K. Samol, *supra* n. 28; C. Gerner-Beuerle & M. Schillig, *supra* n. 31.
33. European Commission, Modernising Company Law and Enhancing Corporate Governance in the European Union – A Plan to Move Forward Action Plan, COM (2003) 284 final, 15.
34. Action Plan: European Company Law and Corporate Governance – a Modern Legal Framework for more Engaged Shareholders and Sustainable Companies, COM(2012) 740 final, 5.
35. Article 38 (2) SE Regulation.
36. C. Gerner-Beuerle & M. Schillig, *supra* n. 31, at 303.
37. S.M. Bainbridge, *supra* n. 30, at 285; A. Vicari, *supra* n. 23, at 76; K.J. Hopt, *supra* n. 27, at 30.

both feature executive and non-executive directors. The executive board does the day-to-day management of the company, and the board of directors is responsible for setting out the overall strategy and monitoring the executive board.[38]

6.16 French private companies (*societé a responsibilité limité, SARL*) have one or more directors who are appointed by the general meeting.[39] Public companies (*sociétés anonymes, SA*) may adopt a one-tier or a two-tier board. In the case of a unitary board structure, the company is managed by a single board of directors (*conseil d'administration*). The *conseil d'administration* determines the orientation of the company's activities and supervises their implementation. It is therefore the supreme management body of the company. In a two-tier board system, there is a management board (*directoire*) and a supervisory board (*conseil de surveillance*). The management function of a company with a one-tier board is, in practice, carried out by the chairman and executive officers, while the other members of the board exercise a monitoring function with only a theoretical right to manage. In a two-tier system, the management board manages the company, whereas the supervisory board monitors the management board. Later reforms of the one-tier board structure called for the separation of the functions of the chairman of the board and the chief executive manager, introducing the position of a chief executive (*directeur général*).[40] This separation is not mandatory, but the board of directors may decide that the chairman cannot at the same time be the general manager of the company.[41] By introducing this separation, the one-tier board moves in the direction of a two-tier system. The role of the separated chairman is to organize the work of the board, which entails convening and chairing the meetings, setting the agenda, etc.[42] The two-tier system must be opted for in the company's articles of association.[43] The company is in that case managed by a management board (*directoire*),[44] which exercises its functions under the control of a supervisory board (*conseil de surveillance*).[45] In companies employing a total of more than 1,000 employees, including those working for subsidiaries with their statutory seat in France, or in companies with foreign subsidiaries, if they employ a total of more than 5,000 employees, employees will have at least one representative on the board (*see* paragraphs 7.42 *et seq.*).

6.17 In a German private limited liability company, a *Geselschaft mit beschräkter Haftung* or GmbH, there are usually only two corporate bodies: the management board and the general meeting. However, any GmbH may choose to also establish a supervisory board to carry out many of the control functions of the general meeting. A

38. C. Gerner-Beuerle & M. Schillig, *supra* n. 31, at 305.
39. Article L. 223-18 French Commercial Code.
40. *Loi sur les Nouvelles Régulations Économiques* n° 2001–420 of 15 May 2001 (NRE).
41. Article L225-51 French Commercial Code. I. Grossi, D. Poracchia & A. Raynouard, 'France', in A. Vicari & A. Schall (eds), *supra* n. 17, at 52 m. 231.
42. I. Grossi, D. Poracchia & A. Raynouard, 'France', in A. Vicari & A. Schall (eds), *supra* n. 17, at 53 m. 232–233.
43. Article L225-57 French Commercial Code.
44. Article L225-58 French Commercial Code.
45. Article L225-68 French Commercial Code.

supervisory board is compulsory if the company has more than 500 employees.[46] This requirement is imposed because of German law's concept of employee participation, which involves the employees, through membership of the supervisory board, in the management structure of companies (and other business organizations) employing more than 500 employees. The concept of employee participation is discussed in paragraph 7.41. Where a GmbH chooses to (voluntarily) have a supervisory board but is not required by law to do so (i.e., it employs fewer than 500 employees), most of the powers of that board, its membership and its relationship with the general meeting are left to the discretion of the company. The German Limited Liability Companies Act does refer to the comparable provisions for an AG unless the articles stipulate otherwise.[47] Where the supervisory board is compulsory due to the regulation of employee participation, the rules applicable to an AG will also apply to the GmbH on a mandatory basis.

The German Stock Corporation Act, applicable to public limited liability companies (*Aktiengesellschaft* or AG), requires all AGs to have a management board, a supervisory board and a general meeting. In general, it is the management board's function to manage, the supervisory board's function to monitor the management board (but not to instruct it on management issues), and the general meetings' function to appoint members of the supervisory board and to approve certain basic transactions, such as amendments of the articles of association and capital changes. Employee participation on the supervisory board is compulsory if the company employs more than 500 employees.[48]

6.18 The Dutch public company (*naamloze vennootschap* (NV)) and private company (*besloten vennootschap* (BV)) are governed mainly by identical statutory provisions regarding their management structure. There are three possible governance regimes applicable: the first consisting of a management board only, the second being a one-tier or two-tier regime on a voluntary basis and the third is the compulsory one-tier or two-tier regime. The first two regimes have a traditional division of powers between management and the shareholders acting in the general meeting, whereas the compulsory regime implies a shift of powers from the general meeting to the supervisory board.

The compulsory one-tier or two-tier regime, commonly called the structure regime or large company regime (*structuurregime),* was introduced in the early 1970s as one of several innovations in Dutch company law. As with the German AG, the structure regime mandates employee participation for the Dutch NV and BV. In the Netherlands, supervisory board members, or non-executive directors in the case of a company that opts for a one-tier system, are compulsory where the company qualifies as a large company. This is the case when a company employs, on a regular basis, at least 100 employees. It is then legally obliged to establish a works council. Another

---

46. Section 1 *Drittelbeteiligungsgesetz.*
47. Section 52 German Limited Liability Companies Act (*GmbH Gesetz*).
48. *See Drittelbeteiligungsgesetz.*

requirement for the structure regime to be applicable is that according to the company's balance sheet, the share capital and reserves together amount to a certain minimum, as determined by royal decree (currently EUR 16 million).[49] It should be noted that individuals employed by subsidiaries and a works council established by a subsidiary must be taken into account when assessing whether or not these criteria are met. The initial obligation is to disclose, via the Commercial Registry, that the criteria mentioned above apply to the company. After a three-year run-in period, such a company must establish a supervisory board or appoint non-executive directors. This kind of compulsory two-tier or one-tier structure is not only subject to the general rules pointed out above but also governed by special rules with regard to the appointment and removal of its members, as well as to its powers. When the structure regime is applicable, the members of the supervisory board are appointed by the general meeting of shareholders, although the procedure considerably reduces the actual influence of the shareholders on the composition of the board.[50] The general meeting receives proposals from the supervisory board as to the individuals to be appointed, and it may only reject such proposal by a majority vote, representing one-third or more of the company's capital. If the general meeting neither appoints the proposed candidates nor expressly rejects them, the supervisory board itself may appoint the proposed members. The procedure includes rules for the supervisory board on how to carry out a proposal for the nomination of its members. The supervisory board must allow both the general meeting and the works council to put forward their candidates. For one-third of its members, the supervisory board must follow the proposal of the works council, unless the supervisory board objects to the candidate(s) on the grounds specified in the statute.[51] This reflects the Dutch system of employee participation which is further discussed in paragraphs 7.41 *et seq*. The position of the general meeting is further weakened by restrictive rules for the dismissal of supervisory board members (or non-executive directors). An individual member of the supervisory board can only be removed by the Enterprise Chamber and only on limited grounds, *inter alia*, for dereliction of his or her duties.[52] By a majority vote representing one-third or more of the company's capital, the general meeting can pass a motion of no confidence that results in the immediate removal of all members of the supervisory board. The management board must then request the Enterprise Chamber of the Amsterdam Court of Appeal to temporarily appoint one or more supervisory board members.[53]

The structure regime confers extended powers to the supervisory board. Apart from the basic tasks and powers of the usual supervisory board, it also has the right to appoint and dismiss the directors of the company. Moreover, several important resolutions of the management board must be approved by the supervisory board, for

49. Articles 2:153 and 2:263 Dutch Civil Code.
50. *See* Articles 2:158 and 2:268 Dutch Civil Code.
51. Articles 2:158 and 2:268 Dutch Civil Code.
52. Articles 2:161 and 2:271 Dutch Civil Code.
53. Articles 2:161a and 2:271a Dutch Civil Code.

example, resolutions concerning issuing shares and bonds or entering into a lasting cooperation with another legal person.[54]

C Types of Directors, Composition and Representation

1 Types of Directors

6.19 The different board structures lead to a distinction between the different types of directors. In a one-tier board, there are two different types of directors in the sense that they each have a different function as the board can consist of executive and non-executive directors. In a two-tier board, all directors in principle have the same function. Nevertheless, a division of tasks can of course still be made. A first distinction that can therefore be made is the distinction between the executive directors and the non-executive directors (and supervisory board members). The non-executive directors in a one-tier board can, to a certain extent and of course taking the allocation of powers in a specific jurisdiction into account, be equated to the supervisory directors in a two-tier board. The executive directors are often in the corporate law literature referred to as inside directors since they generally have an employment or a service contract with the company. Non-executive directors are in some of the literature referred to as outside directors, since they do not have a full-time job with the company.[55] They often take a position that is more remote from the company. The non-executive directors and supervisory board members can have several of these functions at different companies. Even though they meet regularly with the other directors, they are not present on a full-time basis at the company. They can be a representative of a specific (large) shareholder, or in some countries, they are appointed by the employees (*see* paragraph 6.18).

6.20 A further distinction that can be made is between the dependent and independent (supervisory) board members. National laws and/or corporate governance codes often set requirements of independence, requiring a certain number of the non-executive directors in a one-tier structure or supervisory board members in a two-tier structure to be independent. These requirements are often only applicable to listed companies. One of the reasons behind requirements of independence is that they are seen as a tool to reduce agency costs caused by the separation of ownership and control.[56] The goal is to remove a potential conflict of interest *ex ante* to ensure that the agent does not achieve a personal gain from disadvantaging its principal.[57] The idea is that independent directors do not profit from actions that are to the advantage of the controlling shareholder or the managers of the company.[58] They may therefore also serve to

54. Articles 2:164 and 2:274 Dutch Civil Code.
55. This term is often used in the US literature. *See* S.M. Bainbridge, *supra* n. 30, at 275–333.
56. *Ibid.*, 318.
57. J. Armour, H. Hansmann & R. Kraakman, 'Agency Problems and Legal Strategies', in R. Kraakman et al., *supra* n. 1, at 35.
58. *Ibid.*, 35.

protect other stakeholders, not only minority shareholders.[59] As independent directors generally come from outside the company, they may also bring in additional external knowledge and expertise.[60]

6.21 There is no harmonization with regard to board composition requirements at the EU level. However, the Commission did issue a recommendation in 2005 dealing with the role of non-executive directors and supervisory board members of listed companies.[61] This recommendation urged the Member States to set several requirements with regard to the appointment and functioning of non-executive directors and supervisory board members on a comply or explain basis. These types of rules are nowadays incorporated in corporate law and/or national corporate governance codes. The idea behind the recommendation was that non-executive directors/supervisory board members play an important oversight role in providing for the necessary checks and balances in the company. Part of the goal of the recommendation was to ensure that there is a sufficient number of independent non-executive directors or supervisory board members. According to the Commission:[62]

> The presence of independent representatives on the board, capable of challenging the decisions of management, is widely considered as a means of protecting the interests of shareholders and other stakeholders. In companies with a dispersed ownership, the primary concern is how to make managers accountable to weak shareholders. In companies with controlling shareholders, the focus is more on how to make sure that the company will be run in a way that sufficiently takes into account the interests of minority shareholders.

Independence in the Recommendation is defined as:[63]

> (...) free of any business, family or other relationship, with the company, its controlling shareholder or the management of either, that creates a conflict of interest such as to impair his judgement.

Requirements for independence are often further specified in national corporate governance codes. There are different descriptions of what constitutes independence. The Dutch Corporate Governance Code for example provides in Best Practice 2.1.8 a negative list of situations in which a person cannot be regarded as independent. This is the case if a supervisory board member:
(...) or their spouse, registered partner or life companion, foster child or relative by blood or marriage up to the second degree:

(i) has been an employee or member of the management board of the company (...) in the five years prior to the appointment;

59. L. Enriques, H. Hansmann, R. Kraakman & M. Pargendler, 'The Basic Governance Structure: Minority Shareholders and Non-Shareholder Constituencies', in R. Kraakman et al., *supra* n. 1, at 99–100.
60. S.M. Bainbridge, *supra* n. 30, at 315.
61. Recommendation 2005/162/EC.
62. Preamble recital 7 of Recommendation 2005/162/EC.
63. Provision 13.1 of Recommendation 2005/162/EC.

(ii) receives personal financial compensation from the company, or a company associated with it, other than the compensation received for the work performed as a supervisory board member and in so far as this is not in keeping with the normal course of business;
(iii) has had an important business relationship with the company or a company associated with it in the year prior to the appointment. (...);
(iv) is a member of the management board of a company in which a member of the management board of the company which he supervises is a supervisory board member;
(v) has temporarily performed management duties during the previous twelve months in the absence or incapacity of management board members;
(vi) has a shareholding in the company of at least ten percent, taking into account the shareholding of natural persons or legal entities cooperating with him or her on the basis of an express or tacit, verbal or written agreement;
(vii) is a member of the management board or supervisory board - or is a representative in some other way - of a legal entity which holds at least ten percent of the shares in the company, unless the entity is a group company.[64]

Independence in this context relates to not having been employed by the company previously or not having had business relations with the company, but also to the compensation the independent directors or supervisory board member receives. It furthermore concerns things like cross-directorships, being a representative of a 10% or more shareholder or being a 10% or more shareholder in the company itself.

The UK Corporate Governance Code also provides a list of circumstances that are likely to impair independence. These include being an employee of the company for the past five years, having had a material business and having received additional remuneration from the company. Holding cross-directorships in other companies is also mentioned as well as representing a significant shareholder.[65] If one of these circumstances is applicable, then the person is not directly disqualified for the position of independent director. The board may, nevertheless, consider the non-executive director to be independent. However, a clear explanation needs to be provided as to why this is the case.

6.22 The required number of independent directors also differs between jurisdictions. The Commission's recommendation merely requires that there should be a sufficient number of independent directors to ensure that any material conflict of interest involving directors can be dealt with.[66] According to the Dutch Corporate Governance

64. This is also applicable to one-tier boards according to Best Practice 5.1.1 of the Dutch Corporate Governance Code 2016.
65. Provision 2.11 of the UK Corporate Governance Code 2018.
66. Provision 4 of Recommendation 2005/162/EC.

Code, more than half of the supervisory board members/non-executive directors should be independent.[67] In the UK, at least half of the board should be independent.[68]

6.23 Independent directors also play an important role on board committees. In listed companies, the board in the case of a one-tier structure or the supervisory board in a two-tier structure is generally required to have several committees that prepare certain specific decisions. The most common committees are: the audit committee, the nomination committee and the remuneration committee. Corporate governance codes require these committees to be composed of a certain number or even entirely of independent (non-executive) directors as the topics of these committees require independent supervision.[69]

6.24 A last distinction that can be made is between de facto and de jure directors or shadow directors. De jure directors are directors that have been appointed as such by the shareholders or the supervisory board. The latter are the directors discussed in this chapter. De facto directors are a different category. This is a term that is used for someone who presents himself or herself as a director but is not appointed as such due to the fact that there is, for example, an invalidity in the appointment.[70] In addition, the UK distinguishes another type of director: a shadow director. This is a person who has not been appointed as a director and does not present itself as a director but does steer the direction of the company by giving directions based on which the directors are accustomed to acting and taking away any type of judgement from the directors.[71] The UK Companies Act defines a shadow director as: '(...) a person in accordance with whose directions or instructions the directors of the company are accustomed to act.'[72] In other jurisdictions, such as the Netherlands, no distinction is made between *de facto* and shadow directors and these terms are used interchangeably. In the Netherlands, the terms are used to refer to a person who is not appointed as a director but either steers the other directors or acts as if he were a director. These directors can be held liable in the same way as *de jure* directors when the company or third parties are disadvantaged by their actions. Therefore, this topic will mainly surface in most manuals or textbooks when the liability of directors is discussed.

2 *Composition*

6.25 As mentioned before, there are no harmonized EU rules on board composition. Having independent directors may be a national requirement. National law may set a

67. Best Practice 2.1.7.
68. Provision 2.11 of the UK Corporate Governance Code 2018.
69. The Dutch Corporate Governance Code 2016 in Best Practice 2.3.4 requires more than half of the members of these committees to be independent. The UK Corporate Governance Code requires all non-executives on these committees to be independent. *See*, for example, with regard to the audit committee, Provision 24 of the UK Corporate Governance Code 2018.
70. C. Gerner-Beuerle & M. Schillig, *supra* n. 31, at 288.
71. *Ibid.*, 288–289.
72. Section 215(1) UK Companies Act 2006.

minimum requirement with regard to the amount of directors on the (supervisory) board. In the most simple company form generally no requirements of this nature are set. However, depending on the jurisdiction, minimum requirements may be set for certain types of companies. In French public companies for example the board of directors has to be composed of a minimum of three members and a maximum of eighteen.[73] Requirements regarding the number of board and supervisory board members may also be applicable in systems with employee co-determination as further discussed in paragraph 7.41 *et seq.*

6.26 In addition, there may also be diversity requirements in national law and/or corporate governance codes. In France, for example, the board of large companies listed on a regulated market must consist of at least 40% male and 40% female members.[74] The rules for non-listed public companies are less strict. These companies are required to only seek a balanced representation of men and women on the board without the law imposing strict requirements on what this entails.[75] Dutch law has a comparable system. For listed companies, the requirement is that one-third of the supervisory board members/non-executive directors is male and one-third female. If this is not reached, a new appointment that would not lead to a better division cannot take place.[76] Companies that qualify as large private and public companies but whose shares are not listed are submitted to different rules. They have to set their own ambitious goals for an even division.[77] Also here the law does not prescribe what this entails.

6.27 In 2012, the Commission launched a proposal for a directive on balance of gender among non-executive directors in listed companies. Even though it was adopted by the European Parliament by a large majority, it was difficult for a while to find a consensus among the Member States.[78] After several years of discussions, an agreement was finally reached between the Member States in the Council in March 2022 on a general approach for a directive aimed at strengthening gender equality on corporate boards.[79] The earlier proposal for the directive was amended in order to achieve the agreement and to move forward. The proposed directive now sets a minimum target for companies of 40% of non-executive director positions of listed companies to be filled by

73. Article L. 225-53 French Commercial Code.
74. Article L225-18-1 French Commercial Code. This applies to listed companies employing at least 500 employees and having an annual turnover or a balance sheet total of at least EUR 50 million.
75. Article L225-17 French Commercial Code.
76. Article 2:142(b) Dutch Civil Code; Article 2:187 Dutch Civil Code applies this rule also to non-executive directors in the case of a one-tier board.
77. Articles 2:166 and 2:276 Dutch Civil Code.
78. *See* for this information and an overview of the actions taken on this topic https://www.europarl.europa.eu/legislative-train/theme-area-of-justice-and-fundamental-rights/file-gender-balance-on-boards.
79. Brussels, 4 March 2022, 6468/22. A recent study commissioned by the European Parliament for example recommends the adoption of the proposed directive. *See* A. Kirsch, *Women on Board Policies in Member States and the Effects on Corporate Governance* 7 Dec. 2021 https://www.europarl.europa.eu/thinktank/en/document/IPOL_STU(2021)700556.

members of the under-represented sex, or 33% if all board members are included by 2027.

3 *Representation*

6.28 An important power awarded to the board of directors is the power to represent the company. This power of representation is in all jurisdictions discussed within the ambit of the power vested with the board of directors.[80] The point of departure is often that the power of representation is vested with the board as a whole. If the board consists of several individuals, this means that the power to represent is in the hands of the directors acting jointly. It is, however, generally possible to delegate this power in the articles of association to one or more board members acting on their own or together with one or more other board members. Section 78 of the German Stock Corporation Act, for example, stipulates the following:[81]

> (2) Where the management board consists of several persons, any and all members of the management board shall have authority to represent the company only jointly, unless the by-laws stipulate otherwise.
> (3) The by-laws may also stipulate that individual members of the management board shall have authority to represent the company alone or jointly with an officer of the company vested with full commercial power of attorney (*Prokurist*). The supervisory board may make the same stipulation provided the by-laws have granted it authority to do so. In these cases, subsection (2), second sentence, shall apply mutatis mutandis.
> (4) (...).

The abovementioned German example illustrates some of the choices that can be made with regard to distributing the power to represent. As mentioned above, the default rule here is that the board of directors jointly represents the company, and this power cannot be restricted.[82] Second, the power to represent can also be awarded on the basis of the articles of association to one or more directors acting solely or to one or more directors acting jointly or acting with a person who is not a director but is granted the power of attorney. Some jurisdictions allow the power to represent to also be awarded to representatives who are not a director of the company. Often this is done by means of giving a power of attorney.[83] The latter is often based on general rules of agency law. These rules entail that a principal, in this case, the company, delegates the power of attorney to an agent who is then given the power to enter into a certain transaction on the principal's behalf.[84]

80. *See* for the UK section 40 1, 44 2-3 CA 2006 and Germany section 78 (1) German Stock Corporation Act.
81. This translation comes from the German Federal Ministry of Justice retrieved from: https://www.gesetze-im-internet.de/englisch_aktg/
82. Section 82 (1) German Stock Corporation Act.
83. This is generally based not on company law but on general rules regarding agency law.
84. *See* further A. Cahn & D.C. Donald, *Comparative Company Law* (Oxford: Oxford University Press 2018), 371.

6.29 The system of representation described above can also be found, with minor deviations, in several other EU Member States. Dutch company law, for example, includes a provision that is comparable to the German provision mentioned above for private and public limited liability companies with a few differences.[85] The law empowers the board of directors to jointly represent. In addition, it also by default allows each director individually to represent the company. However, the latter can be restricted in the articles of association in the sense that these can stipulate that instead of having representational power individually, one or more directors can only represent the company jointly. The articles of association can also restrict it by stipulating that besides the board only one or a few specific directors can represent individually.[86] The supervisory board in principle does not represent the company.

In the UK, the directors jointly are authorized to bind the company towards third parties and to authorize others to do so. The individual directors may be authorized to do so if this is provided for in the articles of association.[87] A document is validly executed by the company when it is signed on behalf of the company by a director in the presence of a witness who attests to the signature or by two directors.[88] The company's secretary is also given the power of attorney when acting together with a director. Every public company has to have a secretary,[89] while private companies can have a secretary. This role given to the secretary is comparable to the *Prokurist* described above under German law.

In France, in a public company with a one-tier board structure, the board of directors jointly represents the company. The general manager can also represent the company.[90] In a two-tier board system, the management board represents the company; this can also be done by the sole manager or the chairman.[91] The supervisory board can also grant the power to represent other board members if this is provided for in the articles of association.[92] In a private company, the power to represent lies with the general manager.[93]

6.30 The extent to which the board or individual directors can be restricted in their power to represent is rather strict for limited liability companies incorporated in the EU Member States. This has to do with the fact that the system originates from the first

85. The law for private limited liability companies contained in section 35 of the German Limited Liability Companies Act a comparable provision on the basis of which in principle the entire board represents the company unless stipulated otherwise.
86. Articles 2:130 and 2:240 Dutch Civil Code.
87. Section 40 UK Companies Act 2006; *See* C. Gerner-Beuerle & M. Schillig, *supra* n. 31, at 202; P. Davies, S. Worthington & C. Hare, *Gower: Principles of Modern Company Law* (Sweet & Maxwell 2021), 10-003.
88. Section 44 UK Companies Act 2006.
89. Section 271 UK Companies Act 2006.
90. Article L. 225–56 French Commercial Code; *See* C. Gerner-Beuerle & M. Schillig, *supra* n. 31, at 208.
91. Article L. 225–66 French Commercial Code.
92. Article L. 225–55 French Commercial Code. *See* I. Grossi, D. Poracchia & A. Raynouard, 'France', in A. Vicari & A. Schall (eds), *supra* n. 17, at 58, 260; C. Gerner-Beuerle & M. Schillig, *supra* n. 31, at 208–209.
93. Article L. 223-18 French Commercial Code. B. Francois, 'France', in A. Vicari & A. Schall (eds), *supra* n. 17, at 134, m. 669.

company law directive, now incorporated in Article 9 of Directive (EU) 2017/1132, which stipulates that:

> Acts of the organs of a company and its representation
>
> 1. Acts done by the organs of the company shall be binding upon it even if those acts are not within the objects of the company, unless such acts exceed the powers that the law confers or allows to be conferred on those organs. However, Member States may provide that the company shall not be bound where such acts are outside the objects of the company, if it proves that the third party knew that the act was outside those objects or could not in view of the circumstances have been unaware of it. Disclosure of the statutes shall not of itself be sufficient proof thereof.
> 2. The limits on the powers of the organs of the company, arising under the statutes or from a decision of the competent organs, may not be relied on as against third parties, even if they have been disclosed.
> 3. If national law provides that authority to represent a company may, in derogation from the legal rules governing the subject, be conferred by the statutes on a single person or on several persons acting jointly, that law may provide that such a provision in the statutes may be relied on as against third parties on condition that it relates to the general power of representation; the question whether such a provision in the statutes can be relied on as against third parties shall be governed by Article 16.

The underlying idea of this provision is that third parties should be protected. In order to achieve this, the directive puts provisions in place that restrict the grounds on which obligations entered into in the name of the company are not valid.[94] The first section of Article 9 therefore provides that acts done by the corporate bodies of the company are binding. The directive leaves it up to the Member States to decide what the value of the objects of the company is in this respect. The object of a company is generally stated in the articles of association or constitutional documents and describes the company's goal and/or activities. Member States may provide that companies are not bound if acts are outside the objects of the company and the third party was aware of this. However, as the object clause also restricts the possibilities for companies to diversify their activities and investments, object clauses tend to be formulated broadly.[95] Therefore, even if a Member State were to apply this clause, in reality, it would not really provide the company with the possibility to avoid a transaction with third parties. As a consequence, several countries do not regard the objects of the company as a means to limit the power to represent. This is the case for example in Germany and in the UK.[96]

Article 9 furthermore confers a general power to represent on the board and restricts the limitations that can be imposed on this power to represent. The default rule is that the power of the board to represent the company cannot be restricted, for example, by a decision of the board or in the articles of association. Therefore, even if

94. Recital 5 of the preamble of Directive (EU) 2017/1132.
95. A. Cahn & D.C. Donald, *supra* n. 84, at 367.
96. *See* in this respect A. Cahn & D.C. Donald, *supra* n. 84, at 368 who refer to section 39(1) of the UK Companies Act 2006 and section 82 (1) of the German Stock Corporation Act. *See also* about Germany, A. Schall, 'Germany', in A. Vicari & A. Schall (eds), *supra* n. 17, at 269, m. 234.

the power would be limited in such a way and the board were to disregard this limitation, the acts would still be binding on the company and the restrictions could not be used against third parties.[97] The limitations can, however, have internal consequences, for example, in the sense that it can lead to the liability of the directors towards the company. The only restriction that the directive allows can be found in section 3 of Article 9 of the directive, namely that the articles of association provide that the power to represent is conferred on a single person or several persons acting jointly. This restriction can be relied on against third parties. However, it will have to be disclosed. As long as this restriction is not duly disclosed, a third party may rely on the representation by a single board member unless the company proves that the third party had knowledge of the restriction (*see* Article 16(5)). Moreover, the power of a single director or two directors jointly to represent the company should be unrestricted and unconditional. This means that they are awarded the full power of representation. The only possible restriction is a restriction provided for by legal provisions.[98] The UK, for example, protects third parties against restrictions imposed on the power of the board of directors. Section 40 of the UK Companies Act 2006 stipulates that: '(...)the power of the directors to bind the company, or authorise others to do so, is deemed to be free of any limitation under the company's constitution.' Comparable provisions can be found in other jurisdictions.

6.31 There are also exceptions to the general rule of unrestricted representation by the board. These exceptions are generally based on general civil law concepts such as abuse of authority. When the agent, in this case, the director, and the third party intentionally collude to the detriment of the principal (the company in this case) the acts will not be binding on the company. This will be the case where the third party knew or ought to have known that the director was overstepping his or her authority and the third party was acting in bad faith.[99]

D The Duties of the Board of Directors

1 Rules and Standards

6.32 Once the board of directors or supervisory board is installed, company law provides further safeguards regulating their conduct while in office. They have to abide by certain rules and live up to certain expectations. Not performing their duties in a way that is expected may result in liability of directors and supervisors.

Directors have to be able to take business decisions without knowing the outcome of such decisions. On some occasions, a new investment might turn into a

97. *See* in this respect more specifically about the interpretation of this rule in Germany, A. Schall, 'Germany', in A. Vicari & A. Schall (eds), *supra* n. 17, at 271, m. 239–240.
98. P. van Schilfgaarde, J.W. Winter, J.B. Wezeman & J.D.M. Schoonbrood, *Van de BV en de NV* (Deventer: Wolters Kluwer 2017), 52.
99. *See* about Germany, A. Schall, 'Germany', in A. Vicari & A. Schall (eds), *supra* n. 17, at 270, m. 236.

golden opportunity, while in other situations it may turn out to be less beneficial than estimated and lead to losses for the company. On the other hand, directors do operate with other people's money as the capital has been invested by the shareholders.[100] Their actions may also have a large impact on the interests of stakeholders who are affected by the operations of the company. Therefore, checks and balances have to be put in place in order to make sure that the members of the board do not misappropriate these funds or use them for their own benefit instead of the benefit of the company, shareholders and perhaps to the detriment of other stakeholders.[101] Which of these interests they have to serve, those of the company, the shareholders or the stakeholders, depends on national law as is explained in paragraphs 6.36–6.37.

6.33 Comparative law handbooks often distinguish between two potential ways of regulating directors' conduct: either by standards or by rules or by a combination of both.[102] The following description is based on this distinction made by Cahn and Donald. As they explain, rules are generally more prescriptive *ex ante* whereas standards are generally judged *ex post*.[103] Standards are generally less prescriptive than rules. Standards are open-ended norms requiring directors to behave in a certain way. They can, for example, require a director to behave as can be expected of a reasonable businessperson. Standards are generally used when the undesired conduct is difficult to predict and prescribe the way in which directors are expected to discharge their duties and arrive at a business decision.[104] They not only allow boards of directors some leeway and flexibility in their decision making but also require directors to make an informed decision and act diligently. Standards therefore allow for managerial discretion. The law is not able to predict every type of wrongful behaviour that a director might display in the future. Standards therefore allow courts to penalize different forms of misconduct or breach of duties that may occur.[105] From the perspective of directors, the downside of making use of standards to regulate directors' conduct is that it can lead to legal risks. A situation will always require interpretation by the courts, and there are no safe harbours in that respect.[106]

6.34 As Cahn and Donald explain: rules, conversely, prescribe a certain conduct that is expected or which a director should abstain from. They are used in more predictable

100. Directors are often referred to as 'fiduciaries' which means that they have fiduciary duties. The term originates from common law jurisdictions and is therefore something which one mainly finds in the UK and the US. A fiduciary duty emerges when 'one party (the 'fiduciary') acts on behalf of another party (the 'beneficiary') while exercising discretion with respect to a critical resource belonging to the beneficiary.' *See* D.G. Smith, 'The Critical Resource Theory of Fiduciary Duty', *Vanderbilt Law Review* 2002/55:1402 as referred to by A. Cahn & D.C. Donald, *supra* n. 84, at 395. About the background *see* C. Gerner-Beuerle & M. Schillig, *supra* n. 31, at 466–467.
101. *Ibid.*, 465–466; P. Davies, S. Worthington & C. Hare, *supra* n. 87, at 10-001.
102. A. Cahn & D.C. Donald, *supra* n. 84, at 394.
103. *Ibid.*, 393–394.
104. *Ibid.*, 394–395 and C. Gerner-Beuerle & M. Schillig, *supra* n. 31, at 466.
105. *See* about these differences and the way in which they are used A. Cahn & D.C. Donald, *supra* n. 84, at 350 and 393–395.
106. *Ibid.*, 393.

situations when the probability of a breach is high.[107] The downside is that, because the rules are so prescriptive, they can be easily circumvented. An example of rules that can be found in many jurisdictions is that when directors enter into a contractual relationship with the company, the transaction requires the approval of the general meeting or the non-conflicted directors on the board. The rule creates a more clear-cut description of what should be done in order to avoid wrongful behaviour.[108] However, rules can also easily be circumvented when they are only tailored for one specific situation.[109] Rules can also be used next to standards.[110] For example, there can be a general standard requiring directors to act in the best interest of the company, which can be reinforced by a rule as mentioned above that requires transactions between the company and the director to be approved by the general meeting, the supervisory board or the non-conflicted members of the board of directors.

6.35 Jurisdictions differ in how they set standards and rules for directors. Some jurisdictions, for example, use one or two broad standards while other jurisdictions formulate several more specific duties. There are also differences in how the expected standard of conduct is formulated, as is demonstrated in the following paragraphs.[111]

2 *Serving the Company's Interest*

6.36 A first question when discussing directors' duties and potential liability is: to who do directors owe their duties or in whose interest are they required to act?[112] Directors of UK companies must act in accordance with the company's constitution and only exercise powers for the purposes for which they are conferred.[113] Section 170(1) of the Companies Act 2006 mentions explicitly that the directors owe their duties to the company. This is a provision that can be found in many company laws either explicitly in the law itself or established in case law. What the interest of the company entails is, however, rarely codified and depends on the interpretation in the specific country.[114] The discussion on the shareholder versus stakeholder model generally influences this interpretation. In a shareholder-oriented model serving the interest of the company will generally mean mainly serving the interest of the shareholders, whereas in a stakeholder model the interest of the company can be regarded as a more holistic view of the company's interest or a combination of the interest of all stakeholders involved.[115] In the UK traditionally, the company, in this context, was taken to mean the shareholders. However, the Companies Act now stipulates in section 172 that directors must also have regard for the interests of other stakeholders listed in that provision, such as the

107. *Ibid.*, 394.
108. *Ibid.*
109. *Ibid.*
110. *Ibid.*, 393-394.
111. C. Gerner-Beuerle & M. Schillig, *supra* n. 31, at 466.
112. *Ibid.*; A. Cahn & D.C. Donald, *supra* n. 84, at 363 *et seq.*
113. Section 171 UK Companies Act 2006.
114. A. Vicari, *supra* n. 23, at 217.
115. *Ibid.*

employees, customers and the environment.[116] This formula is also known as the 'enlightened shareholder value' approach.[117] Unlike some other systems, such as the Netherlands, this provision does not require the directors to balance all interests involved in the company. It instead expresses that the interests of the shareholders prevail, however, the interests of the stakeholders have to be taken into account when determining how to promote the success of the company for the benefit of its shareholders.[118] The fact that the duties are owed to the company entails that they are not owed to specific persons or stakeholders, such as individual shareholders.[119]

6.37 In Germany, directors owe their duty directly to the company.[120] This duty is interpreted as serving the interest of the company as a whole including the stakeholders, not exclusively or mainly the shareholders of the company.[121] In the Netherlands, directors are responsible for the proper performance of their duties.[122] They must act in the interests of the company, as well as the enterprise that is carried on by the company.[123] They therefore owe their duties to the company. The company's interest is interpreted as a self-standing interest independent of the interest of the shareholders or other stakeholders. It is defined in case law as promoting the lasting success of the enterprise.[124] In France, the stakeholder view is also emphasized. In public companies, the directors have to manage the company in the interest of the company taking into account the social and environmental consequences of its activities.[125]

3 Care and Diligence

6.38 With regard to directors' duties, the jurisdictions under discussion in this book roughly speaking recognize two main types of duties: duty of care and duty of loyalty.[126] These duties are not always explicitly regulated in company law but aspects of these two duties can be found in many jurisdictions, albeit in different forms and to different extents. In order to give directors a certain amount of leeway when making business decisions, when it comes to directors' duties and liability, the focus is generally more on the process of decision-making, whether this was for example on an informed basis and without a conflict of interest on the side of the directors, rather than

116. *See also*, e.g., *Re DKG Contractors Ltd* (1990) BCC 903, where directors were required to make a contribution to the assets of the company.
117. P. Davies & J. Rickford, 'An Introduction to the New UK Companies Act', *ECFR* 5 (2008): 48(65).
118. P. Davies, S. Worthington & C. Hare, *supra* n. 87, at 10–027.
119. European Model Companies Act 2017, comment to section 9.01, 210. With regard to the very limited exceptions to this default rule in the UK, *see* P. Davies, S. Worthington & C. Hare, *supra* n. 87, at 10-005-10-008.
120. C. Gerner-Beuerle & M. Schillig, *supra* n. 31, at 470.
121. For Germany *see* A. Schall, 'Germany', in A. Vicari & A. Schall (eds), *supra* n. 17, at m.250.
122. Article 2:9 Civil Code.
123. Articles 2:129(5) and 2:239(5) Civil Code.
124. Supreme Court (HR) 4 April 2014, NJ 2014/286 (*Cancun*).
125. Article L. 225–35 French Commercial Code.
126. A. Cahn & D.C. Donald, *supra* n. 84, at 393; C. Gerner-Beuerle & M. Schillig, *supra* n. 31, at 466.

the outcome or content of the decision which is reflected in the requirement to act as a diligent director.[127] The duty of care generally reflects the diligence, care and skill expected from a director, while the duty of loyalty encompasses mainly the avoidance of any type of conflict of interest.[128] A duty of care applies to directors in all EU Member States.[129] National laws do differ, however, with regard to how they formulate this duty.[130]

6.39 The UK Companies Act 2006 has the most elaborate codified system of general directors' duties.[131] Sections 170–177 of the Companies Act 2006 set out consecutively: the duty to act within powers, the duty to promote the success of the company, the duty to exercise independent judgment, the duty to exercise reasonable care, skills and diligence, the duty to avoid conflicts of interest and not to accept benefits from third parties and lastly the duty to declare interest in proposed transactions or arrangements. The duty of care is codified in section 174 which requires a director to exercise the care, skill and diligence that would be exercised by a reasonably diligent person with:

> (a) the general knowledge, skill and experience that would reasonable be expected of a person carrying out the functions carried out by the director in relation to the company and (b) the general knowledge, skill and experience that the director has.

The latter provides a subjective standard, based on the skills of the specific director while the former, mentioned above after (a) constitutes an objective standard. The objective standard requires the director to act as could be expected from someone in that position, therefore making clear that at least this minimum standard should be fulfilled while the second, subjective part requires the director to go beyond this minimum level.[132] The subjective standard can only be used to heighten the objective standard if the director has superior skills and knowledge.[133]

6.40 In Germany, section 43 of the German Limited Liability Companies Act sets out the duty of care by requiring directors to conduct the company's affairs with the due care of a prudent businessman. For the AG this is reflected in section 93 of the German Stock Corporation Act which stipulates:[134]

> 'In managing the affairs of the company, the members of the management board are to exercise the due care of a prudent manager faithfully complying with his duties.' This provision is also applicable to members of the supervisory board.[135] The reference to a prudent manager reflects the objective standard that is

127. C. Gerner-Beuerle & M. Schillig, *supra* n. 31, at 466.
128. *Ibid. See* for this division into two main duties also A. Cahn & D.C. Donald, *supra* n. 84, at 393 *et seq.*
129. K.J. Hopt, *supra* n. 27, at 56; A. Vicari, *supra* n. 23, at 211.
130. *See* for an overview the LSE study *Directors' Duties and Liability in the EU 2013*, 74; K.J. Hopt, *supra* n. 27, at 56; A. Vicari, *supra* n. 23, at 211.
131. A. Cahn & D.C. Donald, *supra* n. 84, at 396; the European Model Companies Act 2017, 207.
132. A. Cahn & D.C. Donald, *supra* n. 84, at 410.
133. P. Davies, S. Worthington & C. Hare, *supra* n. 87, at 10–046.
134. This translation comes from the German Federal Ministry of Justice retrieved from: https://www.gesetze-im-internet.de/englisch_aktg/
135. Section 116 German Stock Corporation Act.

applied.[136] Service contracts with the members of the board have to be negotiated by the supervisory board since the supervisory board represents the company in dealings with members of the board of directors in and outside of court proceedings.[137]

6.41 French law is less pronounced than some of the other systems when it comes to setting out the duties of directors. The French Commercial Code does provide a potential basis for liability but the content of directors' duties is not explicitly elaborated on. French law does not contain a general standard of care. However, directors' duties have been further developed in case law.[138] French courts generally require directors to act as 'prudent and diligent managers.'[139]

6.42 Dutch law also does not contain a codified duty of care, good faith or loyalty going beyond the requirement that the directors have to act in the interest of the company. Article 2:9 of the Dutch Civil Code does provide a short reference to what can be described as a duty of care when it prescribes that directors need to properly perform the task assigned to them. What this entails was, however, further developed in Dutch case law which has established a duty of care. An objective test is used to determine whether the director meets the expectations of a director required to act with the care and diligence that can be expected of a reasonable and diligent director.[140]

4 Loyalty and Conflicts of Interest

6.43 As discussed above, national law generally requires directors to act in the interest of the company. This leads to a duty of loyalty towards the company. Part of the duty of loyalty entails avoiding a conflict of interest between the members of the supervisory and the management board and the company.[141] This issue is addressed in various ways. Some jurisdictions make use of a broadly formulated duty of loyalty whereas others may, instead of or in addition to such a broad duty, formulate specific rules designed to avoid a conflict of interest. These rules often entail that the proposed transaction or agreement between a board member and the company has to be disclosed and is subject to approval either by the other board members and/or by the general meeting of shareholders.

6.44 Under UK law, directors are regarded as being in a fiduciary position vis-à-vis the company and therefore are subject to the range of *fiduciary duties* originally designed by equity for trustees. There are three major aspects of such duties:

136. For Germany, *see* A. Schall, 'Germany', in A. Vicari & A. Schall (eds), *supra* n. 17, at m. 241.
137. Section 112 German Stock Corporation Act.
138. French national report in the Annex to the Study on Directors' Duties and Liability, prepared for the European Commission DG Markt by C. Gerner-Beuerle, P. Paech, E. P. Schuster, LSE, 2013, A 298 available at: http://ec.europa, C. Gerner-Beuerle & M. Schillig, *supra* n. 31, at 519.
139. C. Gerner-Beuerle & M. Schillig, *supra* n. 31, at 522 with reference to cass Com, 30 March 2010 (Credit Martiniquais), *Revue des Sociétés* 2010, 304.
140. Supreme Court (HR) 10 Jan. 1997, *NJ* 1997, 360 m.nt. Maeijer (*Staleman/ Van de Ven*).
141. K.J. Hopt, *supra* n. 27, at 55.

- First, directors must exercise their powers of management in a bona fide manner, for the benefit of the company and not for their own personal gain, which is now laid down in section 172 of the act concerning the duty to promote the success of the company.
- The second fiduciary duty imposed on directors is that they must make *no unauthorized profit* from a corporate transaction. This duty is partly covered by section 176, which contains the duty not to accept benefits from third parties.
- The third fiduciary duty requires that directors do not place themselves in a position in which their personal interest and duty to the company may conflict. Accordingly, section 175 provides the duty of directors to avoid *conflicts of interest* and section 177 requires them to declare their interest in a proposed transaction or arrangement. This fiduciary duty is not infringed where the transaction or arrangement has been authorized by independent directors, though for a public company such authorization has to be allowed by the articles of association.[142]

Furthermore, there are specific rules in place which are all related to situations where a conflict of interest may arise.[143] These apply next to the more broadly phrased duty to avoid conflicts of interest in section 175 of the Companies Act 2006. Long-term service contracts between the directors and the company, for example, require the approval of the general meeting of shareholders.[144] There are controls on substantial property transactions involving directors, loans to directors and payments for loss of office which all require approval by the members.[145] A director who has a direct or indirect interest in the proposed transaction with the company has to disclose this to the other directors.[146]

6.45 German law does not explicitly provide for a general duty of loyalty or the duty of good faith, although it is accepted in German case law.[147] The duty of loyalty is considered in German law to form an integral part of the duty of care.[148] Certain elements of the duty of loyalty and good faith are, however, reflected in statutory law. Besides the duty of care already mentioned in the previous section, section 93 continues by stating that:[149]

142. Section 175(4)(5) and (6) UK Companies Act 2006. This duty (partly) applies also to shadow directors, section 187 UK Companies Act 2006.
143. A. Cahn & D.C. Donald, *supra* n. 84, at 405-406.
144. Section 188 UK Companies Act 2006.
145. Sections 190 *et seq.*, 197 *et seq.*, 215 *et seq.* UK Companies Act 2006. Section 223 provides that these controls apply to shadow directors.
146. Section 177 UK Companies Act 2006.
147. A. Cahn & D.C. Donald, *supra* n. 84, at 400; A. Schall, 'Germany', in A. Vicari & A. Schall (eds), *supra* n. 17, at m. 242.
148. For Germany, *see* A. Schall, 'Germany', in A. Vicari & A. Schall (eds), *supra* n. 17, at m. 244.
149. This and all translations of the German Stock Corporation Act used in this chapter come from the German Federal Ministry of Justice retrieved from: https://www.gesetze-im-internet.de/englisch_aktg/

> No dereliction of duties shall be given in those instances in which the member of the management board, in taking an entrepreneurial decision, was within his rights to reasonably assume that he was acting on the basis of adequate information and in the best interests of the company.

This makes clear that directors should act in the best interest of the company, which is comparable to good faith, and on an informed basis which reflects the duty of care.[150] The provision furthermore specifies a duty of confidentiality by stipulating that:[151]

> The members of the management board are to respect the secrecy of any confidential information and secrets of the company, particularly trade secrets or business secrets, of which they have become aware in the context of their activities in the management board.

Section 88 of the German Stock Corporation Act provides for a non-competition clause for the members of the board of directors which can also be seen as derived from the duty of loyalty.[152] Loans granted to the board of directors or the supervisory board, those in a close relationship with the board members or a company that is represented by the director, require the approval of the supervisory board.[153]

With regard to the GmbH, the duty of loyalty and good faith are not codified. Nevertheless, these duties are assumed to exist and consist of the following summarized duties: (i) avoid conflicts of interest, disclose conflicts and ask for the general meeting of shareholders' approval; (ii) not to compete; (iii) abstain from the use of corporate opportunities; and (iv) not to receive benefits from third parties.[154]

6.46 The duty of loyalty is translated into French law in the sense that directors of French companies (both SA and SARL) are expected to act in the interest of the company.[155] The directors are required to act within their statutory powers and in accordance with the articles of association.[156] As mentioned above, Article L 225–35 of the Commercial Code stipulates for the public company that the board has to act in accordance with the corporate interests, taking into account the social and environmental issues of its activity. They are also required not to act for their own personal gain. The Commercial Code does not contain a general duty of loyalty; this has, however, been established in case law, and French law does contain specific rules on

150. A. Schall, 'Germany', in A. Vicari & A. Schall (eds), *supra* n. 17, at mn. 246.
151. This translation comes from the German Federal Ministry of Justice retrieved from: https://www.gesetze-im-internet.de/englisch_aktg/. A duty of confidentiality can also be found in section 85 of the German Limited Liability Companies Act.
152. A. Cahn & D.C. Donald, *supra* n. 84, at 400.
153. Section 89 and 115 German Stock Corporation Act.
154. *See* for this list and further elaboration V. Klappstein, 'Germany', in A. Vicari & A. Schall (eds), *supra* n. 17, at m. 528.
155. I. Grossi, D. Poracchia & A. Raynouard, 'France', in A. Vicari & A. Schall (eds), *supra* n. 17, at m. 222 with reference to Cass. Comm., 12 May 2015, no. 13-28504 and 14-11028, BJS 2015, 650.
156. Article L225-251 French Commercial Code.

avoiding conflicts of interest.[157] The Commercial Code has specific rules for the SARL aimed at avoiding a conflict between managers' personal interest and their duties. The company may for example not lend money to managers or their immediate family or otherwise guarantee or secure their personal debts.[158] Furthermore, any contract between a manager and the company must be ratified by the general meeting, failing which, the manager is liable to indemnify the company for any loss caused to it because of the contract.[159] However, ratification is not prescribed if the company contracts with the manager in the ordinary course of its business and under normal conditions.[160]

There are comparable rules for the directors of an SA.[161] Also here loans and guarantees are prohibited and void. Agreement between a company and one of its directors or between companies with directors in common must be submitted to the board or, in the two-tier structure, to the supervisory board, for approval. The agreement must be reported by the auditor to the general meeting and approved by that meeting.[162] The director concerned cannot vote at any of these meetings. The liability of members of the supervisory board is restricted to personal fault, excluding any liability for management decisions.[163] Proof of a specific fault or negligence by a director and consequential loss to the company is required.

6.47 Dutch law contains specific rules to avoid conflicts of interest. Conflicted directors may not participate in the deliberations and adoption of resolutions if they have a direct or indirect personal interest in that resolution which is in conflict with the interests of the company. If, as a result, no management resolution can be adopted, the resolution will be adopted by the supervisory board. Where there is no supervisory board, the resolution will be adopted by the general meeting, unless the articles otherwise provide.[164] According to its wording, the statutory provision deals with personal interests only, leaving aside a conflict of duties. In its leading *Bruil* case, the Dutch Supreme Court, however, also regarded - apart from interests of a personal nature - other interests as possibly relevant where they do not coincide with the interests of the company.[165] In case law, additional rules have been developed. In *Linders v. Hofstee*, a member of the company's supervisory board held shares in another company. The company bought those shares of the supervisory board member for a rather high price. Consequently, there were serious doubts about whether there had been any serious bargaining, due to the influence that the supervisory board

157. French national report in the Annex to the Study on Directors' Duties and Liability, prepared for the European Commission DG Markt by Carsten Gerner-Beuerle, Philipp Paech, Edmund Philipp Schuster, LSE, 2013, A 301.
158. Article L223-21 French Commercial Code.
159. Article L223-19 French Commercial Code.
160. Article L223-20 French Commercial Code.
161. Article L225-38 *et seq.* (one-tier system) Article L225-86 *et seq.* (two-tier system) French Commercial Code. *See also* M. Cozian, A. Viandier & F. Deboissy, *Droit des sociétés*, 27th edition (Paris: Lexis Nexis, 2014), 349 *et seq.* (SA), 569 *et seq.* (SARL).
162. Article L225-40 French Commercial Code.
163. Article L225-257 French Commercial Code.
164. Articles 2:129(6) and 2:239(6) Dutch Civil Code.
165. HR 29 June 2007, *JOR* 2007/169 (*Bruil*). Confirmed by the Amsterdam Court of Appeal 22 Sep. 2015, *JOR* 2016/117.

member might have had on the decision to buy the shares. It was held that, when such a conflict of interest arises, the conflicted member, as well as the board itself, is under a duty to disclose the interests concerned, and these interests must be kept strictly separated from the interests of the company. In addition, they must seek the advice of an independent expert, if necessary.[166]

E Directors' Liability and Judicial Review

6.48 A violation of directors' and supervisory directors' duties can lead to liability. Liability can be based on several grounds. It can be the result of a breach of one of the duties mentioned in the previous sections. In most jurisdictions (supervisory) directors can be held liable on the basis of civil law, criminal law and tax law. There may also be administrative consequences attached to breaching directors' duties, such as disqualification of directors.[167] Besides the legal basis for (supervisory) directors' liability, jurisdictions also differ with regard to the parties that can initiate liability actions. When it comes to civil liability, several stakeholders may have reasons to hold directors liable. Think for example of the company itself, its creditors and its shareholders. A distinction is often made between internal liability, i.e., liability towards the company, and external liability, i.e. liability towards third parties such as creditors. In several of the jurisdictions discussed above, directors owe a duty to the company. This means that in the first instance, it is up to the company to initiate liability proceedings against the director(s). This can, for example, be done by the supervisory board on behalf of the company, by fellow directors, or new directors can be appointed who then initiate proceedings against former directors in the name, and on behalf, of the company. Creditors can generally also hold the directors liable and in case of bankruptcy, the liquidator or the receiver in bankruptcy. In Germany, for example, if the directors grossly breach their duty of care, creditors who cannot obtain satisfaction from the company are entitled to sue the directors.[168] In the Netherlands, creditors can hold directors liable on the basis of a tort[169] if the board of directors knowingly continued loss-making activities thereby disadvantaging creditors if it can be said that the directors allowed the company to enter into obligations which they knew or ought to have known that the company would not be able to fulfil.[170] There are more differences between jurisdictions where it comes to the question of whether or not shareholders can hold directors directly liable. These derivative actions are discussed in the part of this chapter that relates to the rights and powers of shareholders: paragraph 6.92 *et seq.*

6.49 In addition to the rules setting out the duties of directors, several countries also have specific liability rules for directors where the company is on the brink of

166. Enterprise Chamber of the Amsterdam Court of Appeal, 26 May 1983, *NJ* 1984, 481.
167. *See*, for example, for the UK the Company Directors Disqualification Act 1986.
168. Section 93(5) German Stock Corporation Act.
169. Liability would then be based on general tort law provided for in Article 6:162 of the Dutch Civil Code.
170. Supreme Court (HR) 6 Oct. 1989, *NJ* 1990, 286 (*Beklamel*).

insolvency. In such a situation, directors may be tempted to enter into risky behaviour in an ultimate attempt to make up for past losses. Shareholders are protected by the principles of limited liability from having to share in the losses of the company. Once the company is close to insolvency, the shareholders have generally already lost their investment since the value of their shares has declined, and therefore they may lack the incentive to seize its business activities. Continuing loss-making activities will therefore mainly disadvantage creditors. The longer the company continues to engage in transactions it cannot afford, the larger the group of creditors will become.

6.50 UK law, for example, has specific rules of directors' liability towards a company nearing insolvency. The wrongful trading provision was introduced by section 214 of the Insolvency Act 1986.[171] This section holds a director personally liable to contribute to the assets of an insolvent company the director knew or ought to have concluded that there was no reasonable prospect that the company would avoid going into insolvent liquidation. However, the court may hold otherwise if the director took every step with a view to minimizing the potential loss to the company's creditors, as ought to have been taken. Section 214 furthermore provides a general test for the conclusions that the director ought to reach and the steps that he or she ought to take. These must be comparable to what would be reached or taken by a reasonably diligent person having both: (i) the general knowledge, skill and experience that may reasonably be expected of a person carrying out the same functions as are carried out by that director; and (ii) the general knowledge, skill and experience that that particular director has. This is comparable to the duty of care contained in the UK Companies Act 2006.

Under German law, directors have to compensate the company for payments which are made after the company has become illiquid or after it is deemed to be over-indebted. An exception to liability is made when the director acted with the due care of a prudent businessman.[172]

According to Dutch law, in case of bankruptcy, directors may incur liability for the amount of damages to the company to the extent that these cannot be satisfied out of the liquidation of the assets of the company. This is the case if management has manifestly performed its duties improperly and if it is plausible that this is an important cause of the involuntary liquidation.[173]

6.51 A last important aspect in relation to (supervisory) directors' liability to point out is the standard of judicial review that is used to assess liability. As mentioned above, in many jurisdictions directors' actions are compared to what could be expected of a diligent and knowledgeable director in the same circumstances. However, as we also mentioned above, a part of directors' tasks is to take business decisions of which the

171. *See* Hans H. Hirt, 'The Wrongful Trading Remedy in UK Law: Classification, Application and Practical Significance', *ECFR* 1 (2004): 71 *et seq. See also* section 10.04 of the European Model Company Act (EMCA) proposing a provision that is inspired by the English wrongful trading liability (accessible at http://www.jura.uni-wuerzburg.de/lehrstuehle/teichmann/forschungs projekte/european_model_company_act/)
172. Section 64 German Limited Liability Companies Act and Section 92 German Stock Corporation Act.
173. Articles 2:138 and 2:248 Dutch Civil Code.

outcome is not always predictable. Directors should be able to take (calculated) business risks. Courts are less skilled at taking those decisions or reviewing them *ex post*. Therefore, the main focus when examining directors' actions will be on how the decision came about and whether or not sufficient care has been applied in that respect.[174] Therefore, courts often check directors' behaviour and decisions in a marginal way. A well-known standard for judicial review in this respect is the 'business judgement rule'. The rule originates from the US,[175] the most famous example of which can be found in Delaware. Under Delaware law, this rule presumes that:

> (...) in making a business decision the directors of a corporation acted on an informed basis, in good faith and in the honest believe that the action taken was in the best interest of the company.[176]

If directors did act in good faith and on an informed basis, the business decision will not be second-guessed by the court. A plaintiff who wants to rebut the presumption will have to prove that the director did not act in good faith, with a conflict of interest, or on an uninformed basis.

Some European countries have codified this rule. Germany for example has adopted its own version of the US business judgment rule. The German Stock Corporation Act stipulates in section 93:[177]

> No dereliction of duties shall be given in those instances in which the member of the management board, in taking an entrepreneurial decision, was within his rights to reasonably assume that he was acting on the basis of adequate information and in the best interests of the company. (...)

According to this rule, the directors will be held liable if they mismanage the company or act in breach of their duties or in breach of the articles of the company. Therefore, unlike the Delaware business judgment rule, under the German version of the business judgment rule, the burden of proof is not primarily on the plaintiff but remains with the members of the board.[178] However, they will not be liable for management decisions if they had good reason to assume that they were acting on the basis of adequate information for the benefit of the company.[179] Other jurisdictions have not codified this rule but one can nevertheless see in case law that non-conflicted directors who have made their business decisions in good faith are presumed to have acted in line with their duty of care, of course, absent situations of fraud or obvious mismanagement.[180] This is, for example, the case in France where courts will not easily

174. C. Gerner-Beuerle & M. Schillig, *supra* n. 31, at 466.
175. LSE study *Directors' Duties and Liability in the EU* 2013, 115. *See* this study for an overview of the use of the business judgement rule in EU Member States.
176. Delaware Supreme Court 473 A 2d 805 (1984), *Aronson v Lewis*. *See also* A. Cahn & D.C. Donald, *supra* n. 84, at 445.
177. Translation from the German Federal Ministry of Justice retrieved from: https://www.gesetze-im-internet.de/englisch_aktg/.
178. LSE study *Directors' Duties and Liability in the EU* 2013, A 339.
179. Section 93(1) 2nd sentence German Stock Corporation Act.
180. *See* in this respect A. Cahn & D.C. Donald, *supra* n. 84, at 445.

second-guess directors' decisions.[181] Also in the Netherlands, it is accepted that although there is no business judgment rule, courts will only use a marginal test to check directors' decisions.[182] In the UK courts also give directors a certain margin of discretion.[183]

V SHAREHOLDERS AND THE GENERAL MEETING

6.52 As emphasized in the introduction to this chapter, the separation of ownership and control within the company is a structural characteristic of the capital company. In this section, we focus on the position of shareholders and the corporate body through which shareholders - mainly - exercise their powers within the company: the general meeting of shareholders.

A Why Do Shareholders Have Voting Rights?

6.53 Companies are granted certain legal privileges, such as legal personality and limited liability. In addition, companies profit from social means that are provided by the state, such as a decent infrastructure and a potential workforce with a good education.[184] In return, it is expected that companies contribute to the creation of social value for society.[185] Given this broad societal goal, it may at first glance be considered surprising that one of the structural characteristics of the capital company is that the shareholders are generally considered the 'owners' of the company. Although this statement is incorrect from a legal perspective - shareholders only own the shares in the company, not the company itself; shareholders do hold an extraordinary position in the governance of companies in comparison to other stakeholders.[186] Shareholders have critical control rights within companies, such as the right to appoint and dismiss directors, determine the capital structure of the company, amend the articles of association, approve important board decisions and - albeit in certain jurisdictions to a limited extent - the right to give the board of directors instructions. As a result, shareholders are - at least in theory - able to determine to a significant extent how companies are managed. This raises the question as to why shareholders have this 'privileged' position within the company compared to other stakeholders and how it

181. LSE study *Directors' Duties and Liability in the EU* 2013, 110.
182. *Ibid.*, 111.
183. *Ibid.*
184. N. Hsieh et al., 'The Social Purpose of Corporations', *Journal of the British Academy* 6, no.s1 (2018): 58.
185. J.E. Parkinson, *Corporate Power and Responsibility: Issues in the Theory of Company Law* (Oxford: Clarendon Press 1993), 41 *et seq.*
186. According to Black's Law Dictionary (11th ed. 2019), a stakeholder is '[s]omeone who has an interest or concern in a business or enterprise, though not necessarily as an owner,' or (more generally) '[a] person who has an interest or concern (not necessarily financial) in the success or failure of an organization, system, plan, or strategy, or who is affected by a course of action.'

relates to creating welfare for society. In other words, why are shareholders the (only) stakeholders that have been granted voting rights?

6.54 There are several theories that try to provide an answer to this question. Here, we focus on four theories in particular, (1) the rights-based theory, which can also be viewed as the more doctrinal/traditional reasoning, (2) the contractual theory, that the company has to be viewed as a contract between the shareholders, (3) the economic theory, in which the shareholder is qualified as the residual claimant, and (4) the shareholder democracy theory, which takes inspiration from democratic theory.[187]

1 *The Rights-Based Theory*

6.55 According to the rights-based theory, the right to vote can be viewed as inherent to the fact that shareholders are the members of the company.[188] Since the shareholders are members and having the right to exercise influence over the company is inherent to membership, shareholders have the right to vote. This rights-based theory seems to draw inspiration from the traditional view of the company as an association of members. In the 17th century, companies were an instrument to gather significant funds from investors in order to generate wealth by achieving a purpose as was laid down in a charter granted by the state/crown. As a result, the investors who invested the necessary funds held a prominent position within the governance of these early companies. The fact that shareholders in these companies had comparable characteristics to a member of an association follows, for instance, from the way in which the voting rights were arranged. Whereas nowadays most jurisdictions have the default rule that members have one vote for each share,[189] at the time members with large shareholdings were actively limited in the number of votes they could cast. In the Netherlands, this practice continued into the 20th century,[190] where individual shareholders were not allowed to exercise more than six votes in the general meeting. The purpose of this provision was to limit the influence of majority shareholders and protect minority shareholders.[191]

6.56 There are various legal principles in certain national company laws that are in line with this rights-based theory, such as the principle that shareholders should be treated equally, that shareholders should act reasonably and fairly towards each other, and that the transfer of voting rights is not allowed. First is the equal treatment principle which aims to protect shareholders, at least when these are in a similar

187. *See also* for several of these theories: A. Cahn & D.C. Donald, *supra* n. 84, at 577 *et seq.*
188. *Ibid.*, 566 with references to multiple predominantly German sources.
189. *See* for more detail, paragraph 6.85 *et seq.*, which also demonstrates that there are many exceptions to this rule.
190. Article 54 of the Dutch Commercial Code (1838). Even after 1929, it was still possible in the articles of association to limit the number of votes an individual shareholder could cast. It was, however, not possible to increase the number of votes compared to the number of shares held. *See* E.J.J. van der Heijden, *Handboek voor de Naamlooze vennootschap naar Nederlandsch recht* (Zwolle: W.E.J. Tjeenk Willink 1929), 216.
191. J.G. Kist, *De Maatschap of Vennootschap* (Amsterdam: J.H. Gebhard & Comp., 1863), 189.

position from being treated differently within the organization structure of the company, which fits the idea that the shareholders are members of an association. The equal treatment of shareholders is not only featured in most national laws[192] but also recognized in various EU laws, such as Article 85 of the Directive (EU) 2017/1132 relating to certain aspects of company law[193] and the Takeover Directive.[194]

Second, in part as an extension of the right to equal treatment,[195] many jurisdictions recognize that shareholders can have certain responsibilities towards each other. This is in line with the view that the shareholders are members of the association and, as such, are in a form of collective collaboration with each other.

Third, in various jurisdictions, the sale/transfer of voting rights without transferring the underlying shares themselves is not allowed and/or considered void. Transferring voting rights without also transferring the shares in the company leads to 'empty voting' by a person that does not have the interests that other shareholders have because the person exercising the voting right is not the holder of the shares and does not have an (economic) actual interest in the shares.[196] If voting is considered an inherent part of membership, then separating the legal right to the share and the right to vote should not be allowed. Although Germany[197] and the Netherlands[198] prohibit the transfer of only the voting right, this is not the case for – for instance – France[199] and the UK.

---

192. Article 2:92 and 2:201(2) Dutch Civil Code; section 53a German Stock Corporation Act. Certain jurisdictions take a slightly different approach to the treatment of shareholders. One example of this is the UK, which requires *fair treatment* among shareholders but not *equal treatment*. *See*: D. Kershaw, *Principles of Takeover Regulation* (Oxford: Oxford University Press, 2016), 185. The French Commercial Code includes the principle of equal treatment within the reduction of capital (Article L. 225-204 French Commercial Code) and within the auditor's duties which contain a check on equal treatment (Article L. 823-11 French Commercial Code).
193. Article 85 of Directive (EU) 2017/1132: 'For the purposes of the implementation of this Chapter, the laws of the Member States shall ensure equal treatment to all shareholders who are in the same position.'
194. Article 3(1)(a) of Directive 2004/25/EC: 'all holders of the securities of an offeree company of the same class must be afforded equivalent treatment; moreover, if a person acquires control of a company, the other holders of securities must be protected.'
195. *See* for Germany for instance: A. Schall, 'Germany', in A. Vicari & A. Schall (eds), *supra* n. 17, at 292–293.
196. *See* about empty voting: M.C. Schouten, *The Decoupling of Voting and Economic Ownership* (Deventer: Kluwer 2012); C. Clottens, Proportionaliteit van stemrecht en risico in kapitaalvennootschappen (Antwerp: Biblo 2012).
197. Heider (2016), in Münchener Kommentar zum Aktiengesetz (Munich: C.H. Beck, 2014: § 12 mn. 6).
198. R. Abma et al., *De algemene vergadering van Nederlandse beursvennootschappen* (*Recht en Praktijk* nr. ONR9) (Deventer: Wolters Kluwer, 2017), 118. It should, however, be noted that there are also more nuanced views, arguing that it should be considered whether the transferring of votes is acceptable in the specific case (Asser/Serière 2-IV 2018/114).
199. It should, however, be noted that Article L 225-116 French Commercial Code holds a requirement for persons, who, alone or in concert, hold more than 0.5% of voting rights as a result of stock lending or an agreement with similar effect, to notify this to the AMF and to the company on the record date at the latest (i.e., 3 days before the general meeting). The information to be provided includes the identity of the lender, the expiration date of the agreement, and the voting agreement, if any.

2 *The Contractual Theory*

6.57 A second theory on why shareholders have voting rights is the contractual theory, which is a theory that was predominantly followed in France and countries influenced by French commercial law from the start of the 19th century. Under the French Civil Code (1804) and the *Code de Commerce* (1807), the company law form was explicitly described as a contractual arrangement.[200] In other counties that were influenced by, and in some cases for a period of time part of, the French empire, national law included similar arrangements.[201] Under the contractual theory, the company is - unsurprisingly - viewed as a contract between the shareholders and governed by contract law.[202] As a result, the parties to the contract - the shareholders - are the supreme power within the company. They in principle determine the contractual division of power within the company and hold the power to amend this division of power at any time in accordance with the provisions of the contract.[203] Under the contractual theory, the directors were considered agents of the joint shareholders, who had to act in the interest of the shareholders and could be appointed and dismissed by the shareholders.[204] Given the nature of the company as a contract between the shareholders, the shareholders as contractual parties to the agreement determine the decision-making within the company and thereby have the right to vote. Moreover, this theory also provides a dogmatic justification for viewing the company as an instrument of shareholders to primarily maximize shareholder value, which was also referenced in paragraph 6.56.

6.58 The contractual theory, which was applied in France and the Netherlands, has largely lost its persuasive power as large companies became more institutionalized towards the end of the 19th and during the 20th century.[205] However, for smaller companies with a closed group of shareholders, this theory still holds some merits, especially if the company functions more as an investment vehicle for the sharehold-ers. In such circumstances, the cooperation of the shareholders is very similar to a

200. Article 13 of the Civil Code 1804; Article 18 of the *Code de Commerce* 1807.
201. Under the Commercial Code introduced in the Netherlands in 1838 (which replaced the French legislation that remained in force until then), the company was considered a contract and regulated as such in the Dutch Commercial Code.
202. S. Cools, 'The Dividing Line between Shareholder Democracy and Board Autonomy: Inherent Conflict of Interest as Normative Criterion', *European Company and Financial Review* 11 (2014): 262.
203. M. Gelter, 'Taming or Protecting the Modern Corporation? Shareholder-Stakeholder Debates in a Comparative Light', *NYU Journal of Law and Business* (2011): (641) 665, 667; J. Maeijer, *Het belangenconflict in de naamloze vennootschap* (Deventer: Kluwer, 1964), 3; T. Tilquin, 'La société privée et la société faisant ou ayant fait publiquement appel à l'épargne', *TBH* 92 (1993): 102.
204. S. Cools, De verdeling van beslissingsbevoegdheden tussen algemene vergadering en raad van bestuur in de NV, 2015, 29; B. Kemp, *Aandeelhoudersverantwoordelijkheid: De positie en rol van de aandeelhouder en aandeelhoudersvergadering* (Deventer: Kluwer, 2015), 28.
205. S. Cools, *supra* n. 202, 263.

partnership, which still has a contractual nature.[206] Moreover, it is very common in such circumstances to extensively regulate the cooperation between the shareholders by means of shareholder agreements, which are contracts that regulate the corporate governance in addition to the articles of association and the law.[207]

3 *The Economic Theory*

6.59 A third theory on why shareholders have voting rights follows from economic theory. Under this theory, it is argued that social value for society can be best maximized by allocating decision-making rights to shareholders as they are the residual claimant of the company, meaning that the shareholders bear the risk for the company's success or failure.[208] The underlying proposition for the qualification of the shareholder as residual claimant is that the company should be conceived as a 'nexus of contracts' between the various stakeholders of the company.[209] The reference to contracts should be understood in a normative sense, not in the civil law sense as applied under the contractual theory. The starting point in this nexus of contracts is the freedom of the parties to the contract to structure the company in the way they see fit, with (national) company law providing a 'template' for the governance of the company. This template is, however, never complete because parties cannot foresee all circumstances that could arise within the company, and it is not efficient or possible to provide in the written governance of the company, such as the law, the articles of association and board regulations, for all foreseeable circumstances. As a result, a party should be assigned the residual power to resolve issues that are not foreseen in the contract.

6.60 Under this theory, the shareholders are considered the appropriate party to assign the residual power to make discretionary decisions because shareholders are in a different 'normative relationship' with the company compared to other stakeholders, such as employees, creditors and suppliers.[210] The main difference being that the latter stakeholders have a more or less fixed relationship with a set return, whereas shareholders are incentivized to maximize shareholder value and therefore their return on investment. Moreover, shareholders are most incentivized to avoid negative results for the company, as shareholders are last in line and will under those circumstances receive nothing. Therefore, shareholders have the correct incentives to exercise discretionary power in such a way that their interest is maximized.[211]

---

206. For the Netherlands, the public company during the 19th century was actually considered as an extraordinary partnership and as such regulated jointly with the other partnerships.
207. *See* for more detail, paragraphs 6.96 and 6.97.
208. F.H. Easterbrook & D.R. Fischel, *The Economic Structure of Corporate Law* (Cambridge (Mass.): Harvard University Press, 1991), 67-68.
209. M.C. Jensen & W.H. Meckling, 'The Theory of the Firm: Managerial Behaviour, Agency Costs, and Ownership Structure', *Journal of Financial Economics* 3 (1976): 305-360.
210. F.H. Easterbrook & D.R. Fischel, *supra* n. 208, at 67-68.
211. *Ibid.*, 68.

6.61 Most proponents of the economic theory do not argue that maximizing the interest of shareholders is the ultimate goal of the company and therefore company law but consider this theory as a means by which the social value created by the company can be best maximized.[212] The argument put forward to support this is twofold. First, because shareholders are the last in line, maximizing shareholder value is good for all stakeholders. This follows from the thought that a successful company creates value for all stakeholders and not only for shareholders.[213] Second, although the company should create value for society as a whole, it is near to impossible to monitor the board when that board is serving many masters (i.e. all stakeholders).[214] This problem does not arise - to the same extent - when the board is required to focus on maximizing shareholder interest since this provides for a single metric for the board to focus on and a clear stakeholder, the shareholders, to monitor the board in order to ensure that the board actually focuses on this metric.

4 *Shareholder Democracy Theory*

6.62 A fourth, and for purpose of this overview, final theory on why shareholders should have voting rights within the company is the shareholder democracy theory. By comparing the rights of citizens in a democratic state with those of shareholders, this theory considers voting rights as a reliable tool to hold the board accountable.[215] Although already briefly mentioned by Berle and Means in their well-known book *The Modern Corporation & Private Property*,[216] the foundations for this theory are a combination of increasingly diversified shareholdings, widening separation of ownership and management, and growing managerial power in the mid-20th century.[217] The term 'shareholder democracy' was used to describe corporate governance in which groups of small shareholders attended annual meetings, had sufficient information and exercised their voting rights. In the early stage of the development of the theory in the 20th century, it did not focus on the democratic - horizontal - relationship between shareholders, but mainly on the vertical relationship between the management and the shareholder. In that vertical relationship, the management had to adequately inform the shareholders and enable the shareholders to vote on the basis of the information disclosed.[218] To ensure a representative shareholder base and democratic vote, it was

212. J.E. Fisch, 'Measuring Efficiency in Corporate Law: The Role of Shareholder Primacy', *J. Corp. Fin.* 31 (2005): 637, 656–658; M.J. Roe, 'The Shareholder Wealth Maximization Norm and Industrial Organization', 149 *U. Pa. L. Rev.* 149 (2000): 2063.; H. Hansmann & R. Kraakman, 'The End of History of Corporate Law', *Georgetown Law Journal* 2 (2001): 441.
213. F.H. Easterbrook & D.R. Fischel, *supra* n. 208, at 38.
214. A.A. Berle, 'For Whom Are Managers Trustees: A Note', *Harv. L. Rev.* 45 (1932); M. Jensen, 'Value Maximization, Stakeholder Theory, and the Corporate Objective Function', *J. Applied Corp. Fin.* 14 (2001): 8, 9, 14; H. Hansmann & R. Kraakman, *supra* n. 212, 448.
215. A. Cahn & D.C. Donald, *supra* n. 84, at 582.
216. A.A. Berle & G.C. Means, *supra* n. 2.
217. C.A. Dunlavy, 'Social Conceptions of the Corporation: Insights from the History of Shareholder Voting Rights', *Washington and Lee Law Review* 63, no.4 (2006): 1363.
218. *Ibid.*, 1365.

(and is) important for as many shareholders as possible to have the opportunity to vote.[219] It was not until the 1980s that shareholder democracy came to be perceived more horizontally and being linked to the principle of one share-one vote.[220] It could be argued that shareholders, like citizens, elect a representative body to make daily decisions (indirect democracy) and retain the right to make important decisions on specific matters (direct democracy).[221]

6.63 The shareholder democracy theory has several flaws. For one, shareholders do not each have an equal vote, but – in the one share-one vote system – one vote for each share held. In that sense, there is no such thing as shareholder democracy, but only shareholder plutocracy.[222] It is doubtful whether one would have the same positive attitude towards a plutocracy as towards a democracy. Moreover, shareholders can relatively easily exit the company by selling their shares and reinvesting the capital in another company, while a person will not easily be willing or able to 'switch' to a different democracy.[223] This also changes the 'investment horizon' of a shareholder compared to a citizen.

B Shareholder Rights and Minority Protection

6.64 Above, various theories have been set out as to why within the governance of a company control rights are allocated to shareholders. In practice, all these theories at certain points in time have played a role in policy that led to introducing, retaining or increasing the rights of shareholders within the company. Moreover, these theories explain why crucial control rights tend to be allocated to shareholders, such as the right to appoint and dismiss directors (and/or supervisory board members), the power to amend the articles of association, to approve the annual accounts and to enter into a merger, division or transformation. Below, various shareholders' rights are set out in more detail. It should, however, be noted that while reference is made to shareholder rights, these are control rights that the shareholders can exercise through the corporate body of the general meeting of shareholders. In Section 6(V)(C), we set out the functions and procedures of the general meeting of shareholders. The comparative analysis of shareholder rights demonstrates that while overall shareholders have strong control rights in all jurisdictions, the manner in which these rights are structured is

219. T. Poulson, T. Strand & S. Tompson, 'Voting Power and Shareholder Activism: A Study of Swedish Shareholder Meetings', *Corporate Governance: An international review* 18, no.4 (2010): 334.
220. C.A. Dunlavy, *supra* n. 217, at 1366 referring to A.M. Lamport, 'Readers Report: On Going Private', *Bus. WEEK*, 31 Mar. 1975, at 4. Also: U. Rodrigues, 'The Seductive Comparison of Shareholder and Civic Democracy', *Wash. & Lee L. Rev*. 63 (2006): 1389, 1390; A. Lafarre, *The AGM in Europe: Theory and Practice of Shareholder Behaviour* (Bingley: Emerald Publishing Limited, 2017), 14.
221. A. Lafarre, *supra* n. 220, at 14.
222. C. Clerc, 'Questioning the Legitimacy of Shareholder Power', in J.-P. Touffut (ed.), *Does Company Ownership Matter?* (The Cournot Centre for Economic Studies Series, Cheltenham: Edward Elgar Publishing, 2009), 16.
223. A. Lafarre, *supra* n. 220, at 14.

different, and there are limits to the extent to which shareholders can freely exercise those rights.

6.65 As a starting point, most jurisdictions recognize that shareholders can primarily act in their own interest when exercising shareholder rights. This starting point is in line with the various theories for granting shareholders voting rights (*see* Section 6(V)(A)), which not only explains why shareholders have voting rights but also why the shareholder interest can be a prevailing interest within the company. However, in practice, many jurisdictions have limited this starting point under certain – frequently occurring – circumstances. In France, for example, majority shareholders cannot exercise their voting rights such that they pursue their own interest instead of the interest of the company and in a way that is to the detriment of the company.[224] Similarly, in Germany, majority shareholders are not allowed to vote in a way that is 'disloyal' to the minority shareholders.[225] For example, in the landmark *Linotype* case, the BGH held that the majority shareholders violated their duty of loyalty towards the minority shareholders if they voted to wind up the company with the sole purpose of acquiring the underlying business for themselves.[226] In addition, the minority shareholders can also abuse veto powers, as was the case in *Grimes*.[227] In the Netherlands, the starting point is that shareholders can in principle serve their own interest, which has been stated repeatedly by the Dutch Supreme Court,[228] but this freedom becomes more restricted when a shareholder has a more substantive position in the company. In the Netherlands, this has been described as a 'sliding scale' between a shareholder/ investor with limited actual power and therefore also limited responsibility on the one hand and a majority shareholder with controlling influence and therefore a more far-reaching responsibility on the other.[229]

6.66 When shareholders have a duty towards minority shareholders, that offers minority shareholders a certain level of protection. Similar duties to consider the interest of minority shareholders can exist for the board of directors, as is the case in the Netherlands.[230] Given that resolutions are generally passed by majority vote and – for instance – directors are therefore appointed by the majority shareholders, the company is *de facto* governed by the majority shareholder(s). As a result of the majority voting system, majority shareholders might act mostly in their own interest instead of in the interest of the joint shareholders. Similarly, the directors might be largely focused on the interest of the majority shareholders instead of the interest of the company itself. The aforementioned duties are one of the ways in which minority shareholders can be

224. P.H. Conac, 'France: The Permanent Reform of Corporate Governance', in A.M. Fleckner & K.J. Hopt, *supra* n. 27, at 475.
225. A. Schall, 'Germany', in A. Vicari & A. Schall (eds), *supra* n. 17, at 297.
226. BGHZ 103, 183, 194 = NJW (1988), 1579.
227. BGHZ 129, 136, 143 = NJW (1995), 1739.
228. Dutch Supreme Court 30 June 1944, *NJ* 1944, 465; Dutch Supreme Court 13 Nov. 1959, *NJ* 1960, 472; Dutch Supreme Court 19 Feb. 1960, *NJ* 1960, 473.
229. B. Kemp, *supra* n. 204, 230; M. Olaerts, *Vennootschappelijke beleidsbepaling in geval van financiële moeilijkheden; de positie van bestuurders en aandeelhouders* (Antwerpen-Oxford: Intersentia, 2007), 289.
230. Dutch Supreme Court 1 March 2002, *NJ* 2002/296.

protected against abuse by or on behalf of the majority shareholders. In addition, national laws provide for specific legal instruments that protect minority shareholders, such as derivative suits, information rights and qualified majorities, which are all discussed below.

6.67 Within the main jurisdictions, the exception to the above is the UK, where even majority shareholders do not owe duties towards the minority shareholders, and there are very limited possibilities to set aside shareholder resolutions.[231] There is, however, the obligation for shareholders to be treated fairly, which can make it difficult for majority shareholders to make changes to the governance of the company in a way that is detrimental to the minority shareholders.[232] This is also laid down in the unfair prejudice rules, where a shareholder can petition the court for relief - among others - in case the company's affairs are being or have been conducted in a manner which is unfairly prejudicial to the interest of the shareholders generally or some part of the shareholders.[233] Although majority shareholders are not excluded from using these rules, it primarily acts as a mechanism for minority protection.[234] In addition, specifically, when amending the articles of association, the law requires a supermajority resolution of 75% and the majority must act 'bona fide in the interest of the company'.[235]

1 *The Right to Appoint and Dismiss Directors*

6.68 The right to appoint and dismiss members of the board of directors is arguably one of the most influential rights of shareholders. By exercising this right, shareholders determine who will set the strategy, manage and represent the company. As a result, shareholders have a significant influence on how the company is actually run.

6.69 Interestingly, the main jurisdictions all have their own particular regulations in relation to the appointment of directors, with the UK not having any specific provisions in the Companies Act 2006.[236] However, according to case law, the shareholders have the inherent power to appoint the directors, which may be exercised by ordinary resolution of the general meeting.[237] The articles of association may, however, provide for another appointment mechanism, such as co-optation within the board and the

231. I-M. Esser and J. Loughrey, 'United Kingdom', in A. Vicari & A. Schall (eds), *supra* n. 17, at 1531.
232. D. Prentice, 'The United Kingdom', in S. Bruno & E. Ruggerio (eds), *Public Companies and the Role of Shareholders* (Deventer: Wolters Kluwer, 2011), 222.
233. Section 994 UK Companies Act 2006.
234. P.L. Davies, S. Worthington & C. Hare, *supra* n. 87, at 536.
235. Mutual Life Insurance Co. of New York v. The Rank Organization Ltd. [1985] BCLC 11; Re BSB Holdings Ltd. (no. 2) [1996] 1 BCLC 155.
236. C. Gerner Beuerle & M.A. Schillig, *supra* n. 31, 444; A. Cahn & D.C. Donald, *supra* n. 84, at 589. According to main principle J of the UK Corporate Governance Code 2018, there should be 'a formal, rigorous and transparent procedure' for the appointment of new directors.
237. Worcester Corsetry Ltd. V Witting [1936] Ch 640; Link Agricultural Pty Ltd v Shanahan (1998) 28 ACSR 498.

Model Articles allow for both options.[238] In terms of the period for which directors may be appointed, the Companies Act 2006 does not provide for a maximum or minimum. The Model Articles for public companies do provide for such a term, i.e. until the following annual general meeting, at which time the director can be reappointed.[239] In the other main jurisdictions, statutory law gives more (default) guidance on the appointment of directors. In France, the directors are appointed at the incorporation of the company based on the provisions in the articles of association and subsequently by resolution of the general meeting of shareholders.[240] The resolution to appoint the directors has to be passed by means of a resolution in which more than 50% of the nominal value of the issued capital of the company votes in favour of the resolution.[241] For the private company, the directors are in principle appointed for an undetermined duration, unless the articles of association provide otherwise.[242] For the public company, the directors cannot be appointed for a term of more than six years, with the possibility of re-election.[243] If the company decides to set up a two-tier board, which only a minority of French companies do, the directors are appointed by the supervisory board.[244] In Germany, the appointment of directors differs between the private company (the GmbH) and the public company (the AG), in the sense that the AG is always required to have a supervisory board, whereas the GmbH is not always required to have a supervisory board. In the case of a private company, the directors are appointed by the shareholders, unless this power has been assigned to the supervisory board (which is mandatory if certain employees' thresholds are met).[245] In the case of a public company or a private company where a supervisory board is mandatorily required, the directors are appointed by the supervisory board.[246] The directors can be appointed for a term of up to five years and are eligible for re-election.[247] Under those circumstances, the shareholders therefore have no direct power over the appointment of the members of the board of directors. As for the supervisory board, its members are appointed by the general meeting of shareholders,[248] unless the company is subject to relevant co-determination provisions, in which case up to half of the members are employee representatives. Supervisory board members are appointed for a four-year term, with the possibility of re-election.[249] In the Netherlands, directors are in principle appointed by the general meeting of shareholders. In the case of a private company, the power to appoint certain directors can also be assigned to shareholders of a specific class of shares, as long as all shareholders have the opportunity to be involved in the

238. Model Articles for Private Companies, s 17(1); Model Articles for Public Companies, s 20.
239. Model Articles for Public Companies, s 21(2)(a).
240. Article L223-18(2); L225-18 French Commercial Code.
241. Article L223-29; L225-98 French Commercial Code.
242. Article L223-18(3) French Commercial Code.
243. Article L225-19 French Commercial Code.
244. Article L225-59 French Commercial Code.
245. Sections 46 and 52 German Limited Liability Companies Act.
246. Sections 96 and 101 German Stock Corporation Act.
247. Section 84(1) German Stock Corporation Act.
248. Section 101 German Stock Corporation Act.
249. Section 102 German Stock Corporation Act.

appointment of at least one director.[250] For a public company, all directors have to be appointed by the general meeting of shareholders.[251] In practice, the free determination of the shareholders in relation to the appointment of directors can be severely limited in listed companies by the use of voting thresholds, quorums and (binding) nomination rights.[252] Similar to Germany, the Netherlands has a specific regime for large companies (the *structuurregime*),[253] pursuant to which the company needs to install a mandatory two-tier or one-tier board. If this large company regime applies, then the directors are in the majority of cases appointed by the supervisory board, unless a 'mitigated' version of the large company regime is applied, in which case the directors can still be appointed by the general meeting of shareholders. In the case of the large company regime, the supervisory board members are appointed by the general meeting of shareholders on the nomination of the supervisory board.[254] However, the works council can make a binding proposal for one-third of the members of the supervisory board.[255]

6.70 Unsurprisingly, the rights to dismiss directors largely mirror the right of appointment of directors. There are, however, some minor nuances that should be considered. The most important is that in certain jurisdictions directors may – at least under certain circumstances – only be removed *with cause*, meaning that, briefly stated, there needs to be a proper reason for removing the director. Such is for instance the case for directors in the German public company, where the German Stock Corporation Act provides for a non-exhaustive list of grounds on the basis of which directors can be dismissed.[256] In the Netherlands, under the large company regime (applicable to both private and public companies), individual members of the supervisory board can only be dismissed when the shareholders petition the Enterprise Chamber of the Amsterdam Court of Appeal and the court has limited grounds on which it can award such a petition.[257] Shareholders are allowed to dismiss the entire supervisory board, but should that happen the board of directors needs to petition that same Enterprise Chamber to appoint new (temporary) supervisory board members.[258]

6.71 Provisions that are aimed at limiting the power of the shareholders to freely dismiss directors, such as by requiring a cause to dismiss the directors, serve the purpose of insulating the board of directors against (overly) invasive shareholder

250. Article 2:242(1) Dutch Civil Code.
251. Article 2:132(1) Dutch Civil Code.
252. *See* B. Kemp & S. Renshof, 'The Limited Power to Appoint and Dismiss Management Board Members in Dutch Listed Companies', *European Company Law* 17, no. 2 (2020): 37–44.
253. The large company regime applies if three conditions are met: (i) the shareholder capital and reserves of the company are at least EUR 16 million; (ii) the company or a dependent company has been legally required to establish a works council; and (iii) at the company and its dependent companies at least 100 employees work in the Netherlands (Articles 2:153 and 2:263(2) Dutch Civil Code).
254. Articles 2:155, 2:155a, 2:265a Dutch Civil Code.
255. Articles 2:158 and 2:268(6) Dutch Civil Code.
256. Section 84(3) German Stock Corporation Act.
257. Article 2:161(2) and 2:271(2) Dutch Civil Code.
258. Article 2:161a and 2:271a Dutch Civil Code.

pressure, because such provisions limit the possibilities for the shareholders to intervene in the management of the company by removing directors. This is especially relevant in jurisdictions where the board of directors has to serve the interest of the company and not necessarily the interests of the shareholders, such as in Germany and the Netherlands. Provisions limiting the power of the shareholders to dismiss directors provide more autonomy to the board of directors to (primarily) serve the interests of the company, independent from the position taken by the shareholders. However, it should be kept in mind that the aforementioned instruments are the exceptions to the generally prevailing rule that shareholders (and supervisory board members) are free to dismiss the directors that they appoint, as is the case in the Netherlands for directors and supervisory board members outside of the large company regime, for supervisory board members in Germany, and in both France and the UK. Most laws do provide for a certain level of protection for directors in the form of a procedural rule, primarily by means of a requirement to inform and/or hear the director before a vote to dismiss the director can be passed.[259]

2 *Instruction Rights*

6.72 Another influential right that shareholders can have is the right to instruct the board of directors to perform (or not perform) a certain act. The presence of such a right, to force another corporate body to follow a 'command', demonstrates the supreme position of shareholders within the corporate governance in the given jurisdiction. Given that certain jurisdictions provide the board of directors with more of an autonomous position than others, it is not surprising that instruction rights are treated differently between jurisdictions – or even within one jurisdiction based on the applicable company form (private versus public company). In the UK, although at one time the shareholders had the supreme power to give binding instructions to the board of directors at any time, courts have since then determined that whether or not binding instructions can be issued to the board of directors depends on the articles of association of the company.[260] Shareholders can therefore issue binding instructions if the articles of association provide for it. This, however, needs to be a forward-looking instruction; shareholders cannot instruct the board of directors on matters that have already taken place and only while respecting the company's current obligations.[261] In

259. *See* C. Gerner Beuerle & M.A. Schillig, *supra* n. 31, at 448, 453. In the Netherlands, directors need to be heard before the general meeting can dismiss them. In addition, directors have an advisory vote in relation to the proposed resolution, as they have for any resolution by the general meeting (Articles 2:117 (4); 227(4) Dutch Civil Code). In the UK, a director has the right to make written representations to the members (section 169(3) UK Companies Act 2006). The director may also speak at the meeting (section 169(2) UK Companies Act 2006). The (managing) directors of a (German) GmbH do not have such privileges. The removal of a managing director is possible at any time (sections 38 and 46 German Limited Liability Companies Act).
260. Automatic Self-Cleaning Filter Syndicate Company Ltd. v Cuninghane [1906] 2 CH 43.
261. I-M Esser and J. Loughrey, 'United Kingdom', in A. Vicari & A. Schall (eds), *supra* n. 17, at 1502.

the Model Articles for public companies, shareholders have the right to issue binding instructions by means of a special vote requiring 75 % or more of the votes in favour of the resolution.[262] In Germany, whether the shareholders have the power to instruct the board of directors depends on the company type form, the AG or GmbH. In a public company, shareholders neither have the power to give binding instructions to the board of directors nor does the supervisory board.[263] This fits the autonomy granted to the board of directors.[264] By contrast, in a private company, the shareholders do have the power to issue binding instructions to the board of directors on any matter, even with regard to policy.[265] The binding instruction is a consequence of the concept that the ultimate authority in the GmbH lies with the general meeting of shareholders.[266] The Netherlands formally also makes a distinction between the public company (NV) and the private company (BV). In both cases, instruction rights are only present if the articles of association provide for it.[267] In a public company, shareholders are limited to giving instructions on the general policy in certain areas, which can be further specified in the articles of association. Shareholders therefore cannot give specific instructions to the board of directors, although this fact is debated.[268] For a private company, shareholders can give specific binding instructions to the board of directors. However, the board of directors is only obligated to follow the instruction if this instruction is not in violation of the corporate interest of the company. As a result, the board of directors can ignore instructions which would be against the corporate interest. Although not provided for in statutory law, the prevailing view is that instruction rights in the public company are similarly limited.[269] In Dutch practice, the right to give instructions is therefore a less effective instrument, given that this right is mainly relevant in cases where the shareholders would like the board of directors to act in a manner that is mainly in the shareholders' interest instead of in the company's interest.

3 Approval for Important Board Decisions

6.73 The power to manage the day-to-day operations, determine the policy of the company, and represent the company to third parties is generally assigned to the board of directors of the company. Shareholders hold limited but important control rights, such as those mentioned above. In addition, shareholders generally have a role to play in important board decisions that determine the character and structure of the company, such as mergers, divisions, conversions/transformations, and winding up and liquidation. Amongst these rights is also the right to approve important board

262. The Companies (Model Articles) Regulations 2008, SI (2008) n. 3229, Sched 3, Model Articles for Public Companies.
263. A. Schall, 'Germany', in A. Vicari & A. Schall (eds), *supra* n. 17, at 259.
264. *Ibid.*
265. V. Klappstein, 'Germany', in A. Vicari & A. Schall (eds), *supra* n. 17, at 343.
266. *Ibid.*
267. Articles 2:129(4) and 2:239(4) Dutch Civil Code.
268. *See* for an overview: P. van Schilfgaarde, J.W. Winter, J.B. Wezeman & J.D.M. Schoonbrood, *supra* n. 98, at 42; Asser/Van Solinge & Nieuwe Weme 2-IIb 2019/153.
269. Asser/Van Solinge & Nieuwe Weme 2-IIb 2019/153.

decisions regarding the sale of all or a substantial part of the assets. After all, if the board of directors decides to sell these assets, the very nature of the company in which the shareholders have invested might change, and it is generally considered that shareholders should have a vote in such crucial matters.

Aside from provisions included in the articles of association, the main jurisdictions also provide for statutory rules regarding the approval of important board decisions by the shareholders. Under Dutch law, shareholders of the public company have the statutory right to approve any resolution of the board of directors that leads to a change in the identity or character of the company.[270] The provision also provides for a non-exhaustive list of circumstances under which that is considered the case, which is: (a) a transfer of the enterprise or of practically the entire enterprise to a third party; (b) the start or termination by company or its subsidiary of a long-lasting alliance with another legal entity or a commercial partnership, or the start or termination by company or its subsidiary as a fully liable partner in a limited partnership (*'commanditaire vennootschap'*) or general partnership (*'vennootschap onder firma'*), as long as the start or termination of such alliance or partnership is of fundamental importance for the company; and (c) the acquisition or disposal of a participating interest in the capital of another legal entity to the value of at least one-third of the amount of the assets according to the company's balance sheet.

According to the Dutch Supreme Court, the provisions of Article 2:107a DCC need to be explained in a restrictive manner, such that it should be applied only if the resolution of the board of directors is so drastic that the identity or character of the company and the nature of the shareholding in the company would change.[271] The main argument of the Dutch Supreme Court for this restrictive interpretation was the legal certainty that is required in relation to business transactions, as was also referenced in the parliamentary history for the provision.[272] The Dutch legislature explicitly determined that no similar provisions had to be introduced for the private company. Nevertheless, the predominantly held view is that the rule embodied in Article 2:107a DCC should also be applied by analogy to the private company[273] since the same rationale can be applied to both public and private companies. In case law of the lower courts, courts tend to take different positions on whether or not shareholder approval is required for important board decisions. In several decisions, the Enterprise Chamber ruled that the transactions referred to in Article 2:107a DCC are also subject to the approval of the general meeting in the case of a private company.[274] In a more recent decision, the Amsterdam Court of Appeal, however, ruled contrary to this and

---

270. Article 2:107a Dutch Civil Code.
271. Dutch Supreme Court (HR) 13 July 2007, *NJ* 2007/434.
272. *Kamerstukken II* 2001/02, 28179, nr. 5, 19–20.
273. Asser/Van Solinge & Nieuwe Weme 2-IIb 2019/23; E.J.J. van der Heijden/W.C.L. van der Grinten/P.J. Dortmond, *Handboek voor de naamloze en besloten vennootschap* (Deventer: Kluwer 2013), 203.2.
274. *See* for instance: Amsterdam Court of Appeal (Enterprise Chamber) 16 Nov. 2005, *JOR* 2006/5; Amsterdam Court of Appeal (Enterprise Chamber) 1 Feb. 2006, *JOR* 2006/122; Amsterdam Court of Appeal (Enterprise Chamber) 23 Jan. 2009, *JOR* 2009/69; Amsterdam Court of Appeal (Enterprise Chamber) 5 Apr. 2018, *JOR* 2018/212.

asserted that Article 2:107a DCC cannot be applied by analogy to private companies because a right of approval based on unwritten law would lead to unacceptable legal uncertainty.[275] However, the impact of this decision is not undisputed. This follows from the fact that, after the rejection of the analogous application, the court lists various resolutions that are of such a fundamental nature that shareholders should (still) be able to approve them. Rather striking is the fact that this enumeration corresponds with the resolutions mentioned in Article 2:107a DCC. The consequences of this theoretical distinction have not been clearly stated by the court and therefore remain unclear.

6.74 Under German statutory law for the public company, transactions by the company with third parties are not subject to shareholder approval, even if these transactions are very significant.[276] The only codified exception is when the company sells all its assets to a third party,[277] which requires a special resolution with a qualified majority. This, however, does not mean that under German law shareholders do not have a vote with regard to important transactions since German courts have taken a more proactive approach to the matter, of which the *Holzmuller* and *Gelatine* cases are considered to be the most important.[278] In the *Holzmuller* case, Holzmuller AG was a company primarily active in the wood trade. To further strengthen its business, the company established a port facility in the harbour of Hamburg. Over time, this business proved to be more interesting and lucrative than its original wood trade business, which made the company decide to restructure its business and spin it off into a newly incorporated subsidiary. This restructuring would weaken the position of the shareholders because they would only indirectly have a shareholding in and control rights over the port facility business. Shareholders brought a claim to argue that the company lacked the required consent under Section 179a of the German Stock Corporation Act, which states that shareholder approval is required in case a company transfers its entire assets; according to the shareholders, this should be applied by way of analogy to the restructuring. The BGH dismissed the claim to the extent that it was based on Section 179a of the German Stock Corporation Act, but at the same time determined that the board of directors should have requested the general meeting for approval on a different ground. It ruled that if a fundamental board decision affected the rights and interest of the shareholders so deeply that the directors could not reasonably assume to be allowed to take the decision on their own, then it should refer the matter for approval to the general meeting. A breach of this duty would not lead to a challenge of the transaction but did expose the directors to potential liability.[279] This decision by the BGH caused concern in German legal practice because the rule as formulated by the BGH was difficult to apply (with certainty) in practice. As a result, a significant number of transactions were put forward to the shareholders for approval.[280] In 2004, the BGH

275. Amsterdam Court of Appeal 7 Apr. 2021, *JOR* 2021/201.
276. A. Schall, 'Germany', in A. Vicari & A. Schall (eds), *supra* n. 17, at 414-415.
277. Section 179a German Stock Corporation Act.
278. BGHZ 83, 122 = NJW (1982), 1703; BGHZ 159, 30 = NJW (2004), 1860.
279. A. Schall, 'Germany', in A. Vicari & A. Schall (eds), *supra* n. 17, at 416.
280. *Ibid.*, 417.

took the opportunity to further clarify the doctrine of shareholder approval for important board decisions in the *Gelatine* case. In this case, which concerned the transfer of shares in foreign subsidiaries to a new subsidiary and whether a 75% quorum of the capital present at the meeting was required for the shareholder vote to approve the transfer, the BGH held that the standard for requiring shareholder approval for important board decisions without a specific statutory provision was high and should be applied in a very limited manner. Although shareholders can be negatively affected in their interests as a result of the proposed transaction in Gelatine, as a result of which the subsidiaries would move to a lower level by inserting an intermediary subsidiary, the BGH noted that the volume of the transaction should at least be close to that of *Holzmuller*, which was 80% of the assets of the company.

Based on this case law, German courts and doctrine now take the view that a 75% threshold for the assets of the company is required to trigger the requirement of shareholder approval for important board decisions, although this threshold is still controversial.[281] Moreover, what type of transactions triggers the approval is also up for debate, with it at least being clear that transactions like those in *Holzmuller* and *Gelatine* are relevant. The resolution to approve the transfer then also requires a 75% voting threshold to be approved.

6.75 The French Commercial Code is less generous towards empowering shareholders with the right to approve board resolutions. The doctrinal reason for this is that French company law as part of the distribution of powers makes a clear distinction between the governing bodies of the company. Part of this division is that the management decision-making functions, on a day-to-day basis, are in the hands of the board.[282] The decision to sell an essential asset of the company therefore belongs to the power of the board, even if such a decision may have far-reaching consequences for the company and its shareholders.[283] The lack of influence from the shareholders has, however, not gone unnoticed. The AFM, the French securities regulator, has raised concerns about this practice and recommends that decisions to sell or acquire a significant asset should be submitted to the general meeting.[284] The AFM, however, lacks the powers to regulate this matter. Parties are, however, free to include a provision in the articles of association providing that such a decision has to be authorized by the shareholders, keeping in mind that such a limitation of the powers of the board is not effective against third parties.[285]

281. OLG Hamm, NZG (2008), 155, 158.
282. I. Grossi, D. Poracchia & A. Raynouard, 'France', in A. Vicari & A. Schall (eds), *supra* n. 17, at 71.
283. *Ibid.*
284. Position-Recommandation AMF, DOC n. 2015-05, Les cessions et les acquisitions d'actifs significatifs.
285. I. Grossi, D. Poracchia & A. Raynouard, 'France', in A. Vicari & A. Schall (eds), *supra* n. 17, at 71.

6.76 The premise in the UK is that the division of powers between the board and the shareholders depends entirely on the construction of the articles of association.[286] In general, shareholders have a right of approval concerning three types of resolutions. First, in relation to matters in which directors potentially have a conflict of interest. Second, in relation to decisions that have significant implications for the company (e.g., very large transactions). Third, decisions which will affect shareholder rights.[287] Listed companies on the London Stock Exchange are faced with additional rights of approval. Rule 10 of the Listings Rules provides that transactions that amount to 25% of the company's assets, profits, turnover, market value or gross capital require prior approval of the shareholders.[288] Moreover, shareholders of all public companies are provided with rights of approval in case of a takeover offer being made for the company. These rights will only apply in the scenario when the board of the target company has reason to believe that a *bona fide* offer might be imminent and only for any defensive action that could frustrate the bid or for actions such as selling, disposing of, or acquiring (or agreeing to acquire) assets for a material amount; or entering into agreements other than in the ordinary course of business.[289] Examples of these decisions include the allotment of shares save where the articles authorize the allotment;[290] the disapplication of pre-emption;[291] and altering the rights attached to a class of shares.[292]

C What Are the Functions of the General Meeting?

6.77 Having so far focused on the control rights that shareholders exercise through the general meeting, we now turn to that corporate body and its procedural rules. The general meeting of shareholders is a mandatory corporate body in almost all company forms and fulfils three functions within the corporate governance framework of the company.[293]

First, and probably the most important, the general meeting has a decision-making function. Most of the collective rights of shareholders, such as those set out earlier, will in principle be exercised through the general meeting. As a result, it is important that shareholders are able to have access to a general meeting of shareholders and are able to participate in this general meeting as much as possible. Recent years

286. This premise is based on the fact that the UK Companies Act 2006 is silent about the division of powers between the board and the shareholders which has been emphasized in Automatic Self-Cleansing Filter Syndicate Co Ltd v Cuninghame [1906] 2 Ch 34.
287. D. Kershaw, *Company Law in Context* (Oxford: Oxford University Press, 2021), 195.
288. I-M Esser & J. Loughrey, 'United Kingdom', in A. Vicari & A. Schall (eds), *supra* n. 17, at 1503; referring to Listing Rule 10.2.2; Listing Rule 10 Annex 1.
289. Rule 21 of the City Code on Takeovers and Mergers.
290. Section 551 UK Companies Act 2006.
291. Sections 570–571 UK Companies Act 2006.
292. Section 630 UK Companies Act 2006.
293. A. Lafarre, *supra* n. 220, at 7 *et seq.*; T. Strand, *The Owners and the Power: Insights from Annual General Meetings*, PhD series 25.2012 (Denmark: Copenhagen Business School 2012), 13; R. Strätling, 'General Meetings: A Dispensable Tool for Corporate Governance of Listed Companies?', *Corporate Governance: An International Review*, 11 (2003): 74–82.

have seen several initiatives at enabling shareholders to play an active role within the company by removing barriers to exercising shareholder rights.[294] When considering the decision-making function of the general meeting, it is important to realize that there is a distinction between the general meeting of shareholders as a legal decision-making body within the company and an actual joint meeting of shareholders. For the decision-making function of the general meeting, it is not required to have an actual meeting of shareholders. For instance, the Netherlands,[295] the UK,[296] France[297] and Germany[298] allow for shareholders – mainly of private companies – to pass resolutions outside of an actual meeting of shareholders. While no actual meeting took place, these resolutions are still qualified as resolutions from the general meeting of shareholders. Generally, this way of passing resolutions is only possible with the consent of the shareholders and therefore applied solely in companies where all shareholders can be identified (which is generally – in any event – not the case for listed companies) and are actively cooperating with each other, such family-owned businesses and partnership type companies.

A second function of the general meeting is the information function. The general meeting functions as a venue in which the board of directors can share information with the joint shareholders. A distinct example of this is the fact that the board of directors generally presents the annual accounts during the general meeting, after which the shareholders have to vote on whether or not to approve these annual accounts. Moreover, shareholders have the right to put forward questions to the board of directors, which then in principle need to be answered during the meeting. As a result, the shareholders and directors can discuss items that are considered relevant by both, keeping in mind certain limits, such as that the directors generally cannot be forced to share sensitive information.[299]

The third function of the general meeting is to serve as a forum for shareholders to discuss items among themselves. The general meeting is the main place in which shareholders, as a group, can discuss the company, its performance and other items the shareholders deem relevant. Before voting on a specific item, the board of directors will generally introduce the item and explain relevant considerations, after which shareholders have the opportunity to ask questions to the board of directors and give their own view of the proposed item. In doing so, shareholders can also present their views

294. An example is for instance the amendment of Directive (EU) 2017/828, as a result of which for instance the role of shareholders in setting the remuneration policy has been increased.
295. Article 2:128/238 Dutch Civil Code.
296. However, written resolutions are only permitted within the private company (section 281(1) UK Companies Act 2006). Section 336 UK Companies Act 2006, requiring an AGM, applies only to public companies.
297. Article L223-27 French Commercial Code for private companies, public companies do not have this option. L225-103-1 however does stipulate that general meetings can be held exclusively by videoconference or by means of telecommunication allowing the identification of shareholders.
298. Section 48 (2) German Limited Liability Companies Act for the GmbH. Section 118 of the German Stock Corporation Act does not provide for this option but does allow electronic voting/participation.
299. *See* paragraph 6.90 *et seq.*

to other shareholders in the general meeting and even enter into discussions with shareholders that for instance hold an opposing view to their own. Moreover, the board of directors, supervisory board and shareholders can also proactively request the joint shareholders to share their view on a certain subject by way of an informal vote or poll, even if this item is not a formal voting item on the agenda. A recent example of this is the English company Shell Plc, which put forward a non-binding resolution on the company's energy transition strategy to the shareholders.[300]

6.78 In practice, whether and how these three functions of the general meeting work very much depend on the type of company and its shareholder base. For instance, in a private equity portfolio company, the shareholder(s) will be very involved in the business of the company and how it operates, and the PE fund will usually sidestep the general meeting as a forum for shareholders to collaborate and obtain information by means of nominating supervisory board members from its ranks and agreeing to contractual information rights in a shareholder agreement. As a result, the second and third functions of the general meeting play a limited role in such companies. However, in listed companies with a diversified shareholder base, these two functions will play a more important role, since the general meeting is one of the primary ways to obtain information from the company and to enter into discussions with other shareholders – which in listed companies will not all be known to the shareholders and the company itself. Even in listed companies, however, these functions of the general meeting are criticized because of problems related to rational apathy, free riding and the lack of an actual dialogue during the general meeting.[301]

First, shareholders – and especially small shareholders – do not have an incentive to actively participate in the decision-making process of the general meeting because the marginal gains of making an informed vote do not outweigh the costs of ensuring that the shareholder is adequately informed and votes on the shares.[302] Moreover, the outcome of the vote will likely not be influenced by a vote exercised by these shareholders. This behaviour, which is referred to as 'rational apathy', is the result of the relatively high costs of obtaining information and exercising a vote. This problem might partly be resolved by focusing more on the pooling of assets in the hands of professional parties that hold these assets on behalf of the ultimate beneficiary, which is the case for many institutional investors.[303] Many recent regulatory initiatives have rightly been focused on the position of institutional investors and how these investors can (a) be activated to take a more active position in the corporate governance of the company, and (b) provide more transparency on the nature of their investment and commitment.[304]

---

300. https://www.reuters.com/business/energy/shell-shareholders-overwhelmingly-support-energy-transition-plan-2021-05-18/.
301. *See* for an overview: A. Lafarre, *supra* n. 220, at 7 *et seq.*
302. A. Cahn & D.C. Donald, *supra* n. 84, at 583.
303. C. Gerner Beuerle & M.A. Schillig, *supra* n. 31, at 397.
304. For instance, under the revised Shareholders Rights Directive (Directive 2007/36/EC, amended by Directive (EU) 2017/828), there is a mandatory disclosure obligation on asset managers and institutional investors in order for them to reflect on their medium- to long-term orientation (Articles 3h and 3i of the Directive (EU) 2017/828). Moreover, the directive requires asset

Second, certain shareholders might feel that they are not required to incur these monitoring costs because other shareholders – generally with a more significant shareholding – will make the effort of incurring these monitoring costs and casting an informed vote. Since these active shareholders have the same interests as the non-active shareholders, the non-active shareholders are profiting from the monitoring done by active shareholders without having to incur any monitoring costs themselves. As a result, small shareholders actually have an incentive not to participate in the decision-making of the company and 'free ride' on the decisions taken by the active shareholders.

Third, in practice the general meeting is hardly used as a forum to obtain information and for discussions between shareholders and with the management and supervisory board. The design of the general meeting and aim to have a high participation rate actually frustrates this function. In practice, a significant number of shareholders are not present during the general meeting but cast their votes by way of proxy before the general meeting. For instance, in 2019 during the general meetings of the Dutch companies PostNL, ING Groep, DSM and NN Group only 0.87%, 0.67%, 0.15% and 0.02% respectively of the votes were cast by persons actually present in person at the general meeting, with all other votes being cast by proxy.[305] The low physical attendance rates of shareholders at general meetings impact the functions of the general meeting in various ways. First, shareholders in a general meeting cannot actually discuss items together or with the management and supervisory board when most of the shareholders are not present. Second, questions raised during the general meeting and discussion that take place before shareholders vote on the item on the agenda do not have any material effect on how the shareholders vote, because most shareholders never had the opportunity to hear the answers to the questions, the discussions between the board of directors and shareholders, and the positions taken by their fellow shareholders. To address this problem, some scholars have suggested that the general meeting should be fully in writing with the possibility to ask and answer questions beforehand based on the agenda for the meeting.[306] In addition, the COVID-19 pandemic has forced some changes on general meetings, mainly in relation to the requirement to hold a general meeting that could only be digitally attended by the shareholders.[307]

---

managers and institutional investors to develop and disclose an engagement policy that describes how they monitor the companies in which they invest, and they must publish a description of their voting behaviour and how their investment strategy contributes to the medium- to long-term performance of the company (Article 3g(1)(b) of Directive (EU) 2017/828.

305. R. Abma, 'Kroniek van het seizoen van jaarlijkse algemene vergaderingen 2019', *Ondernemingsrecht* 2019/145.

306. H.J. de Kluiver, De aandeelhoudersvergadering van de beursvennootschap (ZIFO nr. 27), 2019/2.

307. The Institutional Shareholder Services group of companies (ISS) published a report in response to the pandemic containing an overview of the guidance that regulators in several countries have produced on the greater flexibility regarding the type of annual general meeting (AGM) publicly listed companies can hold as well as when it can be held: ISS Governance Research Team, Annual General Meetings & COVID-19: A Review of the Regulatory Landscape, April 2020.

6.79 It should be noted that shareholders do have other ways of entering into discussions with the board of directors and obtaining information, primarily by means of recurring conference calls with investors, road shows and one-on-ones.[308] These ways of obtaining information in order for shareholders to fulfil their monitoring role seem to be less costly and more effective. It might also give shareholders the opportunity to have a more open discussion with boards of directors compared to the very public general meetings.[309]

D The Practice of the General Meeting; How to Call the General Meeting and Vote

6.80 When considering the position of shareholders, the substantive rights of shareholders are important, but just as important are how and when shareholders can exercise these rights. After all, if the shareholders have strong control rights but can only exercise these rights under limited or difficult circumstances, the impact of these rights is still limited. In this section, the rules for how a general meeting is called, how items are put on the agenda and how resolutions are passed (majorities/quorums) are discussed. In addition, how voting rights in the various jurisdictions function is also addressed.

6.81 In each of the main jurisdictions, the board or – in a two-tier system – both the board of directors and the supervisory board are the corporate body that is primarily responsible for calling a general meeting.[310] This is in line with the belief that the board of directors is in practice best placed to call a general meeting because it can determine whether a shareholder vote on a particular item is required since the board is best aware of who the shareholders are and of the fact that the company bears the costs related to calling and holding a general meeting. However, there can also be circumstances in which shareholders themselves would like to call a general meeting, for instance in case of a (potential) conflict with the board of directors. Shareholders therefore also have the right to call general meetings themselves, although there are certain requirements that these shareholders have to meet. In the UK, shareholders can require the board of directors to call a general meeting if the shareholders represent more than 5% of the issued capital carrying the right to vote request such a meeting.[311] Germany also applies a 5% threshold but does not require that the shares are fully paid or carry voting rights, provided that the shareholders have the right to attend the general meeting.[312] Should the board of directors refuse to call the general meeting,

308. J.S.T. Tiemstra & J. de Keijzer, Algemene vergadering van aandeelhouders: Hoeksteen van corporate governance of niet-representatieve formaliteit?, *Ondernemingsrecht* 2008/54.
309. R. Strätling, *supra* n. 293, at 76.
310. Section 121(1) German Stock Corporation Act; section 302 UK Companies Act 2006; Article 2:109 Dutch Civil Code; Article L225-103-I French Commercial Code.
311. Section 303(2) UK Companies Act 2006.
312. Section 122 German Stock Corporation Act.

then the shareholder can petition the court for the authority to call a general meeting.[313] In France, there is as a starting point a similar 5% threshold, with lower thresholds up to 1% being applied depending on the share capital of the company.[314] Shareholders can also request the appointment of a representative to call the general meeting. When ruling on such a request, the court will take into consideration the interest of the company and can refuse the request if it is only in the interest of the requesting shareholder.[315] Dutch law on public companies has a higher threshold for calling a general meeting, requiring the shareholder to alone or jointly hold 10% of the issued capital.[316] For the private company, however, the threshold is only 1% of the issued capital, with the possibility to lower the threshold further in the articles of association.[317] If the directors of a Dutch public or private company refuse to call the general meeting, then the shareholders can petition the court for authorization to call the general meeting themselves. For the public company, the test is whether the shareholders have a reasonable interest in calling the general meeting, although courts have also dismissed requests for a general meeting on the ground that the shareholders need to act reasonably and fairly towards the company, and therefore the court should also consider the corporate interest.[318] For the private company, the court also has the room to refuse the request for authorization on the basis of a compelling interest on the side of the company.[319]

6.82 The main jurisdictions also have different regulations when it comes to calling a general meeting and the conduct during the general meeting. The Shareholder Rights Directive sets minimum standards in relation to calling a general meeting, regulating – for listed companies[320] – that annual general meetings have to be called at least twenty-one days in advance of the meeting and 'extraordinary meetings'[321] have to at least be called fourteen days before the general meeting, provided that the company offers a facility for the shareholders to vote by electronic means accessible to all shareholders.[322] The notice for the general meeting should be disseminated in such a manner that it ensures fast access to it on a non-discriminatory basis.[323] The standards for calling a general meeting are further regulated under national law and also differ for the public and the private company. In the UK, the minimum term for calling an annual general meeting of a public company is twenty-one days, with a fourteen days' notice

313. Section 122(3) German Stock Corporation Act
314. Article L225-103-II; L225-120 French Commercial Code.
315. CA Colmar, 24 Sep. 1975, Dalloz (1976), 348.
316. Article 2:110(1) Dutch Civil Code.
317. Article 2:220(1) Dutch Civil Code.
318. *See*, for instance, the judgment of the Amsterdam District Court on the request of activist shareholders in relation to Akzo Nobel: District Court Amsterdam 10 Aug. 2017, *JOR* 2017/260.
319. Article 2:221(1) Dutch Civil Code.
320. The specific scope of the directive is: 'which have their registered office in a Member State and whose shares are admitted to trading on a regulated market situated or operating within a Member State' (Article 1(1) Directive 2007/36/EC).
321. Extraordinary meetings being all meetings that are not annual general meetings.
322. Article 5(1) Directive 2007/36/EC.
323. Article 5(2) Directive 2007/36/EC.

period for other general meetings.[324] For private companies, the minimum term is always fourteen days with no exception for the annual general meeting. In all cases, the articles of association may determine that a longer minimum term is required.[325] It is possible to apply shorter notice periods. In the case of the annual general meeting, all shareholders will have to consent to this. In the case of other general meetings, 90% (the private company) or 95% (the public company) of the shareholders that have the right to attend and vote at the general meeting need to agree on the shorter term.[326] In Germany, the term for calling a general meeting is slightly longer, with Section 123 of the German Corporation Act determining that the general meeting has to be called at least thirty days before the date set for the meeting. Further, in contrast to the UK, it does not make a distinction between the annual general meeting and other general meetings. In the Netherlands, the term for calling a general meeting is fifteen days for the public company and eight days for the private company.[327] A shorter term is only possible if (a) – for the public company – the entire issued capital is represented in the general meeting[328] or (b) – for the private company – all persons entitled to attend the general meeting approve passing a resolution outside of the general meeting,[329] which means that a shareholder that wants to frustrate the decision making can easily do so by simply staying away from the general meeting. For Dutch listed companies, the term is significantly longer with at least forty-two days before the general meeting.[330] French statutory law provides for listed public companies or companies in which not all shares are held in registered form that the body convening the meeting must have the notice of the general meeting published at least thirty-five days before the meeting.[331] Unlisted companies should publish the notice at least fifteen days before the general meeting.[332]

6.83 Another important right in relation to the general meeting is the right to put items on the agenda. The agenda is generally determined by the corporate body that is competent to call the general meeting, which as discussed earlier is in most cases the board of directors and/or supervisory board. However, other stakeholders, and especially shareholders, might want to include their own agenda items for the general meeting. One of the main provisions of the Shareholder Rights Directive aims to protect the right of the shareholders to put items on the agenda of the general meeting.[333] This

324. Section 307(2) UK Companies Act 2006. For listed companies, the conditions are slightly different, but the terms are the same (*see* section 307A UK Companies Act 2006).
325. Section 307(3) UK Companies Act 2006.
326. Section 307(4), (5), (6) and (7) UK Companies Act 2006.
327. Articles 2:115(1) and 2:225 Dutch Civil Code.
328. Article 2:114(2) Dutch Civil Code.
329. Article 2:224(2) Dutch Civil Code.
330. Article 2:115(2) Dutch Civil Code.
331. Article R225-73 French Commercial Code.
332. Article R225-69 French Commercial Code for public companies and Article R223-20 French Commercial Code for private companies.
333. Point 7 of the recitals states: 'Shareholders should, in principle, have the possibility to put items on the agenda of the general meeting and to table draft resolutions for items on the agenda. Without prejudice to different time-frames and modalities which are currently in use across the Community, the exercise of those rights should be made subject to two basic rules, namely that any threshold required for the exercise of those rights should not exceed 5% of the company's

right can be limited to putting items only on the agenda of the annual general meeting - and not other general meetings. In order to ensure that shareholders can still put items on the agenda, in that case, shareholders need to have the right to call a general meeting which should include the items put forward by those shareholders.[334] Moreover, the Shareholder Rights Directive states that the threshold to exercise these rights may not exceed 5 % of the share capital.[335] Next to this minimum regulation, it is up to national law to further regulate the right of shareholders to put items on the agenda. In the UK, shareholders representing 5 % of the voting rights or 100 members that have the right to vote and holding a sum of GBP 100 each can request the company to include additional items on the agenda.[336] Such a request needs to be received at least six weeks (i.e. forty-two days) before the general meeting or, if later, at the time at which notice is given of the general meeting.[337] In the German public company, shareholders have the right to request items be added to the agenda if these shareholders represent 5 % of the share capital or have an interest of EUR 500,000 in the company.[338] Such a request to add items to the agenda needs to be made to the company at least fourteen days prior to the date of the meeting.[339] France applies the same threshold as the UK and Germany, being 5 % of the share capital[340] and applies lower thresholds up to 0.5 % if the company has a certain amount of share capital.[341] In the Netherlands, until 2013 a 1 % threshold was applied to public companies. However, the threshold was increased to 3 % in order to relate more closely to the practice in other counties and because of the significant impact of the right to put items on the agenda of the general meeting.[342] Whereas the threshold for the public company is therefore now 3 %,[343] for the private company the threshold is still 1 %.[344] Moreover, for the private company, there is the possibility to reject the request to put an item on the agenda if the company has a 'compelling interest' to do so.[345] The term for putting forward items for the agenda is thirty days for the private company and sixty days for the public company.[346]

6.84 What is especially interesting from the above is that although there are many minimum requirements with regard to the general meeting and shareholder rights, there are still significant differences between the main jurisdictions in relation to - for

share capital and that all shareholders should in every case receive the final version of the agenda in sufficient time to prepare for the discussion and voting on each item on the agenda.'

334. Article 6(1) Directive 2007/36/EC.
335. *Ibid.*
336. Sections 338–339 UK Companies Act 2006.
337. Section 338(4) UK Companies Act 2006.
338. Section 122(2) German Stock Corporation Act.
339. Section 126(1) German Stock Corporation Act.
340. Article R225-72(2) and R225-73-II French Commercial Code.
341. Article R225-71(2) French Commercial Code.
342. *Kamerstukken II* 2008/09, 32014, nr. 3, 22–23.
343. Article 2:114a(1) Dutch Civil Code.
344. Article 2:224a(1) Dutch Civil Code.
345. The public company has a similar ground for refusal of proposals to add items to the general meeting, but this ground was removed in anticipation of the Shareholder Rights Directive because it was considered incompatible (*see*: Asser/Van Solinge & Nieuwe Weme 2-IIb 2019/57).
346. Articles 2:114a and 2:224a Dutch Civil Code.

instance – thresholds and to what extent a shareholder can be frustrated in exercising its rights. For instance, in the Netherlands and France, the possibility to call a general meeting seems to be more limited because the court has more discretion to refuse such a request based on the interest of the company. At the same time, thresholds for adding items to the agenda are in a number of cases lower than in for instance Germany and the UK.

E Votes, Majorities and Quorums

1 Voting Rights

6.85 When discussing the rights-based theory (paragraph 6.55), reference was made to the principle of one share-one vote and the deviations from this principle in current practice. In most jurisdictions, one share-one vote is still the default rule. For instance, in France Article L225-122 (1) Code de Commerce states that the voting right is proportional to the capital the share represents. A similar rule applies in the Netherlands, where shares with the same nominal value have the same voting rights.[347] This default rule is also a reflection of the equal treatment principle as commonly accepted in most jurisdictions. However, while being a default rule, there are many possibilities in the main jurisdictions to deviate from this. Broadly, this can be done along the following lines:

1. by issuing shares with additional voting rights; i.e. multiple voting shares;
2. by issuing non-voting shares, which hold an economic right but do not infer voting rights on the holder of the shares; and
3. by limiting the possibility to exercise voting rights on the shares to a certain percentage by using voting caps. As discussed when referring to the rights-based theory, there is the possibility to regulate that one shareholder cannot exercise more than a certain number of votes in the general meeting.

6.86 There can be valid reasons for deviating from the default rule, and all main jurisdictions allow for some type of deviation. For instance, a company might want to reward 'loyal' shareholders by giving these shareholders additional voting or dividend rights or a family-owned business might want to give employees an interest in the company without giving these employees voting rights as a shareholder. In those cases, the possibility to deviate from the default rule might serve a valid business purpose that is in the interest of the company.

6.87 The main jurisdictions – once again – deal with this topic in very different ways. In the UK, the Companies Act 2006 recognizes the possibility of having different classes of shares but does not regulate how voting rights should be structured. In practice,

347. Article 2:118(1) Dutch Civil Code.

using non-voting shares next to voting shares is uncontroversial,[348] and the use of multiple voting rights seems to be permissible in certain situations.[349] In listed companies, the use of multiple voting rights is scrutinized far more heavily, especially by institutional investors. However, in a recent effort to attract more companies to the stock exchanges in the UK, the Financial Conduct Authority announced that it will change the listing rules in order to allow a targeted form of dual-class share structures within the premium listing segment.[350] In Germany, companies are similarly allowed to adopt different classes of shares in order to issue both voting and non-voting shares.[351] Having said that, in contrast to the UK, it is not possible to issue share with multiple voting rights. In France, it is also possible to issue both voting and non-voting shares, keeping in mind that the non-voting shares cannot constitute more than 50% of the share capital (25% in the case of listed companies).[352] French public companies may, however, not issue multiple voting shares, with the exception of the possibility to introduce a loyalty scheme on the basis of which the company can issue a double voting right to shareholders who for at least two years held shares in the company.[353] For listed public companies, the loyalty scheme applies, unless otherwise provided for in the articles of association. For non-listed public companies, it is the other way around. In the Netherlands, the regime for private companies provides the most flexibility for non-voting shares and multiple voting shares.[354] For the public company, there is the possibility to create multiple voting shares by introducing different classes of shares which have different nominal values. It is not possible to create non-voting shares in a public company, although there are contractual mechanisms that achieve the same effect. In short, to achieve this effect, the shares are issued to a legal entity, a foundation, that in turn issues depositary receipts (which are contractual rights) to the beneficial owner. This way the voting rights attached to the shares stay with the foundation, which generally has an independent but company-friendly board, whereas the economic rights are transferred to the beneficial owner.

2 Majorities and Quorums

6.88 Another important item when considering shareholder voting is what requirements actually have to be met in order to pass a resolution. Although individual jurisdictions each have their own rules for when a certain resolution is passed, there are several overarching principles that can be considered. First, a distinction can be made between the required voting majority and any quorum requirements. The voting

348. C. Gerner Beuerle & M.A. Schillig, *supra* n. 31, at 386.
349. *See,* for instance, Bushell v Faith [1970] AC 1099 (House of Lords).
350. *See* https://www.fca.org.uk/news/press-releases/fca-confirms-new-listing-rules-boost-growth-and-innovation.
351. Section 12(1) German Stock Corporate Act.
352. Article L228-11 French Commercial Code.
353. Article L225-123 French Commercial Code. *See* for more detail on how this loyalty scheme is regulated: R. Mortier, 'France, in A. Vicari & A. Schall (eds), *supra* n. 17, at 30–31.
354. Article 2:228 Dutch Civil Code.

majority is simple; it states what percentage of the shareholders present during the general meeting need to vote in favour of the resolution in order for it to be passed. This can, for instance, not only be a simple majority but also extraordinary majorities of two-thirds, three-quarters or 80%, depending on whether it is felt that the resolution is of such importance that it should be resolved by a more significant part of the shareholder base. The required quorum refers to the share capital that needs to be represented in a general meeting in order to validly pass the resolution. For instance, in certain cases, it might be required that at least 50% of the share capital be represented in the general meeting. Quorum requirements can safeguard that resolutions are only passed by a majority that is actually representative of the shareholder base and avoids a marginal group of shareholders having the power to pass a resolution because few shareholders were present during the general meeting. To avoid resolutions not being passed because a required part of the share capital simply repeatedly does not attend the general meeting, many jurisdictions provide for calling a second general meeting if the quorum is not met during the first general meeting, in which second meeting the quorum is not required. Second, the required majorities and quorums do not only differ between jurisdictions but also depend on the matter that has to be resolved. Resolutions related to a major corporate change might justify requiring a higher majority than 'run of the mill' resolutions.

6. 89 In all main jurisdictions, resolutions of the general meeting are passed by a simple majority, unless the law or articles of association explicitly provide otherwise. Supermajorities with various thresholds, for both the majority and quorums, are present for certain resolutions. For instance, the abovementioned shareholder approval for important board decisions in German public companies requires a 75% majority. The law might also set limits to the thresholds that can be applied to certain resolutions. Another example is that under Dutch law, the resolution to dismiss directors cannot be set higher than a two-thirds majority vote in a general meeting in which half of the share capital is represented.[355] The rationale behind this provision is that requiring an even greater majority/quorum would make it too difficult for the shareholders to dismiss members of the board of directors.[356]

F Right to Information

6.90 Within the corporate governance framework, shareholders are granted important control rights. In order for shareholders to properly exercise these rights, it is important that shareholders have sufficient information to make an informed vote. An important element of insuring such a vote is by means of information rights for shareholders. These information rights can come in different forms, including in a very broad sense: (a) specific information requests from shareholders and (b) proactive disclosure of information by the company. Proactive disclosure by the company can take the form of

355. Articles 2:134(2) and 2:224(2) Dutch Civil Code.
356. Asser/Van Solinge & Nieuwe Weme 2-IIb 2019/252.

periodic disclosure, for instance by publishing the annual accounts of the company, or ad hoc disclosure, which is for instance the case for price-sensitive information that must be disclosed to the market. In addition, both for information requests and for the proactive sharing of information, the question can arise about how much information can be shared and on which grounds information could be withheld from shareholders (and the public). A similar question can be raised in relation to documents; should these be shared with shareholders and/or the public?

6.91 Rights to information are regulated in various places. While company law generally deals with information rights of shareholders, and in particular to what extent shareholders can request information from the company, provisions related to the annual accounts and securities law also play an important role in shareholders' right to information. Here, we mainly focus on the first point. Under German law, shareholders in a public company have the right to ask questions during the general meeting in relation to items that are on the agenda for that meeting.[357] The obligation to provide information also extends to include the legal and business relations of the company with an affiliated enterprise. There are limited grounds on which the board can refuse a request for information, which include when providing the information would cause a greater than insignificant disadvantage to the company or when providing information which would make the board of directors liable to punishment under law.[358] In France, shareholders have the right to disclosure of documents at any given time and are entitled to make copies of the documents. This disclosure right covers information about the last three closed accounting periods prior to the request.[359] Moreover, shareholders have the right to submit questions at least four days in advance of the general meeting, which questions need to be answered during the general meeting.[360] The board of directors has the possibility to in general terms answer these questions and/or post the answer on the website before the end of the general meeting. In the Netherlands, shareholders have a right to post questions to the company during the general meeting, which the company then needs to answer unless there is a compelling reason for the company to refuse the request.[361] Outside of the general meeting, shareholders in principle do not have the right to ask questions.[362] This is different for companies where there are a limited number of known shareholders and one or more shareholders also have a representative on the board of directors whereas other shareholders do not. The Enterprise Chamber has assumed broader information right for shareholders and a duty for the board of directors to proactively share information with the minority shareholders that do not have a representative on the board of directors.[363] Whether this information right also includes the right to have

357. Section 131 German Stock Corporation Act.
358. Section 131(3) German Stock Corporation Act.
359. I. Grossi, D. Poracchia & A. Raynouard, 'France', in A. Vicari & A. Schall (eds), *supra* n. 17, at 74.
360. Article L225-108(2) French Commercial Code.
361. Articles 2:106 and 2:216(2) Dutch Civil Code.
362. Dutch Supreme Court 9 July 2010, *NJ* 2020/544.
363. Amsterdam Court of Appeal (Enterprise Chamber) 27 Feb. 2020, *JOR* 2020/203; Amsterdam Court of Appeal (Enterprise Chamber) 24 Aug. 2021, *JOR* 2021/296.

access to documents is debatable, but it has been hinted at by the Enterprise Chamber in one judgment.[364] In the UK, information rights take a different form. Under the UK Companies Act, shareholders may inspect company information, including the register of members[365] and a record of resolutions and minutes at no charge.[366] Shareholders are also allowed to inspect directors' service contracts.[367] UK company law does not include a right to ask questions at the general meeting but leaves it to the best practice of each company.[368]

G Derivative Suits

6.92 An important aspect of corporate governance is the possibility to enforce the rules and regulations that are placed upon the corporate bodies. Such enforcement can take place through the use of control rights, such as the right of the general meeting to appoint and dismiss members of the board of directors. However, it can also take place by giving interested parties the opportunity to challenge the acts of these corporate bodies and their members in court. This is especially relevant where it concerns open norms that regulate the behaviour of corporate bodies, such as the norm to act in the best interest of the company and (other) fiduciary duties.

6.93 In most cases, it is up to the company to bring an action in court against a party that - in its view - violated such a norm against the company. In practice, this means that the actions generally have to be brought by the directors, because they have the decision-making power and represent the company to third parties, which includes starting litigation against a third party.[369] This, however, can lead to several complications. First, what to do in case an action was brought against the current directors of the company? Typically, these types of situations can be solved by means of conflict of interest rules, as a result of which conflicted directors, such as those that would be a defendant in the lawsuit, cannot be involved in the decision making. This is, for instance, the case in the UK and the Netherlands.[370] In Germany, this is further formalized by regulating that the supervisory board enforces claims against the directors and the directors decide on the other claims in the company, including claims against supervisory board members.[371] In addition, various jurisdictions determine that shareholders can also have a role in enforcing claims of the company. In Germany, the general meeting can request the board of directors and supervisory board to bring

364. Amsterdam Court of Appeal (Enterprise Chamber) 13 March 2020, *ARO* 2020/87.
365. Section 116 UK Companies Act 2006.
366. Section 358 UK Companies Act 2006.
367. Section 229 UK Companies Act 2006.
368. E. Ferran, *Company Law and Corporate Finance* (Oxford: Oxford University Press, 1999), 266; P. Davies, 'United Kingdom', in T. Baums & E. Wymeersch, *Shareholder Voting Rights and Practices in Europe and the United States* (London: Kluwer Law International, 1999), 351.
369. C. Gerner Beuerle & M.A. Schillig, *supra* n. 31, at 678.
370. Section 175(1) UK Companies Act 2006; Articles 2:129(6) and 2:239(6) Dutch Civil Code.
371. Sections 78 and 122 German Stock Corporation Act.

a claim or appoint a special representative.[372] In the UK, there is support for the view that the shareholders have an implied unwritten power to decide on litigation.[373] Similarly, French shareholders also have the power to – under certain conditions – bring a claim on behalf of the company.[374]

6.94 Although the board of directors, supervisory board and the general meeting have a role when it comes to deciding whether or not to bring claims on behalf of the company, this does not cover the circumstances in which only a minority shareholder has an interest in the company in bringing a claim against, for instance, the majority shareholders and directors. To provide sufficient safeguard for those situations, many jurisdictions have introduced the possibility of a derivative suit by the minority shareholders on behalf of the company. These derivate suits are regulated differently in the main jurisdictions. In the UK, the Companies Act 2006 provides for a specific derivative action proceedings in sections 260–264. Under these provisions, any member can bring a derivative claim, even if that person was not a member at the time of the challenged act.[375] However, any members that intend to bring a claim should first make an application to the court to request permission to continue the derivative claim. The court may grant the application only if the requesting party has a prima facie case[376] and none of the following dismissal grounds is applicable:

1. a person acting in accordance with the duty to promote the success of the company would not seek to continue the claim, or
2. the cause of action arises from an act or omission that is yet to occur, that the act or omission has been authorized by the company, or
3. where the cause of action arises from an act or omission that has already occurred, that the act or omission:
   a. was authorized by the company before it occurred, or
   b. has been ratified by the company since it occurred.[377]

If the court grants the application and the proceedings may proceed, the court must take into account the factors as set out in sections 263(3) and (4) UK Companies Act, which include whether the shareholder is acting in good faith, the importance which a person under a duty to promote the success of the company would attach to the continuing of the action; whether the wrong could be ratified or authorized; whether the company has decided not to bring a claim; the availability of an alternative remedy; and the view of the independent members of the company. In practice in the UK, the derivative action is a mechanism not often used, in part because any amount due as a result of the litigation has to be paid to the company (and not the claiming shareholder) and because the courts have proven reluctant to grant permission for

372. Section 147 German Stock Companies Act.
373. C. Gerner Beuerle & M.A. Schillig, *supra* n. 31, at 680.
374. *Ibid.*, 712 referring to Article L225-252 French Commercial Code.
375. Section 260(4) UK Companies Act 2006.
376. Section 261(2) UK Companies Act 2006.
377. Section 262 (2) UK Companies Act 2006.

bringing a claim.[378] In Germany, a statutory derivative action mechanism was introduced for shareholders in 2005.[379] Under this regime, shareholders holding at least 1 % of the share capital or EUR 100,000 can initiate proceedings, after which the court – similar to the system in the UK– has to decide on whether to grant permission to continue the claim. It will grant this permission if four conditions are satisfied:

1. the claimant should show that it acquired the shares before it knew or should have known of the alleged breach of duty;
2. a sufficient number of shareholders should have requested the company to enforce the claim and have set a reasonable time limit when doing so (unless the company has already stated that it will not pursue the claim);
3. the claimant should be able to show dishonesty or a gross violation of the law or the articles of association;
4. the claim must not be against the overriding interest of the company.

If permission is granted, the shareholders should again request the company to bring a claim. If the company still refuses to do so, then the shareholders can bring the claim in their own name within three months after the decision by the court. In France, a derivative action can be initiated by any shareholder or group of shareholders holding at least 5% of the share capital.[380] As with more thresholds under French law, this threshold is progressively reduced in the case of higher amounts of share capital.[381] Similar to German law, it matters whether the directors decide to bring a claim on behalf of the company. If this is the case, the claim of the shareholders becomes inadmissible.

6.95 In the Netherlands, there is no similar statutory mechanism for derivative actions as in the UK, France and Germany. Moreover, the Supreme Court has ruled that shareholders can – in principle – not bring a claim for damages if the damages suffered are the result of depreciation in the value of shares in the company and that depreciation is the result of damage inflicted on the company.[382] The starting point is that it is the company that should recover the damages, not the shareholders. Under Dutch law, a shareholder may only bring a claim where it can demonstrate that the party that caused the damage breached a duty of care specifically against the shareholder bringing the claim,[383] which will only be the case in extraordinary circumstances.

378. *See* I-M Esser & J. Loughrey, 'United Kingdom', in A. Vicari & A. Schall (eds), *supra* n. 17, at 1537.
379. Section 245 German Stock Corporation Act.
380. Article L225-252 French Commercial Code.
381. *See* for more detail on the thresholds: C. Gerner Beuerle & M.A. Schillig, *supra* n. 31, at 712.
382. Dutch Supreme Court 2 Dec. 1994, *NJ* 1995/288.
383. *See also,* M.J. Kroeze, *Afgeleide schade en afgeleide actie* (PhD diss. University of Utrecht) (Deventer: Kluwer 2004); W.J. Oostwouder, 'Actualiteiten 'afgeleide schade' – What's in a name?', *O&F* 2018/4.

H Shareholder Agreements

6.96 In company law, when discussing the division of power and the individual rights of the corporate bodies and its members, the main focus generally tends to be on the law and articles of association. However, in practice, contractual instruments are also commonly used to structure the cooperation between shareholders and/or the company. Parties can have a variety of reasons to decide to include provisions regulating their relationship within the company in a contract instead of in the articles of association. First, since shareholder agreements are simply a contract between various private parties, these agreements can generally be kept confidential, whereas the articles of association of a company are publicly available for review. As a result, if parties want to keep a certain arrangement confidential, for instance, the price determination mechanism for a future transfer of shares, they might want to include such an arrangement in a shareholder agreement instead of in the articles of association. The confidentiality of shareholder agreements is treated differently in various jurisdictions. In the Netherlands, the confidentiality of shareholder agreements is relatively absolute, and parties would only have to disclose such an agreement under extraordinary circumstances. Similarly in France, shareholder agreements are in principle also confidential, but under exceptional circumstances, the agreement must be partially or fully disclosed. This is for instance the case when the agreement governs the relationship between shareholders in a listed company, in which case the provisions organizing preferred sales/buy options are to be made public.[384] A similar exception to confidentiality in case of a listed company applies in Spain.[385]

Second, since shareholder agreements are solely contractual in nature, they are amended in the same way that ordinary contracts are, with the consent of all parties to the contract. This is different to the articles of association, which are amended by vote of the general meeting, which can be taken by a simple majority or any other majority that the articles of association prescribe. If only certain shareholders are party to the agreement, this also provides more flexibility to amend the articles of association since it is not necessary to involve all shareholders in the establishment and amendment of the agreement. This can be especially relevant in the case of a listed company with a large number of unknown shareholders.

Third, it could be argued that a shareholder agreement provides for more flexibility to include provisions that are of a contractual nature, such as provisions that regulate non-competition between the parties, price mechanisms for the transfer of shares and drag- and tag-along rights and dispute mechanism clauses, including clauses on buyout/squeeze-out of shareholders.

6.97 When considering the use of shareholder agreements to regulate the relationship between parties in the company, it is important to consider to what extent provisions in such an agreement are binding in nature and can actually be enforced. Although

384. I. Grossi, D. Poracchia & A. Raynouard, 'France', in A. Vicari & A. Schall (eds), *supra* n. 17, at 88.
385. F. Marin de la Barcena Garcimartin, 'Spain', in A. Vicari & A. Schall (eds), *supra* n. 17, at 1114.

both questions are subject to national law, an overarching principle seems to be that shareholder agreements are generally considered valid as long as they do not breach fundamental public policy and mandatory rules of law.[386] Whether or not acting in breach of the shareholders' agreement means that the resolution can be invalidated depends in several jurisdictions on whether the company is a party to the shareholder agreement. If that is not the case, resolutions in breach of the shareholder agreement cannot be annulled in France. In the Netherlands, there is debate on whether or not the company should be a party and lower court case law is divided on the subject.[387] In Spain, a shareholder agreement is considered binding on the company if all the members are a party to the agreement.[388] Voting against a shareholder agreement that is signed by all members may be in violation of the obligation to act in good faith.[389]

386. *See* for France: I. Grossi, D. Poracchia & A. Raynouard, 'France', in A. Vicari & A. Schall (eds), *supra* n. 17, at 87; for Spain, *see* F. Marin de la Barcena Garcimartin, 'Spain', in A. Vicari & A. Schall (eds), *supra* n. 17, at 1113; for the Netherlands, *see* B. Steins Bisschop, H. Roelink & B. Kemp, 'The Netherlands', in A. Vicari & A. Schall (eds), *supra* n. 17, at 1340–1341.
387. *See* Asser/Van Solinge & Nieuwe Weme 2-IIb 2019/107.
388. Article 1257 Spain Commercial Code.
389. STS 24 Feb. 2016.

CHAPTER 7

Involvement of Employees

I INTRODUCTION

7.01 Employees may be involved in the decision-making process within the enterprise (or undertaking) at different levels. The first level of employee involvement starts with informing the employees of corporate decisions. The next level is that of consultation of the employees before making corporate decisions that affect the rights of employees. The highest form of employee involvement is participation at the level of corporate bodies, also known as employee board-level representation. All three concepts are further defined in the definitions sections 7.10–7.13 of this chapter.

7.02 Several directives deal with the right of employees to information and consultation. Of an overall character is Directive 2002/14/EC, establishing a general framework for informing and consulting employees (Framework Directive).[1] This directive was preceded by much older legislation dealing with information and consultation for specific situations, namely, where an undertaking is transferred or collective redundancies are contemplated.[2] In addition, in 1994, a directive was adopted applying to 'Community-scale undertakings' or 'Community-scale groups of undertakings', covering the issue of information and consultation rights in internationalized enterprises. These undertakings or groups are obliged to establish a European works council (EWC) or an alternative procedure for information and consultation of employee representatives.[3] It must be noted that the directives mentioned here are part of the European Union (EU) policy regarding employment and social rights, along with issues such as

1. OJ 2002, L 80.
2. Directive 77/187/EEC (now: Directive 2001/23/EC) and Directive 75/129/EEC (now: Directive 98/59/EC), respectively.
3. Directive 94/45/EC.

safety and health requirements for the organization of working time and the posting of workers.[4]

7.03 In this chapter, we provide a brief overview of the legislative developments first before introducing the legal concepts of information, consultation and participation. We then discuss the Framework Directive harmonizing national information and consultation rights in paragraphs 7.14–7.23, the EWC Directive in paragraphs 7.24–7.34 and employee involvement in the *Societas Europaea* (SE) and *Societas Cooperativa Europaea* (SCE) Directives in paragraphs 7.35–7.36. Subsequently, we address other relevant EU legislative acts concerning employee involvement in paragraphs 7.38 (collective redundancies), 7.39 (transfer of undertakings) and 7.40 (occupational safety and health). In closing, paragraphs 7.41–7.46 address employee participation regimes.

Throughout this chapter, important characteristics of employee involvement in a number of Member States, including France, Germany and the Netherlands, as well as the United Kingdom (UK) are introduced to illustrate employee involvement regimes further.

II DEVELOPMENT OF EMPLOYEE INVOLVEMENT IN THE EU

7.04 Employee involvement has developed in a national context in various forms, but the conditions for its functioning have changed due to the internationalization of business enterprises on a European and global scale. That is not to say that existing channels of employee involvement became totally ineffective in the context of a multinational enterprise (MNE). Where the structure of such an enterprise requires a centralized strategy – because goods and services are sent from the company's home country to its subsidiaries elsewhere – employee involvement may retain some impact on the policy of the enterprise. However, the collectivity of an MNE's employees cannot be represented based on national arrangements; hence, only the employee involvement of the company's home country may be able to exert some influence. No such influence remains, however, where MNEs have another structure and develop their strategy within a multi-centred, network-like setting. Such MNEs do not operate from a home country in the traditional sense but combine local operations with cost price reductions and economies of scale by operations in a global dimension.[5] In general, national procedures for the involvement of employees are not very compatible with the transnational structure of MNEs and may lead to unequal treatment of

4. *See* further information on Employment, Social Affairs & Inclusion on the European Commission's website: https://ec.eu ropa.eu/social/main.jsp?catId = 157&langId = en.
5. W.M.G. Allertz, *Grensoverschrijdende organisatie-ontwikkeling en medezeggenschap* (Assen: Van Gorcum, 2002). For the structures of MNEs: C.A. Bartlett & S. Ghoshal, *Managing Across Borders: The Transnational Solution* (Boston: Harvard Business School Press, 1989). From the same authors: 'The Multinational Corporation as an Interorganizational Network', *The Academy of Management Review* 15, no. 4 (October 1990): 603–625. J.H. Dunning and S.M. Lundan, *Multinational Enterprises and the Global Economy* (Cheltenham: Edward Elgar Publishing, 2008).

employees affected by the decisions of such undertakings.[6] The European Commission already observed, in 1980, that the completion of the internal market was bound to generate a process of internationalization of undertakings, leading to such inconsistency. Against this background, the EU has taken several legislative actions in order to ensure the social dimension of the internal market, and some of the most relevant directives are discussed in this chapter.

7.05 In 1980, the Commission proposed a directive concerning information and consultation of employees in undertakings with a complex structure, particularly MNEs.[7] This draft could be regarded as nothing more than complementary to the directives already enacted with regard to collective redundancies and the safeguarding of workers' rights in the event of a transfer of undertaking.[8] The draft was abandoned after a 'heated debate' during which no political agreement could be reached.[9] At the time, the draft directive was strongly opposed both at governmental and at managerial levels, which also occurred with the draft Fifth Directive.

As Blanpain stated: 'Those proposals are ideologically loaded, touch upon delicate power balances between management and labour (...).'[10] Notwithstanding its political sensitivity, the role of employees is now firmly embedded in Community policy. According to the 1989 Community Charter of the Fundamental Rights of Workers, the involvement of employees must be developed, especially in companies or groups of companies having establishments or subsidiaries in two or more Member States.[11] The European Parliament called on the Commission to adopt a series of measures to guarantee these rights of employees. It urged that there should be a directive 'incorporating in identical forms the rights to information and consultation and in equivalent forms the right to participation, into the statutes of all companies, irrespective of their legal constitution - limited companies, European companies, cooperatives, mutual benefit companies, self-management companies - and also into those of the European Economic Interest Grouping (EEIG)'.[12] Moreover, the Member States, with the exception of the UK, agreed to carry out the policy of the Charter upon the signing of the 1992 Maastricht Treaty. To carry out this policy, the Commission successfully launched a new proposal for information and consultation of employees in enterprises with a Community dimension, which was to become the EWC Directive of 1994 (now Directive 2009/38/EC). By 1997, the Amsterdam European Council agreed to incorporate the agreement on social policy in the EC Treaty and the UK accepted the

6. Further on the economic and social context of employee involvement and on industrial relations J. Calvo et al., *Employee Representatives in an Enlarged Europe*, vol. 1, European Commission, Directorate-General for Employment, Social Affairs and Equal Opportunities, April 2008 (available at http://bookshop.europa.eu), 19 *et seq.*
7. OJ 1980, C 297. The draft was called the 'Vredeling-directive', named after the commissioner who was responsible for it.
8. Directive 75/129/EEC and Directive 77/187/EEC.
9. R. Blanpain, *Labour Law and Industrial Relations of the European Community* (Deventer/Boston: Kluwer Law and Taxation Publishers, 1991), 334–337.
10. R. Blanpain, 'Representation of Employees at the Level of the Enterprise and the EEC', *Recht der Arbeit* 2 (1992): 127.
11. Articles 17 and 18 of the Community Charter, adopted on 9 Dec. 1989.
12. Article 45 Resolution A3-175/90 of 13 Sep. 1990.

EWC Directive.[13] Yet, with the UK's formal withdrawal from the EU on 1 January 2021, the directive is no longer applicable to UK companies, and individual company-level agreements have to be made concerning EWC members from UK subsidiaries.

7.06 Almost 30 years after its first wake-up call, the Commission put the process of globalization on its Renewed Social Agenda of 2008 against the backdrop of the financial and economic crisis. The Commission stressed that technological change, globalization and an ageing population are transforming Europe's societies and that EU policies need to keep pace with these trends and help people adapt to changing circumstances.[14] Yet again, the Commission put social integration on the agenda through the European Pillar of Social Rights proclaimed in Gothenburg in 2017, which should be implemented through the European Pillar of Social Rights Action Plan 2021.[15]

7.07 Employees may express their interest in the company's affairs not only via the means of information and consultation but also by becoming shareholders. Several Member States have a tradition of employee share ownership schemes (ESOS). In its 2012 Action Plan, the Commission announced its objective to identify and investigate potential obstacles to transnational ESOS and to take appropriate action to encourage employee share ownership throughout the EU. A 2014 study revealed that barriers to cross-border employee share ownership arise from differences in regulatory density, application of national legal frameworks or differences in the fiscal treatment of existing schemes. Several policy options were suggested in order to overcome these obstacles, but no policy changes have come into effect to date.[16]

7.08 This book is mainly concerned with legal issues and, therefore, the possible effects of employee involvement on the performance of the enterprise are not discussed here. Nevertheless, the often controversial nature of the topic may justify pointing out findings showing that, for instance in the UK, more responsive management to 'worker voice practices', being any formal mechanism by which workers can communicate their views to the management, will result in improved productivity.[17] According to a survey on the way in which Dutch top management and works councils interact, it seems to make all the difference to the firm's economic position in the sense that a positive attitude of managers towards the works council is positively associated with organizational performance.[18] Apart from this phenomenon, the effects of the presence

13. Directive 97/74/EC of 15 Dec. 1997 extending, to the United Kingdom of Great Britain and Northern Ireland, Directive 94/45/EC.
14. Communication of the Commission: *A Renewed Social Agenda: Opportunities, Access and Solidarity in 21st Century Europe.*
15. European Commission, European Pillar of Social Rights Action Plan (available at https://ec.europa.eu/social/BlobServlet?docId = 23696&langId = en).
16. *The Promotion of Employee Ownership and Participation*, Final report October 2014, EU, available at https://op.europa.eu/s/vMM7.
17. A. Bryson, A. Charlwood & J. Forth, 'Worker Voice, Managerial Response and Labour Productivity: An Empirical Investigation'. *Industrial Relations Journal* 37, no. 5 (2006): 438–455.
18. A. van den Berg, Y. Grift & A. van Witteloostuijn, *Works Councils and Organizational Performance: The Role of Top Managers' and Works Councils' Attitudes in Bad Vis-À-Vis Good*

of a works council on performance depend on factors such as whether the organization is in the process of restructuring and, more generally, the fluctuation of the economy [19] Such positive assessments on the involvement of national and European Works Councils are also shared by managers, according to another study.[20]

III EMPLOYEE INVOLVEMENT: THE CONCEPTS OF INFORMATION, CONSULTATION AND PARTICIPATION

7.09 Before turning to the core concepts of information, consultation and participation, it is worthwhile pointing out what is understood by employee involvement as such. This chapter follows the definition of 'involvement of employees' as stipulated by Article 2(h) of the SE Directive, being 'any mechanism, including information, consultation and participation, through which employees' representatives may exercise an influence on decisions to be taken within the company'. This terminology is also used in the Directive accompanying the SCE Statute and in the Corporate Mobility Directive (EU) 2019/2121.[21] In earlier legal documents and related literature, however, 'participation of workers' features as a generic term and 'co-determination' was used for what is now usually called 'participation'.[22] In legal research, other generic terms may be used, for example, 'employee representation', covering similar issues as 'involvement of employees'.[23] Therefore, reference is made to employee involvement as an overarching term.

A Information and Consultation

7.10 For large Community-scale companies, the right to information was first introduced in the 1994 EWC Directive[24] and was quite rudimentary: the EWC should meet

---

Times (Utrecht University, Tjalling C. Koopmans Research Institute), available at https://link.springer.com/article/10.1007/s12122-011-9105-x.

19. S. Sapulete, *Works Council Effectiveness: Determinants and Outcomes*, Dissertation, Utrecht University, 2013 (ISBN 978-90-816238-7-2).
20. V. Pulignano & J. Turk, *European Works Councils on the Move: Management Perspectives on the Development of a Transnational Institution for Social Dialogue* (Leuven: CeSO, 2016).
21. Directive (EU) 2019/2121 amends Directive (EU) 2017/1132. Article 133 of Directive (EU) 2017/1132 is in essence based on and refers to the SE Directive for the issue of participation rights.
22. *See* for 'participation' in the general sense e.g., the 1989 *Community Charter of the Fundamental Rights of Workers*. K.J. Hopt, 'Labor Representation on Corporate Boards: Impacts and Problems for Corporate Governance and Economic Integration in Europe', *International Review of Law and Economics* 14 (1994): 204 *et seq. See also* Michael Gold, *Direct Communications in European Multinationals: A Case Study Approach* (Dublin: European Foundation, 1994) who discerns 'direct forms of participation' (consultation and delegation at work floor level) and 'representational forms of participation' (information and consultation via employees' representatives).
23. J. Calvo et al., *supra* n. 6, at 17.
24. Council Directive 94/45/EC.

the central management once a year and be informed 'on the progress of the business [...] [of the (group of)] undertaking(s) and its prospects.'[25]

In addition, 'where there are exceptional circumstances affecting the employees' interests to a considerable extent, particularly in the event of relocations, the closure of establishments or undertakings or collective redundancies [...] the European Works Council shall have the right to be informed.'[26] Especially the timing of informing the EWC was unclear and the extent to which employee representatives need to be informed and what constitutes 'exceptional circumstances affecting the employees' interests to a considerable extent', leading to insufficient protection of employees' rights.[27] The more recent 2009 Recast of the EWC Directive defines the right to information as:

> transmission of data by the employer to the employees' representatives in order to enable them to acquaint themselves with the subject matter and to examine it; information shall be given at such time, in such fashion and with such content as are appropriate to enable employees' representatives to undertake an in-depth assessment of the possible impact and, where appropriate, prepare for consultations with the competent organ of the [...] undertaking or group of undertakings.[28]

7.11 In a later phase, both information and consultation within single establishments (as opposed to the Community-scale undertakings mentioned above) were also regulated under Framework Directive 2002/14/EC, which sets minimum levels for information and consultation for all companies in the EU.[29] This also includes the right to establish employee representation bodies in undertakings with at least 50 employees or establishments with more than 20 employees, according to Article 3 of the Framework Directive. This minimum requirement is implemented differently in the various Member States as discussed in paragraphs 7.14–7.20.

It has to be noted that the definition in the 2002 Framework Directive on information and consultation has not been revised yet and thus remains less specific than the definition used in the EWC Directive. This does not pose any direct problems in practice because the Framework Directive sets out only minimum requirements for information and consultation rights. On the other hand, it does give the Member States discretionary room for national legislation.

7.12 Consultation is defined in the EWC Directive as:

> the establishment of dialogue and exchange of views between employees' representatives and central management or any more appropriate level of management, at such time, in such fashion and with such content as enables employees' representatives to express an opinion on the basis of the information provided about the proposed measures to which the consultation is related, without

25. *Ibid.*, Article 2 of the subsidiary requirements.
26. *Ibid.*, Article 3 of the subsidiary requirements.
27. Explanatory memorandum to a proposal on the establishment of a European Works Council of 2008; COM(2008) 419 def.
28. Article 2(1)(f) of Directive 2009/38/EC.
29. Directive 2002/14/EC; *see* further 7.02 above.

prejudice to the responsibilities of the management, and within a reasonable time, which may be taken into account within the Community-scale undertaking or Community-scale group of undertakings.[30]

The older Framework Directive 2002/14/EC is again more concise in Art. 2(g): 'the exchange of views and establishment of dialogue between the employees' representatives and the employer'. However, the elaboration in Article 4(4) of the Framework Directive shows that European legislators already had a clear idea about the concept of consultation in 2002. On the basis of the information provided, the employees' representatives: (1) must be able to express an opinion, to which they (2) must receive a reasoned reply. The aim of the consultation is to reach an agreement. Although the EWC and SE Directives also contain the obligation to consult, the obligation to reach an agreement is missing.

B Employee Participation

7.13 The highest form of employee involvement is participation at the level of corporate bodies: employee board-level representation.[31] Such participation includes involvement in the composition and/or in the decision-making process of these bodies through the election of one or more supervisory board (or non-executive board) members or members of the board of directors (e.g., in the case of Sweden[32]). Employee board-level representation regimes can be found in 18 EU Member States and Norway.[33] Being distinct from information and consultation rights, participation of employees connects labour to the inner mechanics of the company's (or other legal entity's) decision-making process. We further elaborate on employee participation and the various national regimes in paragraphs 7.41–7.46.

30. Article 2(1)(g) of Directive 2009/38/EC; Article 2(j) of the SE Directive 2001/86/EC contains a similar provision.
31. *See also* Chapter 4 for employee board-level representation on European Companies.
32. Based on the 1987 Act on Board Representation for Private Sector Employees (*Lag om styrelserepresentation för de privatanställda*); *see* further a PwC study, 'Svenska styrelsers ersättningar och arbetssätt' (2020) <https://www.pwc.se/sv/pdf-reports/skatt/svenska-styrelsers-ersattningar-och-arbetssatt-2020-ny.pdf> (accessed 10 Feb. 2022); *see also* paragraphs 7.41 *et seq.* concerning employee participation regimes.
33. Austria, Croatia, Czech Republic, Denmark, Finland, France, Germany, Greece, Hungary, Ireland, Luxembourg, the Netherlands, Norway, Poland, Portugal, Slovak Republic, Slovenia, Spain and Sweden; A. Conchon et al., 'Worker board-level participation in the 31 European Economic Area countries'. (2015), available at: <https://www.worker-participation.eu/National-Industrial-Relations/Across-Europe/Board-level-Representation2/TABLE-Worker-board-level-participation-in-the-31-European-Economic-Area-countries> (last accessed 15 Apr. 2022).

IV INFORMATION AND CONSULTATION: WORKS COUNCILS, THE EWC, THE SE AND THE SCE

A Framework Directive on Information and Consultation at National Level

7.14 The Directive establishing a general framework for informing and consulting employees (2002) was adopted with the view of consolidating the principle of information and consultation in the EU.[34] It serves to supplement the, at that time, existing directives discussed in the previous paragraphs and to fill gaps in national laws and practices through the introduction of a minimum level of information and consultation.

7.15 In the Member States, employees are traditionally represented by works councils and/or trade union representatives. Their systems regarding the rights to information and consultation vary considerably.[35] The Framework Directive includes the right to establish employee representation bodies in undertakings with at least 50 employees or establishments with more than 20 employees, according to Article 3 of the Framework Directive. According to Article 3, Member States may choose either option in the implementation process. This minimum requirement is implemented differently in the various Member States as discussed in the following paragraphs.

7.16 In the Netherlands, the establishment of a works council (*ondernemingsraad*) is obligatory if 50 or more people are employed by the undertaking.[36] In smaller companies, employees are entitled to hold a meeting twice a year and to be informed and consulted about major decisions that considerably affect the level of employment.[37] In such a small enterprise, the employer may establish a body of employee representatives (*personeelsvertegenwoordiging*) having partly the same rights as a works council.[38]

7.17 In Germany, the establishment of a works council (*Betriebsrat*) is mandatory for every enterprise where more than five people are employed and when at least three employees or a trade union call for an elective assembly.[39] If an employer has established more than one works council, those councils must form a common works council (*Gesamtbetriebsrat*). If the enterprise or undertaking is part of a group, the common works councils may form a group works council (*Konzernbetriebsrat*).[40] Elections must be held every four years within a period of three months, and candidates may be nominated by 5% of the employees, by 50 employees or by trade

34. 2002/14/EC.
35. J. Calvo et al., *supra* n. 6, at 45.
36. Article 2 Works Councils Act (*Wet op de ondernemingsraden*, WOR).
37. Article 35b WOR.
38. Articles 35b–35d WOR.
39. Section 1 *Betriebsverfassungsgesetz* (BetrVG).
40. Sections 47, 54 *et seq.* BetrVG.

unions.[41] In contrast to French law, German legislators only allow employees to be elected as members of the works council.[42] Those employees may not be at a disadvantage because of their membership and enjoy protection against termination of their contract of employment.[43] The works council has the right to be informed and consulted about major decisions of an economic nature as specified in the statute, *inter alia,* the winding-up of the enterprise or a merger.[44] The same applies to management decisions regarding social policy and, in some cases, the works council even has a right to co-decision which provides a veto right.[45] Conflicts may, and, in some cases, must be submitted to a conciliation committee provided for by the statute *(Einigungsstelle)*.[46] In addition to the works council, there are councils for the representation of employees in management functions *(Sprecherausschüsse)*.[47] Moreover, union representatives may be present within the enterprise but, in practice, they function only within large enterprises.[48]

7.18 In France, employee representation is now largely provided by a single elected committee, the Social and Economic Committee (*Comité Social et Économique* - CSE). This brings together three previously separate bodies representing employees at the workplace - the employee delegates, the works council and the health and safety committee. Only in larger companies with 300 or more employees, must a sub-committee of the Social and Economic Committee dealing specifically with health, safety and working conditions be formed as well. The merger of these three bodies into a new single committee was one of the changes introduced by the government of Emmanuel Macron in September 2017 as Ordonnance No. 2017-1386.[49] Starting from 2018 with a transition period until 2020,[50] the new CSE has to be established in workplaces with 11 or more employees.[51] In companies with 11 to 49 employees, the role of the CSE is relatively limited. Its role is to present the workforce's individual and collective complaints and claims to the employer and to monitor the company's compliance with labour regulations. In companies with 50 or more employees, the CSE carries out these roles, but its rights go beyond this to allow the interests of the workforce to be taken into account when company decisions relating to the economic

41. Sections 13 and 14 BetrVG.
42. Section 5 BetrVG.
43. Section 78 BetrVG and section 15 *Kündigungsschutzgesetz.*
44. Sections 106 and 111 BetrVG.
45. Sections 91 and 99 BetrVG.
46. Section 76 BetrVG.
47. Sections 1 *et seq. Sprecherausschußgesetz.*
48. Sections 2, 23 and 77 BetrVG. J. Calvo et al., *supra* n. 6, at 228–229. G.V. Hoyningen-Huene in Münchener Handbuch zum Arbeitsrecht, 2nd edition (C.H. Beck, 2000), Vol. 3, paragraph 294, Rdnr 28–30; On German employee participation in general: A.M. Koene and H. Slomp, Medezeggenschap van werknemers op ondernemingsniveau: een onderzoek naar de regels en hun toepassing in zes Europese landen (VUGA, 's-Gravenhage 1991), pp. 97–142.
49. Ordonnance n° 2017-1386 du 22 septembre 2017 relative à la nouvelle organisation du dialogue social et économique dans l'entreprise et favorisant l'exercice et la valorisation des responsabilités syndicales < https://www.legifrance.gouv.fr/loda/id/JORFTEXT000035607348/ >.
50. *See* Section 12 of the Ordonnance.
51. *See* further L. Fulton, 'National Industrial Relations, an update (2019–2021)'available at http://www.worker-participation.eu/National-Industrial-Relations (last accessed 1 Feb. 2022).

and financial management of the company, work organization, occupational training and production techniques are taken. This is primarily achieved through its information and consultation rights.

7.19 Subject to a few minor exceptions, no binding legislation in the UK stipulating that employees must be represented at the enterprise level existed prior to the implementation of the Framework Directive under national law.[52] However, where such (voluntary) representation existed, several legal provisions applied providing rights for the representatives. The UK and Ireland are hence regarded as countries with a voluntarist tradition on employee representation. Traditionally, trade unions almost exclusively deal with representation of the employees at enterprise level. However, due to the implementation of the Framework Directive 2002/14/EC, an employer is under a duty to initiate negotiations in order to reach an agreement on, *inter alia*, the circumstances in which the employer must inform and consult the employees. To facilitate these negotiations, the employer should make arrangements for the election or appointment of negotiating representatives.[53] Bodies set up under the terms of the implementing legislation are granted the standard information and consultation rights, as prescribed by the Directive.[54] Such bodies, known as joint consultative committees, function as a complement to, and sometimes as a substitute for, union representation (which is the dominant form of employee representation). They cover a relatively small number of workplaces.[55]

Where the employer formally recognizes a trade union, the majority of employees are represented at enterprise level by trade union representatives, who are generally known as 'shop stewards'.[56] There are no legal rules on the number of these representatives, or on the composition of their committees and the method by which they are elected. These matters may vary from union to union.[57] Even where the union is recognized, its representatives have no general right to finance and the use of various resources, though these may be taken care of by a negotiated agreement. However, trade union representatives do have a legal entitlement to time off from work for

52. The exceptions were issue-specific, covering health and safety, occupational pensions and the training of workers: *see* Section 2(4) and (6) of the Health and Safety at Work etc. Act 1974, regulation 4A of the Safety Representatives and Safety Committees Regulations 1977 (SI 1977/500), the Occupational Pension (Contracting Out) Regulations 1996 (SI 1996/1172), the Occupational and Personal Pension Schemes (Consultation by Employers and Miscellaneous Amendment) Regulations 2006 (SI 2006/349) and section 70B of the Trade Union and Labour Relations (Consolidation) Act 1992.
53. Articles 7, 14 and 16 Information and Consultation of Employees Regulations 2004, Statutory Instrument 2004 No. 3426. It is not expected that many new arrangements will be negotiated, J. Calvo et al., *Employee Representatives in an Enlarged Europe,* vol.2, European Commission, Directorate-General for Employment, Social Affairs and Equal Opportunities, April 2008 (available at http://bookshop.europa.eu), 244. On the effects of Directive 2002/14/EC; *see also* Frank Burchill, *Labour Relations*, Third edition (New York: Palgrave MacMillan, 2008), 171–175.
54. Articles 18 *et seq.* Information and Consultation of Employees Regulations 2004.
55. According to B. Kersley et al., *Inside the Workplace* (London: Routledge, 2006), 126 *et seq.*, such committees are present in 14% of the workplaces (in 2004).
56. Other terms are 'union rep' or 'local rep', J. Calvo et al., *supra* n. 53, at *245*.
57. *Ibid.*, 246.

training.[58] The union representatives enjoy protection against dismissal and detrimental treatment.[59] They have information rights that enable them to conduct collective bargaining, and they must be informed and consulted in cases of collective redundancies and business transfers.[60]

7.20 Overall, it becomes clear that the Member States still have rather different systems of employee involvement, notwithstanding the effects of the harmonizing directives. First, although they are essential connecting factors for the regulation of employee involvement, the concepts of 'undertaking' and 'establishment' are perhaps too vaguely defined in the Framework Directive 2002/14/EC to have any harmonizing impact. Second, in the area of information and consultation, the primary actors may be the works council, being a body of employee representatives, or alternatively, trade union representatives, such as in the UK. These two 'channels' may coexist, partly having separate tasks, but they may also be connected where the membership of the two channels is joined. This may be the case, for example, in France, or where the trade unions have a dominant role in setting up works councils, such as in Poland. The Framework Directive does not show a preference for any of these systems and establishes only a general framework setting out minimum requirements for the right to information and consultation of employees and/or their representatives. The practical arrangements for this right must be defined and implemented in accordance with national law and industrial relations practices in the Member States in such a way as to ensure their effectiveness (Article 1). The rules regarding information and consultation apply where undertakings employ at least 20 or 50 employees in one Member State. The threshold can be set at either level by the Member States (Article 3). Information must be provided at such time and in such a way as to enable employees' representatives to conduct an adequate study and, where necessary, prepare for consultation. Consultation must take place at the appropriate level, *inter alia,* on decisions likely to lead to substantial changes in work organization or in contractual relations, insofar as these decisions are within the scope of the employer's powers. The consultation must take place with a view to reaching an agreement with regard to these changes (Article 4). The Directive also provides that rules on the handling of confidential information must be implemented to the extent that employee representatives may be bound by an obligation of confidentiality. If information is harmful to the functioning of the undertaking's employer, in cases to be specified, it is not obligatory to disclose information to employees or consult with them (Article 6).

7.21 According to the core provision, Article 4, of the Framework Directive, the Member States must ensure that the following rules apply:

58. Section 168 of the Trade Union and Labour Relations (Consolidation) Act 1992 (TULR(C)A 1992).
59. Section 104 of the Employment Rights Act 1996.
60. *Ibid.*, 247 and 248 and Section 181 of TULR(C)A 1992. However, if the relevant employer does not recognize a trade union, the relevant representatives will be elected employment representatives: *see* Sections 188(1B) and 196(1), (2) and (3) of TULR(C)A 1992 and regulations 13(3) and 14 of the Transfer of Undertakings (Protection of Employment) Regulations 2006 (SI 2006/246).

(2) Information and consultation shall cover:
   (a) information on the recent and probable development of the undertaking's or the establishment's activities and economic situation;
   (b) information and consultation on the situation, structure and probable development of employment within the undertaking or establishment and on any anticipatory measures envisaged, in particular where there is a threat to employment;
   (c) information and consultation on decisions likely to lead to substantial changes in work organization or in contractual relations (...);
   (...)

(4) Consultation shall take place:
   (a) while ensuring that the timing, method and content thereof are appropriate;
   (b) at the relevant level of management and representation, depending on the subject under discussion;
   (c) on the basis of information supplied by the employer in accordance with Article 2(f) of the Directive and of the opinion that the employees' representatives are entitled to formulate;
   (d) in such a way as to enable employees' representatives to meet the employer and obtain a response, and the reasons for that response, to any opinion they might formulate;
   (e) with a view to reaching an agreement on decisions within the scope of the employer's powers referred to in paragraph 2(c).

7.22 The directive leaves the Member States the option to grant management and labour representatives the freedom to establish, through negotiated agreement, the practical arrangements for informing and consulting employees. Such arrangements may deviate from the provisions of Article 4, but they should be in accordance with the principles laid down in Article 1. This means that their effectiveness must be ensured and that the 'employer and the employees' representatives shall work in the spirit of cooperation and with due regard for their reciprocal rights and obligations, taking into account the interests both of the undertaking or establishment and of the employees'.

7.23 The directive should have been implemented no later than 23 March 2005. Four Member States declared that no implementation was necessary because national legislation and practice were already in line with the provisions of the directive; however, the Court of Justice of the European Union (CJEU) has ruled differently in two of these cases.[61] Evaluation of the implementation showed that a series of problems remain. Among these is the lack of clarity with reference to the scope of application of the directive due to the vagueness of the definitions of 'undertaking', 'establishment' and 'employee', and the incomplete transposition of Article 6 on the handling of confidential information.[62] These points remain unresolved to date and so far, no revision of the Framework Directive has been put on the European legislative agenda.

61. C-320/06 (regarding Belgium) and C-385/05 (regarding France).
62. *Ibid.*, 34.

B The European Works Council

7.24 Directive 2009/38/EC deals with, as mentioned above, the establishment of an EWC or a procedure for the purpose of informing and consulting employees. It applies to Community-scale undertakings or groups of undertakings.[63] The Community-scale is reached where an undertaking has at least a total of 1,000 employees within the Member States and employs a minimum of 150 employees in at least two Member States each. For a group of undertakings, the latter criterion is replaced by a similar requirement: the group must have at least two group undertakings in different Member States, each having no fewer than 150 employees (Article 2(1)(c)).

7.25 The 2009 EWC Directive is a recast of the original 1994 EWC Directive[64] and addresses a number of shortcomings, which are also further discussed. The adoption of the Recast EWC Directive was stimulated *inter alia* by the *Renault Vilvoorde* case. The management of Renault announced the closure of the production plant at Vilvoorde (Belgium) without prior consultation of employee representatives. At the same time, Renault appeared to be planning to expand its production capacity in Spain, with the envisaged financial aid of both Spanish authorities and the EC. Making a decision affecting the jobs of more than 3,000 employees without due consultation provoked the furious reactions of trade unions and Belgian authorities alike. It also raised interest at the European level, and the Commissioner announced his intention to assess the legality of Renault's actions in terms of the 1994 EWC Directive and the collective redundancies Directive (75/129/EEC).[65] However, Renault had set up a 'European group committee' by voluntary agreement before September 1996 pursuant to Article 13 of the 1994 EWC Directive and consequently was exempted from the obligation to renegotiate the formation of an EWC. The text of this pre-directive voluntary agreement contained no obligation for Renault to order an extraordinary meeting of this committee to consult its members on the closure of Vilvoorde. Confronted with the case, both Belgian and French courts held that information and consultation rights had been violated, notwithstanding the wording of the voluntary agreement. The agreement had to be interpreted in a manner consistent with its preamble, which referred to the EWC Directive and the Community Charter on Fundamental Social Workers' Rights. In terms of the EWC Directive, any decision having a significant effect on the interests of employees must lead to information and consultation of the EWC. The Versailles Court of Appeal held that consultation does not necessarily have to be prior to the decision, but must leave scope for criticism, in order to eventually modify the initial decision.[66]

63. Directive 2009/38/EC.
64. Directive 94/45/EC.
65. The European Parliament adopted a resolution claiming that these directives had been violated, OJ 1997, C 115.
66. F. Dorssemont, 'The Renault Saga (revisited)', *European Company Law* 3, no. 1 (2006): 5 *et seq.* and *Revue de jurisprudence social* 1997, nr. 829.

In the wake of 'Vilvoorde', Belgian legislators enacted stricter rules in order to prevent any further violation of information and consultation rights.[67]

7.26 Such voluntary pre-directive agreements were the result of Article 13 of the 1994 EWC Directive. The directive was adopted on 22 September 1994 and had to be implemented within two years, by 22 September 1996. According to Article 13(1), any 'agreement, covering the entire workforce, providing for the transnational information and consultation of employees' adopted prior to that date resulted in an exemption from the application of the directive. Therefore, the 1994 EWC Directive foresaw a stimulus for negotiations because it respects any agreements reached before the date the directive entered into force, such as the agreement in the *Renault Vilvoorde* case. These Article 13 agreements could also remain in force under the Recast EWC Directive of 2009. The EWC Directive, therefore, may be applicable only if no such agreement exists or if, upon its expiration, the parties concerned do not mutually decide on a renewal (Article 14 EWC Recast Directive).

7.27 The original 1994 EWC Directive was, indeed, preceded by several initiatives to establish Europe-wide employee involvement within French MNEs, such as BSN and Thomson. These pioneers were to be followed by the initiatives of employees within several other multinationals, for example, Ford, Volkswagen and Continental Can. They varied from arrangements for joint exchange visits between employee representatives of European plants to a joint information and consultation forum on a group-wide, European level.[68] More than 400 arrangements with management had been reached before the 1994 EWC Directive came into force.[69]

The primarily contractual nature of the EWC Directive (negotiations combined with a fallback on standardized rules if no agreement is reached) has been copied by both the SE Directive and the Tenth Directive on cross-border mergers[70] (*see* paragraphs 4.35 and 8.98 *et seq.*).

7.28 If no prior agreement existed and the Recast EWC Directive applies, then the central management is responsible for setting up an EWC or an alternative information

---

67. I. Schömann, S. Clauwaert & W. Warneck, *Information and Consultation in the European Community: Implementation Report of Directive 2002/14/EC*, European Trade Union Institute for Research, Education and Health and Safety (ETUI-REHS) (Brussels, 2006), 7 (available at https://www.etui.org/publications).
68. M. Gold, *Direct Communications in European Multinationals* (Luxembourg: Office for Official Publications of the European Communities, 1994), 20 *et seq.*, A. Dikker & A. de Lange, 'Europees Overleg in opmars', *Praktijkblad voor Medezeggenschap* 4 (1994) 8. M. Gold & M. Hall, *Report on European-Level Information and Consultation in Multinational Companies.* An Evaluation of Practice (Dublin: 1992).
69. *The Impact of the European Works Councils* (1998), available at www.eurofound.europa.eu/eiro/index.htm (August 2008), the website of the European Industrial Relations Observatory (EIRO). A database containing transnational company agreements identified and catalogued by the ILO and the European Commission is published on the Commission's website regarding Employment, Social Affairs & Inclusion (retrieved from http://ec.europa.eu/social/main.jsp?catId=978&langId=en, April 2017).
70. From 2023 onwards also cross-border conversions and divisions pursuant to Directive 2019/2121.

and consultation procedure.[71] It may therefore initiate negotiations and is obliged to do so at the written request of no fewer than 100 employees or their representatives in at least two undertakings or establishments in two different Member States. The Directive contains guidelines for the composition of a special negotiating body of employees so as to ensure that the employees in each of the Member States where there is an establishment or an undertaking are represented.[72] The negotiating body has the task, together with the central management, to determine, by a written agreement, the scope, composition, functions and terms of office of the EWC, or of the alternative procedure for information and consultation.[73] Article 6(2) spells out the details that the agreement must determine:

(a) the undertakings of the Community-scale group or the establishments of the Community-scale undertaking which are covered by the agreement;
(b) the composition of the EWC, the number of members, the allocation of seats and the term of office;
(c) the functions and the procedure for information and consultation of the EWC;
(d) the venue, frequency and duration of meetings of the EWC;
(e) where necessary, the composition of the select committee set up within the EWC and rules regarding its functions and procedures;
(f) the financial and material resources to be allocated to the EWC;
(g) the duration of the agreement and the procedure for its renegotiation.

If no agreement can be reached or if the central management and the negotiating body so decide, 'subsidiary' (default) requirements apply, as laid down by the legislation of the Member State in which the central management is situated. Such requirements must at least meet the provisions set out in the Annex to the Directive.[74] Notwithstanding this solid fallback provision, the negotiating body may decide, by at least two-thirds of the votes, not to open negotiations or, alternatively, to terminate negotiations already opened and, as a consequence, the subsidiary requirements would not apply.

7.29 According to the subsidiary requirements in the Annex to the Directive, the right of the EWC to information and consultation is restricted to matters that concern the Community-scale undertaking or group of undertakings as a whole (Annex, paragraph 1(a)). Other provisions concern, *inter alia,* the composition of the EWC, the right to meet with the central management once a year and the right of the EWC to be assisted by experts of its choice (paragraphs 1, 2 and 5). Where exceptional circumstances occur, affecting the employees' interest to a considerable extent, the EWC has the right to be informed and to meet with management. This applies in particular to relocations, closure of establishments or undertakings and collective redundancies (paragraph 3).

7.30 The Member States must provide rules to secure that the members of the negotiating body or the EWC are not authorized to disclose information that has

71. Article 4 Recast Directive 2009/38/EC.
72. Article 5(1 and 2) Recast Directive.
73. Article 5(5) Recast Directive.
74. Article 7 Recast Directive.

expressly been provided to them in confidence. The Member States must additionally provide that the central management is not required to transmit any information which, by its nature, would be seriously prejudicial to any of the undertakings affected. Members States may make such derogation of the duty of information subject to prior administrative or judicial authorization.[75] The directive further provides for protection of the employee representatives. The members of negotiating bodies, EWCs and employee representatives exercising their functions under the alternative procedure for information and consultation enjoy the same protection and guarantees provided for employee representatives by the national legislation and/or practice in force in their country of employment.[76]

7.31 The directive may be implemented by the Member States not only by bringing the necessary laws, regulations and administrative provisions into force but also by ensuring that management and labour representatives introduce the required provisions by way of (collective) agreement. The most common way has been the transposition of the directive into law, although several Member States have consulted social partners before taking legislative measures.[77] The directive does not affect the rights of employees to information and consultation under national law (Article 12(2)). Therefore, its implementation has not had significant influence on existing systems of industrial relations because the EWCs could be fitted into, and are supplementary to, existing arrangements.[78]

7.32 Questions regarding the establishment of an EWC have been referred to the CJEU. In *Anker* (2004), the works council of the German subsidiary of the Swiss-based Anker group requested information from its local management with a view to establishing an EWC. According to Article 5 of the German implementing legislation, the central management of a Community-scale group, upon request, must provide information to the employees' representatives on the average number of employees, the distribution of these employees within the Member States, on the undertakings and establishments, and on the structure of the group of companies. The Anker works council requested this information from its local management, which was supposed to forward the request to the central management. The management of the German subsidiary replied that both its parent company, being a Dutch BV, and the Swiss parent company of the group refused to provide the information. The works council then started proceedings at the labour court at Bielefeld (Germany). The court submitted preliminary questions to the CJEU, in particular, as to whether an undertaking in the group, which is regarded as the central management, is obliged to provide information to other group undertakings established in different Member States when such undertakings received a request for information from the employees' internal representation bodies. The CJEU held that Member States are required to impose on undertakings established within their

75. Article 8 Recast Directive.
76. Article 10(3) Recast Directive.
77. *The Impact of the European Works Councils* (1998), available at <https://www.eurofound.europa.eu/observatories/eurwork>, the website of the EIRO.
78. *Ibid.*

territory and constituting the central management of a Community-scale group the obligation to supply to another undertaking in the group established in another Member State the essential information for opening negotiations with a view to setting up an EWC. The same applies to the 'deemed central management' of groups, where the actual central management is not situated in the EU, which was the case with Anker. In such case, the responsibilities of the central management lie with the central management's representative agent in a Member State, the management of the establishment, or with the group undertaking employing the greatest number of employees in any one Member State (Article 4(2) EWC Directive). The CJEU stressed that any other interpretation of the obligations by which the central management or deemed management is bound 'would be liable to undermine the useful purpose of the Directive'.[79]

7.33 Two earlier cases already demonstrated the difficulties that employee representatives may encounter when requesting information with a view to establishing an EWC. Similar preliminary questions as in *Anker* were referred to the CJEU in *Kühne & Nagel* (2004) and *Bofrost* (2001). In the first case, as in *Anker*, the central management of the group was established in Switzerland. The CJEU held that, if the central management refuses to cooperate, the deemed central management, in order to be able to fulfil its obligation to provide information to the employees' representatives, must request the information from the other undertakings of the group, insofar as they are located in the EU. The deemed central management has the right to receive that information from them, and the management of each of the other group undertakings must supply the deemed central management with the information concerned if it is in possession of it or is in a position to obtain it.[80] In *Bofrost* (2001), the information was refused on the basis that none of the undertakings was in the position to effectuate central management. Within the Bofrost group, a special agreement was concluded, intending to establish parity between the various undertakings, so that none would be dominant and that there would be no hierarchy between them. The CJEU held that:

> an undertaking which is part of a group of undertakings is required to supply information to the internal workers' representative bodies, even where it has not yet been established that the management to which the workers' request is addressed is the management of a controlling undertaking within a group of undertakings.[81]

7.34 These CJEU's judgments on the obligation of undertakings within a Community-scale group are now codified in the Recast Directive; hence the undertakings are obliged to provide information that is required for commencing negotiations with a view to establishing EWCs, in particular information concerning the structure of the undertaking, the group and its workforce (Articles 4 and 5).

79. Case C-349/01 (*ADS Anker*) (2004).
80. Case C-440/00 (*Kühne & Nagel)* (2004).
81. Case C-62/99 *(Bofrost)* (2001), ruling 1.

C The SE and the SCE

7.35 The model of the EWC Directive, giving priority to negotiations with a view to reaching an agreement between the employer and employee representatives in a joint special negotiating body, backed by subsidiary (default) rules where no agreement is reached, was duplicated in the directives accompanying the SE and SCE Statutes. According to the Preamble to the SE Directive, information and consultation procedures at a transnational level should be ensured in all cases of creation of an SE. It should also be defined primarily by means of an agreement between the parties concerned or, in the absence of such agreement, through the application of a set of subsidiary or standard rules. The standard rules are laid down in Part 2 of the Annex to the SE Directive and define the competence and powers of the representative body set up in the SE. Part 1 of the Annex contains the standard rules for the composition of such body. The right to information and consultation is modelled after the rights laid down in the 1994 EWC Directive. These issues and the relationship between the EWC Directive and the SE Directive are dealt with in more detail in paragraph 4.35 *et seq*.

7.36 The SCE Directive is similar to the SE Directive in many respects, and the same standard rules apply where no agreement on employee involvement is reached. In contrast to the SE, however, the SCE may be established by natural persons or by a single legal entity and natural persons. In the event that these persons or the entity employs fewer than 50 employees, or employs 50 or more employees in only one Member State, employee involvement is governed by local rules. For the SCE itself, the provisions of the Member State where the SCE is registered apply, and for its subsidiaries and establishments, the provisions of the Member State in which they are situated apply. After the registration of the SCE, however, a request by one-third of the total number of employees of the SCE, its subsidiaries and establishments will suffice to have the basic rules of the directive applied; that is, starting the negotiating procedure on a transnational information and consultation procedure (Article 8).

V INFORMATION AND CONSULTATION: OTHER DIRECTIVES

7.37 The Directive on collective redundancies, the Directive on protection of employees' rights in the case of a transfer of the undertaking, as well as some directives on safety and health, all contain provisions regarding procedures for information and consultation of employee representatives.[82] However, these directives deal with specific situations, whereas Directive 2002/14/EC establishes a general framework for informing and consulting employees.[83]

82. Directive 75/129/EEC; *inter alia* 89/391/EEC.
83. OJ 2002, L 80.

A Collective Redundancies

7.38 The Directive on collective redundancies (1975, amended 1992 and 1998)[84] applies where dismissals are effectuated by an employer for reasons not related to the individual workers concerned. The threshold can be set by the Member States at a certain number of dismissals with a choice for one of the regimes stipulated in Article 1(1)(a) of Directive 98/59/EC. One of the options is, for example, to apply the rules where, over a period of 90 days, at least 20 dismissals take place, regardless of the number of workers normally employed in the establishments. Information on collective redundancies must be given to employee representatives before the decision is taken and before any notification to the competent authority is given. The employer has the obligation to explain, in writing, *inter alia,* the reason for the redundancies, the number of workers to be made redundant, the number of workers normally employed and the period over which the redundancy is to be effectuated (Article 2(3)). The employer is obliged to notify the competent authority of the projected collective redundancies (Article 3). The consultation must cover ways and means to avoid or reduce redundancy and mitigate its consequences. The employer is also required to consult the employee representatives with a view to reaching an agreement. The collective redundancies may not take effect any earlier than 30 days after notification to the competent authority (Article 4).[85]

B Transfer of Undertakings

7.39 The Directive on the safeguarding of employees' rights in the event of transfers of undertakings (1977, substituted 2001)[86] applies where economic trends lead to changes in the structure of undertakings and businesses, which result in a change of employer. More precisely, this directive applies where an undertaking, business or part of an undertaking or business is transferred to another employer because of a legal transfer or merger (Article 1(a)). For the sake of clarity, it is stipulated that the provisions apply where there is a transfer of an economic entity that retains its identity, meaning an organized grouping of resources that has the objective of pursuing an economic activity, whether or not that activity is central or ancillary (Article 1(b)). This phrase essentially codifies the extensive case law generated by the CJEU on the concept of transfer and the concept of undertaking, or part thereof.[87] The rules set by the directive apply where, and insofar as, the undertaking to be transferred is situated within the EU (Article 1(2)). The directive enables employees to remain employed on

84. *See* the consolidating Directive 98/59/EC.
85. R. Blanpain, *supra* n. 9, at 283–293.
86. Directive 77/187/EEC amended by Directive 98/50/EC, 1998; both directives are repealed by the consolidating Directive 2001/23/EC.
87. C. de Groot, 'The Council Directive on the Safeguarding of Employees' Rights in the Event of Transfers of Undertakings: An Overview of the Case Law', *Common Market Law Review* 30 (1993): 331–350.

the terms and conditions of the existing contract and the transferee becomes the employer (Article 3). The transferor and transferee both must inform the representatives of the employees affected by the transfer about the date of the transfer, the reason behind it, the legal, economic and social implications for the employees and the measures envisaged in relation to the employees. If the transferor or the transferee contemplates measures in relation to its employees, the transferor or the transferee must consult the employee representatives with a view to reaching an agreement (Article 6). More details of the directive are discussed in paragraph 8.100.

C Safety and Health

7.40 What is called the Framework Directive on safety and health (1989, amended 2007) concerns general measures to improve the safety and health of employees while at work.[88] Among other matters, it provides for employee involvement in relation to the enterprise's safety and health policy. According to Article 10, employees must receive all the necessary information concerning the safety and health risks and the measures and activities undertaken in this respect. Article 11(1) requires employers to consult employees and/or their representatives and allow them to take part in discussions on all questions relating to safety and health at work. This includes the right to be consulted and to make proposals. It presupposes a balanced involvement in accordance with national laws and/or practices.[89]

VI EMPLOYEE PARTICIPATION

7.41 Finally, when it comes to employee participation at board level,[90] it must be noted that this is not a common feature in all Member States. Currently, such participation can be found in 18 EU Member States as well as Norway.[91]

Most commonly, employee representatives in these Member States have one-third of the seats on the board (e.g., the Netherlands[92]) or up to 50% in large companies in a number of Members States (e.g., Germany[93] and Austria). Most often the employee

88. Directive 89/391/EEC and 2007/30/EC.
89. These provisions of the 1989 Directive are not amended. Therefore, the old terminology is used: 'participation of workers' (which is equivalent to 'involvement of employees').
90. *See* paragraph 7.13 above for the definition of the concept.
91. Austria, Croatia, Czech Republic, Denmark, Finland, France, Germany, Greece, Hungary, Ireland, Luxembourg, the Netherlands, Norway, Poland, Portugal, Slovak Republic, Slovenia, Spain and Sweden; A. Conchon et al., *supra* n. 33.
92. The Dutch system applies to fairly large public and private companies, that is, companies having a share capital of EUR 16 million and employing at least 100 persons and having a works council (Articles 2:153 and 2:263 Dutch Civil Code).
93. The German Co-determination Act of 1976 (*Mitbestimmungsgesetz*) applies to the German public limited (AG) and private limited (GmbH) company above 2,000 employees. Other company forms are not covered and circumvention of co-determination or participation is subject to academic and policy debate.

representatives have their seats on the supervisory board.[94] In five other Member States, employee participation is limited to state-owned companies or companies owned by municipalities, and two Member States have extended it to privatized companies.[95] Ten Member States have no legal arrangements at all for board-level participation.[96]

7.42 French law, since 2015, also provides for employee representation on the board of large companies. These rules apply to companies employing a total of more than 1,000 employees, including those working for subsidiaries with their statutory seat in France.[97] They also apply to French companies with foreign subsidiaries if they employ a total of more than 5,000 employees. In these cases, employees will have at least one representative on the board, if the size of the board is less than or equals eight members, and two representatives, if the size of the board exceeds eight members. The nomination procedure is determined by the articles of association and can be chosen from four different possibilities regulated by law (e.g., election by the employees or nomination by the works council).

7.43 In Germany, the works council, in principle, deals with affairs at the level of the plant, such as working conditions as outlined above in paragraph 7.17, whereas participation pursuant to the Co-determination Acts regards the economic policy of the company at the level of the supervisory board. Employee representation on the supervisory board is mandatory for certain business organizations, *inter alia,* public and private companies, if they employ more than 500 people. In such case, one-third of the members of the supervisory board are elected by the employees (*see* paragraph 6.17).[98] This rises to one-half if more than 2,000 people are employed. If between 2,000 and 10,000 people are employed, the supervisory board must have 12 members, and 6 of these are reserved for employee representatives, that is, 4 employees of the company and 2 trade union representatives. Different figures apply if more people are employed, and the largest number of supervisory board members (20) must be appointed by companies having more than 20,000 employees. Similarly, half of these seats are designated for employee representatives, of which a part is reserved for trade union representatives.[99] To avoid deadlock, the chairperson has a casting vote. The chairperson has to be elected by the supervisory board by a two-thirds majority, allowing both employee representatives and shareholder representatives on the board to block the

94. J. Calvo et al., *supra* n. 6, 64–65. Swedish legislation, which is not discussed in this book, entitles employees to two permanent representatives and two deputies on the board of directors in companies with at least twenty-five employees. If the company has more than 1,000 employees and operates in at least two different lines of business, the number is three permanent representatives and three deputies.
95. Belgium, Greece, Ireland, Poland and Spain. France and Malta have extended employee participation to privatized companies; J. Calvo et al., *supra* n. 6, at 64.
96. Bulgaria, Cyprus, Estonia, Iceland, Italy, Latvia, Lithuania, Romania, Portugal and the UK (prior to withdrawal); *Ibid.*
97. *See* Article L225-27-1 French Commercial Code.
98. *Gesetz über die Drittelbeteiligung der Arbeitnehmer im Aufsichtsrat* (DrittelbG), s. 1.
99. Sections 1 and 7 *Mitbestimmungsgesetz.* For certain industries, different rules may apply according to the *Montan-Mitbestimmungsgesetz.*

appointment. In such case, however, the shareholder representatives may choose the chairperson. The employee representatives may then choose the vice-chairperson.[100]

7.44 The Co-determination Acts apply, *inter alia,* to the public company AG and private company (GmbH). All members of the supervisory board are equally held to further the interests of the enterprise, and the legal position of the employee representatives does not differ from that of other members.[101] Companies incorporated in other jurisdictions are not covered by the Co-determination Acts, even if the workforce is exclusively or mainly located in Germany. Some German businesses have avoided employee participation by incorporating their company into other European jurisdictions. There is a lively academic and political debate in Germany on whether German legislators should change the Co-determination Acts in a way that foreign legal entities would also be covered and whether such a rule would be compatible with the European freedom of establishment.[102] From another angle, it was challenged whether German co-determination may be in conflict with EU law because only employees working in Germany are entitled to vote and to be nominated for supervisory board mandates. This issue was referred to the CJEU for a preliminary ruling. According to the CJEU, legislation restricting the right to vote and to stand as a candidate to employees of establishments located in the national territory does not violate EU law, specifically not Article 45 Treaty on the Functioning of the European Union (TFEU).[103]

7.45 In the Netherlands, as is the case in Germany, apart from the works council there is a form of employee participation at the level of the supervisory board of certain business organizations.[104] The Dutch system applies to fairly large public and private companies, that is, companies having a share capital of EUR 16 million and employing at least 100 people and having a works council. The members of the supervisory board are appointed according to a rather complicated mechanism, resulting from a statutory review in 2004. Although the members of the supervisory board are appointed by the general meeting upon the proposal of the supervisory board, both the general meeting and the works council may first nominate individuals to be appointed as members of the supervisory board. For one-third of the seats, the candidates proposed by the works council must be accepted by the supervisory board. The supervisory board may object to the proposed candidate, but only if that candidate lacks the abilities to carry out his or her duties, or if the board would be improperly constituted due to that particular appointment. If no agreement can be reached, the supervisory board may request the Enterprise Chamber of the Amsterdam Court of Appeal to decide on the matter.[105] This

100. Sections 27 and 29 MitbestG.
101. Section 25 MitbestG, ss 116 and 93 AktG.
102. *See* C. Teichmann, 'Mitbestimmungserstreckung auf Auslandsgesellschaften', *ZIP* 2016, 899–907.
103. Case C-566/15 (*Erzberger*). For the academic debate in Germany *see*: H.-J- Hellwig & C. Behme, 'Gemeinschaftsrechtliche Probleme der deutschen Unternehmensmitbestimmung', *AG* 2009, 261–278; R. Krause, 'Zur Bedeutung des Unionsrechts für die unternehmerische Mitbestimmung', *AG* 2014, 485–497.
104. Articles 2:152 *et seq.* (public company) and 2:262 *et seq.* (private company) Dutch Civil Code.
105. Articles 2:158 and 2:268 Dutch Civil Code.

so-called structure regime system further differs from the German system in that members of the supervisory board may not be employed by the company, by its subsidiaries or by the trade union that is involved in collective negotiations with the company.[106] Lastly, it must be noted that, *inter alia,* international holding companies are exempt from the structure regime.[107]

7.46 Although employee participation has not been harmonized, it has been taken into account in the directives regulating transactions of a cross-border nature (Tenth Directive on cross-border mergers, the SE Directive and the SCE Directive as well as the corporate mobility package of Directive 2019/2121/EU, which comes into force on 31 January 2023).[108] Participation rights are dealt with at the EU level by the regulations and directives governing EU business organizations and cross-border company mobility transactions: cross-border mergers, conversions and divisions.[109] These rules protect existing participation rights when a SE or SCE is formed or a cross-border transaction takes place. The starting point is the applicable legislation of the country in which the company resulting from the transaction will have its registered office, but the 'before-and-after principle' ensures the protection of existing participation rights.[110]

106. Articles 2:160 and 2:270 Dutch Civil Code.
107. Articles 2:153 and 2:263 Dutch Civil Code.
108. *See* paragraphs 4.35 and 8.100.
109. Directive (EU) 2019/2121 of 27 Nov. 2019 amending Directive (EU) 2017/1132 as regards cross-border conversions, mergers and divisions.
110. Article 133(1) Directive (EU) 2017/1132.

CHAPTER 8

Cross-Border Business Combinations, Takeovers and Restructuring Tools

I INTRODUCTION

8.01 There are many ways in which companies form business combinations, restructure their own operations or an entire corporate group. Companies and business activities develop and grow over time. A company may, for example, acquire a competitor or may have to focus on a specific type of business and therefore disinvest in other parts which will be sold off. A company may also choose to move its business across borders and be subject to the law of a different Member State, for example because its business has developed throughout the years in such a way that its main activities are now situated in that other Member State. This requires the law to cater for tools that make cross-border or national business combinations and restructurings possible.

8.02 There have been efforts at the EU level to harmonize various instruments to enable business combinations and restructurings in a cross-border or a national context. First of all, as mentioned in Chapter 3 (*see* paragraph 3.34 *et seq.*) there is a harmonized procedure for mergers and divisions between companies from the same Member States as well as between companies from different Member States in the form of a cross-border merger or division. In addition, there is a harmonized procedure for cross-border conversions when a company wants to move from one Member State to another. When talking about business combinations, a term that is often used in corporate practice is a takeover. Takeovers in listed companies are also, partly, harmonized by the Takeover Directive.

8.03 This chapter focuses on the tools for (cross-border) business combinations and restructurings mentioned above. We begin by briefly discussing different types of cooperation in corporate practice. From there we provide an overview of the different tools to achieve business combinations: asset transactions, mergers and divisions and share transactions. Subsequently, we discuss a specific type of share transaction, namely a takeover in the context of listed companies. Even though not strictly an instrument to achieve a fully integrated business combination, it can be a means by which one company acquires control over the business of another company. After that, we address national mergers and divisions followed by the cross-border tools: the cross-border merger and division and cross-border conversion. The chapter concludes with several remarks concerning the protection of the rights of employees (*see* paragraph 8.98 *et seq.*) and European Union (EU) merger control (*see* paragraph 8.105 *et seq.*).

II DIFFERENT TYPES OF COOPERATION

8.04 There is a spectrum of different ways in which businesses can combine their activities, ranging from a rather loose cooperation on a contractual basis to a full integration of several previously existing businesses into one company or a group of companies. Companies can, for example, on a contractual basis agree to coordinate their businesses and to buy or sell, lend or hire, etc. This generally requires limited actual long-term cooperation between business enterprises, apart from reaching an agreement on the terms of a contract. Where cooperation has a long-term impact on the competitiveness of the companies involved, while these companies retain their independence and identity, it is generally identified as strategic cooperation.[1] From the viewpoint of the individual companies involved in such an arrangement, the cooperation results in a strategic alliance. On the other side of the spectrum lies the full integration of businesses, where an acquisition of a business, a share purchase or a merger has resulted in complete control by one business enterprise over the activities of another enterprise. In such cases, economic decisions are no longer coordinated by market mechanisms, but by the hierarchy within the combined enterprise. Between these two extremes, there are many other forms of cooperation. They differ, *inter alia,* according to variations in the duration of the arrangement and the commitment of the parties involved. The main focus of this chapter is on the different tools that can be used to achieve a full integration. However, before providing an overview of the tools for combining businesses, we first discuss joint ventures, as joint ventures are generally seen as a form of strategic cooperation where a separate business organization is created without aiming to achieve an integrated business combination of all parties involved. It therefore stands somewhere in the middle of the spectrum mentioned above, ranging from a loose cooperation to a full integration.

8.05 The term 'joint venture' is frequently used in the economic and legal literature, as well as in legal practice. Although based on a literal explanation of the term joint venture, every joint activity of business enterprises can be designated as a joint

1. S.E. Huyzer *et al., Strategische samenwerking. Oriëntatie en Implementatie,* Second edition (Alphen aan den Rijn/Zaventem: Coopers & Lybrand Dijker Van Dien, 1992), 29.

venture, the definition is often narrowed to cooperation, whereby a separate business organization is created. In this case, the cooperating enterprises supply know-how and/or capital to that entity, but they remain independent and outside the scope of the cooperation itself.[2] In this respect, the joint venture differs from the other forms of strategic cooperation, such as contractual agreements, leading to the transfer of technology or co-makership, where no separate entity is formed.

8.06 A joint venture is defined as a separate enterprise (undertaking) that has been created to structure the cooperation of two or more business enterprises. The choice is between the incorporated joint venture or equity joint venture and the unincorporated joint venture or contractual joint venture. The first implies the participation of the joint venture partners in a private or public company, whereas the second is a contractual joint venture, resulting in an entity that most likely will have the form of a partnership.

8.07 A joint venture company may be newly formed, but the partners may also use a company previously owned or acquired by one of them. Likewise, the relationship of joint venture partners may vary considerably. If there are two partners, as a rule, they will each hold 50 % of the shares and votes in the joint venture company. However, the distribution of profits may deviate from that percentage, where an unequal contribution to the assets of the joint venture has to be compensated for. The management of the joint venture business may be attributed to a joint board of directors or to one of the partners exclusively. That, however, may give rise to issues inherent to the law of groups of companies, such as mandatory consolidation of the joint venture by the managing partner,[3] thereby considering the joint venture company as a subsidiary of one of its shareholders (however, this is normally *not* the intention of its shareholders). Contractual joint ventures, as already mentioned, frequently have the form of a partnership. Although commercial partnerships may have legal personality, especially in continental countries, this feature does not affect the essential personal and contractual character of such a partnership, and the same applies to a European economic interest grouping (EEIG). Consequently, the joint venture partners generally enjoy more freedom as to the provisions laid down in the contract or articles, in comparison with the incorporated forms.

Whatever form is chosen, questions may arise as to the seat of the new entity if the joint venture has a cross-border dimension. The options are to have the entity seated in the country of one of the joint venture partners or in a third country. On the basis of Directive (EU) 2019/2121 and once this directive has been transposed into the national laws of the EU Member States by 31 January 2023, companies will be able to rely on a legal framework to transfer their registered office to a different Member State. As a principle, there are no legal restrictions to the transfer of a joint venture's

2. *See*, for example, J. Brodley. 'Joint Ventures and Antitrust Policy', *Harvard Law Review* 95 (1982): 1521, 1527–9; C.M. Schmitthoff, *The Law and Practice of International Trade*, Ninth edition (London: Sweet & Maxwell, 1990), 338, where it is stated that 'The joint venture is a common undertaking created by two or more participants for a specific purpose of commercial, financial or technical nature.'
3. According to Article 22 of Directive 2013/34/EU.

registered office if it has the form of a business organization under EU law, notably the EEIG and the *Societas Europaea* (SE).

8.08 Parallel to the formation of a joint venture entity, the partners will often draw up a separate joint venture contract (JV contract) or several contracts on different subject matters in relation to the joint venture. Such contract, for instance, may regulate commercial transactions between the partners and the joint venture. It may also cover specific contributions, such as the transfer of technology and intellectual property rights or the supply of employees and goods. In addition, the contract may also relate to the transfer of shares, pre-emption rights and the resolution of deadlock situations. Although essential for the joint venture, the articles of a joint venture company very rarely regulate these issues. The main reason is that the articles have to be disclosed, thus making sensitive business information available to competitors if such issues were included. Where the joint venture has an international character, attention should be paid to avoiding divergences between the law governing the legal entity and the law applicable to related contracts. Lastly, it should be noted here that a joint venture may have effects on competition, which must be assessed under Articles 101 and 102 Treaty on the Functioning of the European Union (TFEU), and/or the Merger Regulation (*see* paragraph 8.105 *et seq.*).

8.09 Sophisticated devices are sometimes used for the legal structuring of joint ventures, especially for buyout provisions. An example is the right of first refusal, which prohibits parties from selling their stake to a third party before having offered to the joint venture partner(s) to buy it for the price the third party is willing to pay. If the parties do not mind whether they sell their own interest or buy that of the other party, they may resort to clauses, which have been given fancy names by the business and legal community, such as 'auction clauses' or 'envelope clauses', where the parties aim at letting the party who is willing and able to pay the highest price for the company to take over the company and carry on its business. This is essentially an option for a party (say, A) to put an end to the cooperation by calling the price for which the other party (B) may buy A's share. B may then decide whether to buy A's share or to sell its own share to A for the same price.

III TOOLS FOR BUSINESS COMBINATIONS

A Overview

8.10 As set out in paragraph 8.04, the integration of business enterprises, in full or in parts, goes beyond strategic cooperation. Such integration can be realized, to put it simply, where one business enterprise has acquired the control of another enterprise. There are different methods of acquiring control, which under one common umbrella are named M&A (merger and acquisition): (a) the acquisition of a business (often by way of an Asset Purchase Agreement (APA), or a Business Transfer Agreement (BTA)); (b) the acquisition of a company's shares (often by way of a Share Purchase Agreement

(SPA)); or (c) the completion of a (legal) merger. In addition, a division can also be used to combine parts of already existing businesses.

In the case of an acquisition of a business through an asset transaction, the assets or a separable part of the assets of an undertaking are acquired. In the case of a share transaction, control is acquired by one company over another, and it therefore also entails the acquisition of control over the business carried out by that company.

A legal merger means the winding-up of a company without going into liquidation, while all its assets and liabilities are transferred to the acquiring company (*see* paragraph 3.34 *et seq.*). A division means acquiring a part of a company, often in the form of a business or a part of a business, by way of dividing the company that owns the business.

All the ways of combining a business mentioned above can be used in a national as well as in a cross-border context. Which one of these instruments will be used, depends on the goal of the business combination. For example, a company may only want to take over certain parts of the activities of another company, in which case either a division or an asset transaction may be appropriate. In other circumstances, a company may want to expand geographically and has acquired a competitor in a different Member State, in which case a share transaction may be useful to ensure that the company has a subsidiary incorporated under the laws of a different Member State. Very often tax law will also play an important role in deciding how to structure the deal.[4]

8.11 An important control question, facilitating the choice of the right method of M&A, is often: who receives the consideration for the sale (because an M&A is always some kind of sale)? The answers are that: (a) when acquiring a business, the selling company receives the consideration; (b) when acquiring a majority stake, the individual shareholders receive the consideration; (c) when merging companies A and B, with B as the surviving company, the shareholders of A receive the consideration; and (d) when dividing company A, thereby transferring a part of its assets to company B, the shareholders of A receive the consideration, just as in a merger (and thereby also contrary to the transfer of business, where the selling company receives the consideration).

8.12 Further, it must be noted that share transactions are generally easier to carry out than asset transactions. Mergers, including cross-border mergers, require a specific procedure to be followed. In practice, mergers are often used to restructure companies that already form part of a group, whereas share and asset transactions are more often used as acquisition tools to acquire new activities or companies from third parties outside of the group.

8.13 Cross-border acquisitions are likely to meet several regulatory hurdles, such as taxation, exchange control, investment restrictions, stock exchange requirements and

4. A. Cahn & D.C. Donald, *Comparative Company Law* (Oxford: Oxford University Press, 2018), 768–769.

merger control.[5] Within the EU, however, a lot has been done to facilitate cross-border transactions. Several operations mergers, divisions, formation of a holding company ('exchange of shares') and business transfer ('transfer of assets') are recognized as combination or takeover methods by directives, such as the Merger Tax Directive 2009/133/EC.[6] Consequently, this has diminished tax complications and related directives, which account for the harmonized taxation of transfer of assets, exchange of shares and mergers as well as divisions, if companies from two or more Member States are involved. Furthermore, exchange control and investment restrictions, for the most part, have been removed in order to realize free movement of capital.[7] Stock exchange requirements play a role if an acquisition takes place by a public takeover bid, but here harmonization has had its effects too (*see* paragraphs 3.32 *et seq.* and 8.19 *et seq.*). Lastly, merger control can be exerted by national authorities, but EU control prevails when mergers have a Community dimension (*see* paragraph 8.105 *et seq.*).

In the following paragraphs, we further discuss each of the abovementioned business combination tools.[8]

B Asset Transaction

8.14 Acquisition of a business through the acquisition of its assets (APA or BTA)[9] may have some advantages in comparison with the other methods. It is a flexible method because it does not automatically lead to the acquisition of all the assets of a business, which would happen in a merger and, albeit indirectly, upon the acquisition of the shares in a company. It therefore allows cherry-picking, the acquirer can only purchase the parts of the business that it really wants to acquire. Asset transactions can therefore be useful if one company wants to buy a certain division of another company which seems to be most promising for the future. On the other hand from the perspective of the selling company, an asset transaction may be used to disinvest in a certain line of business by selling it off to a competitor, for example. Moreover, the purchaser, as a rule, does not automatically assume the liabilities of the acquired business, because the purchaser is only liable if it expressly assumes all or part of those liabilities. However, there may be exceptions for tax liability; and under German law, the acquirer of a commercial business is liable for the debts of the former owner, unless an agreement

5. T. E. Cooke, *International Mergers and Acquisitions* (Oxford/New York: Blackwell, 1988); D.J. Ben-Daniel & A.H. Rosenbloom, *The Handbook of International Mergers & Acquisitions* (Englewood Cliffs, NJ: Prentice Hall, 1990).
6. Directive 90/434/EEC amended by Directive 2005/19/EC.
7. Article 63 TFEU.
8. These are in handbooks also referred to as techniques for business combinations *see* A. Cahn & D.C. Donald, *supra*, n. 4, at Chapter 23.
9. The names APA and BTA are often used interchangeably, but there may, for practical reasons, be a slight difference. The APA may refer to a transfer of assets only, i.e., that no transfer takes place of a whole business, regarded as an economic entity having maintained its 'identity', whereas the BTA certainly refers to such transfer of an 'entity'.

to the contrary is registered with the Commercial Registry.[10] In some jurisdictions, liabilities also follow the assets due to specific legal provisions of, for example, consumer or environmental protection.[11]

It depends on national law who decides on the transaction. From the point of view of both the buyer and the seller, this is generally the board of directors. However, where it concerns very large transactions, shareholder approval may be required based either on the division of power envisaged in national company law or on the provisions in the articles of association. Notwithstanding its flexibility, an acquisition of assets may be less attractive due to taxation and the complicated nature of the transfer of assets. It can potentially lead to a lot of transaction costs.[12] There is no universal transfer of title to the purchaser. This means that every single asset has to be transferred in accordance with the applicable rules of national law.[13] It requires specific contracts as well as in some cases rules on conveyance to be taken into account. In the case of a transfer of real estate, for example, a notarial deed may be required. Another potential disadvantage is that for the transfer of important contracts, for example, supply contracts or leases, the consent of the counterparty will be required.[14]

C Mergers and Divisions

8.15 A merger entails that two or more companies, the merging entities, merge their assets and liabilities on the basis of a universal transfer of assets into a surviving entity. The merging entities will be dissolved without going into liquidation, and the shareholders of the merging entities will become shareholders in the surviving entity in proportion to the assets and liabilities transferred to the surviving entity. The shareholders of the disappearing company become shareholders of the acquiring company. However, in groups of companies mergers can also take place at a lower level within the group by means of merging the disappearing company with a subsidiary. This type of merger is often referred to as a triangular merger. In order to ensure that the parent company retains full control over the subsidiary, in such case, the shareholders of the disappearing company often do not get shares in the acquiring company but instead in the parent company.[15]

A universal transfer of assets and liabilities means that the assets and liabilities are transferred together in their entirety to the surviving entity and not on an asset-per-asset basis, which would be much more complicated. For example, for each asset a transfer contract would have to be drafted, each existing contract would have to be analysed as to how to transfer it to the new entity, third-party approvals for

10. Section 25 HGB (Commercial Code). *See* W. Beisel & H.-H. Klump, *Der Unternehmenskauf* (München: C.H. Beck, 2016).
11. A. Cahn & D.C. Donald, *supra* n. 4, at 771.
12. *Ibid.*
13. Some countries allow for a universal title of transfer of a business, such as France. *See* Articles 141-1 *et seq. Code de commerce (fonds de commerce)*.
14. A. Cahn & D.C. Donald, *supra* n. 4, at 771.
15. *Ibid.*, 774.

various different contracts and assets would have to be obtained and so on. That means, however, that a merger is a major transaction for a company, its shareholders, and also for creditors or employees. For example, a shareholder that held a majority of shares and thus also of the votes in a merging entity may be a minority shareholder in the surviving entity or where the credit risk for a creditor in a merging entity has been low, the credit risk may be high in the surviving entity. Consequently, a framework that governs mergers must address the risks for such stakeholders and a cross-border framework must add additional aspects that arise due to the cross-border nature of the transaction.

8.16 A division, also sometimes referred to as 'scission',[16] is based on the same principles as a merger. The main difference is that the company being divided transfers its assets and liabilities to more than one company. Therefore, in the case of divisions, the transfer is effectuated by one company to several others; whereas, for mergers, transfers can be effectuated by either one or more companies, but to one other company only.

D Share Transaction

8.17 Unlike a merger or an asset transaction, a share transaction does not lead to an integration of two pre-existing businesses or parts of businesses. It does, however, allow one company to control the business of another company. Compared to an asset transaction, a share transaction is relatively simple in the sense that the only assets that need to be transferred are the shares in the company. Transaction costs are generally low in cases where there are only a limited number of shareholders. If in that case there are a lot of assets to be transferred, a share transaction may be preferred instead of an asset transaction. The costs increase when there is dispersed ownership and especially when the company is publicly listed.[17] Unlike an asset transaction but similar to a merger, in the case of a share transaction, the acquirer acquires control of the company including all of its assets as well as all its liabilities.

8.18 The decision-making from the point of view of the seller will always be in the hands of the shareholders as they will be the ones selling their shares. However, as discussed in the following section, defensive measures can give the board of directors a stronger position when a takeover is imminent. Since the acquirer takes over the company by buying the shares in that legal entity, all existing contracts between the target and third parties, such as key suppliers, stay in place. However, in practice, the acquirer must be aware that this can trigger change of control clauses incorporated in contracts with third parties. These change of control clauses often cause the contract to terminate or require the contract to be renegotiated once there is a change of control in the company. In that sense one of the disadvantages of an asset deal mentioned above,

16. *See* V. Edwards, *EC Company Law* (Oxford University Press 1999), 91 on the introduction of this word in the English legal language.
17. A. Cahn & D.C. Donald, *supra* n. 4, at 771.

can also arise in a share transaction as important contracts with change of control clauses will have to be renegotiated, and existing contracts that are advantageous to the target may be lost for the future.[18] In the remainder of this chapter, we discuss the European legal framework for each of these types of transactions in more detail.

IV TAKEOVERS

8.19 In this section, we delve into a specific type of share transaction: takeovers. The term takeover is not specifically defined and is often used in a variety of ways. In a broad sense, the term takeover can refer to any type of business combination whether this is through an asset transaction, a merger or a share transaction. In a narrow sense, the term is often used in corporate practice to refer to the situation in which one company acquires control over another company by means of a share transaction. In this section, we focus on takeovers in this narrow sense. Even though the acquisition of shares is relevant for both privately held companies and for publicly listed companies, the part below focuses solely on transactions of shares in listed companies, as there are several mandatory rules at the EU level pertaining to this type of share transaction while uniform rules for share transactions in private companies are lacking. The acquisition of control of a listed company, in general, involves the acquisition of a majority of the shares carrying voting rights, which, in most cases will require a public offer for the outstanding or part of the outstanding shares. To ensure that shareholders receive sufficient information and are treated equally, takeover bids are relatively heavily regulated, compared to private share transactions. At the EU level, the Takeover Directive is in particular focused on disclosure, transparency and proper procedures to ensure that shareholders are able to review and, if so decided, accept the public offer. The Takeover Directive thus has the function of safeguarding the interests of shareholders, securing the proper functioning of the capital market[19] and potentially also safeguarding the interests of other stakeholders.

A The Market for Corporate Control

8.20 The rationale behind doing a takeover may be explained by the pursuance of economies of scale and reduction of agency costs. The first is obvious and also applies to other forms of acquisition, whereas the latter requires further clarification on agency costs and the theory of the market for corporate control. Agency costs are costs incurred by the principal to align the agent to the interests of the principal.[20] Within the company, the shareholders, taken together, have been regarded as the principal and

18. *Ibid.*, 772.
19. *See, e.g.*, Preamble paragraphs 1 and 12 of the Directive 2004/25/EC of 21 Apr. 2004 on takeover bids, OJ 2004, L 142 (Takeover Directive).
20. J. Armour et al., 'What Is Corporate Law', in R. Kraakman et al., *The Anatomy of Corporate Law* (Oxford: Oxford University Press, 2017), 29–30.

the board members as the agents.[21] Shareholders are required to rely on their control rights to monitor the board members. Shareholders are in many cases not able to optimally perform their monitoring function where the company has a dispersed shareholding because of free riding and rational apathy among shareholders. In such cases, a successful takeover by an offeror (i.e., the party making the public offer) should lead to the situation in which the offeror acquires (full) control over the target company. This concentration of power in the hands of the offeror, as the controlling shareholder, leads to a situation in which the controlling shareholder is able to better exercise the monitoring function and replace inefficient board members with more efficient board members, in theory increasing shareholder value in the company. In practice, even the mere threat of a takeover functions as a disciplinary power towards the board of directors, because the directors are aware of the fact that 'their' companies might be taken over, leading to their potential removal by the offeror as the future controlling shareholder, if they underperform and do not create value for the shareholders.[22] This disciplinary effect of takeovers is referred to as the 'market for corporate control'.[23]

8.21 As mentioned in paragraph 8.18 above, the shareholders are the ultimate decision-makers in a takeover. They eventually have to decide whether or not to sell their shares. However, one of the ways in which companies, and boards of directors, can protect themselves from a takeover attempt is by using defensive measures. These defensive measures can already be in place before a public offer is launched, in which case these are considered pre-bid defensive measures. The defensive measures can, however, also be engaged once a public offer is launched/announced, in which case they are referred to as post-bid defensive measures. It is difficult to determine whether granting the power to the board of directors to use defensive measures is positive or negative. On the one hand, it diminishes the disciplinary effect - as set out above - of a public offer. After all, the board of directors knows that as a result of its power to use defensive measures the company cannot be taken over without the board's cooperation. As a result, the board of directors will not feel the disciplinary effect of a potential takeover. Moreover, the board of directors could be considered as having an inherent conflict of interest in relation to defensive measures. The offeror will want to replace the inefficient management with more efficient management, meaning that the current inefficient directors run the risk of being replaced should the takeover bid be successful. As a result, the directors have an incentive to use defensive measures to frustrate a takeover bid in order to save their own position.[24] At the same time, there can also be valid reasons for companies to have/engage in defensive measures in case of a (potential) public offer, especially in jurisdictions where the company and its board of directors should not be focused solely on the (long-term) interest of shareholders, but

21. *See* for more detail Chapter 6, paragraph 6.04 *et seq.*, and the sources cited there.
22. *See*, e.g., the Bangemann memorandum, COM(88)823 final.
23. *See*, for instance, D. Kershaw, *Principles of Takeover Regulation* (Oxford: Oxford University Press, 2016), 1 *et seq.*
24. *See also*, S. Grundmann, *European Company Law* (Cambridge/Antwerp/ Portland: Intersentia, 2012), 739.

should also focus on the interests of other stakeholders. The interests of these other stakeholders can be severely impacted as a result of a takeover bid. If shareholders are allowed to, at their discretion, decide whether or not a takeover bid is attractive and will be successful, the interests of other stakeholders might not be given sufficient consideration. This is an argument in favour of giving boards of directors more power to engage in defensive measures against hostile takeovers.

8.22 It is helpful in broader terms to understand how defensive measures work and what types of defensive measures are generally available for companies. Defensive measures are measures that are aimed at making it difficult or impossible for the offeror to acquire control over the offeree company following a successful takeover bid, which in turn makes it less attractive to launch the offer in the first place and, if necessary, acquire the required financing for the bid. There is a wide array of legal instruments that can be used in takeovers, both pre-bid and post-bid. It goes beyond the scope of this book to go into detail on these measures and how they work from a legal perspective. This would also require a detailed description of national law because the governance mechanisms are part of national law. It is therefore important to note that whether or not a defensive measure is possible depends on national law. However, one could consider the following – non-exhaustive – list of takeover defensive measures:

Pre-bid defensive measures: measures that create barriers for the acquisition of shares in the company or to exercise control over the general meeting that are already in place at the time of launching the public offer (or even when the offeror indicates its interest). These include:[25]

a. shares with multiple voting rights;
b. non-voting shares;
c. pyramid structures;
d. priority shares, conferring extraordinary control rights to specific shares;
e. voting rights ceilings, meaning that shareholders may only vote up to a certain percentage of the share capital;
f. ownership ceilings, meaning that shareholders are not allowed to hold a stake over a certain percentage;
g. supermajority provisions, increasing the voting thresholds for certain decisions and therefore lowering the required majority to exercise a blocking vote;
h. golden shares, conferring a special control right to (local) governments; and
i. cross-shareholdings, in this case, companies hold blocking minority stakes in each other's companies.

Post-bid defensive measures: measures that create barriers for the acquisition of shares in the company or to exercise control over the general meeting that are engaged

25. *See* for more detail on this overview: The takeover bids directive assessment report, which can be accessed at https://op.europa.eu/nl/publication-detail/-/publication/67501b75-7583-4b0d-a551-33051d8e27c1.

after launching the public offer, or after the offeror has indicated its interest. These can include:

a. seeking a white knight, meaning that the company finds a third party that is on friendly terms with the board of directors and is willing to make a competing offer for the company on – for the company – more favourable terms than the initial offeror;
b. seeking a white squire, meaning that the company finds a third party that is on friendly terms with the board of directors and is willing to buy a large minority interest in the company;
c. sale of assets, which includes the 'crown jewel defence', in which the offeree company sells an attractive asset to a friendly third party;
d. 'Pac-Man defence', which entails launching a bid by the offeree company on the offeror company; and
e. issuing warrants, which includes 'poison pills' or 'shareholder rights plans' in which, for instance, the target company facilitates the issuing of shares to its shareholders at a discount.

B Takeover Regulation in the EU

1 Background

8.23 After the above general description of decision-making in relation to takeovers and defensive measures, this section focuses on the Thirteenth Directive, formally called Directive 2004/25/EC of the European Parliament (EP) and of the Council of 21 April 2004 on takeover bids. Important underlying principles for the directive seem to be information and transparency towards shareholders, the protection of minority shareholders and the aim to have the shareholders determine whether or not the takeover bid should be successful. We discuss these principles in more detail below and focus more specifically on the scope and general principles, mandatory bid, information and transparency, how the directive deals with defensive measures and finally the squeeze-out and the sell-out provision.

8.24 In its 1985 White Paper, which focused on completing the internal market, the Commission announced that it would introduce legislation to harmonize the laws of Member States on takeovers and other general bids. The purpose of this legislative initiative was to create a level playing field for takeovers within the single market. The Commission considered takeovers in a positive light, insofar as takeovers encourage the selection by market forces of the most competitive companies. Consequently, in 1989 a proposal for the Thirteenth Directive was launched in order to remove the various obstacles and provide room for market forces when considering takeover bids.[26] This proposal met significant resistance. It was argued that only companies that have to resort to legal defensive measures will be exposed to hostile takeovers as a consequence of the directive, whereas institutional defences, such as crossholdings existing in other Member States, were not covered.[27] After delivering its first report on issues related to the directive, the mandate of the High Level Group was extended by the Commission in order to deal with a number of corporate governance issues. This resulted in a second report: *A Modern Regulatory Framework for Company Law in Europe*.[28] The group assessed the mechanisms and structures under company law that may frustrate or inhibit takeover bids. It was recommended that two principles should guide the creation of a level playing field. First, shareholder decision-making should be decisive in the event of a takeover bid. Second, there must be proportionality between risk-bearing capital and control. The latter principle meant that share capital, which has an unlimited right to participate in the profits of the company or in the residue on liquidation, should normally have decision-making power over whether a company is 'sold' to the offeror.[29] By arguing this, the High Level Group of Company Law Experts followed an economic rationale for the position and rights of shareholders, as set out in paragraph 6.59 *et seq.*

8.25 The directive was finally adopted in April 2004 as Directive 2004/25/EC. Five years later, it was amended by Regulation (EC) No. 219/2009 and, lastly, it was amended in 2014, by Directive 2014/59/EU, the 'Bank Recovery and Resolution Directive' (BRRD).

2 *Scope and General Principles*

8.26 Takeover bids for the securities of companies governed by the laws of Member States, where all or some of those securities are listed on a regulated market, fall within the scope of the directive. The directive does not apply to takeover bids for securities issued by collective investment companies and the Member States' central banks (Article 1).

8.27 By implementing the directive, Member States must comply with a set of general principles. These are laid down in Article 3:

---

26. Obstacles to takeover and other general bids. Communication from the Commission to the Council (COM (88)823 final) and: Amended proposal for a Thirteenth Council Directive on Company Law concerning takeover and other general bids, OJ 1990, C 240/7.
27. OJ 1989, C 64, 14 Mar. 1989, 8; with explanatory memorandum, Suppl. 3/89 - Bull. EC. J.M.M. Maeijer & K. Geens (eds), *Defensive Measures Against Hostile Takeovers in the Common Market* (Dordrecht/Boston/London: Springer, 1990). K. Byttebier, 'Protective and Defensive Measures Against Hostile Take-Overs', in E. Wymeersch (ed.) *Further Perspectives in Financial Integration in Europe* (Berlin/New York: 1994), 181.
28. Brussels, 4 Nov. 2002.
29. *Report on Issues Related to Takeover Bids* (Brussels: 10 Jan. 2002), 2–3. *See* http://ec.europa.eu/internal_market/company/docs/modern/report_en.pdf. The Takeover Directive is criticized for being focused on shareholder primacy, thereby neglecting CSR aspects, *see* B. Sjåfjell, *Towards a Sustainable European Company Law* (Alphen aan den Rijn: Kluwer Law International, 2009).

a) all holders of securities of an offeree company of the same class are to be treated equally and if a person acquires control of a company, the other holders must be protected;[30]
b) the addressees of a bid must have sufficient time and information to enable them to reach a properly informed decision on the bid;
c) the board of an offeree company acts in the interests of the company as a whole and must not deny the holders of securities the opportunity to decide on the merits of the bid;
d) false markets must not be created in the securities of the offeree company, of the offeror company, or of any other company concerned by the bid;
e) an offeror must announce a bid only after ensuring that it can fulfil in full any cash consideration if such consideration is offered and after taking all reasonable measures to secure the implementation of a consideration in securities or a combination of cash and securities;[31] and
f) an offeree company must not be hindered in the conduct of its affairs for longer than is reasonable by a bid for its securities.[32]

3 *Mandatory Bid*

8.28 One of the main provisions of the directive concerns the obligation to launch a mandatory bid.[33] Any person who has acquired a specified percentage of the voting rights in a company, giving that person control over that company, is obliged to launch a mandatory bid to acquire all the securities of that company at an equitable price (Article 5(1)). The percentage of voting rights representing control of the company is determined by the rules of the Member State in which the company has its registered office (Article 5(3)), but it is generally considered to be around 30% or 33%, with Austria, Belgium, Cyprus, Czech Republic, Finland, Germany, Ireland, Italy, the Netherlands and Sweden applying the 30% threshold and Greece, Hungary, Luxembourg, Poland, Portugal, Romania and Slovakia applying the 33% threshold.[34] The mandatory bid rule, however, also has a number of exceptions or 'loopholes'. One of these is that a mandatory offer is not required if control over the offeree company was acquired after a voluntary takeover bid.[35]

---

30. The principle of equal treatment of shareholders bans price differentiation in a takeover situation. *See* R. Skog & E. Lidman, *Equal Treatment of Shareholders – Can There Be Too Much of It?*, Nordic & European Company Law LSN Research Paper Series No. 16-15, https://papers.ssrn.com/abstract=2878773 on the principle's background and its negative effect on furthering long-term shareholder engagement as proposed in 2014/0121 (COD).
31. Article 5(5) of Directive 2004/25/EC allows for such consideration.
32. Terminology used is defined by Article 2 of Directive 2004/25/EC.
33. The mandatory bid is regulated in Article 5 of Directive 2004/25/EC.
34. *See*: The takeover bids directive assessment report, which can be accessed at https://op.europa.eu/nl/publication-detail/-/publication/67501b75-7583-4b0d-a551-33051d8e27c1.
35. *Ibid.*

8.29 For the mandatory bid, there are also rules on the consideration that the (forced) offeror should offer to the remaining shareholders. In short, the offeror must in principle offer the highest price paid for the same securities by it, or a person acting in concert with it, over a term set by the Member States, which cannot be less than six months or more than 12 months (Article 5 (4)). Member States may authorize the supervisory authority to adjust the price under clearly determined circumstances, such as where market prices of the securities have been affected by exceptional occurrences (Article 5 (4)). The consideration of the offer has to be cash, securities or a combination of both. However, if the consideration offered does not consist of liquid securities admitted to trading on a regulated market, it must include a cash alternative (Article 5(5)). Member States can also go further and determine that a cash consideration should *in all cases* be offered as an alternative. By determining that the minority shareholders receive the highest price paid by the offeror over a certain period of time, the minority shareholders are ensured of receiving a 'control premium', which is the premium that an offeror must pay on a functioning market for a share package that gives a controlling majority, in return for the ability, acquired along with ownership of the shares, to influence the business of the company.[36]

8.30 An important aspect in relation to the mandatory bid is the fact that, as already stated, a shareholder can also trigger the threshold for the mandatory bid when acting in concert with other persons (Article 5 (1)). Within the scope of the directive, acting in concert is defined as persons who cooperate on the basis of an agreement, either expressly or tacitly, either oral or written, aimed at either (i) acquiring control of the offeree company or (ii) at frustrating the successful outcome of a bid (Article 2 (d)). This means that, in practice, parties need to be careful when soliciting (other) shareholders in order to frustrate a takeover bid, since it could trigger these shareholders themselves being required to launch a mandatory offer.

4 Information and Transparency

8.31 As can be viewed from the – already discussed – general principles, one of the main objectives of the directive is to provide sufficient information and transparency towards shareholders (Article 3(1)(c)). To achieve this, the directive includes several rules on information and transparency.

8.32 The decision to launch a bid, whether mandatory or voluntary, must be made public without delay and the supervisory authority of the Member State(s) concerned must be informed. This must be followed, in good time, by the publication of the offer document containing the information necessary for the holders of securities to decide on the bid. The offer document, however, must first be communicated to the supervisory authority (Article 6). Article 6(3) of the directive provides for a list of the minimum information that must be encompassed by the offer document.

36. *See* opinion of Advocate-General Kokott Case C-735/19 (2020).

8.33 The directive also requires full transparency of all provisions, whether in the articles of association or in contracts, which may impede the takeover of a listed company through a public offer (i.e., the defensive measures). Article 10 of the directive contains a catalogue of defences, ranging from different classes of shares (section a) to golden parachute agreements with board members or employees in the case of a takeover bid (section k). All these defensive measures must be disclosed in two ways: (1) they must be mentioned in the annual report (Article 10(2)); and (2) they must be explained in an explanatory report to the shareholders at the general meeting (Article 10(3)). The disclosure requirements of Article 10 of the directive effectively force companies to draw up a list of their defensive measures (if they have any), which may eventually lead to discussion, criticism and proposals for their cancellation.

5 *Defensive Measures Within the Context of the Takeover Directive*

8.34 Next, we focus on the use of defensive measures in the case of hostile takeovers and the position taken by the board of directors and the shareholders through the general meeting. In addition to certain key principles of the directive, in the context of defensive measures the most relevant provisions to consider are the rules regulating the neutrality of the board of directors of the offeree company[37] (the board neutrality rule, Article 9 of the directive), the possibility to break through (i.e., the setting aside) defensive measures that the company already has in place (the breakthrough rule, Article 11 of the directive) and the optional arrangements for both Member States and individual companies in relation to both the board neutrality and breakthrough rule.

8.35 Before going into the specific provisions, it is important to note that the recitals of the directive and the general principles (Article 3) – as discussed above – already give an indication as to how the directive deals with defensive measures and the position of the board of directors and shareholders in relation to those measures. For instance, recital 16 refers to the fact that the powers of the board of directors of the offeree company (i.e., the target of the public offer) to engage in operations of an exceptional nature (i.e., defensive measures) should be limited, and recital 19 states that the offeror should have the possibility to acquire majority interests in other companies and acquire control over them, meaning that – in short – legal instruments to limit that control should be suspended and ultimately removed. In addition, Article 3(c) of the directive states that the board of directors of the offeree company should not deny the shareholders the opportunity to decide on the merits of the public offer. These provisions demonstrate that the directive is structured on the premises that an offeror should be able to make a public offer; the shareholders should be able to decide whether or not to accept an offer; and defensive measures, whether already in place (pre-bid defensive measures) or enacted in response to a specific (potential) public offer (post-bid defensive measures) should in principle not be possible, unless these

37. As defined in the directive.

measures are such that the shareholders still ultimately decide on the offer (such as is the case when there is a competing offer).

6 *The Board Neutrality Rule and the Breakthrough Rule*

8.36 Article 9 of the directive states that the Member States must ensure that once the company is subject to a takeover bid, the board of directors refrains from any action that may frustrate the bid. This is called the 'board neutrality rule' because it effectively means that the board of directors needs to take a neutral position towards a takeover bid and let the shareholders decide on the public offer.

8.37 The board neutrality rule as laid down in the directive, however, does not mean that the board of directors may not in any way interfere with a takeover bid. First, there is the general exception that the board of directors can engage in defensive measures if it obtains prior approval from the general meeting of shareholders (Article 9(2)). This is in line with the general principle of the directive that the shareholders decide on whether or not to sell their shares to the offeror and therefore determine whether the takeover bid is successful (Article 3). Second, and also in line with this principle, is the exception that the board of directors is allowed to seek alternative bids (i.e., the white knight defence, as explained above) (Article 9(2)). As the white knight will generally have to make an offer that is more attractive to the shareholders than the hostile offer made by the first offeror, this measure can also be considered in the interest of the shareholders. Moreover, it is ultimately up to the shareholders to decide whether to accept the hostile offer or the friendly competing offer from the white knight.

8.38 The fact that the board of directors has to remain neutral does not mean that the board of directors should not give its view on the public offer. The offeree's board is required to give its opinion, which should include its views on the effects of implementation of the bid on all company interests, specifically employment (Article 9(5)). It should also consider the offeror's strategic plans for the company and the likely repercussions on employment and the locations of the company's places of business, as set out in the offer document. At the same time, the board of the offeree company must communicate that opinion to the representatives of its employees or, where there are no such representatives, to the employees themselves. Where the board of the offeree company receives, in good time, a separate opinion from the representatives of its employees on the effects of the bid on employment, that opinion is to be added to the offer document (Article 9(5)). If a company has a two-tier board structure, the term 'board' means both the management board and the supervisory board (Article 9 (6)).

8.39 Whereas Article 9 focuses on post-bid defensive measures, Article 11 focuses on pre-bid defences. Article 11 of the directive states that pre-bid defensive measures, such as restrictions on the transfer of shares or on voting rights, do not apply, albeit on a temporary basis. Because of its function to set aside pre-bid defensive measures, this provision is referred to as the breakthrough rule.

8.40 The breakthrough rule of Article 11 focuses on the following measures:

a. Restrictions on the transfer of shares (securities) will not apply vis-à-vis the offeror during the period in which the bid can be accepted (Article 11(2)).
b. Restrictions on voting rights will not have effect at the general meeting, which decides on post-bid defensive measures (Article 11(3)).
c. No extraordinary rights of shareholders concerning appointment or removal of board members provided for in the articles will apply (Article 11(4)).
d. Multiple voting rights carry only one vote at the general meeting, which decides on post-bid defensive measures (Article 11(3)), as well as at the first general meeting following the closure of the bid, called by the offeror in order to amend the articles or to remove or appoint board members (Article 11(4)).

If the offeror acquires 75% of the voting share capital, then the various pre-bid defensive measures referred to above will no longer have effect (Article 11(4)).

If any shareholder suffers losses by having its legal rights reduced, equitable compensation must be provided (Article 11(5)).[38] This will apply, for example, to the lapse of special voting rights of class A shares, where domination of the company has previously been upheld via such shares.[39]

7 The Board Neutrality Rule and Breakthrough Rule as Optional Arrangements

8.41 Based on the above, the impression could be that within the Member States the possibility to take defensive measures is very limited. This would, however, be incorrect. Although the default rules under the directive are indeed aimed at limiting the influence of defensive measures in the case of takeover bids, Article 12 of the directive provides for an optional arrangement.

8.42 Article 12(1) of the directive states that the Member States may reserve the right not to require companies to apply the core provisions of the board neutrality and breakthrough rules. In other words, Member States are allowed to opt out of one or both rules. Based on the Takeover Bids Directive Assessment Report from 2013, the overwhelming majority of Member States have decided to apply the opt-out rule, and only Estonia applies both the board neutrality and breakthrough rules, as can be seen from the overview below:[40]

---

38. *See*, e.g., Article 11 of the German Control and Transparency Act, *Gesetz zur Kontrolle und Transparenz im Unternehmensbereich* (BGB, 1998), no. 24.
39. B. Gomard in *Revision & Regnskabsvaesen* (København: Foreningen af Statsautoriserede Revisorer Copenhagen, 1993) No. 1, 8 *et seq.*, and in 'Festskrift til Bertil Bengtsson', 141 *et seq.*, and E. Werlauff in *EU-ret & Menneskeret* (København: Djøf Forlag Copenhagen, 2001), 208 *et seq.*, 'Ownership, Interference in Ownership Requirements Regarding Authority, Predictability, Equality and Proportionality under the European Human Rights Convention' (in Danish); Henrik Zahle in *Juristen* (Copenhagen, 2004), 279 *et seq.*
40. *See* for this overview: *supra* n. 34.

		Neutrality	
		Yes	**No**
Reciprocity	**Yes**	France, Greece, Italy, Portugal, Spain	Belgium, Denmark, Germany, Hungary, Luxembourg, the Netherlands, Poland
	No	Austria, Cyprus, Czech Republic, Estonia, Finland, Ireland, Romania, Slovakia, Sweden, UK	

		Breakthrough	
		Yes	**No**
Reciprocity	**Yes**	France, Greece, Italy, Portugal, Spain	Belgium, Cyprus, Denmark, Germany, Greece, Hungary, Italy, Luxembourg, the Netherlands, Poland, Portugal, Spain
	No	Estonia	Austria, the Czech Republic, Finland, France, Ireland, Romania, Slovakia, Sweden, UK

As a result of this opt-out possibility, the directive has little effect in the way of actually providing a level playing field when it comes to using defensive measures in the Member States.

8.43 Where the Member States have made use of the possibility to opt out of the board neutrality and/or breakthrough rule, Member States need to provide companies with the reversible opportunity to apply the board neutrality and/or breakthrough rule (Article 12(2)).

8.44 In addition to opting out, Member States may also elect to follow an interesting middle path, which was introduced as a compromise during the directive's prolonged progress through the various instances. This middle path is laid down in Article 12(3) of the directive and is sometimes referred to as the *reciprocity principle*. Pursuant to Article 12(3) of the directive, a Member State can formulate its legislation in such a way that companies that are open to a takeover (i.e., companies that comply with Article 9 and/or Article 11 of the directive) can, nonetheless, rely on defences if they become the target of an offer by a company not complying with Article 9 and/or Article 11 of the directive. Such a defence, however, requires authorization by the general meeting, albeit by a decision which may be taken in advance (Article 12(5)). In other words, when a Member State applies Article 12(3) of the directive, it means that a company that applies the board neutrality and/or breakthrough rule cannot be taken over by a company that does not apply the same rules.

8 *Squeeze-Out and Sell-Out*

8.45 Lastly, one of the challenges to a takeover bid is that it is difficult - if not impossible - to obtain 100% of the shares in the company because certain shareholders might knowingly or unknowingly hold out on selling their shares to the offeror. To enable the offeror to obtain 100% of the shares and avoid the remaining minority shareholders from getting stuck, the directive provides for the possibility for the offeror to squeeze out the remaining minority shareholders and for the minority shareholders to sell out their shares to the offeror/(now) majority shareholder (Articles 15 and 16). Member States have the possibility to set this threshold at 90% or higher up to 95% of the capital of the company carrying voting rights.[41]

V DOMESTIC MERGERS AND DIVISIONS

8.46 After having dealt with the European legislation with regard to takeovers, we now turn to EU harmonization with regard to the tools for business combinations starting with domestic mergers and divisions. The cross-border tools for business combinations and restructurings are discussed in the following section.

A Mergers of Public Limited Liability Companies

8.47 The procedure for domestic mergers has been harmonized at the European level initially by the Third or Merger Directive. This directive was adopted in 1978 to introduce provisions on mergers into the laws of every Member State.[42] It provided for the coordination of information and protection of the interests of shareholders and creditors, while protection of employees' rights is regulated in accordance with the directive regarding the transfer of undertakings or parts thereof (Directive 2001/23/EC).[43] The provisions of the directive have now been taken up in the Consolidation Directive (EU) 2017/1132.

The scope of the part of the directive related to (domestic) mergers is limited to public companies. According to Article 88, the directive encompasses two different methods of merger: (1) merger by the acquisition of one or more companies by another company; and (2) merger by the formation of a new company.

8.48 Merger by acquisition occurs when one or more companies are wound up without going into liquidation, while all their assets and liabilities are transferred to

41. *See* for an overview of how Member States apply these thresholds: *supra* n. 34.
42. Third Council Directive 78/855/EEC.
43. Replacing the original Directive EEC 77/187.

another company. In exchange, the shareholders of the acquired company or companies are issued shares in the acquiring company and, if the terms of merger so provide, are paid in cash. The amount may not exceed 10% of the nominal value of the shares or, where they have no nominal value, the accounting par value of the issued shares (Article 89).

In some Member States, shares may be issued without a nominal value. The accounting par value of a share is obtained by dividing the capital of the company by the number of shares issued. Statutory provisions allowing shares without a nominal value are, for example, paragraph 8(3) of the German Stock Corporation Act.

8.49 Merger by formation of a new company results when several companies are wound up without going into liquidation, and all their assets and liabilities are transferred to the newly incorporated company. In exchange, their shareholders are issued shares in the new company and are paid in cash under the same restrictions applicable to mergers by acquisition (Article 90).

8.50 Essentially, the same rules apply to both types of mergers. The administrative or management bodies of the merging companies must, according to Article 91, draw up the draft terms of the merger in writing. These draft terms must specify, *inter alia*, the share exchange ratio and the amount of any cash payment, as well as any special advantage granted to independent experts who examine the draft terms or to members of the merging companies' administrative, management, supervisory or controlling bodies. The draft terms must be published for each of the merging companies at least one month before the date fixed for the general meeting, which will decide on this matter (Article 92). Companies can derogate from this requirement when the draft terms of the merger are publicly available on their website, free of charge, for a period of at least one month before the general meeting that has to decide on them. Member States can require such publication to be made via the central electronic platform or via any other specific website (Article 92).

A merger must have, at least, the approval of the general meeting of each company involved. Member States are to establish provisions requiring a majority of not less than two-thirds of the votes attached to the shares or to the subscribed capital present. They may provide, however, that a simple majority is sufficient when at least half of the subscribed capital is present. Moreover, where appropriate, the rules governing amendments to the memorandum and articles of association apply, because the decision taken covers both an approval of the draft merger terms and any proposed amendment to the memorandum or articles of association necessitated by the merger. Where there is more than one class of shares, a separate vote is necessary for each class of shareholders whose rights are affected by the transaction (Article 93). However, if certain conditions are met, the laws of a Member State need not require the approval of the general meeting of the acquiring company (Article 94).

According to Article 97, all shareholders are entitled to inspect certain documents at the registered office at least one month before the date fixed for the general meeting. Among these are the draft terms of the merger, the financial reports of the merging companies for the preceding three financial years and the management reports of the administrative or management bodies explaining the draft terms of the merger. A report of experts stating whether in their opinion the share exchange ratio is fair and reasonable must be available. A shareholder is entitled to obtain copies of such documents, in a paper or an electronic format (Article 97(3)). Pursuant to Article 97(4), the same derogation mentioned with reference to Article 92 applies here too, meaning it is possible for companies to make the documents available on their website.

8.51 The laws of the Member States must provide for an adequate system of protection of the interests of creditors of the merging companies, whose claims antedate the publication of the draft terms of merger and are not due at the time of such publication. At the very least, they are entitled to obtain adequate safeguards, where the financial situation of the merging companies makes such safeguards necessary (Article 99). Member States are required to lay down the conditions for such protection, and administrative or judicial solutions must be available to safeguard creditors (Article 99(2)). Where the laws of the Member States do not provide for judicial or administrative preventive supervision of the legality of mergers, the minutes of the general meetings, which decide on the merger, and, where appropriate, the merger contract subsequent to such general meetings are to be drawn up and certified in due legal form (Article 102). Employees are protected by means of Directive 2001/23/EC on the transfer of undertakings (Article 98). The laws of the Member States determine the date on which a merger takes effect (Article 103). A merger must be published with respect to each of the merging companies, in accordance with the Codification Directive (Article 104).

8.52 The protection offered by the directive applies not only to mergers but also to operations akin to mergers, that are not fully covered by the definitions of Article 89 (merger by acquisition) and Article 90 (merger by formation of a new company). These articles do not allow for a cash payment exceeding 10% of the nominal value of the shares issued by the merger operation. Furthermore, they provide that one or more companies are wound up without going into liquidation. Where the Member States allow for a cash payment exceeding the percentage mentioned or permit for merger-like operations without all of the transferring companies thereby ceasing to exist, several provisions of the directive nevertheless apply (Articles 116 and 117). The merger provisions in the directive do not cover transactions where only part of the assets is transferred in exchange for shares. Such transactions, however, fall under the ambit of the capital maintenance requirements of the directive because they represent a non-cash contribution. Such a transaction would also be covered by Directive 2001/23/EC on the safeguarding of employees' rights in the event of transfers of undertakings and businesses or part thereof.[44]

8.53 A merger has simultaneous and *ipso jure* legal consequences. In the first place, all the assets and liabilities of any acquired company are transferred. Second, the acquired company shareholders become shareholders of the acquiring company. Third, the acquired company ceases to exist (Article 105). Member States may set out provisions

44. OJ 2001, L 82.

of nullification of mergers only under certain restrictive conditions. Notably, courts may declare a merger null and void only on the grounds that: (1) there has been no preventive supervision of its legality; (2) it has not been drawn up and certified in due legal form; or (3) it can be shown that the decision of the general meeting is void or voidable under national law (Article 108). This will not affect nullification of a merger according to the law of a Member State announced following supervision of the merger procedure (Article 108(3)). An example is the supervision of government agencies exerting merger control. Lastly, it must be pointed out that the provisions of section 4 of the directive alleviate the procedural requirements, where the acquiring company holds 90% or more of the shares in the acquired company, thus facilitating intragroup mergers (*see* paragraph 10.40).

8.54 In the 2013 ACT case,[45] the CJEU was asked, *inter alia*, to determine whether EU law concerning mergers of companies, notably Article 19 of Directive 2011/35/EU, encompassed:

> a system of transfer of liability for administrative offences to the acquiring company for acts committed by the company being acquired before registration of the merger.

In March 2015, the CJEU ruled that:

> Article 19(1) ... must be interpreted as meaning that a 'merger by acquisition' ... results in the transfer to the acquiring company of the obligation to pay a fine imposed by final decision adopted after the merger by acquisition for infringements of employment law committed by the acquired company prior to that merger.

In any case, the court stated that:

> extinguishing such a liability would run contrary to the very notion of merger by acquisition, as defined in Article 3(1) of Directive 78/855/EEC.

and that:

> the category of third parties, whose interests the directive is intended to protect, includes those entities which though not yet creditors or debenture holders at the date of the acquisition may become such post-acquisition as a result of situations predating the acquisition. This is the case, for instance, for infringements of employment law provisions which are found to have been committed in a decision adopted after the merger by acquisition had taken place. ... if such liability were not transferred, a company could use a merger by acquisition as means of escaping the legal consequences of offences it has committed to the detriment of the Member State concerned or other potential interested parties.

45. Case C-343/13 (*Modelo Continente Hipermercados SA v. Autoridade para as COndições de Trabalho – Centro Local do Lis (ACT))* (2015).

B Divisions of Public Limited Liability Companies

8.55 The procedure for divisions of companies has been harmonized by the Sixth Company Law Directive. This directive, in contrast to the Third Directive concerning mergers, did not require the Member States to introduce the division procedure into their legislation.[46] It merely required the Member States to comply with the directive if they permit operations to which the directive applies. These provisions have now also been taken up in Directive (EU) 2017/1132.

8.56 Similar to mergers, shareholders of the company being divided are issued shares in the division in exchange for the transfer of the company's assets and liabilities. Here again, division can take place by acquisition: the company being divided transfers all its assets and liabilities to several existing companies (Article 135(1)) or by the formation of new companies: the company being divided transfers all its assets and liabilities to several newly formed companies (Article 155(1)). The rationale behind the adoption of the directive is to avoid the circumvention of the guarantees provided for mergers by offering equivalent protection in the event of a division. Therefore, it is not surprising that the provisions for mergers and divisions are, in many respects, identical or analogous. The differences originate in the multiplicity of the recipient companies. As a consequence, attention should be drawn to the precise description and allocation of assets and liabilities transferred to each of the recipient companies and the allocation of shares issued in exchange by the recipient companies (Article 137(2)(h)(i)).

8.57 The directive allows the Member States to permit a combined method of division, where a division by acquisition is combined with a division by formation of one or more new companies (Article 135(3)). As is the case for mergers, the directive includes anti-avoidance provisions for divisions. The directive applies even where a Member State permits a cash consideration in excess of 10% of the nominal value of the shares issued (Article 158). In the event that a Member State allows for an operation that falls under the description of Article 135, but without the company being divided or ceasing to exist, most provisions of the directive apply (Article 159).

8.58 Member States may relieve companies from certain obligations if a division operation is subject to the supervision of a judicial authority. This option only applies where the judicial authority has certain powers, *inter alia,* to call a general meeting of shareholders of the company being divided in order to decide on the division (Article 157).

8.59 The directive also provides for an exemption to the requirement of an independent expert's report of the draft division terms if all shareholders agree (Article 144). With regard to the consequences of the division, the rules are comparable to those for mergers (Article 151). The assets and liabilities of the company being divided will be transferred to the acquiring company, the shareholders become shareholders of one or more recipient companies and the company being divided ceases to exist. Employees

46. Sixth Council Directive 82/891/EEC.

are protected by means of Directive 2001/23/EC on the transfer of undertakings (Article 145). The rules on creditor protection are comparable to those applicable for mergers described above and can be found in Article 146.

VI CROSS-BORDER BUSINESS COMBINATIONS AND RESTRUCTURING TOOLS

A Cross-Border Mergers of Companies

8.60 The first legislative act in relation to cross-border mergers (CBMs) was the 2001 enactment of the SE Statute, offering the cross-border merger facility as one of the methods available for formation of an SE (*see* paragraph 4.17 *et seq.*). Subsequently, the Tenth Directive (CBM Directive), adopted in 2005 (*see* paragraph 3.19a *et seq.*), provided for the cross-border merger as a generic instrument for domestic companies, without leading to the formation of an SE. This directive allows both public and private companies to merge across borders on the condition that they may merge under their national laws.[47] Lastly, according to the *Sevic* case,[48] a CBM is permitted based on Articles 49 and 54 of the TFEU, arguably even outside the realm of Directive (EU) 2017/1132 and the SE Regulation (*see* paragraph 3.57a). In 2017, the provisions of the CBM Directive were included in Directive (EU) 2017/1132. Moreover, in 2019, Directive (EU) 2019/2121 modified and reformed the framework for CBMs provided by Directive (EU) 2017/1132, for example concerning aspects such as disclosure, specific contents of the common draft terms or the management report, creditor protection, and the scrutiny of the transaction by the competent authorities. In particular, the competent authorities can refuse to provide merger certificates, which are necessary for the completion of the CBM, if the CBM is set up for abusive or fraudulent purposes leading to or aimed at the evasion or circumvention of EU or national law, or for criminal purposes.[49] The provisions of Directive (EU) 2019/2121 amending Directive (EU) 2017/1132 have to be transposed into the laws of the Member States by 31 January 2023.

8.61 Before tools such as the SE Regulation, the *Sevic* case and the CBM Directive came into play, most jurisdictions did not expressly allow for CBMs. Nevertheless, some of these mergers were completed based on international private law, that is, by cumulative application of the harmonized national merger provisions and the mutual recognition of the results of the operation.[50] A well-known example is the Barclays merger of

47. Article 121(1)(a) of Directive (EU) 2017/1132. Most Member States have introduced merger rules for private companies similar to those introduced by the Third Directive applicable to domestic mergers and as currently in place through Directive (EU) 2017/1132 (*see* paragraph 3.34 *et seq.*), G. van Solinge, *Grensoverschrijdende juridische fusie* (Deventer: Kluwer, 1994), Chapter 3.
48. Case C-411/03 (2005).
49. Article 127(8) of Directive (EU) 2017/1132.
50. *Ibid.*, 204.

1993 between the English holding company and its French subsidiary, the English company being the acquiring party.[51]

8.62 Above, it has been explained in general what the effects of the merger are (*see* paragraph 8.53). A cross-border merger involves the following steps which are in line with the procedure for domestic mergers. The management bodies of the merging companies have to draw up common draft terms of a cross-border merger, in which certain information on the CBM is included, such as the identity of the merging companies, the applicable ratio for the exchange of shares and other securities and so on.[52] Such common draft terms must be disclosed among others through the national registers of the merging companies so that it is available to the stakeholders of the company.[53] The management board must also prepare a report for the shareholders and the employees in which the companies justify and explain the legal and economic aspects of the CBM, also explaining the implications for employees.[54] Thereafter a report has to be drafted by an independent expert, who will scrutinize whether the cash compensation and the share exchange ratios are adequate.[55] Thereafter and within a certain time frame that allows shareholders to take notice of all such information and documents, the shareholders will vote at a general meeting on the CBM.[56] Protections for minority shareholders and creditors are also foreseen in case their situation is at risk.[57] For example, minority shareholders can exit the company by receiving a cash compensation for their shares and creditors can ask for additional guarantees. If the companies have a system of employee participation, a procedure is put in place to ensure that such system is safeguarded in the company resulting from the CBM. In order to ensure that these steps are followed, and to effectuate the CBM, the national authorities of the Member States involved in the CBM must issue certificates that show that all steps have been followed.[58] As a final point, the CBM must be registered in the national registers of the Member States involved in the CBM.[59] On the effective date of the CBM, the assets and liabilities of all merging companies become assets and liabilities of the surviving company, the shareholders of the merging entities become shareholders of the surviving entity and the merging entities cease to exist.[60]

8.63 It should also be noted that the provisions on CBMs apply to four different types of mergers as stipulated in Article 119 of Directive (EU) 2017/1132. Without addressing all technical details, Directive (EU) 2017/1132 applies to the four following merger scenarios. The first scenario is where one more company, on being dissolved without going into liquidation, transfer(s) all assets and liabilities to another existing company,

51. A. Viandier & J. Caussain, *Chronique, Droit des sociétés*, La semaine Juridique (JCP), ed. G (JurisClasseur, Paris, 1993), I-3715, 461, no. 14.
52. Article 122 of Directive (EU) 2017/1132.
53. Article 123 of Directive (EU) 2017/1132.
54. Article 124 of Directive (EU) 2017/1132.
55. Article 125 of Directive (EU) 2017/1132.
56. Article 126 of Directive (EU) 2017/1132.
57. Articles 126a and 126b of Directive (EU) 2017/1132.
58. Articles 127, 127a and 128 of Directive (EU) 2017/1132.
59. Article 130 of Directive (EU) 2017/1132.
60. Article 131 of Directive (EU) 2017/1132.

the acquiring company, and that company issues in exchange shares or other securities to the shareholders of the merging companies. This is called merger by acquisition. The second scenario is where two or more companies, on being dissolved without going into liquidation, transfer all their assets and liabilities to a company which they form, the new company, in exchange for the issuance of shares or other securities by such company to the shareholders of the merging companies. This is called merger by formation of a new company. The third scenario is where a company, on being dissolved without going into liquidation, transfers all its assets and liabilities to the company holding all the securities or shares representing its capital. The fourth and last scenario is when one or more companies, on being dissolved without going into liquidation, transfer all their assets and liabilities to another existing company, the acquiring company, without the issuance of any new shares by the acquiring company, provided that one person holds directly or indirectly all the shares in the merging companies or the members of the merging companies hold their securities and shares in the same proportion in all merging companies.

8.64 Whilst EU legislation provides for an overall framework, Member States have discretion to transpose certain rules differently. Both the SE Regulation and Directive (EU) 2017/1132 refer to provisions of national law for compliance with the formalities of the cross-border merger.[61] Although these provisions are certainly similar, they are not identical as a consequence of the implementation of the various options offered by the Third Directive on domestic mergers when transposed by the Member States at the end of the 1970s regarding important issues, such as: (i) decision-making by the general meeting, (ii) how protection is offered to creditors and (iii) the date on which the merger takes effect. However, the system of creditor protection has further been reformed through Directive 2019/2121 and limits substantially the discretion of Member States.

8.65 Decision-making is one of the issues that may be treated differently by the Member States. According to Article 93 of Directive (EU) 2017/1132, a merger requires the approval of the general meeting of each of the merging companies with a majority of not less than two-thirds of the votes. Member States, however, may provide that a simple majority of the votes is sufficient when at least half of the subscribed capital is represented. Under national law, the required majority may also be higher. The terms of the merger must be approved by resolution of the general meeting of each of the companies merging; however, Member States may leave the decision of the acquiring company to another body if certain conditions are fulfilled.[62] The Netherlands has used this option by empowering the board of directors of the acquiring company to decide on the merger unless otherwise provided by the articles and within the limits that certain further conditions are fulfilled.[63] For cross-border mergers, Directive (EU)

61. Articles 9 and 18 of the SE Regulation (EC) No 2157/2001; Article 121 of Directive (EU) 2017/1132.
62. Article 94 of Directive (EU) 2017/1132 for domestic mergers and Article 126 read together with Article 94 of Directive (EU) 2017/1132 for cross-border mergers.
63. Article 2:331 of the Dutch Civil Code.

2017/1132 requires approval by the general meeting of each of the companies to merge but does not specify a majority or quorum (Article 126).

8.66 Furthermore, systems of creditor protection may differ. According to Article 99 of Directive (EU) 2017/1132, Member States, for domestic mergers, are required to provide for an adequate system of protection of the interests of creditors of the merging companies whose claims predate the publication of the draft terms of merger and have not fallen due at the time of such publication. Such creditors are entitled to obtain adequate safeguards where the financial situation of the merging companies makes such protection necessary and where those creditors do not already have such safeguards. An equal high degree of discretion exists for creditor protection in cross-border formations of an SE under the SE Regulation (Article 24). For cross-border mergers, a similar protection had been offered under the CBM Directive (Article 4(2)).

8.67 Based on the obstacles that such differentiation in creditor protection provides to CBMs and in accordance with reform proposals,[64] it should, however, be mentioned that Directive 2019/2121 has amended the system of creditor protection for CBMs.[65] While the core remains the same as it exists in many Member States, namely that creditors can ask for safeguards, Directive 2019/2121 provides clearer time frames during which the safeguards can be asked, namely within three months of the disclosure of the common draft terms of the CBM. Member States must ensure that the safeguards are conditional on the CBM taking effect. Moreover, as a new measure, Member States may also require the management body of the merging companies to provide a declaration that accurately reflects the financial status of the merging companies at a date not earlier than one month before the disclosure of such declaration. Such declaration must further state that the management body is unaware of any reasons why the company resulting from the merger would be unable to meet its liabilities when they fall due.

8.68 Directive (EU) 2019/2121 has also reformed the system of minority shareholder protection.[66] The CBM Directive had merely provided that a Member State may adopt provisions designed to ensure appropriate protection for minority members who have opposed the cross-border merger,[67] which thus left Member States discretion in the provision of minority shareholder protection or whether they would provide minority

64. T. Biermeyer, Study on the application of the Cross-Border Mergers Directive, 2013, commissioned by the European Commission, carried out together with Lexidale and Brech-Bruun, 31 (main findings) *et seq.*; J. Schmidt, Cross-border mergers and divisions, transfers of seat: is there a need to legislate? Study for the JURI Committee, European Parliament (2016), 19; European Parliament resolution of 13 June 2017 on cross-border mergers and divisions (2016/2065(INI)); *see also* G.T.M.J. Raaijmakers and T.P.H. Olthoff, 'Creditor Protection in Cross-border Mergers: Unfinished Business', *Utrecht Law Review* 4(1) (2008).
65. Article 126b of Directive (EU) 2017/1132.
66. T. Biermeyer, *supra* n. 64, at 47 (main findings) *et seq.*; J. Schmidt, *supra* n. 64, at 19–20; European Parliament resolution of 13 June 2017 on cross-border mergers and divisions (2016/2065(INI)).
67. Article 4(2) of the CBM Directive.

shareholder protection at all.[68] Directive (EU) 2019/2121 does not allow such discretion anymore. In accordance with the directive and as is found in Article 126a of Directive (EU) 2017/1132, Member States must ensure that at least the members of the merging companies who voted against the approval of the common draft terms of the CBM have the right to dispose of their shares for adequate cash compensation, provided that as a result of the merger they would acquire shares in the company resulting from the merger which would be governed by the law of a Member State other than the Member State of their respective merging company.

8.69 The date on which a cross-border merger takes effect may still vary because this is determined by the law of the Member State, whose jurisdiction the company resulting from the cross-border merger is subject to (Article 129 of Directive (EU) 2017/1132).[69]

8.70 Due to their cross-border aspects, both the SE Regulation and the rules on cross-border mergers under Directive (EU) 2017/1132 include additional rules for the execution of a merger in comparison to the regulation of domestic mergers in the directive. The issues concerned are, for instance, the information to be included in the draft terms of the merger and the protection of (minority) shareholders (*see* paragraph 8.50 *et seq.*). Typical of the cross-border aspect is the determination of the choice of law for pre-merger and post-merger issues. The SE Regulation includes rather detailed rules for the formation of an SE by way of a merger and these rules supersede national law. In addition, Article 18 refers to the national law of the companies to be merged, as harmonized by the Third Directive. Likewise, Directive (EU) 2017/1132 refers in Article 121(2) to the provisions and formalities of the national law of the 'merging companies', in particular, those concerning the decision-making process as well as the protection of employees, regarding rights other than those governed by Article 133 (which covers employee participation).[70] Lastly, it must be noted that both the authorities competent to scrutinize the legality of the completion of the cross-border merger and the negotiation procedure with respect to the involvement of employees are governed by the law of the Member State of the registered office of the company resulting from the cross-border merger.[71]

8.71 In relation to the scrutiny by the competent authorities in general, Directive 2019/2121 has modified substantially the procedure for the pre-merger and the merger certificate. A CBM will not be scrutinized by the competent authority issuing a pre-merger certificate only as to whether the steps to complete the CBM have been

68. The implementation study of the CBM Directive shows that seven Member States had not provided for minority shareholder protection. T. Biermeyer, *supra* n. 64, at 97 (main findings).
69. *See also* Article 17 Third Directive. In practice, however, mergers can have different types of effective dates according to: (i) internal effect, (ii) effect towards third parties, (iii) accounting purposes and (iv) tax purposes. Such dates can vary and are also dependent on national legislation.
70. Despite the phrase 'taking into account the cross-border nature of the merger', the national law of a Member State protects only interests connected to the company that is governed by that national law.
71. Article 26(1) SE Regulation and Article 128(1) of Directive (EU) 2017/1132.

followed by the company in question. In principle, the authority also has to examine whether the CBM has been set up for abusive or fraudulent purposes leading to or aimed at the evasion or circumvention of EU or national law, or for criminal purposes, and can refuse on that basis to issue the applicable merger certificate.[72]

B Cross-Border Divisions of Companies

8.72 EU legislation regarding cross-border divisions (CBDs) began with the Sixth Directive on domestic divisions in 1982. It took, however, until 2019 to establish a framework for CBDs by the enactment of Directive (EU) 2019/2121. Different from CBMs, the SE Regulation does not provide rules enabling CBDs.[73] Moreover, different from CBMs or CBDs, there is no case law from the CJEU on CBDs. Yet, arguably *Sevic* (2005),[74] *Vale* (2012)[75] and *Polbud* (2017)[76] can also be applied to CBDs. That means if a Member State provides for domestic legislation on divisions, it is obliged to also allow CBDs.

8.73 Before CBDs were made possible through Directive (EU) 2019/2121, amending Directive (EU) 2017/1132, most Member States did not expressly allow for CBDs.[77] A CBD could, however, for example, be carried out by first executing a domestic division, followed by cross-border transfers of seats of the entities the registered office (and central administration as the case may be) of which were intending to be located in a different jurisdiction. As an illustration, company P from country A seeks to carry out a CBD in which the assets and liabilities of company P are to be divided over company P and the newly to be established company O located in country B. If the national legislation of country A (and country B) do not allow a CBD, then company P can first carry out a domestic division into company P and company O. Thereafter, company O could carry out a cross-border transfer of seat (or conversion as the case may be) to country B.[78]

72. Article 127 (8)-(10) of Directive (EU) 2017/1132.
73. Directive 2019/2121 amended Directive (EU) 2017/1132 and the transposition deadline for the provisions on CBD in such Directive is 31 Jan. 2023.
74. C-411/03.
75. C-378/10.
76. C-106/16.
77. In principle, only the Czech Republic, Denmark, Finland, Italy, Norway and Spain allowed CBD. Further, other countries allowed analogous application of domestic division procedures (such as Austria, Belgium and France) or cross-border merger legislation (such as Austria, Italy and the Netherlands). *See* T. Biermeyer & M. Meyer, 'Cross-Border Corporate Mobility in the EU: Empirical Findings 2020' (Edition 1) (Ernst & Young 2020), available at SSRN: https://ssrn.com/abstract=3674089; DG JUST, Assessment and quantification of drivers, problems and impacts related to cross-border transfers of registered offices and cross-border divisions of companies, 2018, JUST/2015/PR/01/0003, drafted by Ernst & Young, 26.
78. This is of course conditional upon country A and country B allowing cross-border seat transfers/conversions. However, this is mostly the case based on the case law of the CJEU and Directive (EU) 2019/2121 has also provided a legislative framework for CBC. *See* for further specific national options and solutions DG JUST, Assessment and quantification of drivers,

8.74 From a regulatory perspective, CBDs are very similar to CBMs (*see* paragraph 8.60 *et seq.*). This is also logical because whereas in a merger, the assets and liabilities of two or more companies are transferred via a universal transfer of assets and liabilities to one company, in a division, the assets and liabilities of one company are transferred through a universal transfer of assets and liabilities to more than one company. For this reason, the risks to the stakeholders of the company are similar to those involved in a merger. Shareholders may have a different holding percentage of shares in the company(s) resulting from the division and particularly the assets may be different, and creditors may face a higher credit risk depending again on division of the assets and liabilities in the companies resulting from the division. Also, employees may face risks, for example, in relation to the application of an employee participation regime.

8.75 A CBD therefore involves the following steps. The management body of the dividing company must draw up common draft terms of a cross-border division in which certain information on the CBD is included, such as the identity of the companies involved, the applicable ratio for the exchange of shares and other securities, and so on.[79] Such common draft terms must be disclosed through the national register of the company being divided so that it is available to the stakeholders of the company.[80] The management board of such company must also prepare a report for the shareholders and the employees in which the company justifies and explains the legal and economic aspects of the CBM, also explaining the implications for employees.[81] Thereafter an independent expert has to draft a report and scrutinize whether the cash compensation and the share exchange ratios are adequate.[82] Subsequently and within a certain time frame that allows shareholders to take notice of all such information and documents, the shareholders of the dividing company will vote at a general meeting on the CBD.[83] Protections for minority shareholders and creditors are also foreseen in case their interests are at risk.[84] For example, minority shareholders can exit the company by receiving a cash compensation for their shares and creditors can ask for additional guarantees. If the company being divided has a system of employee participation, the directive provides for a procedure ensuring that such system is safeguarded in the companies resulting from the CBD. In order to ensure that these steps are followed, and in order to effectuate the CBD, the national authorities of the Member States involved in the CBD must issue certificates that show that all steps have been followed.[85] As a final point, the CBD must be registered in the national registers of the Member States involved in the CBD.[86] On the effective date of the CBD,

problems and impacts related to cross-border transfers of registered offices and cross-border divisions of companies, 2018, JUST/2015/PR/01/0003, drafted by Ernst &Young, 73 *et seq.*

79. Article 160d of Directive (EU) 2017/1132.
80. Article 160g of Directive (EU) 2017/1132.
81. Article 160e of Directive (EU) 2017/1132.
82. Article 160f of Directive (EU) 2017/1132.
83. Article 160h of Directive (EU) 2017/1132.
84. Articles 160i and 160j of Directive (EU) 2017/1132.
85. Articles 160m, 160n and 160o of Directive (EU) 2017/1132.
86. Article 160p of Directive (EU) 2017/1132.

the assets and liabilities of the dividing company become assets and liabilities of the surviving companies, the shareholders of the dividing company become shareholders of the surviving companies and the dividing company ceases to exist.[87]

8.76 The provisions on CBDs apply to three different cross-border division scenarios. In the first scenario, the company being divided, on being dissolved without going into liquidation, transfers all its assets and liabilities to two or more recipient companies in exchange for the issuance to the members of the company being divided of securities or shares in the recipient companies, i.e., a full division. In the second scenario, a company being divided transfers part of its assets and liabilities to one or more recipient companies in exchange for the issuance to the members of the company being divided of securities or shares in the recipient companies, in the company being divided or in both the recipient companies and the company being divided, i.e., a partial division. In the third scenario, a company being divided transfers part of its assets and liabilities to one or more recipient companies, in exchange for the issuance to the company being divided of securities or shares in the recipient companies, i.e., a division by separation.

8.77 As with the SE Regulation and the CBM, the provisions of Directive (EU) 2017/1132 on CBDs refer to national law for compliance with certain formalities. It is particularly specified that the law of the Member State of the company being divided governs those parts of the procedure and formalities to be complied with in connection with the cross-border division in order to obtain the pre-division certificate, and the laws of the Member States of the recipient companies govern those parts of the procedures and formalities to be complied with following receipt of the pre-division certificate.[88]

8.78 As for CBMs, the approval of a CBD by the shareholders is an issue that may be treated differently by the Member States. However, different to CBMs, for CBDs it is specifically provided that Member States must ensure that the approval of a CBD requires a majority of not less than two-thirds but not more than 90% of the votes attached to the shares represented at the general meeting. Moreover, it is expressly stated that the voting threshold may not be higher than that provided by national law for CBMs. Similar to mergers, the rules on divisions in Directive (EU) 2017/1132 provide that the Member States may leave the decision of the company to be divided to a different company body (i.e., a general meeting of shareholders is not required) if the recipient companies together hold all the shares of the company being divided and all other securities conferring the right to vote at general meetings of the company being divided, and certain conditions are fulfilled. That involves in general terms that all companies involved in the operation must publish certain documents one month before the division takes effect.[89]

87. Article 160r of Directive (EU) 2017/1132.
88. Article 160c of Directive (EU) 2017/1132.
89. Article 154 of Directive (EU) 2017/1132. This provision exists in the section for domestic divisions and not in the section for CBD. Also, the latter section does not make an explicit

8.79 The system for creditor protection for CBDs as provided in Article 160j is basically the same as for CBMs. This means that the Member States must ensure that creditors who are dissatisfied with the safeguards offered in the draft terms of the cross-border division can apply, within three months of the disclosure of the draft terms of cross-border division, to the appropriate administrative or judicial authority for adequate safeguards. The creditors can make such application if they can credibly demonstrate that, due to the cross-border division, the satisfaction of their claims is at stake and that they have not obtained adequate safeguards from the company. Moreover, Member States may also require the management body of the dividing company to provide a declaration that accurately reflects the financial status of the dividing company at a date not earlier than one month before the disclosure of such declaration. Such declaration must further state that the management body is unaware of any reasons why any recipient company, or in the case of a partial division, also the dividing company, would be unable to meet its liabilities when they fall due.[90]

8.80 In relation to the system for minority shareholder protection, in accordance with Article 160i of Directive (EU) 2017/1132, Member States must ensure that at least the members of a company being divided who voted against the approval of the draft terms of the cross-border division have the right to dispose of their shares for adequate cash compensation, provided that, as a result of the crossborder division, they would acquire shares in the recipient companies which would be governed by the law of a Member State other than the Member State of the company being divided.

8.81 Again as with CBMs, also the date on which a CBD takes effect can vary as Article 160q of Directive (EU) 2017/1132 leaves discretion to the Member States to determine such date. Yet, Article 160q provides that the date cannot be earlier than the scrutiny by the national authorities in relation to the division certificates and also not earlier than the national registers of the recipient companies having received from the national register of the dividing company that such company has been struck off the national register.[91]

8.82 Due to the cross-border aspects, the rules in Directive (EU) 2017/1132 on divisions provide additional rules for CBDs compared to domestic divisions, similar to cross-border mergers compared to domestic mergers. The issues concerned are, for instance, the information to be included in the draft terms of the division and the protection of (minority) shareholders. Typical of the cross-border aspect is the determination of the choice of law for pre-division and post-division issues. Lastly, it must be noted that the authorities competent to scrutinize both the legality of the completion

reference in this regard to the section for domestic divisions. Therefore, it remains to be seen how Member States will transpose such provision for CBD in their national laws.

90. Article 160j(3) of Directive (EU) 2017/1132.
91. In practice, however, divisions can have different types of effective dates according to: (i) internal effect, (ii) effect towards third parties, (iii) accounting purposes and (iv) tax purposes. Such dates can vary and are also dependent on national legislation.

of the cross-border division and the negotiation procedure with respect to the involvement of employees are governed by the law of the Member State of the registered office of the company resulting from the cross-border merger.[92]

8.83 With regard to scrutiny of CBDs, a CBD will not be scrutinized by the competent authority issuing a pre-merger certificate only as to whether the steps to complete the CBD have been followed by the company in question. In principle, the authority also has to examine whether the CBD has been set up for abusive or fraudulent purposes leading to or aimed at the evasion or circumvention of EU or national law, or for criminal purposes, and can refuse on that basis to issue the applicable merger certificate.[93]

C Cross-Border Conversions of Companies

8.84 Legislation on cross-border conversions (CBCs) is similar and very much intertwined with the legislation for CBMs and CBDs. However, in terms of the nature of the transaction, it is very different. In a CBM or CBD, there is a transfer of assets and liabilities through a universal transfer, either from the merging companies to the surviving company in a CBM or from the dividing company to the recipient companies in a CBD. In a CBC, companies convert from a company law form governed by country A to a company law form governed by country B. So for example, a Dutch BV may carry out a CBC in order to convert into a German law governed private company (GmbH). Such conversion is carried out through a transfer of the connecting factors to the national company law from Member State A to Member State B. That can be the registered office of the company, i.e., the address under which the company is registered in the national register of a country, and/or the central administration, which is essentially the place where the main decisions of the company are taken.[94]

8.85 From a conceptual perspective, it is important to understand in this context the overlap and also difference between the concepts of a (cross-border) transfer of seat and a (cross-border) conversion. As explained above, the transfer of the seat of a company entails the transfer of its registered office and/or its central administration. Before Directive (EU) 2019/2121 enacted a legislative framework for CBC,[95] EU legislative proposals and case law of the CJEU were not labelled as CBCs but as cross-border company transfers of seat. An example is the proposal of the 14th Company Law Directive on the cross-border transfer of the registered office of limited

92. Article 160o of Directive (EU) 2017/1132.
93. Article 160m (8)-(10) of Directive (EU) 2017/1132.
94. *See* for a more in-depth discussion on this topic for example T. Biermeyer, 'Stakeholder Protection in Cross-Border Seat Transfers in the EU' (WLP, 2015), *27 et seq.*
95. Directive (EU) 2019/2121 amended Directive (EU) 2017/1132 and the provisions on CBC in that directive have to be transposed into the laws of the Member States by 31 Jan. 2023.

liability companies, which was never enacted.[96] In principle, as also reflected above, cross-border transfers of seat and cross-border conversions can have the same result, namely that a company converts from the company law form governed by the law of Member State A to a company law form governed by the law of Member State B. Yet, this conversion does not necessarily have to result in a cross-border transfer of seat if a company seat is not transferred in compliance with the connecting factors of Member State A and Member State B.

8.86 Moreover, considering both concepts in a domestic situation, they are completely different. In a domestic transaction, a transfer of seat means that a company transfers its seat for example from one city to another. A conversion into a different company law form does not take place because the national applicable law governing the company remains the same. In a domestic conversion, the company converts into a different company law form available in a country, for example from a Dutch BV into a Dutch NV. The registered office of the company, however, remains at the same location, unless transferred at the same time.

8.87 CBCs and cross-border transfers of seat have been subject to a number of landmark cases of the CJEU, starting with *Daily Mail* (1988),[97] *Centros* (1999),[98] *Überseering* (2002),[99] *Inspire Art* (2003),[100] *Cartesio* (2008),[101] *Vale* (2012)[102] and *Polbud* (2017)[103] (*see* paragraph 2.54 *et seq.*).

8.88 Traditionally, not all Member States allowed cross-border conversions based on national legislation. Among the countries that allow such conversion are Belgium, Cyprus, Czech Republic, Denmark, France, Greece, Italy, Liechtenstein, Luxembourg, Malta, Poland, Portugal, Slovakia and Spain.[104] However, in recent years cross-border conversions have become increasingly more frequent also in countries without legislation on this topic, such as Germany or the Netherlands, due to the case law of the CJEU.[105] EU legislators had already attempted to enact a framework through the idea of a 14th Company Law Directive on the cross-border transfer of the registered office of limited liability companies.[106] Yet, Member States could not agree on a common approach and therefore the directive was never enacted. Since *Cartesio, Vale* and

96. Still in 2012, the European Parliament labelled the legislation as cross-border seat transfers – European Parliament resolution of 2 Feb. 2012 with recommendations to the Commission on a 14th company law directive on the cross-border transfer of company seats.
97. C-81/87.
98. C-212/97.
99. C-208/00.
100. C-167/01.
101. C-210/06.
102. C-378/10.
103. C-106/16.
104. T. Biermeyer & M. Meyer, *supra* n. 77, at 14–15.
105. For example, the Netherlands and Germany rank fourth and fifth in the amount of CBC (319 and 288 respectively) for the period 2007 to 2019 despite not having a legislative framework on this matter. T. Biermeyer & M. Meyer, *supra* n. 77, at 36.
106. *See* on this topic S. Rammeloo, 'The 14th EC Company Law Directive on the Cross-Border Transfer of the Registered Office of Limited Liability Companies - Now or Never?', *Maastricht Journal of European and Comparative Law* 3, no. 15 (2008).

Polbud together obliged the Member States to allow cross-border conversions, this fact gave a new impulse to EU legislators and the Member States to provide an orderly framework for CBCs on the basis of Directive (EU) 2019/2121.

8.89 It should be noted here that the SE Regulation, which was enacted in 2001, provides for a cross-border transfer of seat framework applicable only to SEs. This means that on this basis, cross-border transfers of seat were possible as of the transposition of the SE Regulation into the national laws of the Member States. However, it entailed that a company governed purely by a national law had to convert into an SE in order to carry out a cross-border transfer of seat. This procedure was cumbersome and costly and consequently has not been applied frequently. A further possibility was to carry out a CBM in order to enable a CBC. As an illustration, company P in Member State A establishes a subsidiary S in Member State B, thereafter merging P into its subsidiary S, with S as the acquiring company. Yet, again, the procedure is rather cumbersome, which is the reason why in recent years most CBCs are carried out based on a combination of national applicable law and the case law of the CJEU.[107]

8.90 Similar to CBMs and CBDs, the provisions of Directive (EU) 2017/1132 on CBCs refer to national law for compliance with formalities. It is expressly specified that the law of the departure Member State governs those parts of the procedures and formalities to be complied with in connection with the CBC in order to obtain the pre-conversion certificate, and the law of the destination Member State governs those parts of the procedures and formalities to be complied with following receipt of the pre-conversion certificate.[108] The SE Regulation does not provide such a provision for cross-border seat transfers.

8.91 For decision-making, Directive (EU) 2017/1132 provides the same rules as for CBDs, which are very similar to those for CBMs. That means the approval of the CBC by the shareholders is an issue that may be treated differently by the Member States, meaning they have discretion to apply the majority and quorum for the approval of the CBC. However, Member States must ensure that the approval of the CBC requires a majority of not less than two-thirds but not more than 90% of the votes attached to the shares represented at the general meeting. Moreover, it is expressly stated that the voting threshold may not be higher than the threshold provided by national law for CBMs. Directive (EU) 2017/1132 does not provide that Member States may leave the decision to carry out a CBC to a different company body than the general meeting of shareholders. Also, the SE Regulation provides discretion for the Member States to apply a majority and quorum for the approval of a cross-border transfer of seat within certain limits. This means that the applicable majority may not be less than two-thirds of the votes cast. Moreover, a Member State may provide that where at least half of an

107. *See* for a discussion of the different possibilities also DG JUST, Assessment and quantification of drivers, problems and impacts related to cross-border transfers of registered offices and cross-border divisions of companies, 2018, JUST/2015/PR/01/0003, drafted by Ernst &Young, 57 *et seq.*
108. Article 86c of Directive (EU) 2017/1132.

SE's subscribed capital is represented, a simple majority of the votes suffices.[109] Equally, the SE Regulation does not give the Member States the possibility for a cross-border transfer of seat to be decided by a different company body.

8.92 The system of creditor protection is set up in a similar way as for CBMs and CBDs. This means that the Member States must ensure that creditors that are dissatisfied with the safeguards offered in the draft terms of the cross-border conversion can apply, within three months of the disclosure of the draft terms of cross-border conversion, to the appropriate administrative or judicial authority for adequate safeguards. The creditors can make such application if they can credibly demonstrate that, due to the CBC, the satisfaction of their claims is at stake and that they have not obtained adequate safeguards from the company. Moreover, Member States may also require the management body of the company to provide a declaration that accurately reflects the financial status of the company at a date not earlier than one month before the disclosure of such declaration. Such declaration must further state that the management body is unaware of any reasons why the company would be unable to meet its liabilities when they fall due.[110] Under the SE Regulation, creditor protection is regulated similarly but in less detail. It is provided that before the competent authority from the Member State in which the SE is located before the cross-border transfer of seat issues its certificate, the SE must ensure that any liabilities arising prior to the publication of the cross-border transfer of seat proposal, the interests of creditors and holders of other rights in respect of the SE (including those of public bodies) have been adequately protected in accordance with requirements laid down by the Member State where the SE has its registered office prior to the transfer.[111]

8.93 In terms of minority shareholder protection, Member States must ensure that at least the members of a company who voted against the approval of the draft terms of the cross-border conversion have the right to dispose of their shares for adequate cash compensation.[112]

8.94 Again as with CBMs and CBDs, the date on which a CBC takes effect can vary as Article 86q of Directive (EU) 2017/1132 leaves discretion to the Member States to determine such date. Yet, Article 86q provides that the date cannot be earlier than the scrutiny by the national authorities in relation to the conversion certificates has taken place.

8.95 As a final point, similar to CBMs and CBDs, a competent authority must examine whether a CBM has been set up for abusive or fraudulent purposes leading to or aimed at the evasion or circumvention of EU or national law, or for criminal purposes, and can refuse on that basis to issue the pre-conversion conversion certificate.[113]

109. Article 8(6) read together with Article 59 of the SE Regulation (EC) No 2157/2001.
110. Article 86j(2) of Directive (EU) 2017/1132.
111. Article 8(6) of the SE Regulation.
112. Article 86i of Directive (EU) 2017/1132.
113. Article 86m of Directive (EU) 2017/1132.

D Cross-Border Operations of Companies: Conclusion

8.96 If one were to regard the *Daily Mail* case as the starting point of the EU legislative journey on CBMs, CBDs and CBCs, then it took 31 years for EU legislators to provide a comprehensive framework on the different modes of cross-border corporate mobility and restructurings through Directive (EU) 2019/2121 in 2019. The time has, however, also provided EU legislators with lessons learned from the evaluations of the SE Regulation and the CBM Directive, which allowed Directive (EU) 2019/2121 to provide more sophisticated mechanisms on certain points, such as creditor or minority shareholder protection. From this perspective, Directive (EU) 2019/2121 has been a major step forward in cross-border company mobility.

8.97 To what extent the frameworks provided in Directive (EU) 2019/2121 will guarantee effective cross-border mobility of companies in the EU remains to be seen. As a first point, Member States only have to transpose the provisions of the Directive into national law by 31 January 2023, and it happens frequently that the Member States are late with their transposition obligations. Moreover, new concepts have been introduced by the directive. An example is that national authorities can refuse to issue a certificate necessary for the completion of the CBM, CBD or CBC if the authority concludes that the transaction has been set up for abusive or fraudulent purposes leading to or aimed at the evasion or circumvention of EU or national law, or for criminal purposes, and can refuse on that basis to issue the pre-conversion certificate. As the Member States have not yet transposed these provisions, it is not yet clear how the mechanism will work. For example, will the competent authority (being for example a district court or a notary) have the necessary expertise to make such determination? To what extent will it delay cross-border operations in general? If competent authorities refuse to issue a certificate more frequently, it can be expected that there will be case law, likely also at the level of the CJEU as to what for example constitutes an abusive or fraudulent purpose.[114]

VII PROTECTION OF RIGHTS OF EMPLOYEES

8.98 To understand to what extent the rights of employees will be protected in the case of a cross-border acquisition or restructuring, one must discern between the various directives for the protection of these rights and the methods of acquisition or restructuring.

8.99 In the first place, national provisions regarding the *right to information and consultation* of employees or their representatives may apply irrespective of the method of acquisition or restructuring tool used. Minimum standards in this respect are

114. *See* on this point for example also J. Schmidt, 'Cross-Border Mergers, Divisions and Conversions: Accomplishments and Deficits of the Company Law Package' *European Company and Financial Law Review* 16 (2019): 222.

set by Directive 2002/14/EC, establishing a general framework for informing and consulting employees in the EU.[115] The directive is meant to prevent serious decisions affecting employees from being taken and made public without adequate procedures having been implemented beforehand to inform and consult employees or their representatives.[116] National legislation on information and consultation can, and it often does, go further than the minimum standards set by this directive. For countries with a voluntarist tradition on employee involvement, this framework directive constituted a significant change.

8.100 Where an *acquisition of assets* can be qualified as a transfer of an undertaking (business) or part thereof, the rights of employees are protected by rules prescribed by Directive 2001/23/EC on the safeguarding of employees' rights in the event of transfers of undertakings (*see also* paragraph 7.39).[117] Such an event occurs when an undertaking or part thereof is transferred to another employer as a result of a legal transfer or merger. This covers any transfer of an economic entity, which retains its identity, meaning an organized grouping of resources that has the objective of pursuing an economic activity, whether or not that activity is central or ancillary (Article 1). According to the directive, the transferor's rights and obligations arising from employment contracts are automatically transferred to the transferee, that is, the company acquiring the business (Article 3). The CJEU held that an existing works council and the protection of employee representatives also constitute rights that are transferred to another employer.[118] The CJEU held in another ruling that transactions may fall within the ambit of the directive if there is a change in the person carrying out the business and incurring the obligations of an employer, 'regardless of whether or not ownership of the undertaking is transferred'.[119] Consequently, even a lease agreement may fall within the meaning of the directive.[120] The transfer of an undertaking does not, in itself, constitute grounds for dismissal by the transferor or the transferee. Nevertheless, dismissals may take place for economic, technical or organizational reasons entailing changes in the workforce (Article 4). The protection offered by the directive does not apply if the transferor is the subject of bankruptcy proceedings or any analogous insolvency proceedings (Article 5).[121] Notwithstanding its scope, Directive 2001/23/EC is not tailored to cases, where undertakings or parts thereof are transferred across

115. Directive 2002/14/EC, establishing a general framework for informing and consulting employees in the European Community, OJ 2002, L 80.
116. Preamble No. 6, Directive 2002/14/EC, OJ 2002, L 80.
117. Directive 2001/23/EC relating to the safeguarding of employees' rights in the event of transfers of undertakings, businesses or parts of undertakings or businesses, OJ 2001, L 82 replacing Directive (EEC) 77/187, OJ 1977, L 61.
118. Case C-151/09 (*UGT-FSP)* (2010), para. 45 *et seq.*
119. Case C-287/86 (*Ny Mølle Kro)* (1987).
120. C. de Groot, 'The Council Directive on the Safeguarding of Employees' Rights in the Event of Transfers of Undertakings: An Overview of the Case Law', *Common Market Law Review* 30 (1993): 339.
121. The issues mentioned here as well as many others are dealt with in the 2007 Commission Services Working Document, *Memorandum on Rights of Workers in Cases of Transfers of Undertakings*, accessible at http://ec.europa.eu/employment_social/labour_law/documentation_en.htm.

borders. According to Article 1(2), the directive applies to the transfer of undertakings 'situated within the territorial scope of the Treaty'. The criterion for the applicability, therefore, is the place where the undertaking is situated at the date of the transfer, irrespective of the nationality of the transferor and the transferee.[122] However, cross-border transfers are not mentioned in the directive and conflicts-of-laws provisions are lacking.[123] Difficulties may arise especially if the transfer of the undertaking implies its relocation to another Member State, or even outside the EU. Against the background of the importance of outsourcing and the increasing mobility of production factors in a globalizing economy, the Commission started exploring the possibility of amending the directive to ensure legal certainty for cross-border transfers of undertakings.[124] The adoption of Directive (EU) 2019/2121 now covers employees' rights in the case of a cross-border conversion (i.e., the cross-border transfer of an undertaking) and safeguards them through the before-and-after principle alongside the employees' rights applicable in the country of destination of the company. The principle, in essence, mandates that rights existing prior to the cross-border transaction must be applicable after the transaction (Articles 86k and 86l). The starting point is the applicable laws in the country of destination, but existing rights – if more favourable regarding the level of protection or the protection of employees abroad – must be retained in light of the before-and-after principle (Article 86l(2)(a) and (b)). The directive's transposition deadline is 31 January 2023.

8.101 A case decided on by the Hamburg Labour Court illustrates the types of issues that arise when an undertaking is transferred across borders. A German company transferred its English news service, which was part of its activities, to its Irish subsidiary. The employee carrying out the publishing of the news service in Hamburg was dismissed. The employee, however, was willing to move to Cork and successfully brought a claim under German law in the Labour Court of Hamburg. The court held the dismissal notice to be invalid.[125] As McMullen remarks, in this case, only the transferor was sued and, therefore, it does not clarify whether the employee could have enforced his or her rights against the transferee, which was situated in another Member State.[126]

8.102 In the case of an acquisition by means of a share transaction, employment contracts to which the acquired company is a party remain with that company. Although the control of the company changes hands, there is no change in the legal

122. Commission, June 2007, *First phase consultation of social partners under Article 138(2) of the EC Treaty concerning cross-border transfers of undertakings, businesses or parts of undertakings or businesses*, retrievable from http://ec.europa.eu/employment_social/social_dialogue/consultations_en.htm.
123. J. McMullen, 'Some Problems and Themes in the Application in Member States of Directive 2001/23/EC on Transfer of Undertakings', *International Journal of Comparative Labour Law and Industrial Relations* 23, no. 3 (2007): 353.
124. Commission, June 2007, *First phase consultation of social partners under Article 138(2) of the EC Treaty concerning cross-border transfers of undertakings, businesses or parts of undertakings or businesses*, s. 9.
125. Landesarbeitsgericht Hamburg, 22 May 2003, as reported by J. McMullen, *supra* n. 123, at 353–354.
126. *Ibid.*, 354.

person that is responsible for carrying out the business and that incurs the obligations of an employer. Nevertheless, national laws of the companies concerned may provide information and consultation rights for the employees or their representatives. Where the acquisition results in a group of companies with a Community dimension ('Community-scale group of undertakings'), an obligation may be triggered for the acquiring company to establish a European works council.[127] Directive 2001/23/EC does not cover acquisitions by a transfer of shares because, in such a case, the identity of the employer remains the same. As a result, employees are not protected by this directive against dismissals that are connected to the transfer of shares.[128] Similarly, the information and consultation rights under Article 7, in the case of a transfer of an undertaking, do not apply to a share transfer, but this may be compensated for by national law.[129]

8.103 In the case of a merger, the automatic transfer of all assets and liabilities as a matter of course pertains to the obligations arising from the contracts between the acquired company and its employees. Nevertheless, Article 12 of the Third Directive explicitly mentions that the protection of the rights of the employees of each of the merging companies has to be regulated in accordance with Directive 2001/23/EC on the safeguarding of employees' rights in the event of transfers of undertakings. The Tenth Directive does not affect employees' rights other than rights of participation. Therefore, in the case of a cross-border merger, the rights of employees are protected to the same extent as to where an (cross-border) asset transaction constitutes the transfer of an undertaking.[130]

8.104 Unlike the Third Directive, both the SE Directive and the Tenth Directive[131] provide additional rules regarding employee participation in the company resulting from the cross-border merger. The concept of employee participation used in the Tenth Directive corresponds with participation, as defined in the SE Directive.[132] And following the implementation of Directive (EU) 2019/2121 by January 2023, this protection will be further extended to cross-border conversions and divisions as well. It points to the rights of employee representatives to elect or appoint some or all of the members of the company's supervisory or administrative body or the right to recommend and/or oppose the appointment of such members. The starting point is that a company resulting from a cross-border merger is subject to the rules in force concerning employee participation, if any, in the Member State in which that company has its registered office (Article 133). If national law does not provide the same level of

127. Directive 2009/38/EC. *See also* Chapter 7 of this book.
128. J. McMullen, *supra* n. 123, at 338.
129. For example, Article 25(1)(a) of the Dutch Works Councils Act confers the right of information and consultation in the case of transfer of control of the enterprise or any part thereof. This may include the transfer of control by the acquisition of shares. *See* R. Fluit, 'What a US Buyer Should Expect in a Dutch M&A Transaction', *European Company Law* 14, no. 1 (2017): 29–42.
130. Preamble No. 12 of the Tenth Directive.
131. Now codified in Article 118 *et seq.* of Directive (EU) 2017/1132.
132. Article 2(k) of the SE Directive defines employee participation. The concept of employee participation of the Tenth Directive corresponds with this definition because Article 16 refers extensively to the SE Directive.

participation as operated in one or more of the merging companies, this matter must then be regulated. The SE Regulation and the SE Directive contain provisions used for this purpose. Details of employee participation in the SE have been set out in paragraph 4.35 *et seq.* The same rules and procedures apply for a cross-border merger, according to the Tenth Directive, albeit with some modifications, because the company resulting from a cross-border merger in accordance with the Tenth Directive is subject to national law.[133] The involvement of employees is discussed in Chapter 7 of this book.

VIII MERGER CONTROL

A The Treaty Provisions

8.105 The TFEU, in Article 101 *et seq.*, provides rules on competition, which is an important area of EU policy. For the subject of cooperation and acquisitions, Articles 101 and 102 TFEU are the most relevant. Article 101 prohibits agreements between undertakings, decisions by associations of undertakings and concerted practices that may affect trade between the Member States and that have as their object competition or effect the prevention, restriction or distortion of competition in the common market. This article applies exclusively to cooperation between undertakings (business enterprises). An example of illegal conduct infringing Article 101 is a secret agreement (cartel) between competitors, leading to price-fixing and/or market sharing.[134] Article 101 also covers cooperative joint ventures and acquisitions of shareholdings, falling short of a concentration as defined by the Merger Regulation (*see* paragraph 8.121). The prohibition does not apply if the agreement, decision or practice has beneficial effects, such as improvement of products or technical progress if a fair share of these is allowed to the consumers (Article 101(3)).

8.106 Cartels are generally not easily detectable. Therefore, the Commission encourages companies to hand over inside evidence in exchange for complete or partial immunity from fines.[135] Individuals are also encouraged to report inside knowledge they may have of a cartel to the Commission. They can do this openly or anonymously through a 'whistleblower' tool established in 2017.[136]

8.107 Cooperation between undertakings (businesses) may negatively affect trade but may also have beneficial effects. Article 101(3) allows for cooperation if it contributes to improving the production or distribution of goods or to promoting technical or economic progress while allowing consumers a fair share of the resulting benefit. In its

133. Recital 66, Preamble of Directive (EU) 2017/1132.
134. *See* the Commission's website: http://ec.europa.eu/competition/cartels/overview/index_en.html.
135. http://ec.europa.eu/competition/cartels/leniency/leniency.html.
136. http://ec.europa.eu/competition/cartels/whistleblower/index.html.

2011 Communication, the Commission explains how it assesses the effects of horizontal cooperation (agreements between actual or potential competitors).[137] In the same vein, certain categories of vertical agreements and concerted practices are acceptable if they meet the conditions laid down in Regulation EU 330/2010.[138]

8.108 Behaviour of undertakings, not leading to cooperation, but to concentration was originally dealt with under Article 102 (at the time Article 82 EC Treaty), which prohibits any abuse by an undertaking of its dominant position within the common market or in a substantial part thereof. In *Continental Can v. Commission*, the court held that this provision, indeed, had to be applied where a company in a dominant position acquired a competitor if the acquisition reinforced the acquirer's position.[139] Obviously, this applies only to concentrations, where one of the parties involved already has a dominant position. However, other concentrations may be equally incompatible with the undistorted competition envisaged by the treaty. Therefore, the position of the Commission was reinforced, initially by Regulation 4064/89 (on the control of concentrations between undertakings), which was based on Articles 83 (87) and 308 (233) of the EC Treaty.[140] This regulation was replaced by Merger Regulation EC No 139/2004.[141]

8.109 Strengthening the position of the Commission must also be viewed against the background of the objectives of the EU, as embodied in Article 9 of the TFEU. This includes, *inter alia*, the promotion of a high-level employment and the guarantee of adequate social protection. The Commission was of the view that European integration could be furthered by competition and merger control policy.[142]

8.110 The dominant position of an undertaking in the internal market or in a substantial part of it is not, by itself, a concern for the competition authorities. It is the abuse of such position that is declared incompatible with the internal market, insofar as it may affect trade between the Member States. Article 102 TFEU further specifies what may, in particular, constitute abuse. Imposing unfair prices or limiting production to the prejudice of consumers are, *inter alia*, mentioned. The growing importance of innovation and high-tech industries have put the effectivity and even the necessity of this part of competition policy under debate.[143]

---

137. Communication from the Commission, *Guidelines on the applicability of Article 101 of the Treaty on the Functioning of the European Union to horizontal co-operation agreements*, OJ 14.1.2011, C 11/1.
138. Commission Regulation (EU) No. 330/2010. The regulation concerns undertakings operating at a different level of the production or distribution chain.
139. C-6/72, *Continental Can v. Commission* ((1973)) ECR 215.
140. Regulation (EEC) No. 4064/89 amended by Regulation (EC) No. 1310/97.
141. Regulation (EC) No. 139/2004.
142. K. van Miert, cited by Haid, in D. C. Mueller, A. Haid & J. Weigand (eds), *Competition, Efficiency and Welfare* (Boston: Kluwer Academic Publishers, 1999), 167.
143. Commission Communication COM(201) 713 final, *A competition policy fit for new challenges*, Brussels 18.11.2021. +*See*, for the original purpose of what is now Article 102, C.S. Rusu, *European Merger Control: The Challenges Raised by 20 Years of Enforcement Experience* (Alphen aan den Rijn: Kluwer Law International, 2010). *See* further M.L. Katz & H.A. Shelanski, 'Schumpeterian Competition and Antitrust Policy in High-Tech Markets', *Competition* 2005; P.

B The Merger Regulation

8.111 According to Article 3(1) of the 2004 Merger Regulation, a concentration is deemed to arise where a change of control on a lasting basis results from:

- a merger of two or more previously independent undertakings or parts of undertakings; or
- the acquisition by one or more undertakings of direct or indirect control of one or more other undertakings (or parts thereof), whether by purchase of securities or assets, by contract or by any other means.

Control is defined in Article 3(2) and 'shall be constituted by rights, contracts or any other means which (...) confer the possibility of exercising decisive influence on an undertaking'. The provision specifies that control is, in particular, realized by ownership or the right to use the assets of an undertaking, as well as by rights or contracts that confer decisive influence on the composition, voting or decisions of the organs of an undertaking.

8.112 It follows from the previous paragraph that the Merger Regulation covers not only mergers in the strict sense but also all operations that lead to a lasting change in the structure of the undertakings concerned. Unlike company law, whose function is to offer a legal structure for entrepreneurial activities without affecting these activities, the Merger Regulation pertains directly to a specific entrepreneurial activity, namely the acquisition of control. It does so irrespective of whether control is acquired by legal instruments like mergers, contracts and majority or controlling voting rights or by *de facto* circumstances, like economic dependence and dominance. As a matter of course, these factual elements of control are especially hard to assess. Not surprisingly, the Merger Regulation gives rise to many questions on how to interpret its provisions. Therefore, the Commission has provided jurisdictional notices in order to explain how the most important concepts have to be applied, most recently in a document called the Consolidated Jurisdictional Notice.[144]

8.113 The scope of the Merger Regulation is limited to concentrations with a Community dimension. The powers of national authorities are limited to cases where, failing intervention by the Commission, effective competition is likely to be significantly impeded within the territory of a Member State.[145] Member States are not permitted to apply their national legislation on competition to concentrations with a Community

Ibáñez Colomo, 'Intel and Article 102 TFEU Case Law: Making Sense of a Perpetual Controversy', *LSE Law, Society and Economy Working Papers* 29/2014; N. Petit, 'Intel, Leveraging Rebates and the Goals of Article 102 TFEU' (20 May 2015), available at SSRN: http://ssrn.com/abstract=2567628.

144. Consolidated Jurisdictional Notice under Council Regulation (EC) No. 139/2004 on the control of concentrations between undertakings, 10 Jul. 2007, OJ 2008, C/95; accessible at http://ec.europa.eu/competition/mergers/legislation/legislation.html. *See* for merger cases examined by the Commission http://ec.europa.eu/competition/mergers/cases/.
145. Preamble, Recital 18 and Article 21(3) of the Merger Directive. An overview of national competition laws can be found in publications like P.F.C. Begg, *Corporate Acquisitions and*

dimension unless the Merger Regulation makes provisions in that respect. According to Article 9, concentrations with a Community dimension may be referred to national authorities when they affect competition in a 'distinct market' within a Member State. The reverse situation – referral to the Commission by the Member States – is dealt with by Article 22. Accordingly, Member States may request the Commission to examine a concentration that does not have a Community dimension if such concentration affects trade between the Member States and threatens to significantly affect competition within the territory of the Member State(s) making the request. In general, the Commission has the duty to carry out the procedures set out in the Merger Regulation in 'close and constant liaison' with the competent authorities of the Member States (Article 19).

8.114 A concentration has a Community dimension where:

Article 1(2):

(a) the combined aggregate worldwide turnover of all the undertakings concerned is more than EUR 5,000 million; and
(b) the aggregate Community-wide turnover of each of at least two of the undertakings concerned is more than EUR 250 million.

Article 1(3):

A concentration below the thresholds of Article 1(2) nevertheless has a Community dimension where:

(a) the combined aggregate worldwide turnover of all the undertakings concerned is more than EUR 2,500 million;
(b) in each of at least three Member States, the combined aggregate turnover of all the undertakings concerned is more than EUR 100 million;
(c) in each of at least three Member States included for the purpose of point (b), the aggregate turnover of each of at least two of the undertakings concerned is more than EUR 25 million; and
(d) the aggregate Community-wide turnover of each of at least two of the undertakings concerned is more than EUR 100 million.

Even if the thresholds, as defined by sections 2 or 3, are met, the Community dimension is deemed to be absent where each of the undertakings concerned achieves more than two-thirds of its aggregate Community-wide turnover within one and the same Member State. Article 5 further specifies the calculation of turnovers.

Mergers (looseleaf) (Aspen Publishers); Baker & McKenzie, *Acquiring Companies and Businesses in Europe*, 5th edition, 2005 and P. Verloop & V. Landes, *Merger Control in Europe*, International Competition Law Series Volume 11 (The Hague: Kluwer Law International, 2003).

1 *The First Phase*

8.115 Notification of a concentration with a Community dimension to the Commission must take place following the conclusion of the agreement, the announcement of the public bid or the acquisition of a controlling interest leading to such concentration (Article 4). Earlier notification is allowed where the undertakings concerned demonstrate to the Commission a good faith intention to conclude an agreement or, in the case of a public bid, where they have publicly announced an intention to make such a bid (Article 4(1)). Such intention can be demonstrated by 'letters of intent' or 'heads of agreement'. However, these, by themselves, do not create binding obligations for the parties concerned. It is standard practice for parties to engage in pre-notification discussions with the Commission, even in an earlier stage, to ensure that the intended concentration does not raise too many concerns and that the notification itself contains the essential information. Although concentrations may not be implemented before notification, or until it has been declared compatible with the common market, the Merger Regulation does not prevent the implementation of a public bid but rather restricts the use of the acquired voting rights instead (Article 7(2)).

8.116 The subject matter and content of the information to be provided in the notification are defined by the implementing Regulation (EC) 802/2004.[146] Annexes to this regulation contain forms to be used by parties notifying a concentration. According to the full notification form (Form CO), parties to the concentration must specify 'the nature of the concentration (e.g., merger, acquisition or joint venture), the areas of activity of the notifying parties, the markets on which the concentration will have an impact (including the main markets affected) and the strategic and economic rationale for the concentration'.[147] In describing the nature of the concentration, parties must state, *inter alia,* 'whether the proposed concentration is a full merger, an acquisition of sole or joint control, a contract or other means of conferring direct or indirect control within the meaning of Article 3(2) of the Merger Regulation or the acquisition of joint control in a full-function joint venture within the meaning of Article 3(4) of the Merger Regulation'.[148] In the case of a joint venture, details about the cooperative effects must be provided.[149] Further guidance can be found in the Commission's Best Practices on the conduct of EC merger control proceedings.[150]

146. The implementing regulation further includes rules for time limits, hearings, confidentiality and the terms of reference of hearing officers in competition proceedings. The regulation is amended by Commission Regulation (EC) No. 1033/2008 (Official Journal L 279, 22.10.2008, 3-12) and by Commission Implementing Regulation (EU) No. 1269/2013 of 5 Dec. 2013 (Official Journal OJ L 336, 14.12.2013, 1-36).
147. Section 1, Article 1.1.
148. Section 3, Article 3.1(a).
149. Section 10, Article 10.
150. Article 1, Form CO. The document is provided for by the DG Competition on its website http://ec.europa.eu/competition/mergers/legislation/legislation.html. A document in PDF,

8.117 After receiving the notification, the Commission, according to Article 6(1), can make several *decisions* by concluding that the concentration:

(a) does not fall within the scope of the Merger Regulation; or
(b) does not raise serious doubts as to its compatibility with the common market; or
(c) in case it raises serious doubts to initiate proceedings.

These decisions must be taken within 25 working days, and it is often referred to as the first phase. The period may be increased up to 35 days where the undertakings concerned offer commitments in order to modify the concentration in such a way as to make it compatible with the common market (Article 10(1)).[151]

In a 2007 notice, the Commission provides guidance on modifications to notified concentrations, including commitments to modify a concentration. The object of such commitments, or 'remedies', as they are more commonly called, is to eliminate the competition concerns identified by the Commission. Such remedies include, for example, divestitures (the commitment to sell a business unit) and granting competitors access to key infrastructures on non-discriminatory terms.[152]

2 *The Second Phase*

8.118 The second phase starts when proceedings have been initiated, because of the serious doubts raised. After investigation, the Commission may decide that the concentration is, nevertheless, declared compatible with the common market (Article 8(1) and (2)). The concentration then has to fulfil the criteria of Article 2(2), meaning that it does not significantly impede effective competition and, where a joint venture is created, that the effects on the coordination of the competitive behaviour of the cooperating undertakings are in accordance with the criteria of Article 101(3) TFEU. During the second phase, modifications may also be made in order to remove the objections of the Commission (Article 8(2)). Where the Commission finds that a concentration would significantly impede effective competition in the common market or in a substantial part of it, in particular as a result of the creation or strengthening of a dominant position, it should then be declared incompatible with the common market (Article 8(3) and (4)). Where the Commission finds that such a concentration has already been completed, it may require the dissolution of the merger or the disposal of the acquired assets or shares. Decisions completing the second phase must be taken within 90 days of the date on which the proceedings were initiated and may be

---

including all relevant legislation, is available on the website and is updated from time to time: *EU Competition Law: Merger Legislation*.

151. The extended period also applies when the undertakings concerned require referral to national authorities, *see* Article 9.
152. Commission Notice (2007) on remedies acceptable under Council Regulation (EC) No. 139/2004 and under Commission Regulation (EC) No. 802/2004, accessible at http://ec.europa.eu/competition/mergers/legislation/legislation.html.

extended to 105 days where the undertakings offer commitments to modify the concentration (Article 10(3)).

8.119 The Merger Regulation not only grants wide powers to the Commission but also provides for some checks and balances. An Advisory Committee on concentrations (consisting of representatives of the competent authorities of the Member States) must be consulted before any decision is taken by the Commission, *inter alia,* on the (in)compatibility of a concentration with the common market and on the imposition of fines (Article 19(3)). Most of the decisions must be published together with the opinion of the Advisory Committee in the *Official Journal of the European Union* (Article 20).[153] Furthermore, decisions of the Commission may be reviewed by the CJEU (*inter alia:* Articles 16 and 21).

8.120 The Commission has adopted guidelines describing the analysis for the substantive test as to whether concentrations are compatible with the common market. The *Horizontal Guidelines* deal with mergers between competing or potentially competing firms.[154] Horizontal mergers generally reduce the number of firms active in the relevant market, and the primary competition concern over these mergers is that the structural changes they create will lead to higher prices in comparison to if the merger would not take place. The Commission's assessment of mergers normally entails a definition of the relevant product and geographic markets, as well as the competitive assessment of the merger. In assessing the competitive effects, the competitive conditions that would result from the notified merger are compared with the conditions that would have prevailed without the merger. Thereby, the Commission may take account of the likely entry or exit of firms if the merger were not to take place when considering what constitutes the relevant comparison.

Vertical and conglomerate concentrations (non-horizontal concentrations) are dealt with by the *Guidelines for merging companies with vertical or conglomerate relationships.*[155] Vertical concentrations involve companies operating at different levels of the supply chain, for example, when a manufacturer merges with one of its distributors. Conglomerate concentrations are mergers or acquisitions of firms that are not in a horizontal relationship (as competitors in the same relevant market) and not operating at different levels of the supply chain. The focus of the guidelines is on mergers between companies that are active in closely related markets, for example, between suppliers of complementary products. According to the guidelines, non-horizontal concentrations are generally less likely to significantly impede effective competition than horizontal mergers, *inter alia,* because they do not imply loss of direct competition as horizontal mergers do. Concerns raised by non-horizontal concentrations are possible 'anti-competitive foreclosure', meaning the hampering or

153. The latest case information can be found at: www.ec.europa.eu/comm/competition/mergers/news.html and/or: ec.europa.eu/comm/competition/mergers/cases.
154. Guidelines on the assessment of horizontal mergers under the Council Regulation on the control of concentrations between undertakings, OJ 2004, C 31.
155. Guidelines on the assessment of non-horizontal mergers under the Council Regulation on the control of concentrations between undertakings, OJ 2008, C 265.

elimination of rivals' access to supplies or markets that may lead to the loss of these companies' abilities to compete. Another concern is that due to the concentration, companies may significantly more likely coordinate their activities to raise prices or otherwise harm effective competition. Pro-competitive effects of non-horizontal concentrations may stem from substantiated efficiencies benefiting consumers.

3 *Joint Ventures*

8.121 Joint ventures, as has been explained in paragraph 8.05 *et seq*, function to structure the cooperation of business enterprises that remain independent. Therefore, they are not automatically covered by the concentration concept. It makes a difference whether a joint venture originates from the joint acquisition of an existing undertaking or from the creation of a new entity, created by the cooperating partners. The first case clearly constitutes a concentration according to Article 3(1)(b) of the Merger Regulation, where the acquisition of control by one or more undertakings is explicitly mentioned. By way of contrast, a joint venture resulting from the creation of a new undertaking will only constitute a concentration if it performs, on a lasting basis, all the functions of an autonomous economic entity (Article 3(4)). Autonomy, in this respect, means that the joint venture must be operationally autonomous, whereas the joint venture partners may direct its strategy.[156] It implies, *inter alia,* that the joint venture has management dedicated to its day-to-day operations, and that the joint venture has access to sufficient staff, finance and assets in order to conduct, on a lasting basis, its business activities within the area provided for in the joint venture agreement.[157]

8.122 To the extent that a joint venture has as its object, or effects, the coordination of the competitive behaviour of undertakings that remain independent, such coordination will be appraised in accordance with the criteria of Article 101(1) and (3) TFEU. In doing so, the Commission must take into account whether the joint venture partners (parent companies) retain activities in the same market, in a market upstream or downstream or in a neighbouring market. Another important aspect is whether the coordination, which is the direct consequence of the joint venture, affords the undertakings concerned to eliminate competition with respect to the relevant products or services (Article 2(4) and (5)).[158] According to Article 101(1) TFEU, agreements between business enterprises (undertakings) leading to the prevention, restriction or distortion of competition within the common market are prohibited. Agreements may be exempted if they contribute to improving the production or distribution of goods or to promoting technical or economic progress while allowing consumers a fair share of

156. Consolidated Jurisdictional Notice, No. 91–93.
157. Consolidated Jurisdictional Notice, No. 94.
158. Further reading: N. Tyson, 'Joint Venture Regulation under European Competition Laws: An update', *European Law Journal* 13, no. 3 (May 2007): 408–423.

the resulting benefit (Article 101(3)).[159] Although joint ventures are not mentioned as such, both the prohibition and the conditions for exemption pertain to joint ventures. The Commission has provided several examples of joint ventures and other arrangements which, although falling under the ambit of Article 101(1) TFEU, may be exempted on the grounds of section 3 of that article.[160]

159. Even then, certain conditions must be met, Article 81(3) and Communication from the Commission - Notice - Guidelines on the application of Article 81(3) of the Treaty, OJ 2004, C 101, 27 Apr. 2004, 0097 - 0118.
160. Guidelines on the application of Article 81(3) of the Treaty, OJ 2004, C 101, 27 Apr. 2004, no. 38 *et seq.*

CHAPTER 9
Financial Statements and Related Reports

I INTRODUCTION

9.01 Directive 2013/34/EU (as amended), also known as the Accounting Directive, combines the previously separate directives for the annual financial statements of companies and the consolidated financial statements of groups of companies.[1] This directive brought about a change in terminology, namely 'financial statements' for 'annual accounts'. As mentioned in paragraph 3.49, the International Accounting Standards (IAS) also play a role in setting standards for financial statements thereby reflecting the global spread of the capital markets. This chapter includes an analysis of the main features of the Accounting Directive and the applicable international standards. First, by way of further introduction, paragraph 9.02 sets out the scope of the directive and additional legislation, and paragraph 9.07 highlights the background of the international standards. Second, this chapter deals with specific requirements of annual financial statements. Paragraph 9.11 outlines the general principles that the annual financial statements have to comply with, after which paragraph 9.15 gives a more detailed description of the balance sheet, paragraph 9.20, the profit and loss account, paragraph 9.21, the notes to the accounts, and paragraph 9.23, the management report. Third, paragraph 9.27 discusses the publication of annual financial statements and paragraph 9.29 addresses any additional reports by listed companies. Lastly, paragraph 9.30 takes an in-depth look at consolidated financial statements and paragraph 9.46 concludes this chapter with a discussion of the statutory audit.

9.02 The corporate bodies must ensure that the annual financial statements and the consolidated financial statements are drawn up and published in accordance with the requirements of the Accounting Directive and, where applicable, in accordance with

1. Fourth Directive 78/660/EEC (as amended) and Seventh Directive 83/349/EEC (as amended) respectively. *See also* paragraph 3.19a of this book.

the IAS. The annual financial statements must be audited in accordance with Directive 2014/56/EU on statutory audits and be published according to Chapter 7 of the Accounting Directive and Chapter III of Directive 2017/1132. The financial reporting obligations are addressed to public and private limited liability companies, public limited partnerships and limited partnerships. These are mentioned in Article 1 and further specified in Annexes I and II of the Accounting Directive. Consequently, entities of the 'GmbH & Co. KG' type fall within the scope of the directive, and partnerships cannot be used to avoid the requirements of the European Union (EU) accounting norms, or the publication of essential data concerning its members, where these members have limited liability.[2] To alleviate the administrative burden for entrepreneurs, simplifications and exemptions are allowed for micro-undertakings, small undertakings and medium-sized undertakings.[3] These categories are defined in Article 3 of the Accounting Directive based on balance sheet total, net turnover and the average number of employees. Lastly, the Transparency Directive 2004/109/EC subjects listed companies to additional obligations in order to ensure that information is published regularly to inform investors (*see also* paragraph 3.54 of this book).

9.03 Each Member State is free to decide on the technical manner in which the requirements of the Accounting Directive are carried out. Member States may incorporate the accounting rules in specific company legislation (e.g., in their Companies Act or Private Companies Act) or set up a common accounting act governing all relevant company types. As a matter of course, the accounting provisions may also be incorporated in a pre-existing act that is common for the various company types, as Germany did when incorporating the provisions of the predecessors of the Accounting Directive in sections 264–315e of its Commercial Code (*Handelsgesetzbuch*). Many provisions of the Accounting Directive give the Member States the leeway to deviate within certain limits. The directive is a minimum insofar as the Member States, in Article 4(1), are allowed to require undertakings, with the exception of small undertakings, to draw up other statements in their annual financial statements besides the balance sheet, the profit and loss account, and the notes to the financial statements. A company may not rely on the fact that other Member States than the state where it is registered have less stringent accounting requirements. In *Blanguernon*, the Court of Justice of the European Union (CJEU) held that a French company must observe the duty to submit financial statements, even if another Member State fails to implement that requirement of the directive. The CJEU rejected the argument of the French company that such a difference between the Member States results in a distortion of competition to the detriment of companies that duly submit their financial statements.[4]

2. The extension to hybrid entities such as the GmbH & Co happened already by the amending Directive 90/605/EEC. Germany, where the use of the GmbH & Co was widespread implemented this directive with prolonged hesitation, C. Luttermann, *ZIP* (2000), 517 *et seq.*
3. Preamble recital 5, Directive 2013/34/EU clarifies what is meant by 'undertakings'. In order to demarcate the scope of the directive the term means 'certain undertakings with limited liability such as public and private limited liability companies' but also to 'partnerships and limited partnerships all the fully liable members of which are constituted either as public or as private limited liability companies'.
4. CJEU 11 Jan. 1990, C-38/89 (Blanguernon).

9.04 Companies whose securities are offered to the public ('listed companies') must prepare their *consolidated financial statements* in conformity with the IAS adopted by the European Commission.[5] By contrast, Member States have the option to allow or require adherence to these standards for the non-consolidated annual financial statements of listed companies. For non-listed companies, almost all Member States require or permit non-listed companies to draw up their *consolidated* financial statements according to the IAS/ International Financial Reporting Standards (IFRS), but most Member States do not permit non-listed companies to use these standards for their annual financial statements.[6]

9.05 According to the Accounting Directive, large undertakings and groups must disclose non-financial and diversity information. The initiative for the inclusion of these elements in the Accounting Directive derives from the resolutions of the EP on 'Corporate Social Responsibility: accountable, transparent and responsible business behaviour and sustainable growth' and 'Corporate Social Responsibility: promoting society's interests and a route to sustainable and inclusive recovery'. EU legislators are of the opinion that disclosure of non-financial information is vital for managing change towards a sustainable global economy by combining long-term profitability with social justice and environmental protection.[7] The non-financial statement should include, *inter alia*, a brief description of the undertaking's business model and its policies and activities relating to environmental, social and employee matters, as well as respect for human rights, anti-corruption and bribery matters. The non-financial statement is dealt with in paragraphs 9.24, 9.25, 9.26 and 9.45 of this chapter.

9.06 Scholars and accounting practitioners have developed several instruments to account for the social, economic and environmental value that result from the activities of businesses. Among these are Integrated Reporting (IR) and Social Return on Investment (SROI). IR means that organizations account for both the financial and non-financial effects of value creation. SROI is an investment appraisal technique that is explicitly designed to include social and environmental effects in the assessment of a project.[8] The effects of the obligation to report on Corporate Social Responsibility (CSR) activities are not considered very significant. This is due to the fact that many organizations already engage in CSR activities and publish such information and, at the same time, the minimum harmonization approach is not supported by detailed rules and standards.[9]

5. The Commission is empowered to adopt these standards by Article 5 Regulation EC 1606/2002 (adopted by the EP and the Council). The Commission Regulation EC 1126/2008 (as amended) summarizes the standards adopted.
6. Report of the Commission, COM(2008) 215 final, 3.
7. Preamble of the amending Directive 2014/95/EU, recital 3.
8. M. Ortega Maldonado & M. Corbey, 'Social Return on Investment (SROI): A Review of the Technique', *MAB, Maandblad voor Accountancy en Bedrijfseconomie* 90 (2016): 80 *et seq.* http://mab-online.nl.
9. J. Quinn & B. Connolly, 'The Non-financial Information Directive: An Assessment of Its Impact on Corporate Social Responsibility', *European Company Law* 14, no. 1 (2017): 15–21. *See also*, Tineke Lambooy, *Corporate Social Responsibility: Legal and Semi-Legal Frameworks Supporting CSR* (Deventer: Kluwer 2010).

II THE IAS/IFRS

9.07 A few remarks concerning IAS may be useful. To begin with, the aim of the two original accounting directives was to ensure that information extracted from the accounting materials is reliable and comparable, regardless of the company that an investor or creditor is looking at. However, full comparability was not achieved due to the considerable number of options offered to the Member States by these directives. In addition, the CJEU could not substantially further harmonize because not many cases concerning accounting standards had been brought before the court.[10] At the same time, IAS were evolving. The Commission initially tried to bridge the gap between these standards and Community law by its Interpretative Communication, concerning certain articles in the Fourth and Seventh Directives.[11] By 1999, however, the Commission in its Communication on Accounting Harmonization recognized both the shortcomings of the accounting directives and the need to set standards that are accepted worldwide.[12] The United States (US) Generally Accepted Accounting Principles (GAAP) were internationally accepted, but they were developed without European input. Therefore, the Commission preferred to cooperate with the International Accounting Standards Committee (IASC) in order to further develop the IAS. The IAS are more oriented to value-based (market-based, future-oriented) annual accounts, rather than transaction-based accounts (historical, retrospective). The roots of the IAS/IFRS go back to 1973 when the IASC was formed. France, Germany, the UK and the Netherlands were among the founding members of the IASC, whereas the Commission had 'a difficult relationship' with the IASC. This changed in 1990 because the Commission then finally became an observer at IASC board meetings.[13] The current International Accounting Standards Board (IASB) succeeded the IASC in 2001 and adopted all IAS that were in force at the time. From then on, standards adopted by the IASB were referred to as the IFRS. The standards are set according to an extended process that may include public consultation.[14]

9.08 The introduction of IAS/IFRS at the EU level dates back to the 2000 Lisbon European Council's endorsement of the Financial Services Action Plan, in order to create a single financial market in Europe. In the aftermath of the Council, Regulation

10. *See*, e.g., ECJ 27 June 1996, C-234/94 (Gebrüder von der Wettern GmbH), ECJ 3 May 2005, C-387, C-391/02 and C-403/02 (Berlusconi). Further Cases: C-161/78 (Conradsen), C-275/97 (DE + ES Bauunternehmung GmbH), C-306/99 (BIAO), C-234/94 (Tomberger).
11. Interpretative communication concerning certain Articles of the fourth and seventh Council Directives on accounting, OJ 1998, C 016.
12. 'Accounting Harmonisation: A New Strategy vis-à-vis International Harmonisation', Com 95 (508).
13. B. J. Epstein with contributions by A. A. Mirza, *IFRS 2006. Interpretation and Application of International Accounting and Financial Reporting Standards (Wiley IFRS 2006)* (Hoboken, NJ: John Wiley & Sons, 2006), 11.
14. More on the background of IFRS can be read in P. Pacter, *Pocket Guide to IFRS® Standards: The Global Financial Reporting Language* (London: IFRS Foundation, 2016). A recent overview of the IFRS can be downloaded at: https://www.iasplus.com/en/publications/global/ifrs-in-your-pocket/2021.

(EC) 1606/2002, more commonly known as the IAS Regulation, was enacted to empower the Commission to identify and adopt the standards that are to be mandatory.[15] Article 6 of the IAS Regulation requires the Commission to act in accordance with the procedure of Council Decision 1999/468/EC for the exercise of its implementing powers. This procedure is made up of several steps. First, the Commission receives recommendations from an advisory group and the opinion of another group before it decides to propose a standard or an interpretation for endorsement. Then, the Accounting Regulatory Committee (with representatives from the Member States) votes on the endorsement. After confirmation by the European Parliament (EP), the Commission makes the final decision on the adoption of standards.[16]

9.09 According to Recital 9 of the Preamble to the IAS Regulation, IAS/IFRS, in order to apply throughout the EU, must meet the basic requirement of the Accounting Directive 2013/34/EU, that is to say that 'its application results in a true and fair view of the financial position and performance of an enterprise'. Furthermore, a standard should be conducive to the European public good and meet basic criteria as to the quality of information required for financial statements to be useful to users. By adopting international standards, the EU contributes toward a 'global accounting convergence'.[17] It must be noted, however, that even if financial statements are prepared according to IFRS, several requirements of the Accounting Directive still have to be applied.[18]

9.10 More than 70 IFRS have been adopted by Commission regulations.[19] In 2015, the Commission published an evaluation of the IAS Regulation. According to the evaluation, IFRS was successful in creating a common accounting language for capital markets, and companies were mostly positive about their experience of using IFRS. Investors also largely supported IFRS for improving the transparency and comparability of financial statements. Lastly, the criteria that all new IFRS should meet to become EU law were deemed appropriate and most stakeholders considered that the process through which IFRS become part of EU law works well.[20] It is estimated that in 2018, on a global scale 27,000 listed companies were using IFRS.[21]

---

15. Regulation (EC) 1606/2002. *See also* the preceding Commission Recommendation *EU Financial Reporting Strategy: The Way Forward*, COM(2000) 359.
16. *Report from the Commission on the operation of Regulation (EC) No. 1606/2002 of 19 Jul. 2002 on the application of international accounting standards*, Brussels, 24 Apr. 2008, COM(2008) 215 final, 4.
17. R.K. Larson & D. L.Street, 'The Roadmap to Global Accounting Convergence', *The CPA Journal* (October 2006).
18. A list is available at: https://ec.europa.eu/info/sites/default/files/ifrs-financial-statements-accounting-rules_en.pdf (accessed January 2022).
19. A list is provided by the consolidated version of Regulation (EC) 1126/2008 (accessible at https://eur-lex.europa.eu/legal-content/EN/TXT/?uri=CELEX%3A02008R1126-20220101).
20. *Evaluation of Regulation (EC) No 1606/2002*, Brussels, 18.6.2015, COM(2015) 301 final.
21. According to www.ifrs.org: https://www.ifrs.org/content/dam/ifrs/around-the-world/adoption/use-of-ifrs-around-the-world-overview-sept-2018.pdf (accessed January 2022).

III GENERAL PRINCIPLES

9.11 The annual financial statements for a public or private limited liability company consist of a balance sheet, a profit and loss account, and notes to the financial statements – together, these documents constitute a 'composite whole' (Article 4(1) of the Accounting Directive). The annual financial statements must give a *true and fair view* (i.e., a reliable and accurate view) of the company's assets, liabilities, financial position and profit or loss (Article 4(3)). If the application of the directive's provisions does not suffice in giving a true and fair view, additional information must be provided (Article 4(3)) and, in exceptional cases, the application of a provision of the directive has to be departed from in order to give a 'true and fair view' (Article 4(4)).

9.12 The Member States must implement provisions into their national law, ensuring that annual financial statements are prepared adhering to the general principles laid down in Article 6 of the directive. This article prescribes the following:

(a) The company is deemed to continue its activities. This principle of a business as a *going concern* implies that the assets may be assessed from the presumption that operating equipment, etc., may continue to be applied for the operation of the company.
(b) The accounting policies and measurement bases shall be applied *consistently* from one financial year to the next.
(c) A *prudence principle* must always be observed. Thus, Article 6(1)(c) of the Directive prescribes, *inter alia*, that recognition and measurement shall be 'on a prudent basis and in particular: only profits made on the balance sheet date may be recognised'. It means that only realized profits may be included, that regard must be given to all liabilities and that all negative value adjustments must be included, irrespective of whether the result of the financial year is a profit or a loss.[22]
According to paragraph 22 of the Preamble of the Accounting Directive, it is inevitable that the recognition and measurement of some items in financial statements are based on estimates, judgments and models, rather than exact depictions. 'This is especially true in the case of provisions, which by their nature are more uncertain than most other items in the balance sheet. Estimates should be based on a prudent judgement of the management of the undertaking and calculated on an objective basis, supplemented by experience of similar transactions and, in some cases, even reports from independent experts. The evidence considered should include any additional evidence provided by events after the balance-sheet date.'

22. *See* ECJ 27 June 1996, C-234/94 (*Tomberger v. Gebrüder von der Wettern GmbH*): it is not contrary to the prudence principle if national law requires from a parent company, whose subsidiary has decided to appropriate profits to its parent, that the profits be entered in the parent company's balance sheet for the financial year in which they were appropriated by the subsidiary, instead of the next financial year in which actual payment has taken place.

(d) The amounts recognized in the balance sheet and the profit and loss account shall be computed on an *accrual basis*. The accrual basis requires recording of transactions in the period in which they actually occur, rather than the period in which the cash flows related to these transactions occur.
(e) The opening balance shall correspond to the closing balance sheet for the preceding financial year.
(f) and (g) The components of asset and liability items shall be valued separately and any set-offs between asset and liability items or between income and expenditure are prohibited. The Directive thus prescribes what is known as the *gross principle*.
(h) Items shall be accounted for and presented having regard to the substance of the transaction or arrangement concerned. This points towards the *substance over form principle*, meaning that items should be accounted for with regard to their commercial reality, rather than their legal form. This may be of importance, for instance, in reporting the consequences of lease contracts. Although the lessor remains the owner of the asset leased, the lease may shift all risks and rewards towards the lessee. In such a case, the les*see* must report on the value of the asset. IFRS 16 specifies how leases must be recognized, measured, presented and disclosed.
(i) The items in the financial statements shall be measured in accordance with the principle of purchase price or production cost.
(j) The requirements regarding recognition, measurement, presentation, disclosure and consolidation need not be complied with when the effect of complying with them is immaterial.

IV CATEGORIES OF UNDERTAKINGS

9.13 The provisions of the Accounting Directive apply, in principle, to large companies (undertakings) and large groups. Member States may permit several exemptions for micro-undertakings, small undertakings, small groups, medium-sized undertakings and medium-sized groups, as defined by the directive. The exemptions allowed for micro-undertakings are substantial, and they are enumerated in Article 36. Exemptions for the small- and medium-sized categories are mentioned throughout the directive, where applicable. For instance, Article 14 summarizes the simplifications that small- and medium-sized undertakings may apply to their balance sheet and profit and loss account. In Article 17, the requirements vary for prescribing what matters must be disclosed in the notes to the annual financial statements for medium-sized undertakings, large undertakings and public-interest entities (these are, *inter alia*, listed companies and credit institutions as defined in Article 2(1)).

9.14 A company is deemed to be a *micro-undertaking* if it meets at least two of the three following criteria on the balance sheet date (Article 3(1)):

- balance sheet total: EUR 350,000;
- net turnover: EUR 700,000;
- average number of employees during the financial year: 10.

A company or group is deemed to be a *small undertaking or small group* if it meets at least two of the three following criteria on the balance sheet date (Article 3(2) and (5)):

- balance sheet total: EUR 4,000,000;
- net turnover: EUR 8,000,000;
- average number of employees during the financial year: 50.

A company or group is deemed to be a *medium-sized undertaking or medium-sized group* if it meets at least two of the three following criteria on the balance sheet date (Article 3(3) and (6)):

- balance sheet total: EUR 20,000,000;
- net turnover: EUR 40,000,000;
- average number of employees during the financial year: 250.

A company or group is deemed to be a *large undertaking or large group* if it meets at least two of the three following criteria on the balance sheet date (Article 3(4)):

- balance sheet total: EUR 20,000,000;
- net turnover: EUR 40,000,000;
- average number of employees during the financial year: 250.

A group, for this purpose, consists of parent and subsidiary undertakings, to be included in a consolidation and which, on a consolidated basis, do not exceed the limits of at least two of the three criteria on the balance sheet date of the parent undertaking.

The figures denoting when a company qualifies for the small size status are revised at five-year intervals (Article 3(13)).

V BALANCE SHEET

9.15 The Accounting Directive contains detailed rules for the drawing up and presentation of the balance sheet in Articles 9–12 and the Annexes. A company has a choice between a presentation in horizontal format (Annex III) or vertical format (Annex IV). The Member States may prescribe one or the other. If a Member State allows both, the choice is left to the individual company (Article 10).

A horizontal balance sheet is characterized by an enumeration of the company's assets, followed by an enumeration of the capital, reserves and liabilities.

A vertical balance sheet will state the assets, followed by the debts and will be concluded by a statement and specification of the equity (capital and reserves). Thus, a balance sheet in a vertical format will 'compute' its way to the equity as an end item emerging from the preceding figures.

Companies must comply with the specifications of the directive when drawing up their statements with regard to both contents and order. However, Members States may permit companies to make even more detailed subdivisions of the items, as long as the prescribed layouts are complied with (Article 9(2)). Some of the items may need to be combined (Article 9(3)). For each item on the balance sheet and profit and loss account, the figures relating to the corresponding item for the preceding financial year must be shown for comparison purposes (Article 9(5)).

9.16 In the following paragraph, the balance sheet according to the Annexes in the directive is briefly discussed. It must be noted, however, that the Accounting Directive offers many options to the Member States and, for that reason, jurisdictions show considerable variations in both presentation and valuation of the balance sheet. In addition, it must be stressed that IFRS differ in many respects from the rules set by the Accounting Directive. In the following paragraphs, differences are addressed by a few remarks in order to provide a general idea regarding the nature of these differences.

9.17 According to Annexes III and IV of the Accounting Directive, the balance sheet must state as assets:

- *Subscribed, but not paid-up capital,* unless the law of the Member State provides that called-up capital must be shown under 'Capital and reserves' (paragraph A of both annexes).
- *Formation expenses* must be listed where national law allows such expenses to be shown as assets (paragraph B). Where the state allows the inclusion of such expenses under 'assets', they must be written off within a maximum period of five years (Article 12(11)).
- Subsequently, the *fixed assets* of the company must be stated (paragraph C). These will generally include assets intended for use on a continuing basis for the company's operation (Article 12(3)). The concept of fixed assets covers intangible assets (e.g., costs of R&D and patents), tangible assets (e.g., land, buildings, equipment) and financial assets (e.g., shares in affiliated companies, investments held as fixed assets).

Under the heading of 'intangible assets', *goodwill* must be shown if such value was acquired against a valuable consideration. The goodwill mentioned is the amount paid as a specified additional price, in excess of the fair value of demonstrable assets at the purchase stage of a business. Where goodwill is capitalized, it must be written off within a maximum period set by the Member State between five and ten years (Article 12(11)). This is one example out of many where IFRS take a different approach by not allowing for this method of write-off. The standard of IFRS 36 requires a yearly review of the activated goodwill in order to determine whether it has suffered any impairment. Only if it has such impairment, may partial or complete write-off of this asset follow.

- The balance sheet's assets must further contain *Current assets* (Annex III, paragraph D: stocks, debtors, investments, cash) and *Prepayments and accrued income* (paragraph E).

An example of an item to be stated under 'current assets' is the debtors of the company, being the (outstanding) claims of the company.

9.18 So far, both layouts specified in Annex III (horizontal layout) and Annex IV (vertical layout) follow the same pattern. The listing, however, subsequently varies according to whether the balance sheet is made in horizontal format or vertical format:

(a) In a horizontal format, an enumeration of capital, reserves and liabilities must follow.
(b) In contrast, the balance sheet in vertical format continues its report of company property matters by stating, under paragraph F, the debts due within one year, followed by the net current assets (paragraph G) and another total in the form of a statement of all the assets, after the deduction of current liabilities (paragraph H), and so on.

9.19 Both Annexes sum up the *capital, reserves and liabilities* that have to be mentioned (albeit positioned differently, depending on the horizontal or vertical layout):

- The amount of subscribed capital must be stated, as well as the premium paid at issue, the revaluation reserve (and other reserves) and the profit or loss for the financial year (paragraph A in the horizontal layout).

  The directive does not mention the concept *of subordinated capital (mezzanine)* (*see* paragraph 5.30). Such capital is a loan and may not be entered under equity, but because it is a debt commitment, it must be reflected under 'debts'. A company may find it useful to enter it as a separate item on the balance sheet and provide more information on the terms of the loan, such as currency, rate of interest, and so forth, in the notes to the accounts.
- Under the next item (B), *Provisions,* the company must state, *inter alia,* pensions and similar obligations and provisions for taxation. In general, provisions are 'liabilities, the nature of which is clearly defined and which at the balance sheet date are either likely to be incurred or certain to be incurred, but uncertain as to their amount or as to the date on which they will arise' (Article 12(12)).

  The IFRS specify detailed rules for the recognition of a provision. According to IAS 37, a provision is a liability of uncertain timing or amount if it is probable that an outflow of cash or other economic resources will be required to settle the provision.[23]
- *Creditors* are the next heading (C) under liabilities and here, like the debtors in the assets part of the balance sheet, several items have to be separately stated, *inter alia,* debenture loans, amounts owed to credit institutions, trade creditors and amounts owed to affiliated undertakings.

23. https://www.ifrs.org/issued-standards/list-of-standards/ias-37-provisions-contingent-liabilities-and-contingent-assets (accessed January 2022).

- Following this, *Accruals and deferred income* (D) are stated, unless national law provides for such items to be shown under *Creditors*.

VI PROFIT AND LOSS ACCOUNT

9.20 EU law also provides options for the layout of the profit and loss account (Article 13). Member States may prescribe one of the options provided, or they may leave the choice to the companies themselves. The choice is between a layout based on the nature of expenses (Annex V) and a layout based on the function of expenses (Annex VI):

(1) The first layout starts with the net turnover and operating income and continues, *inter alia*, with expenses for raw materials, staff and value adjustments, all taken together, in order to close with the profit or loss for the financial year.
(2) The second layout also starts with the net turnover, but continues with entries like cost of sales and administrative expenses and ends, as a matter of course, also with the profit or loss for the financial year.

VII NOTES TO THE ANNUAL FINANCIAL STATEMENTS

9.21 Together with the balance sheet and profit and loss account, the notes to the financial statements make up a composite whole (Article 4(1)). Thus, the notes are an integrated component of the annual financial statements. The content of the notes is partly determined by the items and their order on the balance sheet and the profit and loss account. For example, if application of a provision of the directive is incompatible with the true and fair view requirement, the disapplication of such provision shall be disclosed in the notes, together with an explanation of the reasons for it and of its effect (Article 4(3) and (4)). In the same vein, departures from the prescribed layout of the balance sheet or profit and loss account may be permitted, but the departure and the reasons therefor shall be disclosed in the notes (Article 9(1)). Lastly, value adjustments in respect of financial fixed assets or other fixed assets shall be disclosed separately in the notes if they have not been shown separately in the profit and loss account (Article 12(6)(c)).

9.22 Furthermore, Article 16 lists a large number of matters that must be set out in the notes to the financial statements of *all undertakings*.

Among these matters are:

- the accounting policies adopted;
- detailed information on revaluation of fixed assets and financial instruments;

- the total amount of any financial commitments, guarantees or contingencies that are not included in the balance sheet;
- the amount of advances and credit granted to members of the administrative, managerial and supervisory bodies (note that the extent to which such loans are allowed is a matter of national law).

Article 17 requires additional disclosures for *medium-sized and large undertakings and for public-interest entities* (these are, *inter alia*, listed companies and credit institutions as defined in Article 2(1)).

Among the additional disclosures are:

- more specific information on the valuation of fixed assets and (derivative) financial instruments;
- the name and registered office of each of the undertakings, in which the undertaking, either by itself or through a person acting in his or her own name, but on the undertaking's behalf, holds a participating interest;
- the nature and business purpose of arrangements that are not included in the balance sheet ('off-balance-sheet arrangements'), provided that the risks or benefits arising from such arrangements are material and in so far as the disclosure is necessary for the purposes of assessing the financial position of the undertaking;
- information regarding transactions, which have been entered into with related parties: Members States may permit or require that disclosure is limited, *inter alia*, to transactions that have not been concluded under normal market conditions and/or to intragroup transactions that are exempted from disclosure.

Article 18 requires even more additional disclosures for *large undertakings* and *public-interest entities*.

These additional disclosures concern the following matters:

- the net turnover broken down by categories of activity and into geographical markets;
- the total fees for the financial year charged by each statutory auditor or audit firm for the statutory audit of the annual financial statements, and the total fees charged by each statutory auditor or audit firm for other assurance, tax advisory and for other non-audit services. Members States may allow omission of the additional information on the net turnover if disclosure would be seriously prejudicial to the undertaking (Article 18(2)).

9.22a Article 2(3) of the Accounting Directive refers to IFRS (IAS 24) for the meaning of related parties. These are, *inter alia*, close relatives of key management members if these relatives have or can be expected to have significant influence (via the key management member) on the dealings of the company. Although party relationships are a normal feature of commerce and business, transparency regarding transactions with related parties is deemed necessary because they may be effected on different terms (i.e., not at arm's length) than transactions with unrelated parties. Intragroup transactions are also prone to suboptimal conditions. If, for instance, a subsidiary sells goods to its parent at cost price it might not sell on those terms to another customer. Nevertheless, Member States may exempt intragroup transactions if subsidiaries that are party to the transaction are wholly owned (Article 17(1)(r)).

VIII THE MANAGEMENT REPORT AND REPORT ON PAYMENTS TO GOVERNMENTS

9.23 According to EU law, the management report is not an integral component of the annual financial statements of the company, but rather constitutes a natural 'addendum' to the annual financial statements. Although the statements must be submitted in their entirety to the registration authority and made available to the public, Member States may exempt the management report from mandatory publication, provided that a copy of all or part of the report can be easily obtained upon request (Article 30(1)).

The management report must include, *inter alia*, a fair review of the development and performance of the company's business and its position, including the principal risks and uncertainties it faces. To the extent necessary for an understanding of the company's development, performance or position, both financial and, where appropriate, non-financial key performance indicators must be mentioned. This includes information relating to environmental and employee matters (Article 19(1)).

9.24 Member States may exempt small companies from the obligation of preparing a management report (Article 19(3)). Small- and medium-sized companies may be exempted from the obligation to provide non-financial information on the development and performance of their business (Article 19(4)). Extensive non-financial information must be provided by large undertakings that are public-interest entities and have, on average, more than 500 employees. They must provide a statement concerning the undertaking's development, performance, position and impact of its activity, relating to, as a minimum, environmental, social and employee matters, respect for human rights, anti-corruption and bribery matters. The information has to be provided 'to the extent necessary for an understanding' of these aspects (Article 19a).

9.25 Another category of non-financial information concerns corporate governance. The obligation to include a corporate governance statement in the management report applies to listed companies (Article 20). The statement must include, *inter alia*, a reference to the corporate governance code that the company is subject to, deviations from such a code (where deviation is allowed by national law) and a description of the company's internal control and risk management systems in relation to the financial reporting process. The corporate governance statement must also provide information required by the Takeover Directive, such as restrictions on voting rights, information on the operation of the shareholder meeting and shareholders' rights and information on the composition and operation of the administrative, management and supervisory bodies and their committees. Furthermore, a description of the diversity policy on the company's administrative, management and supervisory bodies must be added. Such policy concerns, for instance, age, gender or educational and professional backgrounds. The objectives and results of that diversity policy must be set out. If no such policy is applied, the statement needs to contain an explanation as to why this is the case (Article 20(1)(g)). The obligation to report on the diversity policy does not apply to small- or medium-sized listed companies (Article 20(5)).

9.26 A separate report on payments to governments must be drawn up and published by large undertakings and public-interest entities active in the extractive industry or the logging of primary forests (Article 41 *et seq.*). The obligation serves to support the implementation of principles set by the Extractive Industries Transparency Initiative[24] (Preamble of the Accounting Directive, paragraphs 44 *et seq.*). The undertakings and entities have to prepare and publish a report on payments of EUR 100,000 or more (on an annual basis) made to governments of countries with rich natural resources. Member States are obligated to ensure that the members of the responsible bodies of an undertaking will, to the best of their knowledge and ability, draw up and publish the report on payments to governments in accordance with the requirements of the Accounting Directive.

IX PUBLICATION OF THE ANNUAL FINANCIAL STATEMENTS

9.27 The members of the administrative, management and supervisory bodies are collectively responsible and liable for drawing up and publishing the annual financial statements. The same collective duties apply in regard to the management report, the corporate governance statement (if provided separately) and the consolidated version of these documents. Where applicable, the content and publication should happen in accordance with the IFRS (IAS), adopted in accordance with Regulation (EC) 1606/2002. Publication must take place within a reasonable period of time, which may not exceed 12 months (Article 30(1)). Member States must further ensure that a breach of these duties may lead to liability of the members of the corporate bodies (Article 33).

9.28 Where the annual financial statements and the management report are published in full, they must be reproduced in the form and with the text on the basis of which the statutory auditor (or an audit firm) has drawn up its opinion. The full text of the audit report must also be published (Article 32(1)). The publication requirements may be alleviated in different ways:

- Member States may make an exemption for the publication of the management report if such a report is easily obtainable upon request (Article 30(1)).
- The audit report shall not be published if the annual financial statements and the management report are published in an abridged form (Article 32(2)).

24. Accessible at: https://eiti.org.

Abridged versions of the annual financial statements are allowed for micro-undertakings, small- and medium-sized undertakings (Article 31; *see also* paragraphs 9.13 - 9.14).

- Member States may exempt general partnerships and limited partnerships from the obligation to publish financial statements. However, this exemption does not fully apply in two situations. First, if all partners having unlimited liability are companies (as mentioned in Annex I of the Accounting Directive) governed by the law of a Member State other than the one whose law governs the partnership and none of these companies publishes the financial statements of the partnership with its own financial statements (Article 30(2)(a)). The second situation that does not allow for exemption of general partnerships occurs when all partners having unlimited liability are companies (undertakings), not governed by the laws of a Member State, but with a legal form comparable to public and private companies and limited partnerships with shares (*see* paragraph 2.47 *et seq.*) (Article 30(2)(b)). [25] If one of those situations occurs, the partnership must provide that the financial statements are available to the public at its head office (Article 30(2)).

X REPORTS TO BE PUBLISHED BY LISTED COMPANIES

9.29 Apart from annual financial statements, listed companies must publish their half-yearly financial reports covering the first six months of the financial year (Article 5 Transparency Directive (*see* paragraph 3.54)). The Transparency Directive applies to listed companies and, in principle, to all other issuers of securities that are admitted to trading on a regulated market in a Member State (Article 1).[26] Technological developments have a bearing on the financial reporting of listed companies. It is envisaged that all annual financial reports must have a single electronic format: the European Single Electronic Format (ESEF). The European Securities and Markets Authority (ESMA) has published standards to specify this format.[27] The power to adopt these standards is delegated to the Commission (Article 4(7)).[28]

9.29a The annual financial report to be made public by listed companies and other issuers of securities must include the audited financial statements, the management

25. Article 30(2)(b)) Accounting Directive actually states: 'a legal form comparable to those referred to in Directive 2009/101/EC.' That directive which sums up the legal forms in Article 1 is repealed, however.
26. Member States may make a few exemptions as described in Articles 1 and 8. Directive 2004/109/EC must be read in conjunction with the amending Directive 2013/50/EU, but a consolidated text is accessible at: https://eur-lex.europa.eu/legal-content/EN/TXT/?uri=CELEX%3A02004L0109-20210318.
27. https://www.esma.europa.eu/policy-activities/corporate-disclosure/european-single-electronic-format (accessed February 2022).
28. Regulation (EU) 2021/337 amended the Transparency Directive in order to grant Member States the option to allow their issuers to apply the ESEF requirements starting from 1 Jan. 2022 instead of 1 Jan. 2021, provided that they notify the European Commission.

report and the statements made by a company's board members[29] that the financial statements, 'to the best of their knowledge', provide a true and fair view. Furthermore, they have to state that the management report includes a fair review of, *inter alia*, the performance of the business of the company and of the principal risks and uncertainties that the company faces (Article 4(2)). The audit report must be disclosed in full, together with the annual financial report (Article 4(4)). If the company is required to prepare consolidated accounts, the audited financial statements must include these accounts (Article 4(3)).

9.29b The half-yearly financial report includes a condensed set of financial statements, an interim management report and statements, similar to the statements by a company's board members,[30] as already mentioned. With regard to the interim management report, the board members have to state that it includes a fair review of, *inter alia*, important events that occurred during the first six months of the financial year and of the principal risks and uncertainties for the remaining six months (Article 5(2) and 5(4)). If the half-yearly report has been audited, the audit report must be reproduced in full (Article 5(5)).

9.29c The Accounting Directive empowers the European Commission to enact delegated regulations in order to deal with more detailed and technical matters (Article 4(6) and (7) and Article 5(6)).[31] In delegated Regulation 2016/1437, the Commission deals with regulatory technical standards on access to regulated information at the EU level. It provides that ESMA will set up a web portal in order to enable end-users to search for regulated information. The portal is called European Electronic Access Point (EEAP) and is accessible through ESMA's website (Article 1 of Regulation 2016/1437).[32] Already in December 2016, ESMA has published a statement setting out the digital format which listed companies must use to report their information. *Inline XBRL* is said to be the most suitable technology for issuers to report their annual financial reports in a single electronic format because it enables both machine and human readability.[33] As pointed out in paragraph 9.29, the obligation for listed companies to use this format (the ESEF) for their annual financial statement applies as of 1 January 2022.

29. Literally: 'the persons responsible within the issuer'. *See also* Article 7 on responsibility and liability.
30. Ibid.
31. Commission Delegated Regulation (EU) 2016/1437, OJ 2016 L 234. *See* further http://ec.europa.eu/finance/company-reporting/legal-framework/index_en.htm#legal-acts-other (accessed May 2017).
32. https://www.esma.europa.eu/document/draft-regulatory-technical-standards-european-electronic-access-point-eeap (accessed February 2022).
33. *Feedback Statement on the Consultation Paper on the Regulatory Technical Standard on the European Single Electronic Format (ESEF)*, 21 Dec. 2016, ESMA/2016/1668.

XI CONSOLIDATED FINANCIAL REPORTS

9.30 The parent undertaking of a group of undertakings is obligated to draw up a consolidated financial statement and a consolidated management report (Article 22 Accounting Directive). The provision presupposes control by the 'parent' of one or more subsidiary undertakings. Control exists if the parent has the majority of the voting rights in the general meeting of the subsidiary or, alternatively, the parent has the power to appoint or dismiss the majority of the members of the administrative, managerial or supervisory bodies of the subsidiary. Hence, the main notion of the group concept of the Accounting Directive is that a group exists when at least one of the corporate bodies or the general meeting of the subsidiary is controlled. It is important to note that EU law contains no mandatory definition of group in company law, with the exception of matters relating to accounting.[34] Member States may therefore set other definitions for group concepts in areas other than in accounting law. These other concepts are further discussed in Chapter 10 of this book.

9.31 The decision-making within the EU on the concept of a group in relation to consolidation of financial statements is described by Diggle and Nobes. They conclude that the first memorandum on consolidation (1970) had several German law features, notably a definition of the group based on central and effective control. The first draft of the Seventh Directive was published in 1976, after the accession of the UK, Ireland and Denmark, in which the Member States together with the Netherlands supported a different accounting method concerning groups in which the power to control was pivotal, whether or not the power was actually utilized. This eventually led to a twofold approach in the Seventh Directive, to be found now in Article 22 of the Accounting Directive. The directive proclaims the parent–subsidiary relationship as the starting point but allows for alternative criteria for the group to be consolidated, among these forms of actual control (Article 22(1)(d)(i) and Article 22(2)).[35]

9.32 The IFRS, of course, also pertain to consolidated reporting. According to IFRS 10, Appendix A, consolidated financial statements are the financial statements of a group, presented as those of a single economic entity. A group is a parent and its subsidiaries. A subsidiary is an entity, including an unincorporated entity such as a partnership, which is controlled by another entity (known as the parent). Interestingly, the IFRS define control not only in terms of power but also requires that the parent is entitled to variable returns and may use its power to affect the amount of returns (IFRS 10.6 and 7).[36]

---

34. Reference is made to paragraph 8.28, the Takeover Directive which uses 'control' with a different meaning. Furthermore, paragraph 8.105, 'control' as defined in the Merger Regulation.
35. G. Diggel & C. Nobes, 'European Rule-Making in Accounting: The Seventh Directive as a Case Study', in *International Accounting and Comparative Financial Reporting: Selected Essays of Christopher Nobes* (Cheltenham (UK)/Northampton (MA, USA): Edward Elgar Publishing, 1999), 177 *et seq.*
36. https://www.ifrs.org/content/dam/ifrs/publications/pdf-standards/english/2021/issued/part-a/ifrs-10-consolidated-financial-statements.pdf (accessed January 2022).

9.33 The parent undertaking and its subsidiaries must be consolidated by the parent undertaking (Article 22 Accounting Directive). The duty to consolidate is, prima facie, not dependent on the legal form of the parent or subsidiary. The main rule prescribes a duty to prepare consolidated financial statements if the parent undertaking is among the undertakings listed in Annex I: a public limited liability company, a private limited company or a public limited partnership (limited partnership with shares) (Article 21 and Article 1). The same applies to undertakings mentioned in Annex II: a partnership or a limited partnership in which all members, having unlimited liability, are public or private limited liability companies from an EU Member State or having a comparable legal form, while being governed by the law of a non-EU state. The duty to prepare consolidated financial statements exists irrespective of where the registered offices of the subsidiaries are situated (Article 22(6)). Thus, a company (undertaking) governed by the law of an EU Member State is bound to consolidate the financial statements of all its subsidiaries, situated within or outside the EU. Member States may exempt a consolidated subsidiary from most of the obligations concerning its own financial statement but only if seven conditions are met. Among these are that the parent undertaking has declared that it guarantees 'the commitments entered into by the subsidiary undertaking' (Article 37). The reason is that consolidated statements aggregate operational and balance sheet figures from a group as if all consolidated undertakings were one single business. The summing up process may obscure information with regard to the individual company's results and balance sheet. Therefore, conditions like the guarantee by the parent serve to protect the interests of creditors and other interested parties.

9.34 Member States have to exempt small groups from the obligation to prepare consolidated financial statements and a consolidated management report. They may allow the same exemption for medium-sized groups, except where an undertaking within the group is a public-interest entity (Article 23(1) and Article 23(2)).[37] Furthermore, an exemption is made for a parent that itself is a subsidiary of another parent governed by the law of a Member State. Such an intermediate-level undertaking is not required to prepare consolidated financial statements on its own and on its subsidiaries' behalf if it is wholly owned by its EU-based parent or at least 90% of it is owned by other shareholders, consenting to exempt the intermediate undertaking from preparing consolidated accounts. The exemption is conditional on, *inter alia*, the intermediate-level company being consolidated by a parent governed by the law of a Member State or even of a non-EU state (Article 23(4) and Article 23(8)). In such case, the non-EU parent, of course, has to draw up the consolidated financial statements in accordance with the Accounting Directive and the IFRS, or in a manner equivalent to these. Article 23(5) offers further options for the Member States regarding the exemption from this requirement for intermediate companies. Listed companies at an intermediate level, however, may not be exempted from the obligation to draw up consolidated financial statements (Article 23(3)).

37. In these provisions, the term 'affiliated undertaking' is used, which is defined as undertaking within a group (Article 2(12)).

A Exclusion of Individual Undertakings

9.35 In certain cases, an undertaking does not need to be included in the consolidation. To start with, an undertaking may be excluded from consolidation if the information necessary to prepare the consolidated financial statements cannot be obtained without disproportionate expense or undue delay. An exemption can further be made if the shares in a company are held exclusively with a view to their subsequent resale. Another case mentioned in Article 23(9) is where severe long-term restrictions substantially hinder the parent company from exercising its rights regarding the management of the undertaking. This exemption reveals that undertakings, although covered by the definition of a subsidiary, cannot always be deemed to be in a group relationship with the parent company. Lastly, undertakings may be excluded on the grounds of immateriality (Article 28(2)(a)). If all subsidiaries are immaterial for compliance with the Accounting Directive, then the parent company is exempted from the obligation to consolidate (Article 23(10)).

9.36 Member States may permit a partly owned subsidiary to only be proportionally included in the consolidated accounts (Article 26). This proportional inclusion - which is a practical device if joint ventures must be included in the annual accounts - also implies that the undertakings holding the rest of the shares in the subsidiary are not included in the consolidation.

B Contents of Consolidated Financial Statements

9.37 The methods that must be applied when drawing up consolidated financial statements are, to a considerable extent, built upon the provisions for the financial statements of the single undertaking. Article 24 starts by providing that Chapters 2 and 3 of the Accounting Directive 'shall apply in respect of consolidated financial statements, taking into account the essential adjustments resulting from the particular characteristics of consolidated financial statements as compared to annual financial statements'. As a consequence, consolidated financial statements consist of a consolidated balance sheet and consolidated profit and loss account, as well as notes to the financial statements, and these documents constitute a composite whole. The consolidated financial statements must give a true and fair view as described in Article 4(3). As previously explained for the annual financial statements, the requirement of a true and fair view is the overriding principle. It can lead to the necessity of providing further information and, if certain provisions in the directive are incompatible with the true and fair view principle, the relevant provision must be departed from. The departure must be disclosed and explained in the notes (Article 4(4)).

9.38 When an undertaking is included in the consolidation, all its assets and liabilities are incorporated in full in the consolidated balance sheet, except, of course, where proportional consolidation is allowed (Article 24(2)). The income and expenditure of all the undertakings included in the consolidation must also be incorporated in full in the consolidated profit and loss account (Article 24(5)). Because the parent must necessarily have entered the value of its share in the capital of a subsidiary, the amount thus entered must be deducted in connection with the consolidation. As Article 24(3) states: 'The book values of shares in the capital of undertakings included in a consolidation shall be set off against the proportion which they represent of the capital and reserves of those undertakings.' Differences arising from such set-offs must be entered in the consolidated balance sheet as a separate item (Article 24(3)(a)). Where the amount is positive, it is to be shown as 'goodwill' in the consolidated balance sheet (Article 24(3)(c)).

9.39 The consolidated financial statements must show the assets, liabilities, financial positions and profits or losses of the consolidated undertakings as if they were a single undertaking (Article 24(7)). This is the key provision in the Accounting Directive. As regards the balance sheet, it implies that mutual claims and debts between the companies have to be eliminated. For the profit and loss account, it means that expenses and income deriving from transactions between the consolidated undertakings are excluded. The same applies to profits or losses deriving from these transactions where they are included in the book value of assets.

9.40 In principle, the consolidated financial statements must be drawn up on the same date as the annual financial statements of the parent company, but exemptions may be allowed (Article 24(8)). The principle of aiming at the same financial year for all undertakings in a group is also present in the tax law of several Member States to avoid time displacements. In accounting law, the fear is usually that profits are brought forward, whereas, in tax law, the fear is for profits to be deferred – in both instances, by exploiting the fact that one company closes its financial year while other companies in the group are still in the middle of their financial year.

9.41 In order to satisfy the key provision of Article 24 of the Accounting Directive that consolidated financial statements must present the undertakings as a single undertaking; the assets and liabilities in the various undertakings must be evaluated using uniform methods (Article 24(10)). However, undertakings included in the consolidation may have varying value assessment methods. To offset this, such assets and liabilities must be revalued by applying the methods used at the consolidation (Article 24(12)).

9.42 Participating interests in associated undertakings, where 20% or more of the voting rights are controlled (Article 2(13)) which are not included in the consolidation, should, as a main rule, be shown as a separate item in the consolidated balance sheet. How the value of such participation is to be calculated is prescribed by Article 27.

9.43 The notes to the consolidated financial statements are subject to the same provisions as the annual financial statements, taking essential adjustments resulting from the characteristics of consolidated financial statements into account. An example is that, in disclosing related-party transactions, transactions between related parties included in the consolidation may not be included (Article 28).

9.44 The requirements with respect to the consolidated management report are basically the same as the requirements for the management report of a single undertaking. Essential adjustments may, of course, result from the characteristics of consolidated financial statements, which facilitate the assessment of the position of consolidated undertakings as a whole (Article 29).

9.45 The obligation to disclose non-financial information of the group is, again, basically the same as prescribed for single undertakings (*see* paragraphs 9.24–9.26). Therefore, a corporate governance statement for the group taken as a whole is required (Article 29 Accounting Directive). For public-interest entities that are parent undertakings of a large group with more than 500 employees, more specific non-financial information is required (Article 29a). Furthermore, parents that are public-interest entities or large undertakings also have to draw up a report on a consolidated basis concerning payments to governments (Article 44).

XII AUDIT

9.46 The annual financial statements and the consolidated financial statements must be audited, and the auditor must verify that the (consolidated) management report is consistent with the consolidated financial statements (Article 34). What the audit report must include is set out in Article 28 of Directive 2014/56/EU. There is no duty of having the consolidated accounts audited by the same person who audits the parent's own annual accounts, though this will often be a more practical solution.

CHAPTER 10
Groups

I INTRODUCTION

10.01 The emphasis in the preceding chapters of this book was on the company as an independent legal entity. However, many businesses form part of a group instead of operating as independent companies.[1] Company groups are therefore an important part of corporate reality in today's economy.[2] One can think of Nestle, Unilever or Shell to name just a few examples of well-known group structures. Groups surface in all forms and sizes: from the multinationals just mentioned to smaller locally run businesses that are divided over a variety of legal entities. Listed companies often head a group of subsidiaries but also medium-sized and even small businesses can operate in a group structure. To the outside world, the group often makes use of the same brand name and reputation. Apart from the group's external image, there are several other features of interconnectedness between the companies, notably financial arrangements and intragroup business transactions. Each group member constitutes a separate legal entity with its own duties and responsibilities and its own corporate bodies. This creates a disparity between economic and legal reality. The combination of legal independence of each company and economic dependence between the companies within the group leads to several questions regarding the need for group management and at the same time stakeholder protection.

10.02 The regulation of company groups and how these issues of group management and stakeholder protection are dealt with differs among jurisdictions. Some countries have specific legal rules dedicated to company groups, whereas other countries leave

1. K.J. Hopt, 'Groups of Companies', in J.N. Gordon & W.G. Ringe (eds), *The Oxford Handbook of Corporate Law and Governance* (Oxford University Press, 2018), 603.
2. According to the Reflection Group on the Future of EU Company Law in 2011, they have become 'the prevailing form of European large-sized enterprises'. *See* Report of the Reflection Group on the Future of EU Company Law, Brussels 5 Apr. 2011, 59.

the group phenomenon largely unregulated. Although a uniform European approach to company groups is lacking, regulation and specific provisions with regard to company groups do surface in specific areas of the law such as accounting, competition law, sector-specific laws such as those applicable to banking and financial institutions, labour law and the laws and regulations concerning the role of works councils.[3]

10.03 This chapter explores how the group phenomenon is dealt with in company law. We first discuss the concept of a group, different types of group structures and the reasons for setting up a group structure. Subsequently, we address the problems that may arise as a result of the fact that the group structure creates a disparity between economic and legal reality. Furthermore, we describe the different approaches to regulating company groups. The chapter proceeds with a section on European Union (EU) group law. Although there is no common EU approach to regulating company groups, European legislators have pursued a piecemeal approach to regulating company groups, which is typical for most of the Member States as well. The lack of harmonization, nevertheless, still leads to specific problems for groups in a cross-border context which is also highlighted in this chapter. Lastly, several national approaches to company groups are elaborated on.

II THE CONCEPT OF A GROUP

10.04 There are many definitions of what constitutes a company group. In general, a group is formed when one company incorporates another company and becomes the sole or majority shareholder of that other company or when one company acquires the majority of the shares in, or a dominant control over, another company. The terms company group and subsidiary are often used to describe a situation in which one company has the ability to dominate the decision-making of the other.

10.05 There is not one harmonized definition of what constitutes a group within the EU. However, the Accounting Directive can be used as a starting point when talking about the concept of a group. It classifies several relationships between interconnected companies and contains definitions of 'parent' and 'subsidiary undertaking'. The directive requires companies to consolidate their annual accounts in situations where actual control is or can be exercised by the parent company or the management of the parent company over its subsidiaries.[4] Article 22 of the directive requires an undertaking to draw up consolidated financial statements if that undertaking:[5]

3. A. Cahn & D.C. Donald, *Comparative Company Law* (Oxford: Oxford University Press, 2018), 831–832.
4. Parent companies of micro-groups and small groups do not have to draw up consolidated financial statements and a consolidated management report. Member States have the option to exempt also the parent companies of medium-sized groups (Article 23(1) and (2) of Directive 2013/34/EU).
5. Directive 2013/34/EU.

> (a) has a majority of the shareholders' or members' voting rights in another undertaking (...); (b) has the right to appoint or remove a majority of the members of the administrative, management or supervisory body of another undertaking (...) and is at the same time a shareholder in or member of that undertaking; (c) has the right to exercise a dominant influence over an undertaking (...) of which it is a shareholder or member, pursuant to a contract entered into with that undertaking or to a provision in its memorandum or articles of association (...). A Member State need not prescribe that a parent undertaking must be a shareholder in or member of its subsidiary undertaking (...).

10.06 The concept of a group under the Accounting Directive does not necessarily coincide with the concepts of a group used in other national and EU legislation. Nevertheless, definitions of the concept used in other areas of the law often resemble the two categories that also surface in the provision of the Accounting Directive mentioned above: they either reflect the legal approach, in which the legal power to control is the central element or they are based on the economic approach, according to which a group exists from the moment an undertaking actually exercises a dominant influence over another (actual control).[6] In terms of the first category, a group is deemed to exist irrespective of whether the power to control is actually used. Under the second category, actual control is the determining factor and that control can emerge from a dominant shareholding: 51 % or more of the voting rights or special provisions in the articles of association providing the parent company far-reaching rights at subsidiary level. Control can also emerge from 'contractual and market-based linkages': such as cooperation agreements or control contracts.[7] Legal definitions of company groups can also include a combination of both categories as is reflected in the provision of the Accounting Directive above.

10.07 Member States often prescribe that control is presumed to exist where criteria of a legal nature are met.[8] These legal criteria correspond largely with those mentioned in the Accounting Directive: notably, the parent has the majority of the voting rights or the right to appoint or remove a majority of the members of the corporate bodies of the subsidiary or has the majority of the voting rights due to an agreement with other shareholders.[9] Although definitions of company groups differ among the Member States, it is nevertheless quite likely that most economically associated enterprises that qualify as parent, subsidiary or group in one Member State, also fall within a similar description in another Member State.

---

6. K.J. Hopt, *supra* n. 1, at 604.
7. This distinction was taken from the Report of the Reflection Group on the Future of EU Company Law, April 2011, 72.
8. Corresponding with Article 22 of the Accounting Directive: Article L233-16 Commercial Code (France), Section 290(1) HGB (Germany); Article 2:406 Dutch Civil Code (Netherlands); Section 1162 of Companies Act 2006 (UK).
9. European Commission, *Implementation of the Seventh Directive in EU Member States Summary of findings from a study on the implementation of Seventh Directive 83/349/EEC in the Member States of the European Union, as per* 1 Jan. 1998 http://ec.europa.eu/internal_market/accounting/docs/studies/1998-seventh-dir_en.pdf.

10.08 The definitions of groups and the concept of parent–subsidiary relationships are not only used in relation to accounting but also surface in other areas of the law, such as company law, tax law, etc. The Dutch Civil Code, for example, defines a 'group' and what constitutes a subsidiary in a way that resembles the two categories reflected in the Accounting Directive as explained above. That definition is subsequently used in several provisions to extend prohibitions normally applicable to single entities also to company groups. This is, for example, the case in the Netherlands with regard to the prohibition of a company from acquiring its own shares. This prohibition is extended to the acquisition of shares in the parent company by its subsidiary.[10] Member States also make use of other group-related concepts, besides the definition of a parent and a subsidiary. The UK Companies Act, for example, contains a definition of a 'holding company'.[11] This definition is used, *inter alia,* in the regulation of transactions involving directors and the provisions containing capital requirements.[12] The concept is similar to that of the parent company which is also defined in the Companies Act, except for the factor of dominant influence, and management on a unified basis.[13] Dutch company law also introduces other group-related concepts beyond those mentioned above. It, for example, makes a distinction between a 'dependent company' and a 'subsidiary company'.[14] A company is regarded as 'dependent' if 50% or more of the issued capital is held by another company regardless of whether or not this represents also 50% of the votes. A company is deemed to be a subsidiary if another company holds more than 50% of such capital, provided that such capital holding corresponds proportionally to the voting rights. Although the two concepts are different, in practice most dependent companies will also fall under the definition of subsidiary.

The examples mentioned above illustrate that when it comes to defining company groups and the relationship between interdependent companies, it should be kept in mind that several definitions are used and that these definitions adapt the ambit of the rule in which the definition is used to the specific needs of that particular legal field.[15] Group-related concepts used in, for example, tax law, labour law, company law, etc., can therefore differ from each other.

10. Article 2:98d Dutch Civil Code.
11. Section 1159(1)(a)-(c) UK Companies Act 2006. With regard to these definitions *see* R. Valsan, 'National Report on the United Kingdom', in R.M. Manovil (ed.), *Groups of Companies, A Comparative Law Overview* (Springer, 2020), 631.
12. Sections 1159, 41 and 136 UK Companies Act 2006.
13. Section 1162 UK Companies Act 2006.
14. The dependent company is defined by Articles 2:152 and 2:262 Dutch Civil Code. These provisions serve exclusively for the application of the Dutch 'structure regime', with a mandatory supervisory board or non-executives in case of a one tier-board, for sizeable companies. The definition of subsidiary is laid down in Article 2:24a Dutch Civil Code.
15. E. Wymeersch (ed.) with a foreword by G.E. Fitchew, *Groups of Companies in the EEC: A Survey Report to the European Commission on the Law Relating to Corporate Groups in Various Member States* (Berlin/New York: Walter de Gruyter, 1993).

III TYPES OF GROUP STRUCTURE

10.09 Company groups can take many different forms. The most straightforward group model is one where the parent company holds all or a majority of the shares in one or more subsidiaries. In turn, these subsidiaries may also have one or more subsidiaries, and so on. The example just mentioned is an example of a vertical group model with a single parent company at the top. Horizontal groups may also occur in practice, with more than one parent company at the top. The latter type of group structure was, for example, previously used by Unilever and Eurotunnel.[16]

10.10 A specific type of vertical group is the pyramid structure. A pyramid exists when there are several layers of companies within the group, and the ultimate control is based on a small total investment thanks to the use of minority shareholders at various layers within the group.[17] This is, for example, the case where only a minority (49%) of the shares of a family-owned parent company A are listed. If company A then forms a subsidiary B, of which, again, a minority of the shares (49%) are listed, the family will retain control, albeit indirectly, over the operations of B and its subsidiaries, notwithstanding the fact that investment by third parties has doubled.[18] The pyramid structure therefore gives the ultimate owner a rather large level of control without having to provide the full share capital also at subsidiary or sub-subsidiary levels. These pyramid structures have raised concerns in the past due to the lack of transparency for outside investors and the fact that they make the acquisition of control in the companies expensive. They may also pose problems for minority shareholders who in the end furnish the majority of the risk-bearing capital at the various group levels but do not have the power to exercise control.[19]

10.11 Group structures can furthermore differ in terms of the legal entities that form part of the group. These legal entities can be incorporated in the same jurisdiction or in different jurisdictions. A parent company in the United States (US) can, for example, have subsidiaries in European countries. Groups can furthermore consist not only of capital companies but also of partnerships or of foundations and associations.[20] Also, the European Economic Interest Grouping (EEIG) or the *Societas Europaea* (SE) can be used in group structures.

---

16. In such case, the parent companies are not dependent on one another but associated on an equal footing and mostly seated in different countries. *See* on such 'bi-national horizontal groups', K. Byttebier & A. Verroken, *Structuring International Cooperation Between Enterprises* (London: Graham & Trotman, 1995).
17. Modernising Company Law and Enhancing Corporate Governance in the European Union – A Plan to Move Forward (Brussels, 21 May 2003), COM(2003) 284 final (Company Law Action Plan 2003), 19.
18. This basically is the ownership structure of Heineken: http://www.theheinekencompany.com /investors/governance/ownership-structure (with diagram).
19. *See* with regard to these risks posed by pyramid structures: High Level Group of Company Law Experts, Report on a Modern Regulatory Framework for Company Law in Europe, Brussels 4 Nov. 2002, 39.
20. This is for example the case in the Netherlands and Germany.

10.12 Lastly, group structures can differ in terms of the intensity of the interconnectedness between the group members and how the group is governed. Many groups have a multi-layered governance structure with sub-holdings and only indirect control by the parent company. The following quote from Lord Briggs in *Vedanta Resources plc v Lungow*[21] is illustrative:

> There is no limit to the models of management and control which may be put in place within a multinational group of companies. At one end, the parent may be no more than a passive investor in separate businesses carried out by its various direct and indirect subsidiaries. At the other extreme, the parent may carry out a thoroughgoing vertical reorganisation of the group's business so that they are, in management terms, carried on as if they were a single commercial undertaking.

In other words, company groups can take all kinds of forms and sizes varying from situations in which the parent company takes a rather passive position to groups with a strong operational and/or financial interconnectedness where the policies that are devised at parent company level, merely have to be implemented at subsidiary level.[22]

IV REASONS FOR SETTING UP A GROUP

10.13 There can be several reasons for forming a group. They can be of an economic or organizational nature or they arise from the aim of spreading entrepreneurial risks or optimizing taxation.[23] In practice, it is often a combination of these motives that leads to a certain group structure.

10.14 A driving force behind forming a group structure is to spread risk.[24] Each company within the group is a separate legal entity with its own assets and liabilities. Shareholders are, in principle, not liable for the debts of the company due to the principle of limited liability. Although this principle was originally designed to encourage investments by individuals in single companies, it is also widely used in company groups.[25] It enables business activities to be isolated in separate limited liability companies. Consequently, financial difficulties or business misfortunes within one of the group members will not automatically affect the rest of the group.

10.15 Forming a group can also be a consequence of a desire to expand a business enterprise and enter new markets. Apart from what is known as organic growth, a company can expand its market share by acquiring a competing company or a company that is a supplier or a customer of its business. When the acquisition is done

21. *Vedanta Resources plc v Lungowe* [2019] 2 WLR 1051 at [51].
22. *See* for different types of groups K.J. Hopt, *supra* n. 1, at 603–605.
23. M. Olaerts, 'Concerndilemma's: laveren tussen de economische werkelijkheid en de juridische benadering van het Concern', in Ph.W. Schreurs et al. (eds), *De curator en het concern*, Insolad Bundel (Deventer: Wolters Kluwer, 2017), 8.
24. About limited liability *see* S.M. Bainbridge & M. T. Henderson, *Limited Liability. A Legal and Economic Analysis* (Edward Elgar Cheltenham/Northampton, 2016).
25. A. Cahn & D.C. Donald, *supra* n. 3, at 828.

by means of a stock purchase, the acquiring company becomes (depending on the number of shares acquired) a parent company of the acquired company. The desire to grow can also entail a territorial expansion facilitating access to a foreign market. Such expansion can, *inter alia*, be realized by taking over a company incorporated in that specific market.[26] A reason for not merging a newly acquired company with the acquiring company can be to enable the parent company to concentrate on setting out the general group policy while the day-to-day business is organized at subsidiary level. It allows the directors of the subsidiary to remain in place after the acquisition.[27] It is also possible that the acquiring company wants to make use of the value, brand and goodwill that was built up by the acquired company without shifting the ownership of these assets.[28]

10.16 Another reason to form a group can be to realize efficiency gains and economies of scale by combining several companies under a central group policy.[29] Group financing can serve as a prime example of this. The possibility to finance the group as a whole instead of financing separate companies within the group makes company groups attractive. In such consolidated financing systems, the assets of the group are pooled in order to achieve larger credit facilities than would normally be granted to the companies separately. Asset pooling also allows for financial means to be invested in the part of the business where it is most needed. The legal entities within the group with a solid financial perspective can post a guarantee or declare themselves jointly and severally liable for the other parts of the group. Intragroup loans furthermore allow the financial means available within the various parts of the group to be used where they are most needed.[30] The siphoning of financial means within the group may, of course, pose a potential threat to creditors and minority shareholders. This problem has caught the attention of the European legislature and has led to regulation regarding related-party transactions.[31]

V GOVERNANCE ISSUES AND RISKS OF GROUP STRUCTURES

10.17 Company groups can lead to several specific group-related 'risks' that require the attention of the legislature and the judiciary. Two types of group-related issues/risks can be distinguished: the first has to do with the internal governance of the group, while the second relates to the need for additional protection of stakeholders, more specifically: the voluntary and involuntary creditors and employees at various

26. *Ibid.*, 830. This obviously depends on the number of shares being acquired.
27. *Ibid.*
28. *Ibid.*
29. K. E. Sorensen, 'The legal position of parent companies: a top-down focus on group governance', *Nordic & European Company Law LSN Research Paper Series* (19-5), 3–4.
30. M. Olaerts, *supra* n. 23, at 9.
31. Directive (EU) 2017/828.

group levels, minority shareholders at subsidiary level and shareholders at parent company level.[32]

10.18 Governance issues emerge in company groups due to the fact that each company within the group is a separate legal entity with its own board of directors and general meeting while at the same time the company at the top of the group in most cases wishes to exercise control over the other companies and set out a group policy.[33] The parent company has the ultimate power to control as it can dismiss the board of directors at subsidiary level. Directors at subsidiary level may find themselves in a difficult dilemma when the interest of the group does not concur with the interest of their own (subsidiary) company. [34] A parent company may, for example as part of the group policy, require a subsidiary to declare itself jointly and severally liable for the financing of the entire group which may be in the interest of the group but, depending on the circumstances, not necessarily in the interest of the subsidiary. On the one hand, the directors at subsidiary level in that case run the risk of being dismissed if they do not act in accordance with the group policy. On the other hand, directors' liability may be looming if the group policy is detrimental to the subsidiary or its stakeholders.

10.19 The second issue mentioned above is the risk groups of companies may represent to the stakeholders of the companies involved. One of these stakeholders is the creditor. As mentioned above, a subsidiary can operate in the group interest which does not necessarily coincide with its own company interest. The proceeds gained by one subsidiary may, for example, be used to finance the losses of another subsidiary, which creates a risk for creditors of the first subsidiary. It should be pointed out that not just the creditors who voluntarily entered into a transaction with a company that is part of the group may be affected. The position of what is known as involuntary creditors should not be overlooked. These are creditors who did not enter into a contract with the company but involuntarily become its counterpart, such as tort creditors.[35] One can think of third parties that are harmed or whose interests are otherwise prejudiced by the activities of one or more companies of the group. When these third parties try to recover their losses or damages from other group companies or the group as a whole, claims are often denied due to the fact that the harmful activity is attributable to a specific company within the group but not to the group as a whole. Limited liability

32. *See* with regard to these issues and the different approaches in various legal systems R.M. Manovil, 'Groups of Companies: les groups de sociétés', in R.M. Manovil (ed.), *supra* n. 11, at 7 *et seq*.
33. *See* about these governance issues also M. Olaerts, *supra* n. 23.
34. P. Blumberg, 'The Transformation of Modern Corporation Law: The Law of Corporate Groups', *Connecticut Law Review* 37, no. 3 (2005), Faculty Articles and Papers. 192; C. Paz-Ares, in *Curso de derecho mercantil I*, Capitulo 55: Rodrigo Uría & Aurelio Menéndez (eds), *Uniones de empresas y grupos de sociedades* (Madrid: Civitors, 2006); J.E. Antunes, *Liability of Corporate Groups* (Deventer/Boston: Kluwer Law and Taxation Publishers, 1994); S.M. Bartman, 'From Autonomy of Interests to Concurrence of Interests in Dutch Group Company Law', *European Company Law* 4, no. 5 (October 2007): 207–210.
35. *See* about this category H. Hansmann & R. Kraakman, 'Towards Unlimited Liability for Corporate Torts', *Yale L.J.*100, no. 7 (1991): 1879–1934.

protects other group members against claims from both voluntary and involuntary creditors.[36]

10.20 Another group of stakeholders whose position requires attention is the shareholders at both parent company and subsidiary levels. To start with the latter, as was mentioned above when describing pyramid structures, groups may have minority shareholders at subsidiary level. As with all minority shareholder positions, they run the risk of being disadvantaged by the decisions of the majority shareholder. This can be problematic in any company, but minority shareholders of a subsidiary run a greater risk because of the supremacy of the group policy.

10.21 With regard to the shareholders of a parent company, their interest may be at stake since they do not have a direct influence on the business activities as all or most of the business of the group is generally not carried on by the parent company but by its subsidiaries and/or sub-subsidiaries. Consequently, the shareholders control a board that is not directly accountable for the business activities of the group but instead for the control of the subsidiaries. One way to mitigate this risk for the shareholders of the parent company is by requiring parent companies to report in their corporate governance statement on the main features of the internal controls and risk management systems for the consolidated undertakings, with those undertakings 'taken as a whole' (Article 29(2)(b), Directive 2013/34/EU).[37] It is obvious that this reporting obligation forces parent companies to install group-wide control mechanisms, reinforcing the position of the board and thereby of the shareholders of the parent company. However, company law, still being based on the view that a company is a single and *independent* legal entity, may be an obstacle to effectuating such a rigid control regime.

10.22 The last group of stakeholders whose interests require attention is the employees. Decisions taken at parent company level may affect the interests of employees located at other levels within the group. As mentioned in Chapter 7, employees can be protected by means of information, consultation and participation rights. In company groups, decisions may be taken at a level different from the level where the workers are employed, and they may therefore lack information and or consultation rights regarding issues that affect them. This issue was addressed at the EU level as discussed further in paragraph 10.39. In cross-border company groups, national rules on participation rights may also lead to diverging positions for employees, depending on where within the group they are employed as can be seen in the *Erzberger* case[38] (*see* paragraph 7.44).

36. S.M. Bainbridge & M. T. Henderson, *supra* n. 24.
37. This provision was inserted in 2006 in the Accounting Directive by the amending Directive 2006/46/EC.
38. Case C-566/15 (*Erzberger*) (2017).

VI REGULATORY APPROACHES TO COMPANY GROUPS

10.23 The previous sections described the variety of group relationships and group structures and highlighted the governance issues and risks inherent to these company groups. The law deals with these issues and risks in many different ways. The approach chosen depends on the jurisdiction and on the type of law involved in regulating groups, which is not only company law but also insolvency law, competition law, labour law, tax law, etc. These areas of the law apply to companies, other legal entities, and, therefore, also groups of companies.[39]

10.24 National legislators have approached group-specific issues in a variety of ways. Some countries have a specific legal system for groups in place.[40] Germany, Portugal, the Czech Republic, Hungary, Slovenia and Croatia serve as examples of this approach.[41] Other countries instead opted for partial regulation of group-related issues. Italy, for example, regulates certain aspects of company groups without putting a comprehensive system in place. Unlike Germany, Italian law does not provide for contractually based groups. It does, however, contain rules on de facto groups that are comparable to the German system.[42] France is a schoolbook example of a country that allows for a certain level of group governance through the recognition of the group interest by what is generally known as the Rozenblum doctrine (developed in case law, *see* paragraph 10.62). Neither the Netherlands nor the UK has a codified law of groups. They instead have a piecemeal approach to dealing with certain aspects of company groups in company law while case law also, to a certain extent, takes the group phenomenon into account. How national laws deal with group-related issues is further discussed in paragraph 10.49 *et seq.*

10.25 As mentioned earlier, not only company law but also other areas of law may have to deal with company groups. One way to approach this is to, not use the entity approach as point of departure as is done in many national company laws, but instead focus on the enterprise. The application of certain type of rules may require to focus on the enterprise which is carried on by the group as a whole instead of the separate legal entities. In those cases an enterprise approach can be used instead of an entity approach. The enterprise approach looks at the business enterprise as a whole instead of its separate legal components.[43] Examples of this approach can be found in labour law and tax law. At the EU level, the concept is, *inter alia*, used in the area of competition law. Article 101 Treaty on the Functioning of the European Union (TFEU) prohibits agreements between undertakings that, in short, prevent, restrict or distort competition. The connecting factor to this prohibition is the 'undertaking.' The term

39. R.M. Manovil, 'Groups of Companies: les groups de sociétés', in R.M. Manovil (ed.), *supra* n. 11, at 29–33.
40. *Ibid.*, 21 *et seq.*
41. EMCA, Chapter 15, 371; A. Vicari, *European Company Law* (Berlin/Boston: De Gruyter 2021), 169.
42. A. Vicari, *supra* n. 41, at 175.
43. P. Blumberg, *supra* n. 34, at 605.

'undertaking' must be understood as 'designating an economic unit, even if, in law, that economic unit consists of several persons'.[44] In its *Akzo Nobel* decision, the CJEU ruled that if a parent company owns 100% of the shares in a subsidiary, the rebuttable presumption is raised that the parent company exercised a decisive influence over its subsidiary's conduct and that therefore the subsidiary's competition law infringement is attributable to the parent company.[45]

10.26 There are also other regulations that take the economic reality of the group as the point of departure, such as the European Works Council (EWC) Directive.[46] The preamble of the directive recognizes that company groups may operate across borders and that as an effect of this:[47]

> Procedures for informing and consulting employees as embodied in legislation or practice in the Member States are often not geared to the transnational structure of the entity which takes the decisions affecting those employees. This may lead to the unequal treatment of employees affected by decisions within one and the same undertaking or group of undertakings.

The directive therefore strives to put procedures in place to ensure that the employees of these undertakings are properly informed and consulted when decisions that affect them are taken in a Member State or in an entity other than that in which they are employed.[48] Therefore, the separate legal entities are partly disregarded and the group (or rather the Community-scale group of undertakings) has to ensure that the information and consultation rights of employees are safeguarded.

10.27 Another example of the enterprise approach is provided by the OECD Guidelines for Multinational Enterprises. The OECD has enacted guidelines to prevent abuses, such as human rights violations and environmental damage. These guidelines are directed at all entities within the group and represent standards of behaviour supplemental to applicable national and international law.[49] This approach is also used by national legislators in order to prevent, for example, human rights abuses. The French 'Devoir de Vigilance' requires companies to adopt a surveillance plan to prevent violations of human rights and fundamental freedoms at company and at subsidiary level as well as within the supply chain.[50] Covering all entities within a group, the French 'Devoir de Vigilance' in fact covers the enterprise as a whole. At the EU level, the proposed Directive on Corporate Sustainability Due Diligence follows this approach. Companies within the scope of the directive will have a duty to carry out

---

44. Case C-97/08 (*Akzo Nobel*) (2009), paragraph 55, preceded by Case C-217/05 *(Confederación Española de Empresarios de Estaciones de Servicio)*, paragraph 40 and Case 170/83 (*Hydrotherm)*, paragraph 11.
45. Case C-97/08 (*Akzo Nobel*) (2009). Furthermore, group companies is a starting point for many rules set by the Insolvency Regulation (EU) 2015/848.
46. Directive 2009/38/EC.
47. Recital 11 of preamble of Directive 2009/38/EC.
48. Recital 12 of preamble of Directive 2009/38/EC.
49. The OECD Guidelines for Multinational Enterprises, 2011 edition. Accessible at www.oecd.org.
50. *LOI n° 2017-399 du 27 mars 2017 relative au devoir de vigilance des sociétés mères et des entreprises donneuses d'ordre.*

human rights and environmental due diligence with regard to their own operations, those of their subsidiaries and of their value chains.[51] In other words, the parent company has to set out a group-wide due diligence strategy. [52]

VII EU GROUP LAW

10.28 As mentioned in the introduction of this chapter, there is no harmonized group law at the EU level. Nevertheless, the topic of company groups did attract the European Commission's interest as a possible subject for harmonization and regulation a long time ago. Over the years many formal and informal committees have studied the subject matter and made proposals for potential harmonization. So far none of these proposals has been adopted. The Commission has, however, addressed several issues relating to company groups over the years, and therefore the concept of group does emerge in several parts of EU regulation despite there not being one overarching approach. In the following section, we first discuss the various attempts to come to an overarching harmonization of company groups, after which we examine the issues related to group law which have been harmonized. We also point out in which parts of EU law company groups mainly surface.

A Attempts at Harmonization

10.29 Articles dealing with group relationships were included in the original draft statute for the European company (1970). In 1985, the Commission published a preliminary draft Ninth Directive on the Law of Groups. Support, however, was lukewarm in most Member States, and the Commission withdrew the group-related provisions from the *Societas Europaea* (SE) Statute (*see* paragraphs 4.13 and 4.14). In 1990, even before its formal submission to the Council of Ministers, the proposal for the Ninth Directive was also withdrawn (*see* paragraph 3.19a). In the 1998 Forum Europaeum Konzernrecht, a group of law professors conducted and presented another study containing a proposal for a directive on European group law.[53] The proposal initiated by the Forum Europaeum Konzernrecht, however, never led to a directive being adopted.

10.30 The next committee to advise on group law was the High Level Group of Company Law Experts, installed by the Commission in 2001 for the purpose of designing a modern regulatory framework for company law. The High Level Group of Company Law experts took the view that the enactment of an autonomous body of law,

---

51. Article 6 of the Proposal for a Directive on Corporate Sustainability Due Diligence and amending Directive (EU) 2019/1937COM (2022) 71 final.
52. Article 5 of the proposed directive.
53. Forum Europaeum Konzernrecht, 'Konzernrecht für Europa', *ZGR* 4 (1998): 672–772. In 2000, a version was published in English: 'Corporate Group Law for Europe', Forum Europaeum Konzernrecht, Stockholm (Corporate Governance Forum) 2000 and also in the *European Business Organization Law Review* (EBOR) I (2000): 165–264.

specifically dealing with groups, was not advisable at the EU level. In other words, a new attempt to bring about the Ninth Company Law Directive on group relationships was not recommended. Instead, they suggested the introduction of rules to address specific issues that are characteristic to company groups rather than an overall harmonization. These issues concerned: (i) the transparency of a group's structure and relationships; (ii) the conflicts between the interests of the group and its parts; and (iii) the special problems arising from 'pyramid structures'.[54] The Commission accepted the recommendations in its 2003 Company Law Action Plan.[55]

10.31 In the wake of the 2003 Company Law Action Plan, several formal and informal expert groups were installed. Their reports drew attention to several recurring issues in company groups. In 2010, the 'Reflection Group on the Future of EU Company Law', for example, again dealt with the topic at the EU level. The results were published in its 2011 report,[56] which deals with three measures in relation to groups. Several issues which were already signalled in earlier reports resurfaced. In order to deal with the potentially conflicting interests at stake in company groups, the experts again proposed the recognition of the group interest at the EU level. It was proposed to achieve this by means of the introduction of a modified version of the French *Rozenblum* doctrine. Moreover, the issue of group transparency was raised once more. Following the experts' report, the Commission dealt with the topic in its 2012 Action Plan,[57] in which it announced an initiative on the recognition of the group interest by 2014. Unfortunately, so far harmonizing regulation supporting the recognition of the group interest has not been introduced at the EU level, although an exception has to be made for EU law concerning the recovery of banking groups (*see* paragraph 10.42).

10.32 One of the informal expert groups, the Forum Europaeum on Company Groups, which is an association of academics and practitioners from all over Europe, published a proposal to facilitate the management of cross-border company groups in Europe in 2015.[58] This proposal distinguishes between two types of subsidiaries, taking their size and function into account. Based on this distinction between service companies and ordinary companies, the proposal suggests introducing two different frameworks by means of an EU directive. In March 2016, the *Informal Company Law Expert Group* released a report on the information on groups,[59] which was followed by a report

54. Report of the High Level Group of Company Law Experts on *A Modern Regulatory Framework for Company Law in Europe* (Brussels, 4 Nov. 2002), 94 *et seq.*
55. *Modernising Company Law and Enhancing Corporate Governance in the European Union – A Plan to Move Forward* (Brussels, 21 May 2003), COM(2003) 284 final (Company Law Action Plan 2003).
56. Reflection Group on the Future of EU Company Law, *Report of the Reflection Group On the Future of EU Company Law*, Brussels, April 2011, http://ec.europa.eu/internal_market/company/docs/modern/reflectiongroup_report_en.pdf.
57. European company law and corporate governance – a modern legal framework for more engaged shareholders and sustainable companies, Com(2012) 740/2.
58. Forum Europaeum on Company Groups, *European Company and Financial Law Review* (ECFR) 2015, 299.
59. Informal Company Law Expert Group, *Report on information on groups*, March 2016, http://ec.europa.eu/justice/civil/files/company-law/icleg-report-on-information-of-groups-march-2016_en.pdf. *See* about the European developments, these proposals and the recognition of the group

concerning the recognition of the interest of the group.[60] The latter discusses three options. Each option sets out different criteria, the observance of which allows the manager of a subsidiary to take the group interest into account. It should be noted, however, that the proposal is restricted (at least in its ambitions for harmonization) to wholly owned subsidiaries. Eventually, another proposal for reforming group law in the EU came about, which was published by the *European Company Law Experts*.[61] Besides confirming the need to recognize the group interest at the EU level, this proposal mainly dealt with the handling of related-party transactions (*see* paragraph 10.43).

10.33 The issue of company groups has also been addressed in the European Model Company Act (EMCA), which was released in early 2017. As mentioned in paragraph 3.18 of this book, the EMCA offers the Member States a model company law that can be enacted in its entirety or just in parts. It aims to provide the Member States with a modern, low cost and easy-to-use alternative to the drafting of national company laws. Chapter 15 of the EMCA deals with groups of companies and combines a Rozenblum-inspired approach for recognizing the interest of the group with a liability for *wrongful trading* against the parent.[62]

10.34 So far none of the abovementioned proposals has led to an extensive harmonization of group law or to the recognition of the group interest at the EU level. Nowadays, the idea of a systematic harmonization of group law at the EU level seems to have been abandoned. Nevertheless, as is discussed in the following section, piecemeal harmonization in relation to company groups has occurred at the EU level.

B Company Groups in EU Law

10.35 The search for a common approach to the development of group law at the EU level has not been successful, as is illustrated in the previous paragraphs. Several single issues of group law are dealt with by a number of directives and by the introduction of the SE and the EEIG. Grouped together, these provisions pertain to the formation of groups as well as their functioning and are described below.

---

interest at EU level M. Olaerts, 'The Elephant in the Room: Over verbondenheid, macht en belangenafweging in het ondernemingsrecht' 2017. Maastricht University (inaugural lecture) accessible at https://doi.org/10.26481/spe.20170915mo

60. Informal Company Law Expert Group, *Report on the recognition of the interest of the group*, October 2016, http://ec.europa.eu/justice/civil/files/companylaw/icleg_recommendations_interest_group_final_en.pdf.
61. European Company Law Experts, *A proposal for reforming group law in the European Union – Comparative Observations on the way forward*, https://europeancompanylawexperts.wordpress.com/papers_trashed/reforming-group-law-in-the-eu/.
62. For an analysis *see* P.H.Conac, 'The Chapter on Groups of Companies of the European Model Company Act (EMCA)', *European Company and Financial Law Review* (ECFR) (2016), 301 *et seq*.

1 *The Formation of Groups*

10.36 Several provisions of EU legislation in the area of company law and employee involvement pertain to the formation or the functioning of groups.[63] To start with, Articles 40 and 54 TFEU are essential for the formation of a group because they grant companies the *right of secondary establishment*, enabling the formation of cross-border subsidiaries or partnerships (*see* paragraphs 2.54 *et seq.*). According to Article 49 TFEU, the parent company, having established a subsidiary in another Member State, must not be placed in a weaker position than a parent company from that other Member State.[64] In addition, the provisions in relation to capital requirements in Directive (EU) 2017/1132 facilitate the formation of a subsidiary because the Member States have the option not to apply the requirements for non-cash contributions at the incorporation of a subsidiary. Where the formation (or expansion) of a group is realized through the acquisition of shares in listed companies, the Transparency Directive and the Directive on Takeover Bids impose obligations on the acquirer. Shareholders – or persons holding (potential) voting rights – should inform issuers of the acquisition or disposal of major holdings in listed companies. The objectives of the Transparency Directive are, *inter alia*, to improve and equalize investor protection throughout the Community and to curb secret takeovers (*see* paragraph 3.50 *et seq.*). The Takeover Directive (*see* paragraphs 3.09, 3.19a and 8.19 *et seq.*) serves similar objectives. The mandatory bid is aimed at protecting minority shareholders' interests that, according to the theory of conflicting interests, are most adversely affected by the fact that the formerly independent company will operate as part of a group. Directive 2009/102/EC (previously the Twelfth Directive) also has to be mentioned here, because it allows for single-member companies. This facilitates the structuring of groups in the Member States because restrictions as to the use of single-member companies have been abolished (*see* paragraph 3.20).

10.37 The SE Regulation also facilitates the formation of groups because the methods of formation of an SE may lead to the creation or expansion of a group structure. This applies when an SE is formed as a holding company or a subsidiary (*see* paragraph 4.17 *et seq.*). Here, the accompanying SE Directive on the involvement of employees has an ancillary function because it regulates the transformation from the pre-existing system in place for the involvement of employees to their involvement in the structure emerging upon the formation of an SE which can be a group structure in the case of, for example, a holding or a subsidiary SE (*see* paragraphs 4.35 *et seq.*).[65]

---

63. E. Werlauff, 'Group and Community – The European Court's Development of an Independent Community Law Concept of the Group and Its Significance for National Company Law', *European Company Law* 4, no. 5 (October 2007): 201–206.
64. Whether or not the foreign company is qualified as a parent company is, of course, determined by the law governing the subsidiary, E. Werlauff, 'Group and Community' *supra* n. 63, at 203.
65. To secure the proper implementation of the SE Directive, it defines some concepts, *inter alia*, that of a subsidiary, meaning an undertaking over which a company exercises a dominant influence as defined in accordance with Articles 3(2)–(7) of the EWC Directive 94/45/EC.

10.38 Similar to the SE, the *Societas Cooperativa Europaea* (SCE) may operate through subsidiaries; hence, it can function as the parent company of a group.[66] The SCE will, however, generally not be able to qualify as a subsidiary in group structures because the members of the SCE, in principle, each have one vote. Consequently, an SCE can only qualify as a subsidiary if the majority of the members of the SCE are already entities of the same group. The remarks made above for the SE also apply with regard to the position of the employees in the SCE. Lastly, it must be noted that the EEIG, owing to its ancillary nature, cannot act as a parent entity in a group structure. However, companies within a group may structure their cooperation by using the EEIG form (*see* paragraph 4.08).

2 *The Functioning of Groups*

10.39 Several directives include elements that regulate or facilitate the functioning of groups. Two of these directives were specifically drafted to deal with certain aspects of groups. These are the directive on consolidated accounts (previously referred to as the Seventh Directive 83/349/EEC, now integrated into directive 2013/34/ EU) and the EWC Directive.[67] Since these directives specifically deal with the phenomenon of groups, the elements that need to be fulfilled in order to constitute group falling within the ambit of the directive, need to be defined. As already explained in section II of this chapter, for accounting purposes the Accounting Directive classifies several relationships between 'members of a body of undertakings'. Article 2 contains definitions of 'parent undertaking' and 'subsidiary undertaking' (an undertaking can be considered synonymous with an enterprise). As explained in section II of this chapter, the definitions reflect the legal approach, in which the legal power to control is the central element, combined with the economic approach, according to which a group exists from the moment an undertaking actually exercises a dominant influence over another (*see also* paragraphs 9.30 *et seq.*). The Accounting Directive requires the parent undertaking to draw up consolidated financial statements and a consolidated management report for itself and for its subsidiaries. In the EWC Directive, the economic approach prevails because it requires that the controlling undertaking (parent undertaking) actually exercises a dominant influence over another undertaking (the 'controlled undertaking'). However, the legal approach has a supportive role because the dominant influence is presumed, without prejudice to proof to the contrary, when an undertaking holds a majority of another undertaking's capital, controls a majority of ‘e votes, or can appoint more than half of the members of that undertaking's ıinistrative, management or supervisory body. The EWC Directive[68] requires the ıl management of the controlling undertaking to set up an EWC, or an alternative ·tion and consultation procedure if the group is defined as having a Community ıt is, if it employs at least 1,000 persons within the Member States and has at

---

SCE Regulation.
'5/EC.
ctive 2009/38/EC.

least two subsidiaries in different Member States, each having at least 150 employees (Article 2(1)). The application of the EWC Directive to certain group structures has generated some CJEU case law, as explained in paragraphs 7.32–7.34.

10.40 As mentioned above, several other directives, even though not specifically drafted for group structures, contain provisions pertaining to the functioning of groups. These include:

- Capital (maintenance) requirements in Directive (EU) 2017/1132: According to Article 49, Member States may waive the independent expert's report on consideration other than in cash upon the formation of a subsidiary (*see* also paragraph 5.13). Article 67 of the directive also refers to group relationships. It contains a rather restrictive provision because it extends the prohibition for a company on subscribing for its own shares (and the restrictions to acquire such shares) to its subsidiaries. To apply this prohibition, Article 67(2) defines the relevant parent–subsidiary relationship in terms of a mixture of the legal and economic group concept. More precisely, it applies to companies in which the parent company holds, even indirectly, a majority of the voting rights or upon which it can exercise a dominant influence. Member States may define the cases in which a company is deemed to exercise a dominant influence. They must, in any event, specify that such influence can be exercised if a company has the right to appoint or dismiss the majority of the directors or if it has control of a majority of the voting rights under an agreement concluded with the other shareholders (Article 67(2)(a)). Notwithstanding the criterion of the dominant influence, it is the legal approach that seemingly prevails. The required specifications are rather similar to those mentioned in the Accounting Directive.
- The provisions related to (cross-border) mergers in Directive (EU) 2017/1132: The merger procedure may be simplified if the acquiring company holds 90% or more of the shares in the acquired company. Article 113 provides for the exceptions. For example, if the acquiring company holds all the shares, entries in the draft terms of the merger are not required, as well as the report on the share exchange ratio and the control by an independent expert. Where the acquiring company holds 90% or more of the shares in the company being acquired, the Member States need not require approval of the merger by the general meeting of the acquiring company. The directive allows for similar simplifications as mentioned above in a cross-border merger when the acquiring company holds 90% or more of the shares in the company being acquired (Article 132).
- Takeover Directive: for the application of the rules regarding takeover bids, 'persons acting in concert' constitute natural or legal persons who cooperate with the offeror or the offeree company on the basis of an agreement (Article 2(1)(d)). The person or entity that controls an undertaking, together with that controlled undertaking, are deemed to be persons acting in concert (Article 2(2)). For the criterion of control, reference is made to the definition of Article

87 of Directive 2001/34/EC,[69] now Article 2(1)(f) of the Transparency Directive.[70] The controlled undertaking is defined as any undertaking in which another entity has the power to exercise or actually exercises dominant influence. Furthermore, a controlled undertaking subsists if another entity has majority voting rights, or controls such majority due to an agreement or has the right to appoint or remove a majority of the directors. This is basically the same approach as laid down in the Accounting Directive.

10.41 The functioning of groups is, of course, subject to many other rules of EU origin, which are not discussed in this book. For example, tax treaties between the Member States (to prevent double taxation and double non-taxation) may contain rules that facilitate cross-border activities and establishments. The EU has taken initiatives to coordinate taxation issues and enacted the Anti-Tax Avoidance Directive (EU) 2016/1164.[71] Reference may also be made to rules pertaining to merger control, as discussed in Chapter 8 in relation to joint ventures and mergers as well as takeovers. In determining whether a concentration is deemed to arise, the decisive factor is the acquisition of control. This may be established by legal instruments such as mergers, contracts and majority or controlling voting rights or by *de facto* circumstances, such as economic dependence and dominance (*see* paragraphs 8.105 *et seq.*). The Capital Requirements Directive (CRD IV) relates to credit institutions and investment firms[72] and also takes group structures into account. It prescribes that the parent company is responsible for the organization and management of the whole group and for establishing effective controls, especially with regard to risk management.[73] Reference can also be made to the Insolvency Regulation (Recast) which includes a chapter on insolvency of members of groups of companies.[74] This is briefly discussed in the section dealing with cross-border group issues below (*see* paragraph 10.48) as the Insolvency Regulation deals with insolvency proceedings across borders.

10.42 As mentioned in the previous section, recognition of the group interest at the EU level was proposed several times but so far has not been adopted. Nevertheless, in some areas of EU law, the group interest is recognized, for example in banking law. During the financial crisis of 2007–2008, it became apparent that national company law often prohibited financial support from one subsidiary to another in a cross-border context.[75] The Bank Recovery and Resolution Directive (BRRD) allows banking groups to provide financial support to a group member that requires early intervention due to emerging financial difficulties.[76] This measure can be taken in order to ensure financial

69. Directive 2001/34/EC.
70. Directive 2004/109/EC.
71. Directive 2016/1164/EU. For initiatives regarding company taxation, *see* the Commission's website Company Tax, https://ec.europa.eu/taxation_customs/business/company-tax_en.
72. Report of the ICLEG on the recognition of the interest of the group, October 2016, 15.
73. Articles 74 and 88 jo. 109 of CRD IV Directive 2013/36/EU. The directive was introduced following the banking crisis in 2008 to strengthen the EU banking sector.
74. Chapter V of Regulation (EU) 2015/848 (recast).
75. Report of the ICLEG on the recognition of the interest of the group, October 2016, 15–16.
76. Directive 2014/59/EU.

stability of the group. The conditions for providing financial support closely resemble the French Rozenblum doctrine. The agreement should have the objective of restoring the financial stability of the group, there should be a reasonable prospect of reimbursement or a consideration for the financial support provided, and the liquidity or solvency of the group member providing the support should not be affected.[77]

10.43 The economic reality of a group of companies is something the law has to deal with. As we have seen in the previous sections, it may result in obligations for the group as a whole, even if it will be the parent that primarily has to account for compliance. But we have also seen exceptions where application of obligations to each company within a group would be meaningless because of their economic interconnectedness (for example, the simplified merger procedure, *see* paragraph 10.40). An exception is also provided in the case of related-party transactions that are regulated by Article 9c of the Shareholder Rights Directive.[78] The article requires the Member States to ensure that listed companies publicly announce material transactions with related parties at the latest at the time of the conclusion of the transaction. It also requires these transactions to be approved by the general meeting or the administrative or supervisory body. However, Member States are allowed to exempt transactions entered into between the company and its wholly owned subsidiaries. The exception can also be made for transactions with other companies in the group provided that no other related party of the company has an interest in the subsidiary or that national law provides for adequate protection of the interests of those involved in the transaction: the company, the subsidiary and shareholders who are not a related party.[79]

VIII GROUPS OPERATING ACROSS BORDERS

10.44 Groups of companies can operate across borders in different ways. Companies within a group can, for example, be incorporated in one Member State but also have activities in another Member State. It is also possible that a parent company is incorporated in one Member State while its subsidiary is incorporated in a different Member State. In that case, the company law of the latter will be applicable to the subsidiary and to the rights of the parent company as a shareholder in that subsidiary. The same principle applies if the parent is incorporated in a third country, for instance, the US, but its subsidiary is incorporated in one of the EU Member States.

10.45 Cross-border groups involving companies incorporated in different jurisdictions can lead to several complications. One of these is the level of control and influence of a parent company on its subsidiary. The extent to which the parent company can enforce its group policy will depend on the law of the Member State where a subsidiary is incorporated and to what extent instruction rights are available to shareholders in that jurisdiction (*see* paragraph 6.72 *et seq.* for a discussion of instruction rights). It may

77. *See* Article 23(1)(a-i) of Directive 2014/59/EU for these and other requirements.
78. Directive (EU) 2017/828.
79. Article 9c(6a).

be difficult for the parent to set out a group policy if subsidiaries are incorporated in several jurisdictions with different company laws and different rules regarding the duties and rights of shareholder(s).

10.46 Another complication may be differences in creditor protection depending on where the subsidiary and the parent company each are incorporated. Illustrative is the *Impacto Azul* case brought before the CJEU. In this case, a creditor wanted to hold a parent company liable for the debts of its subsidiary.[80] The subsidiary was a company incorporated in Portugal whereas the (grand)parent company was incorporated outside of Portugal. Portuguese law contains provisions of group law on the basis of which a parent company can be held liable for the debts of its subsidiary. These liability rules were, however, not applicable in this case because the parent company was not located in Portugal. Portuguese law provides that the rule of parental liability is not applicable if the parent company has its seat in another Member State. The CJEU held that this exception does not constitute an infringement of the freedom of establishment. Parental liability could also have been achieved, according to the court, on the basis of a contract. According to the literature, the CJEU did not take all aspects of the Portuguese law on parental liability into account as it establishes not only a duty for the parent company but, by way of counterbalance, also the right for the parent company to give instructions in the group interest.[81]

10.47 Complicated questions with regard to jurisdictional matters may also arise in the case of insolvency of cross-border groups. Before insolvency, companies belonging to the same group are often run in a centralised way, as one single enterprise with a common group policy. Once insolvency occurs, each member of the group is involved in its own insolvency proceedings, often under the guidance of its own insolvency practitioner who has to give priority to the interests of the creditors in that specific insolvency proceeding. There is no consolidated system for group insolvencies at the EU level.[82] It may furthermore be difficult to establish the group's Centre of Main Interests (COMI) which determines the law applicable to insolvency proceedings.[83] In company groups, the COMI of the parent and the subsidiary may be located in different Member States. A theory that is sometimes used by national courts to simplify group

80. Case C-186/12 (2013). S. Rammeloo, 'CJEU C-186/12 (*Impacto Azul*). Company Law: Parental Liability and Article 49 TFEU- A Plea for a 'Soft Law' Oriented EU Law Approach on Company Groups', *European Company Law* 11, no. 1 (2014): 20–29.
81. C. Teichmann, 'Towards a European Framework for Cross-Border Group Management', *European Company Law* 13, no. 5 (2016): 152.
82. C. Litt & M. Olaerts, 'Company Groups in the Recast of the EU Insolvency Regulation- The First Regulation Attempt and Future Prospects', in J.J.A. Hamers et al. (eds), *Young Corporate Lawyers* (Zutphen: Uitgeverij Paris 2016), 93–108.
83. Article 3 of Regulation (EU) 2015/848, OJ 2015; L 141. E.T. Bicker, *Gläubigerschutz in der grenzüberschreitenden Konzerngesellschaft. Eine international-privatrechtliche Untersuchung am Beispiel der abhängigen englischen Kapitalgesellschaft mit Verwaltungssitz in Deutschland* (Berlin: Duncker & Humblot, 2007), 84 *et seq.*

agreement. The registration of the agreement with the Commercial Registry is conditional for the contract to have legal effect.[102] There are several types of enterprise agreements, but the most important is the control agreement (Section 291 German Stock Corporation Act). Concluding a control agreement *(Beherrschungsvertrag)* provides the legal basis for the exertion of control by the controlling enterprise, as well as for the application of rules protecting creditors and minority shareholders of the controlled company (enterprise). The main reason for entering into an enterprise agreement is that it allows the parent to give instructions to the board of the controlled company and therefore lead the group as one enterprise. Control agreements and agreements regarding profit and loss absorption are often entered into for reasons of taxation, in order to create a tax unity between the companies concerned, leading to taxation of the pooled profits and losses at the level of the dominating company.[103] The main characteristic of a contractual group is therefore the parent's express power to induce its subsidiary to act for the benefit of the group or another group company, even if that implies acting against the subsidiary's interest. The parent has the right to issue binding instructions to the board of a public company contractually subordinated to it *(Weisungsrecht)*.[104] The instruction may not, however: (i) alter the line of business, (ii) entail the instruction to enter into another enterprise agreement and (iii) endanger the economic existence of the subsidiary.[105]

In order to protect the subsidiary's creditors and outside shareholders, the parent has to compensate the subsidiary's losses whether or not the losses have been caused by the instructions of the parent company.[106] The parent also has to offer to the outside shareholders of the subsidiary a guaranteed annual compensation payment as well as the opportunity to withdraw, in exchange for an equitable compensation in cash or in the form of shares in the parent company.[107]

10.55 The second method of forming a group is the integration of a subsidiary company *(Eingliederung)*. The result can be regarded as a special type of the contractual group. The integration, like a control agreement, empowers the parent to give binding instructions to the board of the integrated company but the consequences are even more far-reaching. Although an integrated company remains legally independent, it functions economically and organizationally as a branch of its parent. The parent has an unrestricted right to issue instructions and is also allowed to dispose of the integrated company's assets and profits. As a counterpart, the parent becomes jointly and severally liable for all acts and debts of the integrated company. Integration by majority resolution is possible even against the minority's will when the parent holds at least 95% of the subsidiary's shares. In such case, minority shareholders must be

---

102. Section 294 German Stock Corporation Act.
103. G. Wirth, M. Arnold & M. Greene, *Corporate Law in Germany* (Beck, 2016), 144 and 146; U. Immenga, 'The Law of Groups in the FRG', in E. Wymeersch (ed.), *supra* n. 15, at 96; S. Mock, 'National Report on Germany', in R.M. Manovil (ed.), *supra* n. 11, at 306, mn. 9.
104. Section 308 German Stock Corporation Act.
105. J. Lieder, 'Germany', in A. Vicari & A. Schall (eds), *supra* n. 94, at 388, mn. 613.
106. *Ibid.*, 389, mn. 615.
107. Sections 300–307 German Stock Corporation Act, especially 302, 304 and 305. U. Immenga, 'The Law of Groups in the FRG', in E. Wymeersch (ed.), *supra* n. 15, at 104.

bought out against an adequate settlement.[108] The reasons for integrating are comparable to those for concluding an enterprise agreement: namely the power to give instructions.[109]

10.56 The third situation in which interconnected companies can qualify as a group according to the German Stock Corporation Act is when one company exerts actual control over the other without an agreement. Despite the fact that *de facto* groups are treated less favourably than contractual groups in German law, they are more common because they allow[110] for more flexible ways of combining companies within the group.[111] In the absence of an enterprise agreement, the parent company may in principle not use its dominant influence to cause the subsidiary (the dependent/controlled AG or KGaA) to enter into disadvantageous transactions unless the controlling enterprise compensates the subsidiary for it *(Nachteilsausgleich)*. The compensation must take place during the fiscal year in which the controlled company caused the disadvantage. Alternatively, it must be stated when and how compensation will follow no later than by the end of the fiscal year.[112] The controlling enterprise can avoid compensation by operating at arm's length if transactions are concluded with its subsidiaries. The board of the controlled entity in a de facto group is not released of its obligations under this scenario. The main difference between the contractual group and the de facto group is that in the latter, directors of the subsidiary do not have to follow instructions from the parent company and that compensation for the harm caused by the parent has to be calculated by analysing each disadvantage and the compensation offered for it.[113] To this end, the board of the controlled entity has to prepare a report on the relations of the company with affiliated enterprises in the first three months of the financial year. It has to set out all legal transactions that the company has entered into with the controlling enterprise or at the instigation or in the interests of the controlling enterprise and its affiliated enterprises as well as all other measures it has taken or refrained from at the instigation or in the interests of these enterprises. Failing to do so can result in directors' liability.[114] The goal of the report is to protect outside stakeholders, such as minority shareholders, of the subsidiary and creditors. Another aim is to provide transparency on intragroup transactions.[115] Controlling an entity without compensating for it can lead to directors' liability both at the level of the controlled entity as well as at the level of the controlling entity.

The controlling company and its legal representatives will be liable if it disadvantages the controlled entity without compensating for this disadvantage.[116] Members of the management board of the controlled company may also be liable if they

108. Sections 319–327 German Stock Corporation Act.
109. S. Mock, 'National Report on Germany', in R.M. Manovil (ed.), *supra* n. 11, at 308, mn. 12.
110. J. Lieder, 'Germany', in A. Vicari & A. Schall (eds), *supra* n. 94, at 393, mn. 631.
111. T.H. Tröger, Corporate Groups, A German's European Perspective, *Safe Working Paper Series* no. 66 (2014), 8.
112. Section 311 German Stock Corporation Act.
113. A. Vicari, *supra* n. 41, at 174.
114. Section 318 German Stock Corporation Act.
115. J. Lieder, 'Germany', in A. Vicari & A. Schall (eds), *supra* n. 94, at 395, mn. 640.
116. Section 317 (1) and (3) German Stock Corporation Act.

'failed (...) to set out the disadvantageous legal transaction or the disadvantageous measure in the report on the relations of the company with affiliated enterprises, or have failed to state that the company suffered a disadvantage by the legal transaction or the measure and that the disadvantage was not compensated (...)'.[117]

2 *Groups Involving Private Limited Liability Companies*

10.57 The single or majority shareholder of a GmbH can, in principle, exercise a dominant influence on the company's management because German law allows shareholders to issue binding instructions to the management without the prerequisite of a specific contract (*see* paragraph 6.72). With respect to groups, this means that a dominant enterprise can control its GmbH subsidiary without the need for further justification, and the dominant influence creates a *de facto* group relationship. The rules of the German Stock Corporation Act on *de facto* groups are, however, not applicable as long as there are no public companies involved as subsidiaries. Minority shareholders of GmbH subsidiaries are instead protected, *inter alia,* by the fiduciary duty *(Treuepflicht)* that the majority shareholder owes towards the GmbH and the other shareholders if there are any. Breach of this duty when influencing management imposes a liability on the dominant shareholder, and individual shareholders may lodge claims for injunctions and compensation for damages caused by the influence exerted.[118] Creditors' interests should also be taken into account. There may be circumstances justifying the liability of the parent company towards the creditors of the subsidiary.[119] Parental liability on the basis of tort may arise if the parent exerts a permanent and comprehensive influence on the subsidiary's management culminating in detrimental interventions. Since the *Trihotel* decision in 2007, this is known as the *Existenzvernichtungshaftung.*[120] The reasoning behind this judgment is that the rules on capital maintenance are insufficient to protect the subsidiary against disadvantageous interference by the parent company in *de facto* groups. The assets of the subsidiary require further protection than only ensuring the minimum capital requirements and when these are depleted, the doctrine can be triggered.[121]

B The Law of Groups in Other Jurisdictions

10.58 As already mentioned, the German legislative example was followed by only a few EU jurisdictions. Most jurisdictions have developed legal techniques to deal with

117. Section 318 (1) German Stock Corporation Act. This translation comes from the German Federal Ministry of Justice retrieved from: https://www.gesetze-im-internet.de/englisch_aktg/
118. *ITT* (1975) BGHZ 65, 15; *Autokran* (1985) BGHZ 95, 330.
119. *Tiefbau* (1989) BGHZ 107, 7.
120. BGHZ 173, 246; confirmed in *Gamma* (2008) BGHZ 176, 204.
121. J. Lieder, 'Germany', in A. Vicari & A. Schall (eds), *supra* n. 94, at 397, mn. 649.

company groups without creating an overarching law of groups.[122] Originally, the emphasis in national law was on protecting minority shareholders and creditors by means of specific provisions of company law and insolvency law.[123] More recently, the debate concerning the regulation of company groups seems to be shifting and more emphasis is put on the enabling of company groups and the management of such groups.[124] Three aspects are relevant in this respect: the right to give instructions and the recognition of the group interest, as part of the enabling policy, and parental liability as an element of protection. These aspects are discussed in the following paragraphs.

1 *Group Governance and Instruction Rights*

10.59 Groups are, if not by definition, often characterized by a form of central management. As mentioned above, in German law, for instance, uniform management or central management of companies leads to the qualification as a group. Central management implies a strategy or policy set out by the parent company. The extent to which central management leaves room for autonomous setting of strategy at subsidiary level can vary from one group to another.[125] There may be requirements at national level expecting the parent company to have a group policy with regard to specific subject matters. The Dutch Corporate Governance Code, for example, requires listed companies to have adequate risk management and control systems in place. Best practice 1.2.1 of the code provides that the management board should identify and analyse the risks associated with the strategy and activities of the company *'and its affiliated enterprises'*. Likewise, the UK 2018 Corporate Governance Code requires the board of the parent company to ensure compliance within the whole group:[126]

> For parent companies with a premium listing, the board should ensure that there is adequate co-operation within the group to enable it to discharge its governance responsibilities under the Code effectively. This includes the communication of the parent company's purpose, values and strategy.

---

122. *See* for a comparative overview K.J. Hopt, *supra* n. 1, at 603–633; R.M. Manovil, 'Groups of Companies: les groups de sociétés', in R.M. Manovil (ed.), *supra* n. 11; A. Vicari, *supra* n. 41, at 167.
123. R.M. Manovil, 'Groups of Companies: les groups de sociétés', in R.M. Manovil (ed.), *supra* n. 11, at 3; K. E. Sorensen, *supra* n. 29.
124. The European Model Companies Act, for example, contains a chapter on company groups. The focus is on the management of the group. The consideration states that the protection of subsidiaries and related interests such as shareholders and creditors should not be ignored but that this should also not be achieved through burdensome regulation. EMCA, Chapter 15, 373. *See also* the recommendations of the Reflection Group on the Future of EU Company Law, 5 April 2011, 60. According to the ICLEG, there is a trend in national law towards the recognition of the group interest. Such recognition would make group management possible. *See* the report of the ICLEG on the recognition of the interest of the group, October 2016, 25. *See* C. Teichmann, *supra* n. 81, at 150–157; K. E. Sorensen, *supra* n. 29; About the enabling and protective side, *see* M. Olaerts, *supra* n. 59.
125. K.J. Hopt, *supra* n. 1, at 604.
126. *See* the introduction to the UK Corporate Governance Code 2018, 3.

The same approach is taken by the German Corporate Governance Code. It highlights the obligation of management boards and supervisory boards to take the interests of the shareholders, the enterprise's workforce and the other groups related to the enterprise (stakeholders) into account to ensure the continued existence of the enterprise and its sustainable value creation (the enterprise's best interests). The foreword to the code makes clear that the term enterprise refers not only to the listed company itself but also to its group entities.[127]

10.60 The parent company has the power to control subsidiaries in the first place because it can appoint and dismiss the directors at subsidiary level. National law may also provide tools enabling the parent company not only to set out a joint strategy but also to give instructions to the board of the subsidiary in order to execute that strategy. Such instruction rights are recognized in Germany for private companies[128] and in the Netherlands for both private and public companies. It must be noted, however, that in Dutch law instructions to the board of a private company can be far-reaching, whereas for public companies they can be of a general nature only.[129] In the United Kingdom (UK), courts have determined that whether or not binding instructions can be issued to the management board depends on the articles of association of the company[130] (*see* paragraph 6.72 for further discussion of instruction rights). An important question is whether in jurisdictions where instruction rights are recognized, the subsidiary should always follow the instructions from the parent company. This is where the recognition of the group interest comes into play, as is explained in the following paragraphs.

2 Recognition of the Group Interest

10.61 Several Member States recognize the interest of a group as a whole. The recognition of the group interest was also suggested several times in reports at the EU level as a tool to enable group management (*see* paragraphs 10.31–10.34). As briefly explained above, the recognition of the group interest can create a safe harbour for directors of the parent company as well as for directors at subsidiary level because it allows the parent company to issue instructions that may not be primarily in the interest of the subsidiary but nevertheless serve the interest of the group as a whole. It relieves the directors of the subsidiary of the duty to manage the subsidiary as an independent company and protects them from liability for letting the group interest prevail.[131] Recognition of the group interest would further imply that the parent company is allowed to manage the group as a whole towards a common goal. There are, however, limits to what can be justified on the basis of the group interest, and

127. *See* the German Corporate Governance Code 2019, 2. *See also* K. E. Sorensen, *supra* n. 29, at 16.
128. Section 37(1) German Limited Liability Companies Act.
129. *See* Article 2:129(4) Dutch Civil Code for a public company and Article 2:239(4) Dutch Civil Code for a private limited liability company.
130. *Automatic Self-Cleaning Filter Syndicate Company Ltd. V Cuninghane* [1906] 2 CH 43.
131. Report of the Reflection Group on the Future of EU Company Law, 5 April 2011, 61. M. Olaerts, *supra* n. 59.

overstepping these limitations can lead to liability, in the first place not only for the parent and its directors but also for directors at subsidiary level.[132] The group interest is used to define the limits and conditions under which group influence is acceptable.[133]

10.62 France is mentioned as the schoolbook example of a national law system that recognizes the group interest. The Rozenblum doctrine serves as a defence against claims based on the misappropriation of corporate assets. This means that a director can take measures that are against the interest of a subsidiary but in the interest of the group as long as the following conditions are met:

- the company forms part of a group,
- there is a common economic interest in relation to a group policy,[134]
- the transaction is not inadequate or there is no imbalance of mutual obligations, and
- the transaction does not exceed the financial capacity of the company.[135] Overstepping these limitations may lead to liability for misappropriation of corporate assets.

The Rozenblum doctrine was formulated by the French Supreme Court *(Cour de cassation)* in the *Rozenblum* case.[136] Mr Rozenblum controlled a number of companies that were not related by a common policy. Nevertheless, assets were transferred from some of these companies to other companies that were suffering losses. Mr Rozenblum

132. European Company Law Experts, A proposal for reforming group law in the European Union-Comprehensive Observations on the way forward, October 2016, 15.
133. *Ibid.*
134. This can also be translated into a requirement of having a 'balanced and firmly established group structure'. *See* in this respect P. -H. Conac, *supra* n. 62, at 312.
135. Cass. Crim., 4 Feb. 1985, Bull. Crim. No. 54, JCP G, 1986, II, 20585. *See* P.-H. Conac, 'National Report on France', in R.M. Manovil (ed.), *supra* n. 11, at 92 *et seq.* These requirements are often summarized in comparable ways but with different wording. The Reflection Group for example mentions the following requirements: 'First, there must be a group characterized by capital links between the companies. Second, there must be strong, effective business integration among the companies within the group. Third, the financial support from one company to another company must have an economic *quid pro quo* and may not break the balance of mutual commitments between the companies concerned. Fourth, the support from the company must not exceed its possibilities. In other words, it should not create a risk of bankruptcy for the company.' Report of the Reflection Group on the Future of EU Company Law 2011, 62–63. The Club des Juristes describes the first two requirements as follows: 'there must be a group: the legal and financial links among the companies of the group must be demonstrated, as well as the implementation of a common strategy aiming at the realisation of a common project; the operation must originate in a common economic, social or financial interest, which is to be assessed in relation to a policy that has been elaborated for the whole group (…).' Report of the Club des Juristes, Report Towards Recognition of the Group Interest in the European Union, June 2015, 16–17. *See* about these differences also M. Olaerts, *supra* n. 59.
136. Cour de Cassation, Chambre criminelle du 4 février 1985, 84–91.581, *Revue des sociétés* 1985, 648, note Bouloc. For an account on later developments *see* P.-H. Conac 'Das französische Recht zur Anerkennung des Gruppeninteresses seit der Rozenblum-Entscheidung' in P. Hommelhoff, M. Lutter & C. Teichmann (eds), *Corporate Governance im grenzübeschreitenden Konzern* (de Gruyter, Berlin, 2017), 89.

was prosecuted for the criminal act of abuse of a company's assets *(abus de biens sociaux)*. The French Supreme Court held that such transfers were only permissible if certain requirements were met. The Supreme Court held:

> (...) the financial assistance given by the 'de iure' or '*de facto*' directors of a company to other group companies in which they held a direct or indirect interest, should be supported by an economic social or financial common interest, to be evaluated in the light of a policy developed with regard to the group as a whole and should not be devoid of any return or disrupt the balance of the mutual obligations of the companies involved, nor exceed the financial capacity of the company that is supporting the burden.[137]

It must be noted that this is fundamentally different from the approach as laid down in the German Stock Corporations Act. As explained above, under German law the parent is not allowed to impose any disadvantage on the subsidiary - if it is a public company - without compensating for it. In that sense, Germany does not recognize the group interest.[138]

10.63 Certain elements of the Rozenblum doctrine appear in other jurisdictions. In the Netherlands, the point of departure remains that the board of directors has to manage the company primarily in the interest of the company itself, thus promoting the lasting success of the company's enterprise.[139] Therefore, when it comes to assessing the liability of directors at subsidiary level, the Dutch Supreme Court's leading case law still looks at whether the director has served the interest of the individual subsidiary rather than the group as a whole.[140] Nevertheless, it is accepted in case law and the literature that the interest of a company belonging to a group will be influenced by the group interest.[141] Certain acts taken primarily in the interest of the group are therefore acceptable as long as they have a connection with the interest of that subsidiary and insofar as concurrence of interests is assumed.[142] Consequently, serving the group interest should never lead to the discontinuity of the subsidiary.[143]

137. Translation quoted from E. Wymeersch, 'Conflicts of Interest in Financial Services Groups', Financial Law Institute Working Paper No. 2007-05 (University of Ghent, 2008), 4, accessible at www.papers.ssrn.com.
138. This is at least the conclusion of the ICLEG in their report on the recognition of the interest of the group, October 2016, 24.
139. Articles 2:129(5) and 2:239(5) Dutch Civil Code.
140. Supreme Court, 26 Oct. 2001, *JOR* 2002/2 m.nt. S.M. Bartman (*Juno Properties*).
141. *See*, for example, Asser/Van Solinge & Nieuwe Weme 2-IIb 2019/122; J.B. Huizink, 'Bestuursautonomie na Cancun', in A.F. Verdam et al., *Autonomie van het bestuur en haar grenzen voor en na de Cancun-uitspraak* (Deventer: Wolters Kluwer, 2015), 42; G.J.H. van der Sangen, 'Concernleiding en aansprakelijkheid: het delicate evenwicht tussen unitaire leiding en juridische zelfstandigheid', *TvOB* 2009/6, 147; A.F. Verdam, 'Het bestuur van de dochter in concernverband', *Ondernemingsrecht* 2019/77; Enterprise Chamber, Amsterdam Court of Appeal (*Ondernemingskamer*) 13 March 2003, *JOR* 2003/85 (*Corus*).
142. S. M. Bartman, *supra* n. 34, at 207–210.
143. This was for example one of the important factors when the Enterprise Chamber was asked to decide on whether a subsidiary should follow the parent's instructions: Enterprise Chamber 23 Jan. 2017, ECLI:NL:GHAMS:2017:209, *JOR* 2017/96 m.nt. S.M. Bartman (*Kaal Masten*) and 4 Apr. 2018, ECLI:NL:GHAMS:2018:1088, *JOR* 2018/179 m.nt. F. Eikelboom (*MFH/Marinoffs*).

The Dutch approach shares characteristics with the Rozenblum doctrine and the philosophy behind the *'existenzvernichtender Eingriff'* in Germany (*see* paragraph 10.57). Also in the UK, the default rule remains that directors at subsidiary level have to serve the interest of that company. This means that they have to assess whether an instruction from the parent company is in the interest of that subsidiary; they cannot simply follow an instruction without exercising their discretion.[144] It is, however, also accepted that there can be concurrence between the company and the group interest.[145]

3 Parental Liability

10.64 A commonly used approach in case law to protect creditors and minority shareholders of a subsidiary is by holding the parent company liable for disadvantages due to its interference in the subsidiary's business. Vandekerckhove carried out an impressive comparative study on parental liability, and much of what is discussed in this section is based on her findings and still paints the common denominator of what the legal landscape in this area looks like today.[146] To begin with, norms serving as a basis for liability may originate from company law, insolvency law, criminal law or civil law, depending on the jurisdiction. This complicates the description of the phenomenon of parental liability as well as the fact that the authors do not use consistent terminology.[147] Below, we first explain the difference between voluntary and involuntary liability. Following Vandekerckhove, a distinction can further be made between liability based on statutory provisions and liability based on general principles such as a duty of care.

a Voluntary and Involuntary Parental Liability

10.65 Creditors can have a claim on the parent of a group either on the basis of a commitment the parent has voluntarily entered into (voluntary liability) or because the parent has caused damage giving rise to a claim by a third party (involuntary liability). The first type can, for example, occur when one company within the group guarantees the other's debt or provide security for it.[148] Assuming liability by the parent or other companies in the group for the obligations of other group members can be part of a

---

See M. Olaerts, *supra* n. 59, also M. Olaerts, 'The Netherlands', in A.Vicari & A. Schall (eds.), supra n. 94, at 1400 *et seq.* M. Olaerts, 'National Report on the Netherlands', in R.M. Manovil (ed.), *supra* n. 11, at 423–456.

144. B. Hannigan, 'United Kingdom', in A. Vicari & A. Schall (eds.), *supra* n. 94, at 1589, mn. 476.
145. *Ibid.*, 1588, mn. 473 *et seq.*
146. K. Vandekerckhove, 'Piercing the Corporate Veil', *European Company Law* 4, no. 5 (2007): 191 *et seq.*
147. Which cases where liability is established should exactly be called piercing the corporate veil is debatable as explained above, K. Vandekerckhove, *Piercing the Corporate Veil* (Alphen aan den Rijn: Kluwer Law International, 2007), 12–13.
148. Because the conclusion of a control contract under German law is, as explained above, completely at the option of the dominant enterprise, the liabilities resulting from it can be said to be of a voluntary nature.

centralized financial policy of the group. The assumption of parental liability is sometimes made a statutory condition for certain group facilities, such as the subsidiary's exemption from financial reporting requirements (Article 37(3) Directive 2013/34/EU). The second type of parental liability, involuntary liability, is further explored in the following paragraphs.

b *Liability Based on Statutory Provisions*

10.66 As mentioned in paragraph 10.64, a distinction can be made between liability based on statutory provisions and liability based on general principles in case law. An example of the first type of liability that can be found in many jurisdictions is the liability that occurs when a parent company is a director or a de facto director (shadow director) of its subsidiary, and statutory duties have been violated, for example in the case of mismanagement leading to insolvency. This type of liability is laid down in statutory provisions in France, the UK and the Netherlands.[149] Under French law, liability arises when the parent company mismanaged the subsidiary and this contributed to the subsidiary's lack of assets.[150] The parent company has to qualify as a de facto manager (*dirigeant de fait*) which is the case when the parent actively manages the company and binds it to third parties.[151] Furthermore, there has to be a causal link between the mismanagement and the lack of assets of the subsidiary.[152] Also in Dutch law a parent company may qualify as a shadow director or de facto director[153] at subsidiary level and be held liable if it has led the subsidiary into bankruptcy.[154] A comparable rule can be found in the UK where directors may be liable for wrongful trading, and this rule applies *mutatis mutandis* to shadow directors. The provision implies liability of (shadow) directors if at some time before the commencement of the winding-up of the company, the directors 'knew or ought to have concluded that there was no reasonable prospect that the company would avoid going into insolvent liquidation'.[155]

c *Liability Based on General Principles in Case Law*

Duty of Care based on Parental Interference

10.67 A second type of (involuntary) liability occurs when courts make an exception to the basic rule that a company's shareholders, and directors, are not liable for the

149. Art. L. 241-9, art. L. 245-16 and L. 246-2 of the French Commercial Code; Articles 2:138 and 2:248(7) Dutch Civil Code.
150. Art. L. 651-2 of the French Commercial Code.
151. S. Schiller & I. Barsan, 'France', in A Vicari & A. Schall (eds.), *supra* n. 94, at 162, mn. 815.
152. *Ibid.*, 164, mn. 824 with reference to Cass. Comm. 22 June 2010 no. 09-14.214.
153. Dutch law does not distinguish between *de facto* and shadow directorship. These terms are used here interchangeably.
154. Article 2:138/248-7 Dutch Civil Code. *See* further M. Olaerts, 'The Netherlands', in A. Vicari & A. Schall (eds.), *supra* n. 94, at 1424, mn. 536.
155. Section 214 UK Insolvency Act 1986.

debts of a company. As a matter of course, this rule applies equally to companies that serve as a subsidiary within a group structure. This type of liability is often based on general principles of the law or open norms such as the prohibition on abusing one's rights or the acceptance of a general duty of care. There is no set of precise criteria justifying involuntary group liability, and case law dealing with this topic is rather casuistic.[156] The starting point, however, is that the mere existence of a group relationship will not establish liability and that additional factual circumstances are required. These represent some form of abuse of power by the parent when controlling its subsidiary. To put it differently, no liability is imposed on the parent solely because of its status as a parent company. This reflects the theoretical approach of concurring interests, which assumes that what is in the interest of the group will as a rule be in the interest of the separate group members as well.[157] This is, of course, the reverse of the conflict-of-interests approach of the German Stock Corporation Act (*see* paragraph 10.51 *et seq.*). The idea of concurring interests, as already mentioned in paragraph 10.61 *et seq.*, has led some jurisdictions to recognize the group interest but not without setting limits to the extent to which the subsidiary's interest can be subordinated to the group interest. Parental liability nevertheless emerges when these limits are disregarded.

10.68 In the UK the principle that a company is a distinct legal entity, separated from its shareholders even in case of a single shareholding company, was established in *Salomon v Salomon & Co Ltd.*[158] In *Adams v Cape Plc,*[159] it was established that the use of group structures to isolate the group from liabilities caused by a specific group member is allowed. UK courts will therefore not easily hold a parent company liable.[160] Parental liability may nevertheless occur where a parent company interferes with the operations of its subsidiary while it has a duty of care towards a third party that is harmed by the operations of the subsidiary.[161] In *Chandler v Cape Plc,*[162] it was held that the parent company had a duty of care towards the employees of the subsidiary. Contributing factors were that the business of parent and subsidiary were the same, the parent company had or ought to have had superior knowledge and expertise regarding the employees' health, it knew or ought to have known that the work practices at subsidiary level were unsafe, and it knew or ought to have known that the subsidiary

156. J.E. Antunes, *supra* n. 34, at 486.
157. A thorough analysis of the issues related to group liability within the EU is presented by E. Werlauff, 'The Debtor Behind the Debtor, the Tortfeaser Behind the Tortfeasor: On Liability for Another Company's Default and Other Debts', *European Company Law* 5, no. 5 (October 2008): 207–219.
158. [1897] AC 22, HL.
159. [1990] BCLC 479.
160. *See* for this explanation B. Hannigan, 'United Kingdom', in A. Vicari & A. Schall, *supra* n. 94, at 1580–1581, mn. 450.
161. *Ibid.*, at 1582–1584, mn. 457.
162. [2012] EWCA Civ. 525.

or its employees relied on the parent company for protection.[163] The criteria formulated in *Chandler v Cape Plc* are rather restricted, and the question was therefore whether such a duty of care could only arise in cases where the abovementioned requirements were met. In the later *Vedanta* case, the Supreme Court confirmed the duty of care of a parent company. This case concerned a duty of care of the parent company towards the neighbours of the copper mine operated by one of its subsidiaries.[164] The main reason for accepting a duty of care was the parent company's interference or control and supervision over the operations of the subsidiary.[165] The court however made clear that there is no special test applicable to tortious responsibility of the parent company. This was later confirmed by the Supreme Court in *Okpabi v Shell*.[166] Therefore, the acceptance of a duty of care of the parent company is not limited to the rather strict criteria used in *Chandler v Cape Plc* and it may arise depending on:

> the extent to which, and the way in which, the parent availed itself of the opportunity to take over, intervene in, control, supervise or advise the management of the relevant operations (...) of the subsidiary.[167]

In other words, interference is necessary but can also stem from group policies and is not restricted to situations where the parent company exercised actual control over certain operations of its subsidiary.[168]

10.69 In Dutch case law, the level of interference by the parent company also plays a role in establishing a duty of care towards the creditors of its subsidiary. Important factors are whether the parent company had insight into and control over the subsidiary's activities and knew or ought to have known that the creditors of its subsidiary would be disadvantaged by its interference.[169] In the *Albada Jelgersma* case, the Supreme Court held that the parent was liable towards the creditors of its subsidiary when that subsidiary after being taken over by the parent was unable to pay its main suppliers. According to the Supreme Court, the parent company had intensively and substantially interfered with the activities at subsidiary level which constituted a ground for accepting a duty of care of the parent company towards the creditors at subsidiary level.[170]

163. Para. 80 of the case.
164. *Vedanta Resources PLC and another (Appellants) v Lungowe and others (Respondents)*, Supreme Court 10 Apr. 2019, [2019] UKSC 20.
165. B. Hannigan, 'United Kingdom', in A. Vicari & A. Schall (eds.), *supra* n. 94, at 1583–1584, mn. 457.
166. *Okpabi and others v Royal Dutch Shell plc and another* [2021] UKSC 3.
167. *Supra* n. 165, at para. 49 repeated in *Okpabi and others v Royal Dutch Shell plc and another* [2021] UKSC 3, para.149.
168. L. Roorda & D. Leader, 'Okpabi v Shell and Four Nigerian Farmers v Shell: Parent Company Liability Back in Court', *Business and Human Rights Journal* 6 (2021): 368–376.
169. Supreme Court, 25 Sep. 1981, *NJ* 1982/443 m.nt. Maeijer (*Osby*).
170. Supreme Court, 19 Feb. 1988, *NJ* 1988/487 m.nt. van der Grinten (*Albada Jelgersma*). *See* with regard to intensive interference of the parent company with the operations at subsidiary level Supreme Court, 12 June 1998, *NJ* 1998/727 m.nt. Van Schilfgaarde (*Coral/Stalt*). M. Olaerts, 'The Netherlands', in A. Vicari & A. Schall (eds.), *supra* n. 94, at 1423, mn. 531 and M. Olaerts, 'National Report on the Netherlands', in R.M. Manovil (ed.), *supra* n. 11, at 423–456.

10.70 There are various circumstances that can lead to parental liability, and national case law differs in this respect. However, as a common denominator, the following typical situations can lead to liability:

1. undercapitalization,
2. transfers of assets that endanger the continued existence of the subsidiary and
3. unduly continuing loss-making activities.[171] It should be kept in mind that these situations can often overlap. Furthermore, in order to justify parental liability, the emergence of these situations at the subsidiary level must be due to the interference of the parent company (*see* the previous paragraphs).

10.71 First, if a subsidiary is undercapitalized, that is by not having sufficient financial means (equity) in relation to its operations, then the parent company may be liable. In several Member States, undercapitalization, as such, is not an issue regulated by statutory law.[172] It may, however, be among a set of circumstances giving rise to claims on the grounds of tort, such as in Germany and the Netherlands.[173] In the previous sections we saw that in Germany in groups with private limited liability companies, a parent company may be held liable on the basis of tort if the assets of the subsidiary are depleted. In the UK and France, manifest undercapitalization is generally not seen as a basis for parental liability, however.[174]

10.72 Second, the parent company may initiate transfers of assets that endanger the continued existence of the subsidiary. These transfers may vary from the distribution of funds of the subsidiary and intragroup transactions on terms that are unfavourable for the subsidiary to outright asset stripping.[175] Note that for accounting purposes, intragroup transactions are covered by the concept of related-party transactions, but the Member States may exempt these transactions from the provisions dealing with related-party transactions (*see* paragraph 9.22a). Intragroup transactions with a high-risk profile are especially likely to occur where the parent company uses a central cash management system to finance the operations of the group as a whole. This may even lead to withdrawals destroying the economic base of a subsidiary.[176] Intragroup transactions may, in general, be covered not only by statutory rules restricting distributions to shareholders, the actio pauliana (or similar instruments) but also by

171. This distinction is based on K. Vandekerckhove, *supra* n. 146, at 191–200. Although other situations may also lead to liability, this is not meant as an exhaustive list of circumstances that can lead to liability.
172. K. Vandekerckhove, *supra* n. 147, at 124.
173. *Ibid.*, 124–156. With regard to parental liability under Dutch law *see* S.M. Bartman, A.F.M. Dorresteijn & M. Olaerts, *Van het concern* (Deventer: Wolters Kluwer, 2020), 268 *et seq.*
174. K. Vandekerckhove, *supra* n. 147, at 156–163; K. Vandekerckhove, *supra* n. 146, at 193; S. Schiller & I. Barsan, 'France', in A. Vicari & A. Schall, *supra* n. 94, at 164, mn. 827, 828.
175. K. Vandekerckhove, *supra* n. 147, at 179 *et seq.*
176. M. Casper, 'Liability of the Managing Director and the Shareholder in the GmbH (Private Limited Company) in Crisis', *German Law Journal* 9, no. 9 (1 Sep. 2008), available at www.germanlawjournal.com.

parental liability on grounds of tort or abuse of legal personality.[177] In France, for example, the misuse of corporate assets can lead to criminal liability (*abus de biens sociaux*).[178] As mentioned earlier in this chapter, the Rozenblum doctrine (*see* paragraph 10.62) serves to evaluate contested transactions in the case of groups.[179] Based on French case law, liability may also occur on the basis of theories on fictitious companies and asset commingling.[180] German law traditionally deals with intragroup transactions by applying the group law of the German Stock Corporation Act for groups in which public companies function as subsidiaries. Thus, intragroup transactions may obligate the parent company to compensate the subsidiary for losses or disadvantages caused by these transactions. If the parent violates this duty, it may be liable towards the subsidiary's creditors. In de facto groups, parental liability may be based on tort and abuse.[181] We already referred to the fact that in groups with private limited liability companies, the doctrine of *Existenzvernichtungshaftung* can be triggered when the assets of the subsidiary are depleted (*see* paragraph 10.57). In the Netherlands, most cases of parental liability are based on the tortious behaviour of the parent company.[182] Case law shows several circumstances in which a parent company can be held liable due to asset commingling or a combination between asset commingling and the unduly continuing of loss-making activities. Parent companies have, for example, been held liable in cases in which they (i) created the appearance of creditworthiness of the subsidiary,[183] (ii) extracted funds from the subsidiary for example by means of dividend payments or caused the subsidiary to pay only certain creditors such as fellow group members to the disadvantage of external creditors[184] or (iii) they discontinued the existing financial aid provided to the subsidiary.[185]

177. K. Vandekerckhove, *supra* n. 147, at 13.
178. Articles L. 241-3, no. 4 of the French Commercial Code for private limited liability companies and L.242-6, no. 4 for public limited liability companies. About these provisions *see* S.Schiller & I.Barsan, 'France' in A. Vicari & A. Schall (eds.), *supra* n. 94, at 165–167, mn. 834 *et seq.*
179. K. Vandekerckhove, *supra* n. 147, at 183 and 227 *et seq.*
180. *Ibid.*, 242 and 243.
181. This approach initially assumed an external liability (claims by creditors of the subsidiary): BGHZ 149, 10 *(Bremer Vulkan)*; BGHZ 151, 181 (*KBV*). In recent case law, it has been modified into a liability towards the subsidiary (the administrator in bankruptcy): BGHZ 173, 246 *(Trihotel)*; BGHZ 176, 204 *(Gamma)* (decisions are accessible at http://dejure.org). *See* further J. Lieder, 'Germany', in A. Vicari & A. Schall (eds), *supra* n. 94, at 398, mn. 650. Also Section 64 German Limited Liability Companies Act; Section 826 BGB; Section 93 Insolvenzordnung.
182. For instance, Dutch Supreme Court in *Comsys*, 11 Sep. 2009, *NJ* 2009/565. *See* G. Potjewijd & J. van der Kroon, 'Report from the Netherlands', *European Company Law* 4, no. 5 (October 2007): 235–237.
183. Supreme Court, 18 Nov. 1994, *NJ* 1995/170 (*NBM/Securicor*). In this case a representative of the parent company raised the expectation that the parent company would pay for the debts of its subsidiary.
184. Supreme Court, 12 June 1998, *NJ* 1998/727 (*Coral/Stalt*); Supreme Court, 8 Nov. 1991, *NJ* 1992/174 (*Nimox*).
185. *See* for various categories Assink-Slagter, *Compendium Ondernemingsrecht* (Deel 2) (Deventer: Wolters Kluwer, 2013), § 115.3, 2263. For further elaboration *see* M. Olaerts, 'The Netherlands', in A. Vicari & A. Schall (eds), *supra* n. 94, at 1422, mn. 529 and M. Olaerts, 'National Report on the Netherlands', in R.M. Manovil (ed.), *supra* n. 11, at 433 *et seq.*

10.73 The third ground for parental liability is unduly continuing loss-making activities. This may occur where the economic and financial situation of a company implies that its existence is endangered, unless appropriate action is taken by the directors and/or parent company to counteract this development. If the loss-making activities are nevertheless continued and the company goes bankrupt, the parent company may be liable because it has caused the insolvency and/or damaged creditors' interests. We have already mentioned above that there are statutory provisions in France, the UK and the Netherlands that can lead to liability of the parent company in case of bankruptcy of the subsidiary if it acts as the director of its subsidiary or as its *de facto* director. Claims by individual creditors may also be made but they should be based on tort where the parent company has violated standards of care which may apply when its subsidiary is continuously generating losses.[186] In addition, there might be provisions obliging that the general meeting be convened if the net assets of the company have fallen below certain thresholds.[187] German group law partly deals with the issue of the obligations and liabilities of the parent company by means of the legislation designed for contractual groups and qualified *de facto* groups.

Piercing the Corporate Veil and Identification

10.74 A term often used in legal literature to refer to parental liability is piercing the corporate veil because this liability implies that the protection offered by limited liability is pierced.[188] One should keep in mind that piercing the corporate veil not only occurs where a group of companies is involved, but it may also occur in companies with individuals as shareholders. Furthermore, piercing the corporate veil as a doctrine emerged against a specific background, namely as an equitable action under common law in the UK (and the US) and as such it has a narrower meaning than parental liability. UK law, for example, is very reticent to pierce the corporate veil, and it can be justified in case of evasion in order to prevent corporate abuse. It is seen as a remedy of last resort.[189] The closest to piercing the veil in this narrow sense that can be found in other legal systems is identification, in Dutch case law recognized as *vereenzelviging*.[190] It occurs when the court is willing to disregard the separate legal personality and identifies the subsidiary with the parent company.[191] In the Netherlands, as in many countries, piercing the corporate veil in this sense is only accepted under very exceptional circumstances.[192]

186. K. Vandekerckhove, *supra* n. 147, at 324 *et seq.*, 335 *et seq.*, 348 *et seq.*
187. This is for example the case for public companies in the Netherlands based on Article 2:108a Dutch Civil Code.
188. S.M. Bainbridge & M. T. Henderson, *supra* n. 24, at 4.
189. *Prest v Petrodel Resources Ltd & Others* [2013] UKSC 34; A. Schall, 'The New Law of Piercing the Corporate Veil in the UK', *ECFR* 2016/4, 549–574.
190. Supreme Court, 13 Oct. 2000, *NJ* 2000/698 m.nt. Ma (*Rainbow*).
191. K. Vandekerckhove, *supra* n. 146, at 195.
192. R.M. Manovil, 'Groups of Companies: les groups de sociétés', in R.M. Manovil (ed.), *supra* n. 11, at 65.

X CONCLUDING REMARKS

10.75 The EU Member States have regulated the formation, functioning and dissolution of companies as single legal entities governed by their civil code, companies code or companies act, but they often do not deal with groups of companies (or other entities) through a coherent and comprehensive set of statutory rules. With the exception of Germany, the other jurisdictions discussed in this book created solutions for specific issues involving groups, thereby producing a variety of definitions of groups and group relationships. Where Germany has provided a framework for the formation of groups and has acknowledged the inherent risks for minority shareholders and creditors of the group's subsidiaries by providing, in the *Konzernrecht,* a framework for contractual arrangements and liability of the parent undertaking, the other Member States as well as the EU have only dealt with these issues on a piecemeal basis. To name a few, groups may enjoy facilitating provisions regarding mergers or formation of subsidiaries, they have obligations such as drawing up consolidated accounts, and certain transactions with subsidiaries are prohibited, such as issuing shares to a subsidiary.

10.76 Lastly, it can be observed that the courts have been filling in the gaps by dealing with cases where the risks of group structures are not, or not completely, covered by legislation. Although jurisdictions are far from similar in this respect, it is very likely that, in extreme cases, courts in the Member States will not adjudicate very differently in cases characterized by an accumulation of circumstances and events, such as manifest undercapitalization, harmful intragroup transactions and unduly continuing loss-making operations, due to interference by the parent company. It should be noted that parental liability is a broad concept, covering rather different grounds for establishing liability: the tortious behaviour of the parent company, its qualification as a de facto director or the abuse of legal personality.

Bibliography

Armour, J. & McCahery, J.A. *After Enron: Improving Corporate Law and Modernising Securities Regulation in Europe and the US*. Oxford: Hart Publishing, 2006

Bartman, S.M. (ed.). *European Company Law in Accelerated Progress*. European Company Law Series, Volume 1. Alphen aan den Rijn: Kluwer Law International, 2006

Berle, A. & G.C. Means. *The Modern Corporation and Private Property*. With a new introduction by Murray L. Weidenbaum & Mark Jensen. New Brunswick/London: Transaction Publishers, 1991

Blumberg, P.I. Blumberg. *The Multinational Challenge to Corporation Law*. New York/Oxford: Oxford University Press, 1993

Boucourechliev, J. (direction). *Propositions pour une société fermée européenne*. Luxembourg: Office des publications officielles des Communautés européennes, 1997

Brans, E.H.P. *Liability for Damage to Public Natural Resources: Standing, Damage and Damage Assessment*. The Hague/London/New York: Kluwer Law International, 2001

Buxbaum, R.M. & Hopt, K.J. *Legal Harmonisation and the Business Enterprise*. Berlin/New York: Walter de Gruyter, 1988

Buxbaum, R. M., R. Hertig, A. Hirsch & K.J. Hopt (eds). *European Economic and Business Law, Legal and Economic Analyses on Integration and Harmonization*. Berlin/New York: De Gruyter, 1996

Cahn, A. & D.C. Donald, *Comparative Company Law*, Cambridge: Cambridge University Press, 2018

Calvo, J., et al. *Employee Representatives in an Enlarged Europe*. Volumes 1 and 2. Brussels: European Commission, Directorate-General for Employment, Social Affairs and Equal Opportunities, 2008 < http://bookshop.europa.eu >

Dunning, J.H & Sarianna M. Lundan. *Multinational Enterprises and the Global Economy*. Cheltenham: Edward Elger Publishing, 2008

Edwards, V. *EC Company Law*. Oxford EC Law Library, Oxford: Clarendon Press, 1999

Emmerich, V. & Habersack, M. *Aktien- und GmbH-Konzernrecht.* 8. Auflage München: C.H. Beck, 2016

Enriques, L. *EC Company Law Directives and Regulations: How Trivial are They?.* ECGI – Law Working Paper No. 39/2005

Epstein, B.J. with contributions by Ali Mirza, Abbas. IFRS 2006. *Interpretation and Application of International Accounting and Financial Reporting Standards.* Somerset, NJ: John Wiley & Sons, 2006

Forum Europaeum Konzernrecht, *Corporate Group Law for Europe.* Stockholm: Forum Europaeum Konzernrecht, 2000

Fulton, L. *Worker Representation in Europe.* Labour Research Department and ETUI. Produced with the assistance of the SEEurope Network, online publication 2015. available at http://www.worker-participation.eu/National-Industrial-Relations

Gerner-Beuerle, C & M. Schillig, *Comparative Company Law.* Oxford: Oxford University Press, 2019

Gerner-Beuerle, C.P. Paech & E.P. Schuster. *Study on Directors' Duties and Liability, Prepared for the European Commission DG Markt.* London School of Economics, April 2013

Gonzalez, J.V. & C. Teichmann (eds). *Private Company Law Reform in Europe: The Race for Flexibility.* Cizur Menor: Thomson Reuters, 2015

Gronden, J. W. van de and C. S. Rusu, *Competition Law in the EU. Principles, Substance, Enforcement,* Cheltenham: Edward Elgar Publishing, 2021

Grundmann, S. *European Company Law,* Second edition. Cambridge/Antwerp/ Portland: Intersentia, 2012

High Level Group of Company Law Experts. *A Modern Regulatory Framework for Company Law in Europe.* Brussels, 4 November 2002, <http://ec.europa.eu/ internal_market/company/modern/index_en.htm>

Kraakman, R. et al. *The Anatomy of Corporate Law: A Comparative and Functional Approach.* Third edition. Oxford: Oxford University Press, 2017

Lambooy, T. *Corporate Social Responsibility: Legal and Semi-Legal Frameworks Supporting CSR.* Deventer: Kluwer, 2010

Lecher, W, et al. *European Works Councils. Developments, Types and Networking.* Aldershot/Burlington: Gower Publishing, 2001

Luca, N. De, *European Company Law: Text, Cases and Materials.* Cambridge: Cambridge University Press, 2017

Luca, N., De, *European Company Law.* Cambridge: Cambridge University Press 2021

Lutter, M. *Europaisches Unternehmensrecht.* vierte, neubearbeitete Auflage, Berlin/New York: De Gruyter, 1996

Lutter, M. (ed.). *Legal Capital in Europe.* European Company and Financial Law Review, Special Volume 1, 2006

Manovil (ed.), R.M., *Groups of Companies, A Comparative Law Overview.* Cham: Springer, 2020

Marks, Robbins, Fernandez & Funkhouser. *The Handbook of Financing Growth: Strategies and Capital Structure.* Hoboken, NJ: John Wiley & Sons, 2005

McCahery, J.A., Th. Raaijmakers & E.P.M. Vermeulen. *The Governance of Close Corporations and Partnerships*. Oxford: Oxford University Press, 2004

Pacter, P. *Pocket Guide to IFRS® Standards: The Global Financial Reporting Language*. London: IFRS Foundation, 2016Rickford, J. (ed.). *The European Company: Developing a Community Law of Corporations: Collected Papers from the Leiden University Unilever Programme 2002*. Antwerp/Oxford/New York: Intersentia, 2003

Rusu, C.S. *European Merger Control: The Challenges Raised by 20 Years of Enforcement Experience*. Alphen aan den Rijn: Kluwer Law International, 2010

Sapulete, S. *Works Council Effectiveness: Determinants and Outcomes*. Utrecht: Tjalling C. Koopmans Institute, Utrecht University, 2013Schömann, I. S. Clauwaert & W. Warneck. *Information and Consultation in the European Community. Implementation Report of Directive 2002/14/EC*. Brussels: European Trade Union Institute for Research, Education and Health and Safety (ETUI-REHS), 2006 <www.worker-participation.eu>

Seidl-Hohenveldern, I. *Corporations in and under International Law*. Cambridge: Grotius Publications, 1987

Sjåfjell, B. *Towards a Sustainable European Company Law*. Alphen aan den Rijn: Kluwer Law International, 2009

Sun, W., J. Stewart & D. Pollard (eds). *Corporate Governance and the Global Financial Crisis*. First edition. Cambridge: Cambridge University Press, 2011

Tavares da Costa, C. & A. De Meester Bilreiro. *The European Company Statute*. The Hague/London/New York: Kluwer Law International, 2003

Teichmann, C. *Binnenmarktkonformes Gesellschaftsrecht*. Berlin/New York: De Gruyter, 2006

Van Solinge, G. & Nieuwe Weme, M.P. (m.m.v. mr. drs. R.G.J. Nowak, mr. T. Salemink), *Mr. C. Assers Handleiding tot de beoefening van het Nederlands burgerlijk recht. 2. Rechtspersonenrecht. Deel IIb. NV en BV. Corporate Governance*. Deventer: Wolters Kluwer 2019

Vandekerckhove, K. *Piercing the Corporate Veil: A Transnational Approach*. Alphen aan den Rijn: Kluwer Law International, 2007

Verloop, P & V. Landes. *Merger Control in Europe*. International Competition Law Series Volume 11. The Hague, London, New York: Kluwer Law International, 2003

Vicari, A. *European Company Law*. Berlin/Boston: De Gruyter, 2021

Vicari, A. & A. Schall (eds), *Company Laws of the EU*. Munchen/Oxford/Baden-Baden: C.H. Beck, Hart, Nomos, 2020

Werlauff, E. *EU Company Law. Common Business Law of 28 States*. Second edition. Copenhagen: DJØF Publishing, 2003Werlauff, E. *International Contracts – The UNIDROIT Principles as an Alternative to Clauses on Governing Law*. Copenhagen: Ex Tuto Publishing, 2013

Werlauff, E. *SE – The Law of the European Company*. Copenhagen: DJØF Publishing, 2003

Wood, P. *Project Finance, Securitisations and Subordinated Debt*. The Law and Practice of International Finance Series, Volume 5. Hong Kong: Thomson/Sweet & Maxwell, 2007

Table of CJEU Cases

Index

D

E

H

I

J

K

Q

R

S

T

V

W

EUROPEAN COMPANY LAW SERIES

1. Steef M. Bartman (ed.), *European Company Law in Accelerated Progress*, 2006 (ISBN 978-90-411-2529-3)
2. Karen Vandekerckhove, *Piercing The Corporate Veil: A Transnational Approach*, 2007 (ISBN 978-90-411-2591-0)
3. Beate Sjåfjell, *Towards a Sustainable European Company Law: A Normative Analysis of the Objectives of EU Law, with the Takeover Directive as a Test Case*, 2009 (ISBN 978-90-411-2768-6)
4. Cornelis de Groot, *Corporate Governance as a Limited Legal Concept*, 2009 (ISBN 978-90-411-2873-7)
5. Adriaan Dorresteijn, Mieke Olaerts, Bastiaan Kemp, Thomas Biermeyer, Marcus Meyer-Erdmann & Tomas Arons, *European Corporate Law*, Fourth Edition, 2022 (ISBN 978-94-035-3223-3)
6. Gert-Jan Vossestein, *Modernization of European Company Law and Corporate Governance: Some Considerations on its Legal Limits*, 2010 (ISBN 978-90-411-2592-7)
7. Catalin Stefan Rusu, *European Merger Control: The Challenges Raised by Twenty Years of Enforcement Experience*, 2010 (ISBN 978-90-411-3259-8)
8. Sabrina Bruno & Eugenio Ruggiero, *Public Companies and the Role of Shareholders: National Models Towards Global Integration*, 2011 (ISBN 978-90-411-3423-3)
9. Hanne S. Birkmose, Mette Neville & Karsten Engsig Sørensen (eds), *The European Financial Market in Transition*, 2012 (ISBN 978-90-411-3360-1)
10. Hanne S. Birkmose, Mette Neville & Karsten Engsig Sørensen (eds), *Boards of Directors in European Companies: Reshaping and Harmonising Their Organisation and Duties*, 2013 (ISBN 978-90-411-4141-5)
11. Christoph Van der Elst, *Executive Directors' Remuneration in Comparative Corporate Perspective*, 2015 (ISBN 978-90-411-5607-5)
12. Hanne S. Birkmose, *Shareholders' Duties*, 2017 (ISBN 978-90-411-6670-8)
13. Alan S. Gutterman, *Sustainability and Corporate Governance: A Practice Guide to Implementing a Sustainability Governance System*, 2018 (ISBN 978-90-411-9975-1)
14. Jan De Bruyne, *Third-Party Certifiers*, 2019 (ISBN 978-94-035-1091-0)
15. Hanne S. Birkmose, Mette Neville & Karsten Engsig Sørensen (eds), *Abuse of Companies*, 2019 (ISBN 978-94-035-0892-4)
16. Ivan Romashchenko, *Related Party Transactions and Corporate Groups: When Eastern Europe Meets the West*, 2020 (ISBN 978-94-035-1701-8)

17. Patryk Filipiak & Anna Hrycaj, *European Insolvency Proceedings: Commentary on Regulation (EU) 2015/848 of the European Parliament and of the Council of 20 May 2015 on Insolvency Proceedings (Recast)*, 2021 (ISBN 978-94-035-3410-7)
18. Alexandros Seretakis, *Regulating Hedge Funds in the EU*, 2022 (ISBN 978-94-035-3512-8)

www.ingramcontent.com/pod-product-compliance
Ingram Content Group UK Ltd.
Pitfield, Milton Keynes, MK11 3LW, UK
UKHW020234290926
15470UKWH00002B/543

9 789403 532233